ON TROTSKYISM
Problems of theory and history

KOSTAS MAVRAKIS

Translated by John McGreal

ROUTLEDGE & KEGAN PAUL
London and Boston

First published in 1976
by Routledge & Kegan Paul Ltd
Broadway House, 68-74 Carter Lane
London EC4V 5EL and
9 Park Street,
Boston, Mass. 02108, USA
Manuscript typed by Jennifer R. Poole
Printed and bound in Great Britain
by Unwin Brothers Limited,
The Gresham Press, Old Woking, Surrey
A member of the Staples Printing Group

ISBN 0 7100 8277 0

CONTENTS

ABBREVIATIONS

The following abbreviations occur in the text:

AJS	Alliance des Jeunes pour le Socialisme (France)
CC	Central Committee
CCP	Chinese Communist Party
CGT	Confederation Generale du Travail (France)
CI	Communist International
CLER	Committee for the Liaison of Revolutionary Students (France)
CPG	Communist Party of Greece
CPSU	Communist Party of the Soviet Union
DRNV	Democratic Republic of North Vietnam
EAM	National Liberation Front (Greece)
ECCI	Executive Committee of the Communist International
EDES	Greek National Democratic Union
ELAS	Greek National Liberation Army
FER	Fédération des Etudiants Révolutionnaire
GDR	German Democratic Republic
Gosplan	State Planning Commission (USSR)
GPU	State Political Administration of USSR 1922-4, when changed to OGPU
JCR	Jeunesse Communiste Révolutionnaire (France)
NEP	New Economic Policy
NKVD	People's Commissariat of Internal Affairs (USSR)
NLF	National Liberation Front (South Vietnam)
OCI	Communist International Organization (France)
OGPU	United State Political Administration (USSR)
PCF	French Communist Party
PCI	Italian Communist Party; International Communist Party (France)
PLA	People's Liberation Army (China)
POUM	Partido Obrera de Unificacion Marxista (Spain)
PSU	United Socialist Party (France)
RCP(B)	Russian Communist Party (Bolshevik)
RSDLP	Russian Social Democratic Labour Party (Bolsheviks)
RSFSR	Russian Soviet Federated Socialist Republic

SLL   Socialist Labour League (UK)
SWP   Socialist Workers' Party
UJCML   Union des Jeunesses Communistes (Marxiste-Léniniste)
UNEF   Union Nationale des Etudiants de France

INTRODUCTION

Trotsky and his successors have always denied the existence of
'Trotskyism'. They profess to be the faithful disciples of Lenin.
According to them the term was invented by the 'Stalinists' to
designate a so-called theory of Trotsky's with the intention of
making it a target for their attacks, which are really directed
against the revolution in the USSR and the world. Trotsky protested that his concept of the permanent revolution was taken from
Marx and that Lenin 'tacitly' went over to it in his 'April
Theses'. Certain Trotskyists or Trotskysants, notably Isaac
Deutscher and Alfred Rosmer, have argued that there is no
difference between their mentor's permanent revolution and Mao's
uninterrupted revolution by stages. Trotsky himself said, 'I have
never claimed and I do not claim to have created a special doctrine.
In theory, I am a pupil of Marx. As for revolutionary method, I
went through Lenin's school.' (1)

It would seem that Trotskyism's defence implies its disavowal
and the misrecognition of the theoretical contribution of Lenin.
However, there is some truth in Trotsky's denials. Deutscher has
insisted on his attachment to 'classical Marxism'. We shall show
in what follows that this is a euphemism designating an approach
that is at once dogmatic and empirical, the theoretical impotence
implied by the dogmatism leading those who are afflicted by it to
revert to empiricism. Bukharin said of Trotsky that he 'excelled
... in tracing general revolutionary perspectives'. In fact, that
is where his talents as a 'theoretician' end. In contrast to Lenin
and Mao he was never able to analyse a conjuncture in its specificity, or to determine the principal contradiction and the
principal slogan. As he never established the laws of the
revolution in a social formation by applying the universal
principle of historical materialism in the practice of the class
struggle, his contribution to this science was nil. Moreover, his
few original 'ideas' are not his own, for above all he vulgarised
those of others. What is more, he did not demonstrate much dis-
cernment in his borrowings, as we shall see in the case of
'primitive socialist accumulation'. Even his most ardent
supporters are embarrassed when they are asked to name the concepts
he produced.

1

For all these reasons, it is possible to speak of Trotskyism as an ideological current but only with difficulty as a body of doctrine, and not at all as a 'guide to action'. Trotsky's retractions on the subject of the 'Thermidorian reaction' are a perfect illustration of his complete theoretical impotence. As for the Trotskyists today, they practise the dogmatism of a dogmatism. In the era of the cultural revolution and of the thought of Mao Tse-tung, the third stage of Marxism, they are the fossils of a past epoch - Marxists of the first stage. In other words, they are not Marxists at all.

The bourgeois propagandists and Trotskyist ideologues are united by a community of goods. The former provide the latter with their dens of research and documentation. Kremlinology, Pekinology and the publications of the US Consul-General in Hong Kong are the principal sources of Trotskyist diatribes against the socialist countries. (2) For their part, the Trotskyists are important purveyors of 'theoretical' hypotheses, historical schemas and falsifications that make it possible to attack Stalin and People's China from an apparently 'left-wing' standpoint, which is an important resource for certain journalists who claim to be enlightened. This is a matter of a 'pre-established harmony', not a deliberate collusion. For different reasons both propagate the idea that the Communist Parties were only puppets manipulated by Moscow and Stalin, the source of all evil.

One of the most curious arguments of Trotsky's apologists consists of comparing their idol's wit and sparkling prose with the heavy and inharmonious style of the auto-didact Stalin, concluding that the latter could not have been right against the former. As if a solid position in Marxist-Leninist science were a matter of literary talent. This idea runs like a black thread through every page of Isaac Deutscher's biography of Trotsky. Deutscher insistently emphasises that Stalin did not command attention as a theoretician before 1924. In fact, from this point of view, it was Bukharin who enjoyed the most prestige after Lenin. Does this mean that he was right to support the kulaks, to proclaim to them the slogan 'Get rich' and to preach the construction of socialism 'at a snail's pace'? Such logic borders on the grotesque at times, as when Deutscher declares that Ch'en Tu-hsiu was a 'theoretician' much superior to Mao.

The bourgeois publicists argue in the same way. Cadar, the anarcho-Trotskysant, attacks Mao for his 'primary-school outlook'. His thought is not 'refined'. It is incomprehensible to him that writers as 'sophisticated' as Althusser, Glucksmann or Sollers hold Mao in such high esteem. (3) L. Bianco (4) declares that Mao is not 'a profound thinker' but only a 'mediocre theoretician'. It is true that for Bianco (p.135) to be a 'thinker' is to be a 'contemplative'. He observes that Mao has been able to 'emancipate himself from dogma and see reality for what it is', but it does not seem to occur to him that in order 'to see reality for what it is' singularly powerful theoretical spectacles are required, as well as the ability to lead the struggles of the masses who transform this reality in a revolutionary way (if you want to know the taste of a pear, you must change the pear by eating it yourself). Like Trotsky, what these authors are unable to conceive is the link between theory and practice and the concrete form of this link: the mass-line. Did not Trotsky claim to judge revolutionaries the world over from his offices at Prinkipo and Coyoacan, without even having led, as Stalin did, a true International rooted in the masses?

If the result (his articles) sometimes sparkles like glass it is also just as fragile.

Having style and a wide culture, he drew from it the conviction that his ideas were as profound and well-based as they were brilliantly formulated. With him, comparison is very often substituted for argument, and rhetoric for concrete thought. Hence it may be said that he was a victim of his strengths as much as of his weaknesses, the former giving him the illusion that he possessed precisely the powers he lacked: those of the political strategist and theoretician. Mao said: 'The more one thinks one is superior, the more mediocre the results one gets.' Those who have been close to Trotsky have noted his ambition, his pride, and indeed his arrogance. He placed himself high above the rest of humanity, conceding only one exception and that only in the single period from 1917 to 1924. In his writings Trotsky has the good taste not to stress the high opinion he had of himself. In contrast, he does not hide from us the contempt in which he holds the most eminent Bolshevik leaders. One day the texts in which he condemned, denigrated and ridiculed his communist adversaries or fellow combatants should be brought together into an anthology. The polemicist makes fun of his victims but the last laugh will be on him.

I shall not use the same weapons. I shall submit his theses to a severe, but fair critical examination. It is easy to compile a voluminous 'catalogue of errors' out of extracts from his books, and there is a great temptation to pass over in silence his merits in so far as he accepted Lenin's leadership during the first five years of the revolution: revisionist writers generally proceed in this fashion. For my part, I prefer to take on the Trotsky phenomenon face-to-face since, after all, despite all the exorcisms, it lives on.

It is clear that Trotsky was endowed with great talents. As a brilliant publicist, enthusiastic speaker, organiser of the Red Army, he rendered eminent services to the revolution after joining the Bolshevik Party. The reverse of the medal was his extreme individualism, his pride, his arrogance and the fact that the rigour of his thought was that of a barrister, not that of a theoretician who derives his strength from his link with the masses and from his ability to lead them. His best-known works, 'The New Course', 'The Revolution Betrayed', 'The Permanent Revolution', are skilful and brilliant pleas 'pro domo suo', but they are of limited interest because they demonstrate at most that certain of the criticisms directed at him were unfounded. In fact, not everything that he said in his polemic with Stalin was false. But as we shall see, he was mistaken about the essentials. His rival had a decisive advantage over him which a comparison of their respective contributions to the debate makes plain: Stalin was a Leninist, a revolutionary leader in the second stage of Marxism; as his biographer says, Trotsky was a 'classical' revolutionary surviving in a post-classical world.

These old controversies would be of only historical interest if
the Trotskyists did not derive from them a part of their argument.
In so far as they have a certain influence in the student movement
and thrive on and foster the ideological confusion that reigns
there, it is a contribution to hygiene to compare the main themes
of their propaganda with the facts. These main themes start from
'theoretical principles'; we shall examine their scientific status;
that is, their ability to think reality with a view to its transformation. In addition they mobilise examples drawn from the
history of the workers' movement. Never having assumed the
autonomous direction of a victorious revolution in the forty years
that their organisations have existed on an international scale,
the Trotskyists cannot rely on exemplary cases of the application
of their principles. Their argumentation is therefore based on a
critique of the experience of others.

We shall see that in each case their version of history is a
schema very remote from reality. The books in which Trotsky, his
followers and those whom they have influenced, accuse (often
correctly) the 'Stalinist' historians of having falsified history
are innumerable. Should we be surprised if they themselves falsify
it still more in their propagandist literature? (5)

Lies and invective have taken the place of a serious refutation
of Trotskyism for too long. The Soviet historical works present
such an expurgated and one-sided version of the facts that they are
useless to a public which has access to complementary, even
contradictory, information. Aragon's 'L'Histoire de l'USSR' is
worse than the rest from this point of view. Suffice it to mention
the cavalier way he conjures away the polemic on the Chinese
revolution in 1927. It is important to clarify these problems,
notably in the youth movement, an important sector of the popular
revolutionary movement.

In fact the opportunist degeneration of numerous Communist
Parties, notably in Latin America and Europe from 1945 onwards, and
then the adoption of the revisionist theses of the 20th Congress of
the CPSU have contributed to give Trotskyism a 'second wind'.
Counter-revolutionary as it used to be (in the period 1929-45), it
now tends to embody the revolt of the intellectual petty bourgeoisie
in the 'revolutionist' mode. The constant and general advance of
Trotskyist movements since 1960 is thus explained. The unprincipled
attacks made by Krushchev against Stalin's person and the absence of
a scientific self-criticism by the CPSU provided the Trotskyists
with the possibility of presenting their 'prophet's' appraisals of
the USSR in the 1920s and 1930s as predictions of its evolution in
the 1950s and 1960s. They are thus able to justify retrospectively
their attitude in Stalin's day while duping the young whose
historical knowledge is meagre and who are consequently susceptible
to seduction by explanatory schemas which have the merit of
simplicity, if not of rigour.

Profiting from this favourable conjuncture, they intrepidly
proclaim that '"Trotskyism" ... has once more become the touchstone
... of all contemporary revolutionary movements'. (6)

The appearance of Léo Figuères's book, 'Le Trotskyisme, cet
antileninisme', shows that henceforth the PCF is obliged to
recognise this new situation. It faces up to it with its usual

methods. Léo Figuères entitles one chapter 'Trotsky the populist'
but he avoids drawing the reader's attention to the fact that this
'first part' of Trotsky's 'militant life' of which he speaks relates
to the period when Trotsky was less than nineteen years old!
Referring to the Spanish Civil War, our author attributes the sins
of the POUM to Trotskyism - whereas the leader of the Fourth
International had jeered at those in the POUM as 'impotent
centrists'. (7) Lastly, Léo Figuères attributes to Trotsky an
opinion he always refuted, namely that the bureaucracy is a 'new
class'. These few minor dishonesties (I have ignored even better
ones) show well enough that such a book can only convince the
ignorant or those who are already convinced. Criticising Trotskyism
from a rightist standpoint, Figuères helps to give it a left-wing
halo it scarcely deserves.

The object of this book is not to weigh the historical role of
Stalin or of Trotsky and his movement. I propose only:

(a)   to isolate what I believe to be the essence of Trotskyism
      in order to show how it is opposed to Leninism, and how it
      is anti-dialectical and anti-scientific (and therefore non-
      revolutionary) when it is not counter-revolutionary.
(b)   to dissipate the legends and myths of its so-called
      historical argument by showing how the latter is
      contradicted by the facts, in other words by a scientific
      analysis of the class struggle in the period concerned.

I take Stalin's part solely within the limits of the debate between
him and Trotsky. The critique of the latter is to be found in the
writings of the former but the reverse is not true. No refutation
of Trotsky can be conclusive unless it is accompanied by a critique
of Stalin. The latter requires the concepts produced by Mao
Tse-tung. Thanks to him and to the cultural revolution it is
possible today to go beyond 'Stalinism' and consequently, on the
theoretical and practical level, to weigh it up definitively
against Trotskyism.

Once beyond the point of departure constituted by the refutation
of Trotskyism, it turns out that there are more questions than
answers. The reader is warned in advance so that he may not be led
astray by the occasionally overconfident tones of these pages. My
aim has been to advance the debate, not to close it.

Chapter 1

BIOGRAPHICAL LANDMARKS

This chronology provides some details on certain points of Trotsky's career which are not dealt with in the pages which follow and offers a framework to help in understanding them. Everything which is not absolutely necessary for this purpose has been omitted.

1879 26 October	Birth of Lev Davidovich Bronstein.
1897	First military activity in Odessa.
1898	Arrest. Influenced for a while by populism, he becomes a Marxist after reading Lenin's 'The Development of Capitalism in Russia' in prison.
1902	Escapes from deportation in Siberia and arrives in London.
1903 July	2nd Congress of Russian Social Democratic Labour Party. The outcome is a split. Sides with the opportunist wing who are from then on called Mensheviks (minority) and against Lenin and the Bolsheviks (majority).
1904	Makes his way to Munich, meets Helphand (Parvus), German social-democratic theoretician of Russian origin. Borrowed from him elements of his theory of the permanent revolution.
1905 9 January	Bloody Sunday. 'Forces of order' fire on peaceful demonstration led by the priest Father Gapon.
February	Arrives in Kiev; shortly afterwards makes his way to St Petersburg.
October	General strike in St Petersburg. The workers form a soviet (council) of delegates and Trotsky is elected president. Taking fright, Tsar publishes 'Manifesto' promising constitution, civil liberties and

	universal suffrage but has no intention whatsoever of keeping his word.
3 December	Police arrest all members of the soviet. In response Moscow workers rise under leadership of the Bolsheviks, but are crushed by army after ten days of fighting on barricades. Numerous other risings. Social democrats boycott Duma elections.
1906 19 September - 2 November	Trial of Petersburg Soviet. Accused condemned to deportation for life.
1907 February	Trotsky escapes before convoy of prisoners reaches destination.
April	3rd Congress of Social Democratic Party in London. Trotsky denies the seriousness of the differences between Bolsheviks and Mensheviks. He adopts attitude of conciliator 'above the melée' but joins the Mensheviks in their attach on Lenin over the Bolshevik commandos' guerilla activities, particularly in the Caucasus under Stalin's leadership. Trotsky settles in Vienna with journalism his main occupation.
1908 October	Trotsky publishes first number of 'Pravda'.
1910 January	Bolshevik and Menshevik leaders meet in Paris and decide:

1 to expel the 'Otzovists' (boycotters of the Duma), who condemned all legal activity, and the 'Liquidators', who opposed clandestine work.
2 to dissolve their organisations and amalgamate. However, Mensheviks break the agreement straight away. They refuse to expel Liquidators and maintain separate organisation. Lenin, on the contrary, keeps to his side of the agreement.

In his 'Pravda', Trotsky fails to condemn Mensheviks' splittist attitude. Whatever his professions of faith, it is not unity but his position as the arbitrator between the two camps he holds to be important.

| 1912 January | Prague Conference of Bolsheviks, who decide to break with Mensheviks. |

	Trotsky denounces them violently. In April 1912 his anger rises to extremes when Bolsheviks bring out daily paper called 'Pravda' in St Petersburg with Stalin as editor-in-chief. After threatening to 'take other measures' if their paper's name is not changed, he gives up publication of his own 'Pravda'.
1912 August	On his initiative, Mensheviks, Liquidators, Left Bolsheviks (or Otzovists), the Jewish Bund and his group meet at conference in Vienna and form what is known as the 'August Bloc'. The aim of this manoeuvre is to lay the blame on Lenin for the split. August bloc necessarily breaks up very quickly.
1913 April	Trotsky's letter to Chkeidze (Menshevik leader) stating that: 'All Leninism at this moment is based on lies and falsifications and bears within the germ of its own decomposition'.
1914 5 August	Outbreak of First World War. Apart from the Bolsheviks, the social democratic parties of the belligerent powers betray the commitments which they made at the Congress of the Second International, vote for war credits and come out for 'national defence' and the 'Holy Alliance' of capital and labour.
1915 January	Together with Martov, Trotsky becomes joint editor-in-chief of 'Nashe Slovo' in Paris. In this paper he defends slogan 'Neither victory nor defeat' which he counterposes to Lenin's revolutionary defeatism or 'transformation of imperialist war into civil war'. Lenin replied that supporters of slogan 'Neither victory nor defeat' in fact side with bourgeois and opportunists for 'they do not believe' in possibility of international revolutionary actions of working class against its respective governments and do not wish to contribute to development of these actions.
September	Zimmerwald Conference (Switzerland) of socialists opposed to the war

	(the majority pacifists). Manifesto adopted at conference conforms to Trotsky's centrist position.
1916 April	French police ban 'Nashe Slovo'.
30 October	Trotsky deported to Spain from where he makes his way to USA.
1917 8-15 March	The people overthrow Tsarism. Bourgeoisie cheats it out of victory and sets up a provisional government under presidency of Prince Lvov. Soviet of workers' and soldiers' deputies which is dominated by Socialist-Revolutionaries and Mensheviks hand over power to it.
16 April	Lenin returns to Petrograd; publishes 'April Theses'.
17 May	Trotsky arrives in Petrograd.
3 July	Armed demonstrations demanding 'All power to the Soviets'. Outrun by the masses, Bolsheviks just succeed in preventing demonstration turning into insurrection. Repression of Bolsheviks. 'Pravda' banned. Warrant issued for arrest of Lenin, who goes into hiding. Trotsky insistently demands that Lenin give himself up, but of course his 'History of the Russian Revolution' does not breathe a word about this dispute.
23 July	Trotsky arrested.
26 July	6th Congress of Bolshevik Party. Stalin presents Central Committee's political report. The Congress admits Trotsky's 'Interdistrict' organisation into the Party. Trotsky elected to Central Committee.
24 August	General Kornilov tries to seize power but troops he launches against Petrograd are won over by Bolshevik propaganda and join the people.
4 September	Trotsky freed.
9 September	Bolsheviks win majority in Petrograd Soviet; Bolshevik Central Committee decides on immediate preparation for insurrection. Trotsky is opposed, insisting that they should wait until the 3rd Congress of Soviets. In 'History of the Russian Revolution' Trotsky silently passes over this fact while minutely exposing every error of Stalin and other Bolshevik leaders.

17 October	Hostile to the insurrection, Zinoviev and Kamenev reveal Central Committee's decision on it in Gorky's paper 'Novaya Zhizn'.
24 October	Lenin arrives in Petrograd and makes his way to the Smolny Institute, seat of the Soviet and headquarters of the insurrection, which he leads with help of Trotsky and Antonov Ovseenko – members of Bolshevik Party's military revolutionary committee. On night of 24/25 all strategic points in the capital are occupied.
25 October	Appeal drawn up by Lenin to 'the citizens of Russia' announces dismissal of Provisional Government and seizure of power by Petrograd Soviet. 2nd Congress of Soviets meets in evening. Two-thirds of delegates are Bolsheviks.
2 December	Opening of Brest-Litovsk peace negotiations between representatives of central powers and those of Soviet government led by Trotsky, Commissar for Foreign Affairs. Decree on creation of Red Army.
1918 28 January	Soviets (following Trotsky's plan) break off negotiations declaring their intention to demobilise but without signing peace.
1 February	Adoption of Gregorian calendar.
18 February	Germans break through front and advance towards the capital without meeting resistance.
23 February	New Red Army temporarily stops Germans before Pakov and Narva ('Red Army Day').
24 February	Trotsky resigns as Commissar for Foreign Affairs.
3 March	Signature at Brest-Litovsk of new German Diktat.
13 March	Trotsky appointed Commissar of War.
25 May	At French instigation, Czechoslovak Legion and White Guards seize Siberia and advance as far as Kazan. Japanese and Americans land at Vladivostock and English take Baku and Archangel.
11 November	End of First World War.
1919 2-7 March	1st Congress of Communist International.
November	Defeat of White armies of Yudenich

	(south of Petrograd) and Denikin (in Ukraine).
1920 January	Collapse of Whites in Siberia.
24 April	Poles, with Anglo-French support, attack Soviet Russia and seize Kiev.
21 July - 6 August	2nd Congress of Communist International.
12 October	Peace Treaty with Poland.
November	Defeat of Wrangel and end of Civil War.
1921 2-17 March	Kronstadt rising.
8-16 March	10th Bolshevik Party Congress, adoption of NEP; prohibition of factions. Trotsky defeated on trade-union question.
22 June - 12 July	3rd Congress of Communist International.
1922 3 April	Stalin elected Secretary-General.
26 May	Lenin's first stroke.
16 December	Lenin's second stroke.
25 December	Lenin's 'Testament'.
1923 January-March	Lenin's last articles.
15 October	Letter of forty-six oppositionists criticising economic policy and absence of democracy in Party. Behind the scenes, Trotsky is their inspiration.
7 November	Opening of public debate on Letter of the Forty-six.
December	Publication of Trotsky's 'The New Course' attacking Bolshevik 'Old Guard' whose bureaucratic degeneration he fears and appealing to youth. Zinoviev calls for Trotsky's expulsion from the Party and for his arrest. Stalin categorically opposed to this.
1924 16-18 January	13th Party Conference condemns Trotsky and the Forty-six.
21 January	Lenin's death.
October	Trotsky publishes 'The Lessons of October' in which he tries to discredit Zinoviev and Kamenev, leaders of the Party together with Stalin, by recalling their past mistakes. His main achievement is to arouse general outcry against himself for 'Literary debate'.
1925 15 January	Trotsky resigns as Commissar of War. Kamenev tries to make Stalin give up his general-secretaryship by proposing that he replace Trotsky.
27-29 April	14th Party Conference. First

	differences between Stalin on the one hand, arguing that it is possible to construct socialism in one country, and Zinoviev and Kamenev on the other, denying this possibility.
	During the summer Zinovievists attack Bukharinists whom they accuse of defending kulaks. Stalin supports Bukharin but rejects his slogan to peasants, 'Get rich'. Bukharin makes a self-criticism on this point.
18-31 December	14th Congress of Bolshevik Party: Zinoviev and Kamenev defeated. Trotsky makes no intervention. Having taken no part in politics for a year he has not even noticed the birth of a new opposition.
1926 April	Zinoviev and Kamenev form united Opposition with Trotsky.
14-23 July	Trotsky presents Opposition programme to Central Committee. Zinoviev loses seat on Political Bureau.
23-26 October	Trotsky and Kamenev expelled from Political Bureau. Bukharin replaces Zinoviev as head of International.
31 March	Trotsky attacks Political Bureau's Chinese policy.
July	Trotsky's 'Clemenceau declaration'. Gives notice that in event of war Opposition will do its utmost to seize power in order to provide better guarantee for defence of the country.
27 September	Trotsky expelled from Executive Committee of International.
21-28 October	Trotsky and Zinoviev expelled from Central Committee.
7 November	Opposition attempts to take part in official demonstrations with its own slogans: 'Strike against the kulak, the NEP-man and the bureaucrat!'; 'Carry out Lenin's Testament!'; 'Preserve Bolshevik unity'.
15 November	Trotsky and Zinoviev expelled from Bolshevik Party.
2-19 December	15th Congress of Bolshevik Party. Opposition programme signed by only 6,000 of 725,000 members. Zinoviev and Kamenev acknowledge that their positions are 'erroneous and anti-Leninist'.

1928	17 January	Trotsky exiled to Alma Ata. The kulaks having refused to hand over their corn at fixed prices, famine makes itself felt more and more in the towns.
	6-11 April	Central Committee calls for struggle against kulak danger. Orders requisitioning of stocks of corn. Beginning of anti-rightist orientation.
	September	Kuibyshev's speech on accelerated industrialisation. Moscow rightists eliminated. Bukharin criticises left-turn in 'Remarques d'un économiste'.
	10 February	Trotsky exiled from USSR. Settles in the Princes' Isles near Constantinople.
	16-23 April	Central Committee condemns right deviation.
	23-25 April	14th Party Conference adopts First Five-Year Plan.
	24 October	Wall Street crash; beginning of the great crisis.
	10-17 November	Bukharin expelled from Political Bureau; makes a self-criticism.
	27 December	Stalin issues call for acceleration of collectivisation and liquidation of kulaks as a class.
1930		Trotsky publishes 'La Révolution défigurée' and 'The Permanent Revolution'; issues first number of 'Bulletin Oppozitsii'.
1931-2		Trotsky warns against rise of Nazism and criticises tactics of German Communist Party.
1933	30 January	Hitler in power.
1935	15-18 January	First trial of Zinoviev and Kamenev, accused of complicity in Kirov's assassination.
		Trotsky publishes 'The Workers' State and the Question of Thermidor and Bonapartism'.
	June	Expelled from France, Trotsky is granted entry to Norway.
1936	February	Publication of 'The Revolution Betrayed'.
	June	Victory of Popular Front in France.
	17 July	Beginning of Spanish Civil War.
	19-24 August	First Moscow Trials. Zinoviev and Kamenev condemned to death.
	September	USSR gives aid to Republican Spain.
	27 September	Yezhov replaces Yagoda as head of NKVD.

	November	Extraordinary 8th Congress of Soviets adopts new constitution, 'the most democratic in the world'.
1937	January	Trotsky arrives in Mexico.
	23–30 January	Trials of Piatakov and Radek.
	3 March	Stalin presents his report 'Pour une formation bolchevique' to the Central Committee.
	11 June	Communiqué announcing execution of Tukhachevsky and other Red Army leaders.
1938	2–13 March	Trial of Bukharin and Rykov.
	3 September	Founding Conference of the Fourth International.
	30 September	Munich Agreement.
	December	Yezhov replaced by Beria. End of Great Purge.
1939	28 February	End of Spanish Civil War.
	22 August	Soviet-German Pact.
1939	September – 1940 August	Trotsky writes 'In Defence of Marxism'.
1940	May–June	German invasion of France.
	20 August	Assassination of Trotsky in his house at Coyoacan by a supposed agent of Soviet Secret Service.

Chapter 2

AN ATEMPORAL DOGMATISM

TROTSKY'S 'ORIGINAL' THEORY

In May 1904 Trotsky had just been excluded from the editorial board
of 'Iskra' at Plekhanov's insistence. He continued, nevertheless,
to collaborate with the Menshevik journal. At this time he made his
way to Munich where he met the Russian social democrat, Alexander
Helphand, whose nom de plume was Parvus. He was to remain with him
until February 1905 and to fall strongly under his influence. Like
him, while his sympathy went to the Mensheviks, he was to claim the
role of arbiter, judge and pacifier of the two factions of the
Russian Social Democratic Party, and in order to do this he was to
keep himself apart from both sides. The 'theory' of the permanent
revolution in its essential traits is due to Parvus. He was the
first person to set out some of the ideas which continue to
structure Trotskyist thought up to the present day.

In a series of articles entitled 'War and revolution' he argued
that the national state, the birth of which corresponded to the
needs of industrial capitalism, was henceforth superseded. The
development of a world market shattered this compartmentalisation by
accentuating the interdependence of nations.

At the beginning of the 1905 revolution Parvus wrote a preface to
Trotsky's book 'Our Political Tasks' in which he argued: 'The
Provisional Revolutionary Government of Russia will be a workers'
democratic government ... As the Social Democratic Party is at the
head of the revolutionary movement ... this government will be
social democratic ... a coherent government with a social democratic
majority.'

Trotsky was to conclude quite naturally that such a government
could not but carry out a specifically social democratic policy and
would therefore immediately commit itself to the road of socialist
transformation. In this he was as much opposed to the Mensheviks
who, arguing the bourgeois-democratic character of the revolution,
supported the big liberal bourgeoisie who were seeking a compromise
with Tsarism, as to the Bolsheviks who, while distinguishing the
democratic stage from the socialist stage, considered that the
proletariat had to mobilise the peasantry in order to take up the
leadership of the democratic revolution and to carry out its tasks

radically, which by no means implied that social democracy would be in a majority in a government set up after a victory of the people. (1)

At first sight it may seem that Trotsky's theses are left-wing, those of Martov right-wing and those of Lenin centrist, but extremes converge and Martov agrees with Trotsky on more than one point. As we shall see further on, Lenin devoted an article to refuting the ideas of Trotsky which Martov had adopted on his own account.

Trotsky, the eloquent tribune, was accepted as the head of the Petrograd Soviet by the Mensheviks and the Bolsheviks precisely because he represented only himself and did not impede them in the pursuit of their policies. This was so true that, while both sides polemicised a great deal among themselves, afterwards they hardly ever bothered to refute his ideas.

Before going on to discuss the 'permanent revolution' in the basis of an analysis of the concrete situation in 1905, let us recall that Trotsky was not long to remain proud of having been Parvus's disciple. The latter revealed himself a social chauvinist in 1914, and in addition an arms dealer and shady speculator. That is why Trotsky traced his theory back to Marx although he did not dare to deny his debt to Parvus.

It is true that Marx uses the term 'permanent revolution', particularly in 'The Class Struggles in France', but what he says about it is at such a level of generality that it cannot be relied upon to confer the palm of orthodoxy on Parvus and Trotsky, nor on Lenin and Mao. The former and the latter agree with Marx while differing among themselves. Besides, Marx was aware of the relatively general and abstract character of his definition of the permanent revolution since he apologises for not having the space to develop it. (2) It was only after 1905 that a differentiation occurs among those calling themselves Marxist over this concept. In any case, the reference to Marx is deceptive, for in the passages where the words 'declaration of the permanent revolution' appear, what is at issue is more reminiscent of the cultural revolution in China than the tactics advocated in 1905 by Trotsky. The latter explicitly invoked Lassalle, who had drawn from the events of 1848-9 the unshakable conviction that 'no struggle in Europe can be successful unless, from the very start, it declares itself to be purely socialist'. (3) If Parvus is the father of Trotskyist theory, Lassalle is its grandfather. The notion of the permanent revolution peculiar to Parvus and Trotsky was an attempt to respond to the problems posed by the 1905 revolution. In what follows I shall endeavour to study the concrete situation at that time.

FROM DEMOCRATIC TO SOCIALIST REVOLUTION

(A summary of 'Que faire?', pp.16-24, UJC (M.L.) pamphlet no.3, Paris, 1967, translated as 'What Is To Be Done?')

In 1905 the imminent revolution had to accomplish bourgeois democratic tasks, that is, to sweep away the Tsarist state and its social basis - feudal property - which were holding back the development of capitalism. However, the bourgeoisie could not lead this revolution, given its alliance with the landowners and its infiltration into the state apparatus which it was gradually transforming from within. Hence the obvious paradox: the bourgeoisie had no interest in the bourgeois revolution; it inevitably preferred a compromise with Tsarism. In the countryside, however, the rural bourgeoisie, fettered as it was by feudal relations, had not developed freely. All the categories of peasants which were beginning to differentiate themselves still had a common interest in the overthrow of Tsarism.

The proletariat and the peasantry were thus the principal revolutionary forces at this time. An alliance between these two classes was necessary to overthrow Tsarism in a revolutionary way. The proletariat had to lead this alliance: it alone had the organisational ability which made its hegemony possible and necessary. For the proletariat to lead the revolution meant: to win over the peasantry, to rely on the revolutionary initiative of the peasant masses, to prevent the bourgeoisie from gaining the leadership of the peasant movement and defeating it by an incomplete and bureaucratic agrarian reform (decreed from above). The slogan of the revolutionary democratic dictatorship of the proletariat and the peasantry expressed this alliance and this hegemony. Further- more, proletarian leadership, guaranteeing the consistency of the revolution (its radical character), would institute the conditions that would prepare the socialist revolution. This slogan made it possible for the Bolsheviks to participate in a provisional revolutionary government which would exercise this dictatorship. Which parties would be long-term members of this government? This was an abstract question in the following sense: only practice could resolve the question, only the real development of the revolution could provide the elements of an answer. This precise question lost its meaning after the defeat of the revolution and the appearance of a new alignment of class forces. The point is essential. The slogan 'revolutionary democratic dictatorship of the proletariat and peasantry' corresponded adequately to the objective situation of the 1905 revolution. It expressed with total accuracy the immediate tasks of the proletariat: the organisation of the peasants for the achievement of their joint dictatorship. It did not leave room for any 'riddle' (Trotsky). A slogan corresponds to the tasks of the moment. Like all slogans, the Bolshevik slogan in 1905 was an instrument of agitation and propaganda; it showed the workers the principal path that the revolution had to follow: the organisation of the peasants for the conquest of consistent democratic power; it oriented the proletarian revolution and freed the initiative of the peasantry. Trotsky, on the other hand, proposed to the proletariat that they should take over state power and afterwards make use of it to rouse the peasants: 'Many sections of the working masses, particularly in the countryside, will be drawn into the revolution and become politically organised only after the advance-guard of the revolution, the urban proletariat, stands at the helm of the state.' (4)

In 1917 the second revolution triumphed in the midst of imperialist war. The latter had accelerated social development. Capitalism had been transformed into state monopoly capitalism. In the countryside the process of differentiation had made headway.

The Tsarist agrarian reform of Stolypin had strengthened the rural
bourgeoisie. The war had united workers and peasants in uniform.
It was mutinous soldiers who overthrew the Tsarist government. The
revolution of February 1917 led to the installation of a dual power:
on the one side, the provisional government representing the
imperialist republican bourgeoisie; on the other, the soviets.
These differed from the soviets invented by the masses in 1905 in
that:

    (a)   they had arms;
    (b)   there were soviets of soldiers (mainly peasant conscripts),
          as Russia was at war.

Lenin explains in his 'April Theses' that the revolutionary
situation presented specific features in relation to that of 1905.
Democratic dictatorship became a reality in the soviets, although
incompletely, since their power co-existed with that of the
imperialist bourgeoisie. The immediate task was how to shift all
power to the soviets. Hence the slogan put forward by the
revolutionary democrats. Concretely, this revolutionary democracy
had to resolve the agrarian question (an identical task in principle
in 1905 and 1917) and tasks which were already socialist in the
towns. It was the imperialist war which put these tasks of
socialism on the agenda. The 1917 revolution was therefore a
proletarian revolution which had to take the socialist road after
carrying out the democratic tasks.

    Trotsky rewrites history. He isolates two moments: 1905 and
1917; he disregards the period that separates them (an episode no
doubt of little use to his argument); and this is what the history
of Bolshevism becomes. According to him, in 1905, Lenin formulated
'a hypothesis': revolutionary democratic dictatorship of the
proletariat and peasantry. This hypothesis depended on an
'unknown': the political role of the peasantry. October 1917
reduced the unknown and Lenin's hypothesis (which envisaged the
possibility of a peasant party with a majority in the revolutionary
government) was invalidated since it was the dictatorship of the
proletariat alone which triumphed! On the contrary, it was
Trotsky's 'prognosis' that was confirmed.

    October 1917 did not invalidate July 1905. The Leninist slogan
was correct at that time because it corresponded to the tasks of the
moment and was an adequate instrument of agitation and propaganda.
The new Leninist slogan was correct in 1917 because it corresponded
to the new tasks of the moment (war, differentiation in the
countryside, development of monopoly capitalism, the current
practical development which produced this unforseeable concrete
form of dual power). Trotsky's construction presupposes the
identity of conditions in 1905 and 1917: indeed, in order to find
in 1917 the confirmation of what he said in 1905, Trotsky has to
assume that nothing changed between the two moments. Such is the
basis of Trotskyist abstraction. The result: Trotsky is forced to
falsify the meaning of Lenin's 1917 texts. Lenin said in fact that
democratic dictatorship was realised to some extent in 1917 (in the
form of the soviets). Trotsky pretends to believe that if
democratic dictatorship was achieved it was in the form of
Kerensky's imperialist regime:

    If the democratic dictatorship had only been realised in our country in the form of Kerenskyism, which played the role of errand-boy to Lloyd George and Clemenceau, then we should have to say that history indulged in cruel mockery of the strategic slogan of Bolshevism. (5)

This is false. Lenin regarded the soviet form as the achievement of democratic dictatorship.

Trotsky tries in vain to dress Leninist theory in his cloak, relying on the apparent coincidence between his slogan in 1905 and Lenin's in 1917. Lenin did not hesitate to describe 'All power to the soviets!' as the slogan, not of socialism, but of 'advanced revolutionary democracy'; he did not allow himself to play with words and abstractions. The dictatorship of the proletariat was not an abstraction for him and he did not hesitate after the revolution to explain how the Soviet state was a workers' and peasants' state.

By common consent of Trotsky and his successors the 'permanent revolution' is not a dated quarrel. Its importance lies in its current value. As a general theory formed on the basis of the lessons of October, it should constitute the universal path of Bolshevism. The 'colonial revolutions - China yesterday, and Vietnam today - should demonstrate it brilliantly. The Trotskyists have acquired a stupefying theoretical ease in reducing specific experiences to applications of the theory of the permanent revolution. This 'ease' must be explained: it results from the very content of the theory. It was formed by reducing the concrete modif- ications in the Russian situation; it has developed in the same way.

Let us take the example of China: for nearly twenty years the Chinese Communist Party mobilised the masses with the slogans of New Democracy, and the struggle against imperialism, feudalism and bureaucratic capitalism. The victory of this new type of democracy, which accomplishes the radical agrarian revolution under the leader- ship of the proletariat, opens up the road to socialism. To achieve this victory, it was necessary to distinguish accurately the stages of the revolution: the fundamentally economic bourgeois stage and the socialist stage; to prepare in the first the conditions for the second. All this supposes a firm leadership of the struggle, which is capable at every moment of winning the largest possible number of allies by its slogans, and of isolating the principal enemy. The Trotskyists contemplate the result - socialist China - and make the following subtle remark: the revolution did not halt, it developed continuously. In short, it is quite clearly a permanent revolution. For twenty years the 'Stalinist' slogan was inadequate: it contained an 'algebraic' unknown, as Trotsky said about the Leninist slogan of the revolutionary democratic dictatorship of the proletariat and peasantry. Its solution is 'arithmetic', the socialist revolution. He who can do more can also do less. Once one has made the socialist revolution (the maximum) one will at the same stroke have made the democratic revolution (the minimum). From the fact that, at a determinate stage, the democratic revolution is transformed into a socialist revolution, the Trotskyists deduce that the socialist revolution is democratic in the first place. This little game of reciprocity exalts their revolutionism. Clearly, it is bankrupt, for it is necessary to prepare the stage in which the revolution is transformed; which supposes that the stages are distinguished. This is a particular condition for freeing the peasants' initiative.

The agrarian revolution is a primordial task in countries dominated by imperialism. The process of the subordination of the landowning class to imperialism gives a new concrete meaning to the thesis: the agrarian revolution is basically a national revolution. Strategically, the Vietnamese example outstandingly bears this out: the principal enemy of a consistent democratic revolution is imperialism. A concrete imperialism: the American one, in Vietnam. The first stage of the uninterrupted revolution is therefore national democratic. Delivering blows at the same enemy as the world proletarian revolution, it forms a part of this revolution. This provides the best guarantee for the necessary leadership by the proletariat without which the national democratic revolution will not be consistent and cannot be transformed into a socialist revolution. This necessary leadership is not inevitable, as is shown by the victory of a non-democratic national revolution in Egypt or Algeria. Trotsky excluded all possibility of a revolutionary national victory led by the democratic petty bourgeoisie. (6) Life gives the lie to Trotskyist formalism.

Proletarian leadership pre-supposes the liberation of the revolutionary initiative of the peasants as they set out for the conquest of power - and not after the workers' seizure of power (Trotsky's thesis). This leadership assumes methods of peasant organisation for the conquest of power. Baldly denying the peasants' ability to organise an 'independent party', Trotsky excluded the possibility of organising them for the seizure of power. To recognise this condition clearly is to acknowledge the revolutionary democratic composition of the power to be won. The Trotskyists are unable to recognise the necessity (the correctness) of a democratic government (the NLF thesis) arising out of the ruins of the old, feudal and colonial or neo-colonial state apparatus. To recognise the necessity to devise forms of leadership which free the initiative of the peasant masses is to make possible the people's war and its infinite capacity for revolutionary creativity.

WAS LENIN CONVERTED TO TROTSKYISM?

Defining the general orientation of the struggle, the objective to which all the efforts of the social democrats had to be directed, Lenin declared in 'Two Tactics': 'the only force capable of gaining a "decisive victory over Tsarism" is the people, i.e. the proletariat and the peasantry ... the "decisive victory" ... means the establishment of the revolutionary-democratic dictatorship of the proletariat and the peasantry.'

The task of this dictatorship is to accomplish 'the changes urgently and absolutely indispensable to the proletariat and the peasantry', that is, the Party's 'minimum programme'.

'But of course', Lenin added, 'it will be a democratic, not a socialist dictatorship. It will be unable (without a series of intermediary stages of revolutionary development) to affect the foundations of capitalism.' (7)

What does Trotsky say on the subject?

The very fact of the proletariat's representatives entering the government, not as powerless hostages, but as the leading force, destroys the borderline between maximum and minimum programme; that is to say, it places collectivism on the order of the day ... For this reason there can be no talk of any sort of special form of proletarian dictatorship (or dictatorship of the proletariat and the peasantry). (8)

A few pages earlier, he has stressed: 'The whole problem consists in this: who will determine the content of the government's policy, who will form within it a solid majority?' (9)

This is why Lenin could plausibly attribute to him the slogan, 'No Tsar but a workers' government', which adequately sums up his position. (10)

Expounding on the resolution of the 3rd Congress of the RSDLP, Lenin declared, on the contrary: (11)

The resolution deals with a provisional revolutionary government only, and with nothing else; consequently, the question of the 'conquest of power' in general, etc., does not at all come into the picture ... because the political situation in Russia does not by any means turn such questions into immediate issues. On the contrary, the whole people have now raised the issue of the overthrow of the autocracy and the convocation of a constituent assembly. Party congresses should take up and decide not the issues which this or that writer has happened to mention opportunely or inopportunely, but such as are of vital political importance by reason of the prevailing conditions.

As for the participation of the social democrats in the provisional revolutionary government, the 3rd Congress had only decided that it could be entered, 'subject to the alignment of forces and other factors which cannot be exactly predetermined'. (12)

We see that Lenin was by no means inclined to make 'prognoses' or to build castles in the air. His sole preoccupation was to formulate the slogans which met the tasks of the moment by pointing out 'the essential, the general'.

Trotsky later explained: 'I came out against the formula "democratic dictatorship of the proletariat and the peasantry", because I saw its shortcoming in the fact that it left open the question of which class would wield the real dictatorship.' (13)

This argument is correct if Trotsky meant by it that Lenin did not fix in advance the composition of the government 'which must exercise the democratic dictatorship'. (14) But it is false if he was suggesting that Lenin did not speak of the hegemonic role of the working class. The Bolshevik leader expressed his view on the subject more than once in 'Two Tactics': 'We intend to guide ... not only the proletariat, organised by the Social Democratic Party, but also this petty bourgeoisie, which is capable of marching side by side with us.' (15) And also: 'The proletariat must be class conscious and strong enough to rouse the peasantry to revolutionary consciousness, guide its assault, and thereby independently pursue the line of consistent proletarian democratism.' (16)

However, when Martov took up an idea of Trotsky's, Lenin made it clear that 'The question of the revolutionary classes, however, cannot be reduced to a question of the "majority" in any particular revolutionary government'. (17)

Trotsky's criticisms are therefore devoid of any basis. By holding fast to the prospect of a homogeneous social democratic

government he overestimated the level of the Russian workers'
political consciousness while underestimating the revolutionary
potential of the peasant masses, who in 1905 were not yet
differentiated.

In April 1917 the situation was profoundly different. Lenin
observes 'the deeper cleavage between the agricultural labourers
and the poor peasants on the one hand and the peasant proprietors
on the other'. (18) He emphasises 'a struggle for influence within
the Soviets of Workers', Agricultural Labourers', Peasants' and
Soldiers' Deputies'. (19)

The formula of 'the democratic dictatorship' was outdated in 1917
for two reasons:
1 It was realised in a way in the soviets: 'The Soviet is the
   implementation of the dictatorship of the proletariat and the
   soldiers; among the latter the majority are peasants. It is
   therefore a dictatorship of the proletariat and the peasantry.'
   (20)
2 Under the leadership of the petty bourgeoisie the soviets had
   ceded power to the provisional government, that is, to the
   bourgeoisie.
In the particular conjuncture of 1917 it was against the political
representatives of this petty bourgeoisie that the principal blow
had to be struck, for it was deceiving the masses and consolidating
the rule of the imperialist bourgeoisie. We know that Stalin
generalised this particular case, while Mao has followed the
opposite (and general) principle of winning over the intermediary
forces while isolating the diehard reactionaries.

The Trotskyists claim that Lenin 'tacitly' went over to Trotsky's
point of view in April 1917. (21) Lenin had already given them the
lie in texts such as the following, which dates precisely from April
1917: 'Trotskyism: "No Tsar but a Workers' Government". But it is
in two parts. The poorer of the two is with the working class';
(22) and also this one which dates from 1918:
   Things have turned out just as we said they would. The course of
   the revolution has confirmed the correctness of our reasoning.
   First with the whole of the peasants against the monarchy,
   against the landlords, against the medieval regime (and to that
   extent the revolution remains bourgeois, bourgeois-democratic).
   Then, with the poor peasants, the semi-proletarians, with all the
   exploited against capitalism ... and to that extent the
   revolution becomes a socialist one. (23)
It is plain what credence is to be given to the legend hawked about
by the Trotskyists that in 1917 Lenin was converted to Trotskyism
and recognised that he had been mistaken in distinguishing the
democratic stage from the socialist stage. As we have just shown,
things were quite different. This is why they are forced to attempt
to confer some credibility on their thesis by going even further
along the road of falsification and fabricating a Lenin denying the
'interpenetration' (transcroissance) of one stage into the other.
Thus Isaac Deutscher's readers are informed: 'His (Lenin's) policy
was based firmly on the premiss that the Russian revolution would
confine itself to its anti-feudal objectives.' (24)

Anyone who takes the trouble to check this will find that Lenin
said exactly the opposite in 'Two Tactics of Social Democracy':

> The revolutionary-democratic dictatorship of the proletariat and
> the peasantry has a past and a future. Its past is autocracy,
> serfdom, monarchy and privilege ... Its future is the struggle
> against private property, the struggle of the wage-worker against
> the employer, the struggle for socialism. (25)

Having introduced a first untruth into the minds of his unsuspecting
readers, Deutscher makes them accept all the more easily a second
(the important one for him) which seems to follow naturally: 'In
1917 ... Lenin changed his mind. In all essentials the thesis of
the permanent revolution (though not, of course, its somewhat
bookish nomenclature) was adopted by his party.' (26)

Thus, to declare Trotsky correct, we must attribute to Lenin a
crude opportunist error in 1905 which then enables us to falsify
Lenin's positions in 1917 in the opposite direction. Finally, let
us admire the 'of course' which saves Deutscher from having to
explain to us why Lenin did not take over the term 'permanent
revolution' if it were true that it corresponded to a scientific
concept. Was Lenin afraid of Marxist terms; was he afraid of
Marxist works?

All the false and nonsensical Trotskyist constructions are
summarised in a short note of Ernest Mandel's:

> Between 1905 and 1917 the Bolshevik Party was educated in the
> spirit of achieving the 'democratic dictatorship of the workers
> and peasants', i.e. in the spirit of a formula with its eye on
> the possibility of a coalition between a workers' party and a
> peasant party ... Only in 1917 did he (Lenin) realise that
> Trotsky had been correct back in 1905 when he predicted that the
> agrarian question could only be solved by the dictatorship of the
> proletariat and the socialisation of the Russian economy. (27)

Lenin has long since refuted this interpretation of his political
line in 1905 by showing that the problem of class alliances cannot
be reduced to that of alliances between parties - which completely
undermines Trotsky's objection that there could not be an
independent peasant party:

> A 'coalition' of classes does not at all presuppose either the
> existence of any particular powerful party, or parties in
> general. This is only confusing classes with parties ... The
> experience of the Russian revolution shows that the 'coalitions'
> of the proletariat and the peasantry were formed scores and
> hundred of times, in the most diverse forms, without any
> 'powerful independent party' of the peasantry. (28)

Mandel could have disputed this argument of Lenin's. He decided
that it was more prudent to pass it over in silence, hoping that his
readers would not come across it in Lenin's voluminous works. In
fact, Mandel not only claims that Lenin's policy was wrong, he
falsifies this policy by arguing that it presupposed a coalition
between parties. Mandel also repeats the old Trotskyist confusion
between socialism and the dictatorship of the proletariat, between
the character (the social content) of the stages and the class
nature of the power. (29) This is what enables him to conclude
that, after the 'April Theses', there was no better Trotskyist than
Lenin.

TROTSKY AND THE PEASANTRY

With his pretension to be a better Leninist than Lenin, Trotsky
vehemently denied that he wanted to 'skip over the peasantry' or
that he underestimated its revolutionary potential. He accused
Lenin of having criticised him on this point without having read his
work. In reality, in the chapter of 'Results and Prospects' devoted
to relations between the proletariat in power and the peasantry, he
openly showed his contempt for the latter. (30) A few quotations
will prove it:

> Many sections of the working masses, particularly in the
> countryside will be drawn into the revolution and become
> politically organised only after the advance-guard of the
> revolution, the urban proletariat, stands at the helm of the
> state. Revolutionary agitation and organisation will then be
> conducted with the help of state resources. (pp. 202-3)
>
>   In such a situation, created by the transference of power to
> the proletariat, nothing remains for the peasantry to do but to
> rally to the regime of the workers' democracy. It will not
> matter much even if the peasantry does this with a degree of
> consciousness no larger than that with which it usually rallies
> to the bourgeois regime. (p. 205)

Alluding to Lenin's policy, he also wrote: 'Lenin now proposes that
the proletariat's political self-limitation should be supplemented
with an objective anti-socialist "safeguard" in the form of the
muzhik as collaborator or co-director'. (31)

In fact, according to Lenin, the proletariat 'can become a
victorious fighter for democracy only if the peasant masses join its
revolutionary struggle'. (32)

Let us note first of all that the chapter from which we have
taken the first two quotations is entitled 'The proletariat in power
and the peasantry'. Trotsky says nothing about the alliance of the
proletariat and the peasantry with a view to taking power.

We can summarise Trotsky's ideas before 1917 on this subject as
follows:

The proletariat emancipates the peasantry and conducts agitation
and organisational work within it after the seizure of power.

For Lenin, on the contrary, the revolutionary mobilisation of the
peasantry is a condition of victory.

The peasantry rallies to the proletariat with more or less as
much fatalism and ignorance of its own interests as when it supports
a reactionary regime.

According to Lenin, 'The proletariat cannot count on the
ignorance and prejudices of the peasantry as the powers that be
under a bourgeois regime count on and depend on them'. (33)

For Trotsky there was no question of making concessions to the
peasantry in order to ensure that the contradiction between it and
the proletariat remained secondary, because he did not distinguish,
in fact, between the democratic stage and the socialist stage of the
revolution. (34) Rather, he considered that the transition to the
socialist stage presupposes a conflict between the two classes.

Lenin's definition of the dictatorship of the proletariat makes
it obvious how anti-Leninist this position is: (35)

> The dictatorship of the proletariat is a special sort of class

> alliance between the proletariat (the vanguard of the workers),
> and the non-proletarian strata of those who labour (petty
> bourgeoisie, small employers, peasants, intelligentsia, and so
> forth) ... for the complete overthrow of capitalism ... for the
> definitive inauguration and consolidation of socialism.

In a country like Russia the 'non-proletarian strata of those who
labour' were mainly the broad peasant masses. For Lenin, the
dictatorship of the proletariat in Russia was therefore a particular
form of the class alliance between the proletariat and the working
peasants and we know that before his death one of his main concerns
was the strengthening of this alliance. Here, on the contrary, is
what Trotsky wrote in 1922, in the preface to his '1905':

> Precisely in order to guarantee its victory, the proletarian
> vanguard in the very earliest stages of its rule would have to
> make extremely deep inroads not only into feudal but also into
> bourgeois property relations. While doing so it would enter into
> hostile conflict not only with all those bourgeois groups which
> had supported it during the first stage of the revolutionary
> struggle but also with the broad masses of the peasantry with
> whose collaboration it - the proletariat - had come into power.

SOCIALISM IN ONE COUNTRY

While formally declaring himself in agreement with Lenin about the
law of uneven development, Trotsky never accepted all its
implications, especially the following:

1 With wars breaking out among the imperialist countries for the
   division of the world, the revolution can triumph first in a
   relatively backward country (the weakest link) such as Russia,
   thanks to the alliance between the proletariat and the peasantry,
   and can hold out, notably on account of the violent contradictions between its enemies.
2 This revolution is not necessarily the immediate prelude to
   world revolution but the latter will continue as it began with
   new victories in particular countries (where capitalism is weak)
   for a long historical period. The uneven ripening of the
   conditions for a revolutionary explosion excludes its simul-
   taneous occurrence in every country.

From as early as 1906, Trotsky reckoned that a revolution in Russia
would lead to an intervention of the European powers, Germany and
Austria-Hungary in particular. This war would inevitably lead to a
revolution in these countries and step by step to the triumph of
world socialism. (36) This mechanism is one of the aspects of the
permanence of the revolution.

It was also necessary for the revolution to go immediately beyond
the borders of Russia in another sense. For Trotsky, the revolution
will be global or not at all. In fact, if it remained isolated in a
predominantly agricultural country it would succumb very quickly to
the blows of external intervention or internal counter-revolution.
(37)

> Without the direct State support of the European proletariat the
> working class of Russia cannot remain in power and convert its
> temporary domination into a lasting socialistic dictatorship.
> (38)

Left to its own resources, the working class of Russia will
inevitably be crushed by the counter-revolution the moment the
peasantry turns its back on it. It will have no alternative but
to link the fate of its political rule, and, hence, the fate of
the whole Russian revolution, with the fate of the socialist
revolution in Europe.(39)

Trotsky did not believe that it would be possible to maintain
workers' power in Russia without external aid, especially because
he was convinced that the logic of the proletariat's revolutionary
action would lead it into conflict with the peasantry.

He returned to this question in 1917 in his pamphlet 'Program of
Peace' (republished in 1924 in the collection 'The Year 1917'). He
declared in it that 'a victorious revolution in Russia or England is
inconceivable without revolution in Germany and vice versa'. To
avoid any ambiguity he specified moreover that: 'It would be futile
to expect ... for instance, that revolutionary Russia could hold its
own in face of a conservative Europe'. (40)

In 1926 he again recalled the position he held in October 1917:
'it was clear to us that the victory of the proletarian revolution
is impossible without the international world revolution'. (41)

During the two years that followed the seizure of power, Lenin
may have feared lest foreign intervention crush the young Soviet
republic. (42) Later, his fears and doubts were allayed, whereas
Zinoviev made a dogma of them five years after at the time of his
dispute with Stalin over the possibility of building socialism in
one country. As for Trotsky, he proved to be remarkably obstinate
in error. In 1922 he no longer spoke of an impending 'inevitable'
defeat of the proletarian power in the absence of a revolution in
Europe, but he expressed the same idea in a more cautious form: 'The
contradiction between a workers' government and an overwhelming
majority of peasants in a backward country could be resolved only on
an international scale, in the arena of a world proletarian
revolution'. (43)

In the same year, Trotsky wrote in the postscript to his pamphlet
'Program of Peace': 'A genuine advance of socialist economy in
Russia will become possible only after the victory of the
proletariat in the most important countries of Europe.'

History having decided, comment is unnecessary - more especially
as Trotsky provided the best one in 1939 in his 'Transitional
Program', in which we read: 'The nationalisation of the means of
production, a necessary condition for socialist development, opened
up the possibility of a rapid growth of the productive forces.'

While being very proud of his 'prognoses', Trotsky constantly
altered his conception of the permanent revolution. 1905, 1917,
1922, 1929, 1939 - these dates mark not the stages of a deeper
knowledge of the laws of revolution but the contortions of a
'theoretician' striving to make something stand up in a schema
undermined, breached and ground to dust by inconsiderate opponents
and merciless historical events.

When, at the beginning of 1925, the dispute over socialism in one
country broke out between Zinoviev and Kamenev on the one hand and
Bukharin on the other, Trotsky kept apart from it. He seems even
not to have been aware of anything for a year. He himself said
later that he was caught unawares by the formidable conflict

dividing the majority and the minority at the 14th Congress in December 1925. He distrusted Zinoviev, who had been the most virulent of his opponents and whom he considered to be the leader of the right wing. He did not believe his differences with Stalin to be serious. However, Zinoviev's argument coincided with his own to a certain extent (except on the question of the alliance with the peasantry) and that is why Stalin had already refuted it in advance in the so-called 'literary' debate at the end of 1924.

Given Trotsky's argument that 'the safety (of the proletarian state) rests solely on the victory of the proletariat in the advanced countries', Stalin concluded that, according to his opponent, 'there is but one prospect left for our revolution: to vegetate in its own contradictions and rot away while waiting for the world revolution'.

He opposed to 'this permanent hopelessness' Lenin's ideas on the construction of socialism in one country. Lenin said, among other things: (44)

Socialism is no longer a matter of the distant future or an abstract picture ... difficult as this task may be, new as it is ... and numerous as the difficulties may be that it entails, we shall – not in a day but in a few years – all of us together fulfil it whatever the cost, so that NEP Russia will become Socialist Russia.

Lenin also said: (45)

Indeed the power of the State over all the large-scale means of production, political power in the hands of the proletariat, the alliance of the proletariat with many millions of the small and very small peasants, the assured proletarian leadership of the peasantry etc – is this not all that is necessary to build a complete socialist society ... out of co-operatives, out of co-operatives alone, which we formerly ridiculed as huckstering and which from a certain aspect we have the right to treat as such now, under NEP? Is this not all that is necessary to build a complete socialist society? It is still not the building of socialist society but it is all that is necessary and sufficient for it.

In the same article, we read the sentence: 'With most of the population organised in co-operatives, socialism ... will achieve its aims automatically.'

Trotsky did his utmost to interpret this text in a sense favourable to his theses. According to him, when Lenin said 'We have all that is necessary and sufficient for the construction of socialism', he was referring to the first political fruits. It would also be necessary to solve the problem of the culture that the Russian people lacked. Culture presupposes a 'certain material base'. Therefore, (according to Trotsky's Lenin), we need the victorious European proletariat to come to our aid with its superior technology. (46)

This is an absolutely unwarranted deflection of Lenin's arguments. In fact, in his article, Lenin was far from denying that the Russian people could raise the level of their culture and technology by their own efforts, otherwise he would have written 'all that is necessary but not sufficient'.

Trotsky was very careful not to enter into a polemic on this

question during Lenin's lifetime. When such a polemic did break out
in 1925 between Zinoviev on the one hand and Stalin and Bukharin
on the other, Stalin was easily able to prove that his view
rigorously conformed to Lenin's ideas. In 'On Co-operation', Lenin
defined what he meant by socialism: 'Given social ownership of the
means of production, given the class victory of the proletariat over
the bourgeoisie, the system of civilised co-operators is the system
of socialism.' (47)

It seems that by 'building a complete socialist society' Stalin
understood fundamentally the same thing, i.e. 'victory over the
capitalist elements in our economy', in the strict sense (linked to
the private ownership of the means of production). As often as not
Zinoviev did not attribute any other meaning to the 'final' victory
of socialism and neither did Trotsky to the 'completion of the
construction of socialism' which they denied was possible in one
country. Taking up Lenin's formula again, Stalin argued against
them that it was possible to construct 'the complete socialist
society' in the USSR. He denied, however, that this victory could
be 'final', that is, guaranteed against external intervention as
long as the proletariat had not taken power 'in at least a number
of countries'. (48)

In 'Leninism', Zinoviev exercises his sleight of hand on
quotations from Lenin. He does not distinguish between the final
victory of socialism in so far as it implies the abolition of
classes, the abolition of the state and the transition to communism
on the one hand, and socialism as 'the transition from a small,
isolated, individual, market economy to a big collective economy',
as Lenin said, on the other. The Bolshevik leader did not believe
that the former was possible without the world victory of the
revolution but he held that it was possible to construct socialism
in one country in the second sense, since for him Russia possessed
'all that is necessary to build a complete socialist society', which
he defined as 'Soviets plus electrification throughout the country',
or 'the system of civilised co-operators'.

According to Ernest Mandel, 'all Trotsky stated ... was the fact
that a fully-fledged socialist society, i.e. a society without
classes, commodities, money and state, could never be accomplished
within the boundaries of a single state'. (49) We have seen that
until 1918 Trotsky denied 'that a revolutionary Russia ... could
hold its own in the face of a conservative Europe'; that, later, he
did not believe that the socialisation of the means of production or
the advance of a socialist economy were possible in one country. It
was only after 1929 that historical experience forced him
occasionally to come close to the position which Mandel attributes
to him. Even then, it is quite simply false to say that this is
'all Trotsky stated'. Let me provide even more proof.

If we place ourselves in the framework of this controversy
(1925-6) we can conclude:
1 that Stalin's position largely conformed to Lenin's views;
2 that it was confirmed in practice when the kulaks and the nepmen
   were liquidated as classes after 1928 and that consequently
   enormous progress was made on the economic and cultural levels;
3 that Stalin went further than Lenin and erred in arguing that the
   victory of the proletariat in several countries was enough to
   enable one to speak of a final victory of socialism. (50)

In his book 'The Permanent Revolution' (1928-31), Trotsky once again beat a retreat. He set up his line of defence on positions which Zinoviev had earlier prepared for him. He was content from then on to deny the possibility of a final construction of socialism in one country. Events decided against him very rapidly, for it was clear (given the context) that his 'final socialism' was identical to Lenin's 'complete socialism'; that is to say, with the measure of socialism realised under Stalin. Let us look, therefore, at what Trotsky wrote at the time when the First Five-Year Plan was already being carried out: (51)

> To aim at building a nationally isolated socialist society means, in spite of all passing successes, to pull the productive forces backward even as compared with capitalism. To attempt, regardless of the geographical, cultural and historical conditions of the country's development which constitutes a part of the world unity, to realise ... all the branches of economy within a national framework, means to pursue a reactionary utopia. If the heralds and supporters of this theory never-theless participate in the international revolutionary struggle (with what success is a different question) it is because, as hopeless eclectics, they mechanically combine abstract internationalism with reactionary utopian national socialism.

Let the reader judge for himself: did the Five-Year Plans pull the productive forces backward even as compared with capitalism? Did the geographical, historical and cultural conditions prevent the realisation of all the branches of the economy within a national framework? The Trotskyists have never told us what they think about this example of their mentor's 'prognoses'. The most interesting thing about the passage that we have just quoted is that it offers us a striking example of the complete about-turns in which Trotsky, the rigid critic of Stalinist zigzags, was adept. In this passage he declares that internally the Soviet leaders were reactionary utopians but that internationally they participated in the revolutionary struggle. Some years later he was to argue the opposite: that as a degenerated workers' state, the Soviet Union presents a two-fold character: it is progressive internally as it maintains socialist relations of production and develops the productive forces; it is reactionary internationally as it systematically betrays all revolutionary struggles.

In 'The Permanent Revolution', Trotsky formulated another 'prognosis' which is extremely embarrassing for his disciples, who continue to denounce the evils of socialism in one country: 'The theory of the kulak growing into socialism and the theory of the 'neutralisation' of the world bourgeoisie are ... inseparable from the theory of socialism in one country. They stand or fall together.' (52)

We consider contemporary Trotskyists to be more qualified than ourselves to comment on this text, which we shall leave to them to think about.

However, it is necessary to emphasise a curious argument of Trotsky's in this new dispute. After 'Pravda' had written that 'the final victory of socialism, guaranteed against the intervention of the capitalist camp effectively (demanded) the triumph of the proletarian revolution in several advanced countries', he claimed to

prove that this was absurd, for if it were possible to build
socialism in the USSR its final victory in that country and even in
the world would 'ipso facto' be achieved because
> The example of a backward country, which in the course of several
> Five-Year Plans was able to construct a mighty socialist society
> with its own forces, would mean a death blow to world capitalism,
> and would reduce to a minimum, if not to zero, the costs of the
> world proletarian revolution. (53)

Here the reader will recognise the Khrushchevite argument. When the
USSR has caught up with the USA in 'per capita' production of
consumption goods, the peoples of the world will choose socialism
and vote accordingly. The only difference is that Khrushchev
thought this overtaking possible given the Soviet Union's faster
rate of growth, whereas Trotsky thought it impossible. For both the
link between the cause (economic success of the USSR) and the effect
(more or less peaceful world revolution) is identical. This
coincidence reflects a common theoretical basis. Neither of them
realised that the development of contradictions in those partial
totalities, in concrete social formations, is fundamentally
explained by the action of internal causes and not by external
influences. (54)

In fact, Trotskyism is characterised particularly by the tendency
to attribute an undue significance to the unity of the world market
which is supposed to constitute the objective basis for proletarian
internationalism. One of the obstacles to the building of socialism
in one country is supposed to be the pressure of cheap commodities
produced in the advanced capitalist countries; capitalism's ability
to subordinate all the other modes of production, even the socialist
mode of production, if its technical basis is insufficiently
developed at the start. 'But, in elaborating the theoretical
prognosis of the October Revolution, I did not at all believe that,
by conquering state power, the Russian proletariat would exclude the
former Tsarist empire from the orbit of the world economy'. (55)

This, however, is what happened. The USSR lived in semi-autarchy
for several decades. The impetuous industrial development of the
USSR during the 1930s, at the very time of the great crisis, shows
that the economy of a country under the dictatorship of the
proletariat in which the means of production and foreign trade are
nationalised, is no longer subject to the repercussions of the
cyclical fluctuations of the world market nor any longer ruled by
the economic law of capitalism (profit maximisation), but develops
according to its own fundamental law.

In the 'Economic Problems of Socialism in the USSR' (p. 333),
Stalin emphasised that after the Second World War the socialist camp
appeared, 'so that we now have two parallel world markets
confronting one another'.

The monopoly of foreign trade retained by proletarian power does
not allow capitalism to become an integral part of the production of
a country which is building socialism, or thereby to eat away the
nascent socialist relations of production by virtue of its temporary
technical superiority.

Trotsky's internationalism was really only a refusal to
acknowledge the discontinuities of the world sociological space:
distinct social formations, national particularities, unevenness in

the development of the objective and subjective conditions for
revolution and, finally, the possibility of a relatively separate
socialist market contemporaneous with the capitalist market.

However, on the practical level and only if we consider the
immediate perspectives, he apparently agreed with Stalin that the
construction of the economic basis of socialism in the USSR should
not be subordinated to the vicissitudes of proletarian struggles in
the advanced capitalist countries. Thus one might think he is
picking an artificial quarrel with him, assuming him in the wrong
from the start. In fact, it was nothing of the sort. As conceived
by Trotsky, industrialisation was only a 'sort of emergency measure
until the advent of international revolution saved the situation',
(56) hence its vague and abstract character. This is all the more
true since, as we have just seen, he considered 'a genuine advance
of socialist economy in Russia' before 'the victory of the
proletariat in the most important countries of Europe' to be
impossible.

Trotsky and his disciples have presented the thesis of socialism
in one country as an expression of a narrow outlook, indeed of a
messianic nationalism (Trotsky made analogous complaints about the
Bolshevik Party before 1917) and even as proceeding from a
deliberate wish to betray the world revolution. A reading of Stalin
does not corroborate this accusation. Just one quotation will
suffice: (57)

> While it is true that the final victory of Socialism in the first
> country to emancipate itself is impossible without the combined
> efforts of the proletarians of several countries, it is equally
> true that the development of the world revolution will be the
> more rapid and thorough the more effective the assistance
> rendered by the first Socialist country to the workers and
> labouring masses of all other countries.

He follows this immediately by quoting a text from 'On the Slogan of
a United States of Europe' in which Lenin advocated armed intervention by the first socialist state to aid the people against their
oppressors! The revisionists and Trotskyists are in league to hide
these aspects of Lenin's and Stalin's thought. The least one can
say about them is that they call into question the usual idea of
socialism in one country.

One would surmise that Stalin, who made so many mistakes in the
construction of socialism in the USSR, is not free from all blame
as leader of the International. Let us be more precise: he was not
always capable of a correct combination of reinforcement of the
socialist bastion and support for revolutionary peoples. We shall
deal with this question later. Investigations and historical
research are required to determine what were Stalin's mistakes in
this domain. The answer to this type of question has no connection
with an examination of the thesis of socialism in one country which,
as we have sufficiently demonstrated, is compatible as such (on the
theoretical level) with the boldest and most intransigent
internationalism. Besides, it is noteworthy that Stalin, who was
its promoter, 'later showed himself rather prudent and reserved in
its accreditation', (58) given that it was taken up by Bukharin who
attached it to his idea of the construction of socialism 'at a
snail's pace'. Stalin, on the contrary, soon came to emphasise the

first term of the formula, 'socialism in one country', on the eve of
the attack on the kulaks and the First Five-Year Plan.

The thesis according to which it was possible 'to build a
complete socialist society' by counting on the forces of the USSR
alone was explicitly presented by Stalin as necessary with a view to
encouraging the people to commit themselves to this construction.
For him it therefore had a practical value.

The process of the restoration of capitalism in the USSR and the
cultural revolution in China have led us to a more rigorous
conception of the advance towards communism. We know that for Marx
the latter comprises two stages: the lower is characterised by the
principle, 'From each according to his ability, to each according to
his work'. A certain inequality thus survives, along with the
bourgeois right which is its corollary. In the 'higher phase' of
communist society (59)

> after the enslaving subordination of the individual to the
> division of labour, and therewith also the antithesis between
> mental and physical labour, has vanished; after labour has become
> not only a means of life but life's prime want; after the
> productive forces have also increased with the all-round
> development of the individual and all the springs of co-operative
> wealth flow more abundantly – only then can the narrow horizon of
> bourgeois right be crossed in its entirety and society inscribe
> on its banners: From each according to his ability, to each
> according to his needs!

By that time the state will have withered away, social classes will
have disappeared along with the three fundamental inequalities
bequeathed by capitalism: the differences between manual and mental
labour, town and country, and agriculture and industry. A profound
transformation in outlook, customs and ideology will have eradicated
egoism and individualism.

It is certain that the transition to the higher stage of
socialism, communism, will only be able to take place on a world
scale after the elimination of capitalist encirclement. This
question (different from that debated in the 1920s) must be
connected to the problematic of the class struggle after the
suppression of private ownership of the means of production.
Trotsky (like Stalin), hardly suspected it, and then only very
confusedly.

If we have said that Stalin was correct to think that it was
possible to construct socialism in one country, we cannot go along
with him when, in his report to the 18th Congress (1939), he
envisaged the transition to communism in one country. He even
argued in it that the state would survive 'in the period of
communism', 'if capitalist encirclement is not liquidated'.   In 1946
Stalin reiterated this thesis according to which 'communism in one
country is perfectly conceivable particularly in a country such as
the Soviet Union'. (60) On this point, Mao has expressed a
diametrically opposite point of view: the transition to communism,
he has said, will only be realisable after several generations when
'the division of labour which is at the basis of class division'
(Engels) has been eliminated and when the state has consequently
'withered away' (Engels).

In 'Economic Problems of Socialism in the USSR', Stalin set out three conditions which must be fulfilled to prepare the transition to communism:

1   continuous expansion of production with priority for the means of production;
2   replacement of commodity circulation by a system of product-exchange which will raise collective-farm property to the level of national property (collective farmers will no longer be able to sell their surpluses on the market but will 'receive products in much greater quantities from the State');
3   cultural advancement so that members of society 'are not tied all their lives, owing to the existing division of labour, to some one occupation'. For this, it is necessary, 'to shorten the working day ... that housing conditions should be radically improved, and that real wages of workers ... should be at least doubled'. (61)

Under the dictatorship of the proletariat, the last two conditions in fact amount to the first one. In short, to move to communism it is enough to increase production!

As for the elimination of the three differences bequeathed by capitalism, Stalin interpreted Marx and Engels's doctrine somewhat freely. We read in his last work, for example: (62)

The ground for antithesis between town and country, between industry and agriculture, has already been eliminated by our socialist system. This, of course, does not mean that the effect of the abolition of the antithesis between town and country will be that 'the great towns' will perish. (Engels, 'Anti-Dühring) Not only will the great towns not perish, but new great towns will appear.

Stalin quoted Engels in order to contradict him. In fact, here is what we read in 'Anti-Dühring': 'It is true that in the great towns civilisation has bequeathed us a heritage which it will take us some time and trouble to get rid of. But it must and will be got rid of.' (p. 352.)

In fact, Stalin denied that it was possible to make 'all' the differences between industry and agriculture, between manual and mental labour disappear because he did not think that the division of labour could be overcome. He declared: 'The essential distinction between mental and physical labour ... the difference in their cultural and technical levels, will certainly disappear. But some distinction, even if inessential, will remain, if only because the conditions of labour of the managerial staffs and those of the workers are not identical'. (63)

Even if the cultural and technical level of the workers is very high, can we consider the distinction maintained between management personnel and workers 'insignificant'?

With such ideas it was impossible for Stalin to prepare the conditions for the transition to the higher stage of communism as the Chinese are doing even now. However, Stalin tackled the problem with at least the minimum of seriousness, which is precisely not the case with the present leaders in the Soviet Union who, since the 22nd Congress (1961), under Khrushchev, boast of constructing full-scale communism there. It is well known that in 1957 Molotov, the last of the 'Stalinists', opposed the thesis of the final completion of socialism in the USSR which was proclaimed by Stalin as early as

1936 in his report on the Draft Constitution. Today the Chinese
insist on the necessity for a people who want to construct socialism
to rely above all on their own forces. This formula can be
considered as an avatar of 'socialism in one country' which the
Chinese only rarely mention. In a certain sense it fulfils the same
function: 'on s'engage et puis on voit'. (64) Rely on oneself, not
on others. It is true that the Chinese situate the complete
realisation of socialism further away than Stalin did in 1926. 'In
five or ten generations or even more', they have written. In fact,
they know, as Lenin did, that the nationalisation of the means of
production is not enough.

    With the clarity and rigour that distinguishes him, Mao Tse-tung
has recently defined the Marxist-Leninist position on this subject.
He poses the problem correctly and thus puts paid to an old
controversy: (65)

> We have won great victories. But the defeated class will still
> struggle. These people are still around and this class still
> exists. Therefore, we cannot speak of final victory. Not even
> for decades. We must not lose our vigilance. According to the
> Leninist viewpoint, the final victory of a socialist country not
> only requires the efforts of the proletariat and the broad masses
> of the people at home, but also involves the victory of the world
> revolution and the abolition of the system of exploitation of man
> by man over the whole globe, upon which all mankind will be
> emancipated.

Back in 1962, Mao had said: (66)

> The next 50 to 100 years or so, beginning from now, will be a
> great era of radical change in the social system throughout the
> world, an earth-shaking era without equal in any previous
> historical period. Living in such an era, we must be prepared
> to engage in great struggles which will have many features
> different in form from those of the past.

At the end of his life the old fighter, who has just carried off his
greatest victory, reveals to us the prospective thunder and
lightning of future revolutionary storms. Once again he invites us
to throw off our illusions and to prepare ourselves for the
struggle. New vanguards will be forged in the flames of their
struggle, new developments in Marxism-Leninism will spring from
their practice. This call and this message are directed to the
entire world. China is a fragment of the international
revolutionary movement and at the same time its principal Red base.
The Chinese consider that Stalin's thesis that it is possible to
construct socialism in one country is an important contribution to
the development of Marxism-Leninism. Is any other proof necessary
to show that adherence to this thesis does not imply opposition to
world revolutions?

PERMANENT REVOLUTION OR UNINTERRUPTED REVOLUTION BY STAGES?

At a lecture and debate on the crisis of the international communist
movement bringing together Pierre Cot, Lelio Basso, Isaac Deutscher
and Jacques Vergès, Vergès's reply to a listener who asked him about
the 'permanent revolution' in China had the merit of infuriating

Pierre Frank (67) who hurled himself towards the platform, his face purple, his eyes popping and foam on his lips. After him, Deutscher calmly explained that he had examined the Chinese and Trotskyist ideas of the permanent revolution very closely, that he had resorted to the strongest 'theoretical lenses', without, however, discovering the slightest difference between them. (68)

We do not believe that lenses of great 'separating power' are necessary to see the opposition between certain aspects of these two theories unless one is suffering from a very advanced intellectual myopia. I have shown above that Lenin did not 'tacitly' become Trotskyist in 1917. I shall now go into the differences between the Chinese uninterrupted revolution and Trotsky's permanent revolution.

Comparing these two concepts, we shall show that they are distinguishable and even opposed to one another. That is why we designate them by different terms, dismissing philological quibbles as irrelevant to the question that the Chinese language possesses only a single expression for both concepts, (69) or that in Russia a single word is translated sometimes by 'stages' and sometimes by 'phases'. (Trotskyists like speaking about 'phases' but not 'stages'.)

For my part, I shall conform to the elementary logical principles stated by Pascal when he said 'I never quarrel about a name as long as I am told what meaning is given it'.

In their translation into foreign languages the Chinese are always careful to use the expression 'uninterrupted revolution' (by stages) to avoid any confusion with Trotsky's ideas.
1 Trotsky wrote:
> It is nonsense to say that stages in general cannot be skipped. The living historical process always makes leaps over isolated 'stages' which derive from the theoretical breakdown into its component parts of the process of development in its entirety ... (70)
>
> The third Chinese revolution ... will not have a 'democratic' period ... It will be forced ... to abolish (from the start) bourgeois ownership in the towns and countryside. (71)

In contrast, Mao argues that the revolution is at once uninterrupted and that it passes through determined stages. These stages can neither be leapt over, nor can the tasks of a stage be embarked upon before those of the preceding one have been accomplished: (72)
> Taken as a whole, the Chinese revolutionary movement led by the Communist Party embraces two stages, i.e. the democratic and the socialist revolutions ... The second process can only be carried through after the first has been completed. The democratic revolution is the necessary preparation for the socialist revolution, and the socialist revolution is the inevitable sequel to the democratic revolution.

Mao emphasises that it is necessary to understand both 'the difference and the connection' between these two stages. The Trotskyists saw the connection but not the difference, while the opportunists of the Chinese Right (Ch'en Tu-hsiu) saw the difference but not the connection.

Under the leadership of the Communist Party the Chinese people carried out the tasks of the democratic stage in a consistent and radical manner, thus ensuring the uninterrupted transition (the interpenetration, as Lenin said) of the revolution to the socialist stage.

2 The displacements of the principal contradiction are the objective basis for the distinction between the stages. A different system of class alliances corresponds to each one of them. During the democratic revolution the party of the proletariat, supported by the fundamental masses of workers and peasants (73) and regrouping under its leadership all the forces which can be united, especially the petty bourgeoisie and a part of the national bourgeoisie, carries to completion the struggle against imperialism, bureaucratic and comprador capital and feudalism. This stage goes beyond the liberation of China (1949) to the completion of agrarian reform (1952), when the principal contradiction becomes that between the working class and the bourgeoisie. The revolution has entered its socialist stage, during which the proletariat is principally in alliance with the poor peasants and the lower stratum of the middle peasants.

For Trotsky, the principal contradiction remains the same during the whole period of the transition from capitalism to socialism: the capital/labour contradiction.

It follows that, for him, the bourgeoisie confronting the workers always and everywhere constitutes one reactionary mass. This being true for the entire world it is also therefore true for China.

The Chinese Communists have been able to distinguish between two groups in the bourgeoisie of their country. One consisted of bureaucratic capital (the four great families who controlled the state apparatus) and comprador capital which acted as an intermediary between the international monopolies and the Chinese market. This group was the instrument of imperialism and the ally of the landlords. The other comprised the middle or national bourgeoisie which displayed a revolutionary character on the one hand and a tendency towards compromise with the enemy on the other. Imperialism, feudalism, and bureaucratic capital were crushing and stifling the middle bourgeoisie. It had a vital interest in the elimination of semi-feudal relations in the countryside in order to enlarge the market, and in national independence to free it from imperialist dumping. It follows that at certain times and to a certain extent it was able to participate in the revolution. In other respects it was an exploiting class as it retained links with imperialism and feudalism and was economically and politically weak, so that there was a risk that it would go over to the side of counter-revolution, particularly after a period of successful popular struggle (for example 1927-31).

Even when it was an ally of the proletariat it remained hesitant and vacillating; hence the necessity to adopt towards it a policy of unity and struggle, that is, to criticise it in order to induce it to prove more steadfast in the anti-imperialist struggle. Given the fact that China was a backward country it was necessary to maintain on the economic level a united front with the national bourgeoisie after the victory of the revolution. In the people's democratic dictatorship then set up, this class constituted a part of the people. (74) The contradication between it and the working class which it continued to exploit presented, in addition to an antagonistic component, a non-antagonistic component. This means that in the concrete conditions in China this contradiction could be solved peacefully by a policy of unity, criticism and education. (75)

This is, in fact, what was done. The national bourgeoisie ceased to exist as a class in 1966, after a fairly long transitional period.

It is hardly necessary to point out that, for the Trotskyists, any alliance with a fraction of the bourgeoisie, whatever the concrete conditions, is an abominable betrayal of principles, as is the formula 'democratic dictatorship of the people'.

Trotsky had learned from Lenin that the stages of a revolution are distinguished by the nature of the socio-economic formations on its agenda, not by that of the political power. In Russia, the democratic stage lasted from February 1917 to July 1918. Trotsky himself acknowledged that the period from November 1917 to July 1918 was democratic. (76) The Trotskyists today have forgotten this. Ernest Mandel does not understand that the democratic stage in China might have lasted until 1952, although the power established in 1949 was in its essence a dictatorship of the proletariat, for the latter had first to complete the democratic transformation before going on to socialist measures.

3 According to Trotsky: (77)

> in a country where the proletariat has power in its hands as the result of the democratic revolution, the subsequent fate of the dictatorship and socialism depends in the last analysis not only and not so much upon the national productive process as upon the development of the international socialist revolution.

The reason for this is 'The world division of labour, the dependence of Soviet industry upon foreign technology, the dependence of the productive forces of the advanced countries of Europe upon Asiatic raw materials'. (78)

As I have shown, Trotsky was convinced that the dictatorship of the proletariat in an economically backward country would quickly be crushed by foreign intervention and internal counter-revolution unless help came from the victorious proletariat in one or several advanced countries. For forty years history has daily contradicted this prognosis of Trotsky's which he presented, moreover, in the mode of 'That's how it is', with no explanation of either how or why.

The Chinese conceive the solidarity between their revolution and the world revolution quite differently:

> (a) When they were still in the democratic and national liberation stage they were deeply conscious of the truth of the theory developed by Lenin and Stalin according to which, after the October revolution, 'the liberation movements of oppressed nations play an integral part in the world socialist revolution': because both have a common enemy, imperialism; because the leadership of the proletariat exercised through the Communist Party guarantees the transition to the socialist revolution after the complete victory of the democratic revolution; because the achievement of economic independence and 'a fortiori' the building of a socialist economy require relations of mutual assistance and solidarity with the socialist camp.

(b)   The revolutionary struggles in the world undermine the rear
of imperialism and are one of the factors that prevent it
from attacking the socialist countries and contribute to its
defeat when it ventures to do so.   The Chinese communists
have pointed out that the vast regions of Asia, Africa and
Latin America dominated by imperialism are the nodal point
at which the contradictions of the contemporary world
converge, the storm centre where the revolutionary peoples
have reaped numerous victories since 1945, where partisan
armies are rooted in the masses and are becoming
progressively stronger, and where, in the present
circumstances, a people's war has the best chance of
victory.   They have recalled what Stalin said in 1925:
(79)

The colonial countries constitute the principal rear of
imperialism.   The revolutionisation of this rear is bound to
undermine imperialism not only in the sense that imperialism will
be deprived of its rear, but also in the sense that the
revolutionisation of the East is bound to give a powerful impulse
to the intensification of the revolutionary crisis in the West.
Lin Piao's theory of the encirclement of the cities of the world
(imperialist countries) by the countryside of the world (dominated
countries) means just this.

Since 1963 the Chinese have said: (80)
We believe that, with the ... struggle between the proletariat
and the bourgeoisie in Western Europe and North America, the
momentous day of battle will arrive in these homes of capitalism
and heartlands of imperialism.   When that day comes, Western
Europe and North America will undoubtedly become the centre of
world political struggles, of world contradictions.

The signs heralding this great future struggle became clear in
1967-8.   The revolt of the youth and the revolutionary awakening of
the broad masses in the imperialist metropolises themselves are new,
universal phenomena which mark the entry of the world into a new
historical era.   The Chinese immediately saw the significance of
these great struggles and gave them enthusiastic support.

This turning-point in history must be connected with the war in
Vietnam which has discredited reactionary ideologies (the Free
World, American democracy, etc.) in the eyes of youth.   For its part
the cultural revolution showed youth the way forward.   The formula
in which Mao Tse-tung summed up the numerous principles of Marxism-
Leninism, 'It is right to rebel', has become the motto of
revolutionary youth throughout the world.

Trotsky's internationalism was based on the unity of the world
market from which he deduced the necessary supremacy of the advanced
capitalist countries.   If he acknowledged that the imperialist chain
could be broken at its weakest link, this could only happen, under
pain of defeat, as an immediate prelude to the revolution in the
more developed countries.   His theory was therefore that of the
strongest link. (81)   On this basis he formulated a pious wish; he
hoped that the revolution would triumph very quickly in these
countries, otherwise all would be lost.

The Chinese do not think that all is lost if the revolution is
late in coming.   They know, in the meantime, that history does not

ask for our preferences and that it generally progresses by its bad
side. (82)   Their internationalism is based on the structuring of
the system of international relations by the political class
struggle on a global scale.   They show that there are four
fundamental contradictions, all equally important, which form a
system (each one is present in the other three).   These
contradictions oppose:
  (a)   the oppressed nations to imperialism and social-imperialism;
  (b)   the proletariat to the bourgeoisie in the capitalist and
        revisionist countries;
  (c)   the imperialists to each other and to social-imperialism;
  (d)   the socialist countries to the imperialist and social-
        imperialist countries.
At the moment, the first is the most explosive.

As for Trotsky, he granted an exorbitant privilege to the
proletariats in the advanced countries in his idea of the world
revolution.   He understood neither the laws of revolution in the
colonial and semi-colonial countries, nor did he concede that for a
long time they could be in the vanguard of the struggle.

The Chinese communists know that it is the peoples of the
advanced capitalist countries who will deliver the final blow to
imperialism.   They also know that the final victory of socialism and
the transition to communism will only be carried out on a world
scale but they cannot accept formulations such as this one: 'The
maintenance of the proletarian revolution within a national
framework can only be a provisional state of affairs ... The way out
for it lies only in the victory of the proletariat of the advanced
countries'. (83)

They would even be tempted to invert the formula: the security of
the proletariat in the advanced countries depends on the victory of
the peoples dominated by imperialism.   This inversion had already
been executed by Marx.   He wrote to Engels on 10 December 1869:
  I long believed that it would be possible to overthrow the Irish
  regime through English working-class ascendancy ... more thorough
  study has now convinced me of the exact opposite.   The English
  working class will never accomplish anything before it has got
  rid of Ireland.   The lever must be applied in Ireland. (84)
4   According to Mao Tse-tung, contradictions are the motor of
    history.
He has written: (85)
  The law of the unity of opposites is the fundamental law of the
  inverse.   This law operates universally, whether in the natural
  world, or in human society, or in man's thinking.   Between the
  opposites in a contradiction there is at once unity and struggle,
  and it is this that impels things to move and change.
As Lenin had already pointed out in a note criticising Bukharin,
contradiction and antagonism must not be confused.   The former will
exist in communist society.   According to Mao, the development of
these contradictions and their resolution will give rise to sudden
qualitative changes, that is, to revolutions.   The revolutionary
process will continue indefinitely.   There will be no end to
history.   Trotsky was totally unaware of this aspect of the theory
of the uninterrupted revolution which is derived from the
dialectical nature of the real.

In the debate cited at the beginning of this section, Vergès had
no time to express himself as clearly as this, for the chairman
allowed him only one sentence to reply to Frank and Deutscher. His
reply was : 'Marxist-Leninists are not the "Monsieur Jourdains" of
Trotskyism.'

In fact, as Trotskyism has no hold on the real as a result of its
original sin - the fact that it is cut off from the masses - its
supporters console themselves by explaining others' victories by an
unconscious application of the only revolutionary doctrine: their
own. They do not bring about the revolution but are very fond of
distributing praise and blame. When they approve of Marxist-
Leninists it is because they supposedly practise Trotskyism without
knowing it. How else can they account for the logical scandal
presented by their opponents' revolutionary successes except by
attributing them to the occult influence of their own ideas? 'Since
these mysteries are beyond us, let us pretend to shape them,' they
say, imitating Figaro.

Chapter 3

TROTSKY'S INCAPACITY FOR CONCRETE ANALYSIS

The incapacity for concrete analysis which afflicted Trotsky throughout his militant life resulted from his failure to comprehend the materialist dialectic, an incomprehension even worse than Bukharin's, although less flagrant, for, prudently, he ventured only rarely into the higher spheres of Marxist philosophy. When he did so, particularly at the time of his polemic against Burnham, the results reach no more than an elementary level. He disparages formal logic but knows nothing of the developments in symbolic logic since Hilbert, Peano and Russell. He assumes that to acknowledge the dialectic implies rejecting the principle of identity or its restriction to elementary and subordinate tasks. For him, 'the dialectic and formal logic bear a relationship similar to that between higher and lower mathematics'. (1) Furthermore, formal logic is supposedly inapplicable, even approximately, to phenomena exhibiting appreciable quantitative changes. He would be at a loss to explain to us how mathematics (based on the principles of identity and non-contradiction) could be applied to nearly instantaneous physical transformations like those which occur at the moment of a nuclear explosion. In fact, Trotsky confused Aristotelian logic with the metaphysical inferences which are wrongly drawn from it by certain philosophers and which deny movement and change.

He had so little idea of the dialectic that he imagined Marx's mode of exposition in 'Capital' to be a vain display of philosophical pedantry. He was reduced to regretting that the creator of the theory of value was 'the doctor of philosophy' Marx and not 'Bebel the turner' who 'could have formulated it in a more popular, simple and direct form'. (2)

Trotsky was more serious when he argued as a politician. His conception of materialism is none the less very schematic. He conflated the instances of the social formation (economic, legal-political, ideological) and saw neither how these instances are articulated, how the contradictions proper to each of them can converge and fuse, nor that contradictions displace one another, a secondary contradiction being able to become temporarily the principal one at a given stage, pushing the principal contradiction 'de jure' into the background within the framework of a wider

historical period. (3)   It follows that the necessity for detours
in the revolutionary struggle generally escapes him and even when he
accepts it in principle he is unable to understand its nature and
implications.

It is Mao Tse-tung who has systematised this dialectical logic
and produced its concepts but it was already active in Lenin's
writings, models of concrete analysis leading to the definition of a
scientific strategy and tactics: cf. for example, 'Two Tactics of
Social Democracy in the Democratic Revolution'. Trotsky, on the
other hand, although in his own terms he 'went through Lenin's
school', was failed by history in the most important subject,
political science. Lenin made a fundamental criticism of him when
he said that 'in all his theses, he looks at the question' from the
angle of 'general principles'. (4)

With a few examples we shall show in greater detail his inability
to rise to the concrete in thought, which is neither the immediate
empirical nor abstract principles cut off from practice.

BREST-LITOVSK

It is well known that in 1917 the Bolsheviks seized power by
inscribing on their banners this triple slogan: 'Peace to the
people, bread to the workers, land to the peasants'.

However, the peace which they sought was 'without annexations and
indemnities'. The Germans were deaf to such a conception.

Even before October the Russian soldiers had started to 'vote for
peace with their feet'. The trenches at the front were deserted.
Lenin was therefore faced with this problem: how could the survival
of proletarian power be ensured without an army at a time when
German imperialism was preparing to take it by storm. He opted for
the acceptance of the German conditions, disastrous as they were,
thus giving up space in order to win time. He was then defeated in
the Central Committee by a coalition composed on the one hand of the
left wing of the party led by Bukharin, supporters of revolutionary
war; and on the other hand, of Trotsky, whose point of view (which
prevailed at the time) was summed up in the slogan: 'Neither peace
nor war', or more precisely: 'We interrupt the war and do not sign
the peace - we demobilise the army'. (5)

It was a bluff based on three postulates, all of which turned out
to be false:
1   that the attitude of the Soviet government would incite the
    German proletariat to rise before the Kaiser's troops attacked;
2   that Bolshevik power could not be sustained in Russia unless it
    received assistance from victorious proletariats in the countries
    of Western Europe: 'The only way out of the current situation is
    to act on the German proletariat in a revolutionary way'; and
    lastly
3   formulated in a letter to Lenin at the end of January 1918: 'We
    shall declare that we end (the Brest-Litovsk) negotiations but do
    not sign a peace. They will be unable to make an offensive
    against us'. (6)
The facts soon called this bluff, to Russia's great cost. In short,
Trotsky was incapable of analysing the concrete situation.

The army opposing them having evaporated, the Germans merely had to get into a train to go to Petrograd. This is what they did. They had to be halted by a hurried acceptance of their new conditions and these were much more onerous than the previous ones. However, by signing the peace, the Soviet government obtained a respite which enabled it to mobilise 'a new army into which there was an influx of peasants eager to defend the expropriated lands' (Bukharin).

A few months later, the consequences of the Brest-Litovsk peace were erased.

In retrospect, Lenin's position seems obvious to us and Trotsky's seems absurd. Even if this is an optical illusion, the face remains that in those serious circumstances, when the future of the revolution was at stake, Trotsky's formalism, i.e., proceeding from principles and not from reality, led to errors all along the line. These principles were, moreover, those of the permanent revolution, which can be summarised under the formula: 'The Russian proletariat cannot possibly maintain itself in power unless it is aided by a triumph of the revolution in the West'. For Trotsky, the principal contradiction was always the fundamental contradiction of our whole epoch, namely the one between capital and labour. For him, the alternative was therefore: world revolution or world defeat of the proletariat. On the other hand, Lenin saw that in the conjuncture at the beginning of 1918, the principal contradiction was the one between the necessity of maintaining Soviet power and the temporary impossibility of making the peasant majority fight in its defence. The alternatives were therefore immediate peace at any price (an indispensable respite for the Bolsheviks) or the destruction of their power. Resolutely grasping the first alternative was the condition for all later success.

ADMINISTRATIVE PLANNING OR POLITICAL ECONOMY

The same weaknesses, abstract dogmatism and incapacity for concrete analysis were even more apparent when Trotsky was confronted with economic problems, pedestrian perhaps but decisive for the survival of Soviet power. Better equipped than anyone to ensure the application of the line adopted by Lenin and the Central Committee, he became dangerous when he tried to arrive at his own solutions to these problems.

During the Civil War, then as Commissar of Transport, Trotsky demonstrated remarkable abilities as an organiser and leader. He effectively combatted disorder and slovenliness, firing his subordinates with his own zeal, and in this way redressing very dangerous situations in a very short time. But this gives no one the right to conclude, as the Trotskyists do, that he was capable of stepping into Lenin's shoes. The latter attacked him in his 'Testament' for his 'excessive preoccupation with the purely administrative side of things'. (7) From Lenin's pen, this criticism has a precise significance which refers to a latent defect in the person at whom it is aimed. Lenin's thoughts on this point are explicit when he made the same complaint about Piatakov, 'unquestionably ... of outstanding ability, but shows too much zeal

for administrating and the administrative side of the work to be
relied on in a serious political situation'. (8)

In other words, 'to show too much zeal for administrating', means
to claim to resolve problems which are posed at the highest central
level without taking into consideration the repercussions of any
decisions in the arena of the class struggle or its effects as to
the strengthening or weakening of proletarian power.

How right Lenin was can be confirmed by considering some of the
positions adopted by Trotsky on the questions of the economic
reconstruction of the USSR after the introduction of the NEP.

In the period of 'war communism', he had advocated the
militarisation of labour, which undoubtedly corresponded to a
necessity in the conditions of the period. But, while Lenin called
'war communism' a 'necessary error' (that is to say, one imposed by
the circumstances) but an error nevertheless in the sense that it
was impossible to draw from it a universal norm applicable to one of
the stages on the transition to socialism, and also in the sense
that this policy had to be abandoned as soon as this became
possible, Trotsky himself retained and generalised his ideas at the
10th Congress, the Congress at which the New Economic Policy had
been announced. (9) According to Trotsky, forced labour 'would
reach its highest degree of intensity during the transition from
capitalism to socialism'. (10) The militarisation of labour, he
said, 'is the basis of socialism'. He did not hesitate to
assimilate this forced labour to that of slaves and to the serf's
corvée. (11)

Elated with his success at putting transport back on its feet
during the Polish campaign by using authoritarian, indeed
bureaucratic methods, Trotsky aspired to erect into a rule what was
only an expedient designed to meet a critical situation. He
threatened 'to shake up' the elected leaders of the different unions
as he had those in the transport unions. In other words he wanted
to replace these elected leaders by others appointed by the state.
He incurred a firm retort from Lenin but refused to be convinced and
pushed blindness and obstinacy so far as to initiate a factional
struggle against the Central Committee. During this controversy,
Lenin showed that Trotsky was 'forgetting the ABC of Marxism' in
wanting to keep the debate on 'economic' grounds. 'Politics must
have precedence over economics ... without a proper political
approach to the subject the given class cannot maintain its rule,
and consequently, cannot solve its production problems.' Now, 'the
political mistake expressed in the shaking up policy that permeates
the whole of Trotsky's pamphlet-platform ... will lead to the
downfall of the dictatorship of the proletariat'. (12)

In short, it was a question of practising not economic
administration but political economy, which can only be economically
advantageous to the extent that it does not contain any political
mistakes.

It was these recent struggles which Lenin had in mind when he
wrote in his letter to the Central Committee about Trotsky's
preoccupation with the administrative side of things. He was
thereby attacking him for being incapable of analysing concretely
and dialectically the conjuncture of the class struggle in all its
breadth and complexity in order to define the tasks of the moment.

At the time of the dispute over planning under the NEP Lenin had been able to state, moreover, that Trotsky's method of thinking consisted of deducing from the most general principles of socialism the 'solutions' to economic problems posed by life, without any mediation between the two levels (without any concrete theoretical analysis), which occasionally gives the impression that he is skipping from one subject to another.

Lenin, on the other hand, knew that in the situation of total destitution and semi-barbarity of Russia in 1921, in which small peasant production was broadly predominant, 'a complete integrated plan for us at the moment = a bureaucratic utopia'. (13) In the following section we shall see how Lenin, as opposed to Trotsky, was able to determine the link which had to be grasped in order to draw the whole chain to him - in other words, how to go about restoring to health a Russian economy drained by eight years of foreign and civil war in order to create the premises of effective planning.

PLANNING AND THE NEP (14)

In 'The New Course' (January 1924), Trotsky described what a planned socialist economy ought to be. He then introduced what he called a 'complication', namely the existence of the market. He laid down a certain number of secondary exigencies to overcome it.

Now the very essence of the NEP as it was defined by Lenin includes a procedure and a deduction which were exactly opposite to those of Trotsky, namely:
1 that Trotsky's 'complication' is its principal determination. It is the market which is the centre of gravity of the unity to be realised between industry and agriculture; henceforth it is the means through which the agricultural surplus has to be realised; industry works for and as a function of the peasant market;
2 that systematic planning - 'de jure' the principal determination of the socialist mode of production - is only relevant at this stage as a secondary determination.
How could a true centralised state plan be built on an immense, scattered, private, peasant market developing and reacting spontaneously on the basis of the laws of capitalism? Trotsky got around the difficulty by a new abstract demand: 'An exact knowledge of the market conditions and correct economic forecasts'.

This demand is abstract:
1 because Trotsky does not establish the means by which to realise it, except in part - this is the question of 'the dictatorship of finance' which we shall consider later;
2 because even if some realistic means were given, the minimum of knowledge and forecasts (without which planning is only a joke or a utopia) required a radical upheaval of the structure of agricultural production and of the agricultural market (the upheaval which historically took the form of collectivisation in 1929).
Now in 1924 Trotsky did not consider collectivisation and the abandonment of the NEP. He thought that it would be possible for the state economy to adapt itself to the peasant market by a few 'corrections' and 'necessary modifications' as its development

proceeded. He did not explain how it would be possible to obtain this result.

Trotsky moves from the deductive definition of the socialist mode of production to the problem of its 'application' pure and simple – conceived, what is more, in an ultra-modest fashion: some detailed adjustments, a progressive adaptation – and thus entirely liquidates the Leninist science of strategy and tactics. He annihilates the phases, stages, moments and successive displacements of the contradictions; hence the atemporal character of his analysis.

The abstract character of his argument is also revealed in the absence of any consideration of the concrete conditions of 'the current situation', the absence of any analysis into levels and instances – the 'de jure' principal contradiction being the 'de facto' principal contradiction, it being presupposed that the instruments of social practice are adequate to their object.

Trotsky called for a centralised plan as early as 1922-3: but who was going to do the planning? Not an ideal state apparatus, not an ideal Gosplan, but the bureaucratic apparatus inherited from Tsarism which Lenin pitilessly criticised. When the state apparatus was still largely in solidarity with the former state of the social formation, it could not be the principal link in the economic offensive of Soviet power.

Trotsky's position on the question of 'the dictatorship of finance or the dictatorship of industry' is a significant example of his method.

In 1923 and 1924, a conflict developed between Gosplan and the People's Commissariat of Finance (Narkomfin). The former demanded the acknowledgment of the subordination of finance to industrial planning; that is to say, the power to fix the policy of credits to industry as a function not of the needs of a sound monetary policy, but of the necessities of industrial development. Narkomfin, for its part, defended its autonomy.

'De jure', Gosplan's position was the only correct one for a socialist economy. But the NEP was not socialism; it was only a preliminary phase laying the groundwork for the offensive to come. By allowing the market to operate in almost normal conditions, the Soviet power restored the spontaneous process of accumulation interrupted by the war; moreover, in this way, it prepared the elementary stock of information without which a plan is impossible.

As the principal tool of the market, money plays a decisive role at this level. Its stabilisation appears as a fundamental objective in relation to which the others are subordinate, as the ultimate aim is in relation to preliminary circumstances.

Now Trotsky entirely supported Gosplan's claims, did not attribute any importance to the problem of money and was content to affirm without any justification that the stabilisation of money depended on the dictatorship of industry.

The essence of the attitude of the Trotskyist opposition is visible here: an attitude of all or nothing which lays it down in principle that if the fundamental contradictions of socialism and the fundamental determinations of socialism are not put on the immediate agenda, anything else is simply unprincipled empiricism.

In his refutation of the Trotskyist line in his report to the session of the expanded Executive on 3 April 1925, Bukharin

exclaimed: 'To demand the dictatorship of industry over finance is
to fail to see that industry depends on its agricultural outlets.'

The inflation in 1923 - indispensable at the time for the
realisation of the agricultural surplus - would normally have
worried the private peasant and prompted him in the following year,
if the situation was not stabilised, to hoard stocks of agricultural
products rather than a steadily depreciating currency. Now, as it
was taking place on the basis of the market, accumulation was easily
jeopardised. In a general way, to acknowledge the market as the
meeting point of the two economies without giving attention to the
practical conditions for the functioning of the market - in the
first place, money - was to talk abstractly. Furthermore, since
money was invested under the NEP, in the framework of the market and
of the normal functioning of the law of value, with the role of an
'indicator' of the broad lines of the structure of production,
consumption and reproduction, its depreciation seriously prejudiced
the preparatory work of planning. (15)

'De facto', what the Opposition globally challenged in the name
of 'a general schema of socialism', rigorous 'de jure' but presented
as a 'preliminary "de facto" demand' (nothing can be done without
centralised and planned accumulation for industry), was the very
principle of a reformist (in the sense of non-revolutionary) stage;
that is, one not bearing on what is essential in the long run and in
a general theory of the modes of production. Now it is precisely
the principle of a reformist phase (with all the incoherent,
contradictory, apparently unprincipled aspects implied by such a
phase) that was the great innovation theorised by Lenin under the
name of the NEP - a phase of tactical retreat preparing the
conditions necessary 'de facto' for the socialist offensive to come.

It was this setting to work, at the level of the NEP, of the
Leninist science of strategy and tactics as the revelation of the
specific contradictions of the stage (contradictions which were not
the principal contradictions in the phase of the NEP and even less
those of socialism), that is denied in the Trotskyist explanation.

In all questions of current political interest Trotskyism appears
as a set of radical demands deduced from a general schema of the
socialist mode of production - without consideration of stages and
phases - and a refusal to accept any partial measures, as well as a
systematic neglect of everything which relates to practical
realisation.

The principal characteristic of Trotskyism is the absence of a
theory of contradiction, the absence of a theory of phases and
stages and consequently the absence of a theory of strategy and
tactics.

THE 'GREAT TURN' OF 1929

Marxist theory did not have any ready-made formula to solve the
concrete problem which Stalin came up against in 1928. The kulaks,
who were the only farmers to have appreciable surpluses at their
disposal, were hoarding their grain and threatening to starve the
towns, as they were dissatisfied with being unable to get enough
industrial goods at the prices which they were being offered for it.

On the other hand, the development of industry forecast by the First Five-Year Plan assumed an increase in the urban population and therefore an increased need for foodstuffs.

There were two ways out of this vicious circle: one consisted of giving the kulaks a free rein, helping them to ruin the small peasants and to set up big capitalist farms with high productivity. Trotsky and his supporters (particularly Rakovsky) were absolutely convinced that Stalin would take this road. They obstinately clung to this prognosis even after the launching of the great offensive against the kulaks designed to liquidate them as a class. It was only at the beginning of 1930 that they began to take into consideration the historical upheavals taking place in the USSR. Even then, Trotsky considered that industrialisation and collect- ivisation were only a passing phase in Stalin's policy. Precisely because Stalin was not the counter-revolutionary Trotsky saw him as, this road - that of the development of traditional forms of capitalism - was closed to him.

The other was collectivisation and accelerated industrialisation. Speed was essential otherwise there was a risk that the tensions produced by a struggle against the kulaks would become too dangerous. In fact, the kulaks had succeeded in uniting the majority of the peasants around them. They let loose a White terror against communist cadres and the poor peasants who wanted to join the kolkhozy. This resistance had to be smashed immediately, otherwise it would have smashed the proletarian power. If the communists had joined in a war of attrition with the kulaks they, not their enemies, would have been worn down. What was needed was a quick decisive engagement. Collectivisation and industrialisation had to keep pace, moreover, even if this initially demanded sacrifices. The former made possible the extraction of the surpluses thanks to which one could invest; the latter provided tractors and agricultural machines which made the kolkhozy attractive and led to an even higher productivity.

As we have suggested, the line followed by Stalin in this conjuncture resembled in more respects than one the line advocated by Trotsky in 1924, which does not, however, make the latter right retrospectively, as is claimed by his supporters whose thought is as atemporal as their master's since the combined conditions in 1929 were not there in 1924. Declaring that Stalin had 'plagiarised' his programme (Lenin did as much to that of the Social Revolutionaries), Trotsky did not conclude from this that he should rally to the Central Committee as thousands of his supporters had at the time, but opted for a complete shift in his own ideas. In this way he continued to set himself apart from Stalin and preserved his 'raison d'être' as leader of 'the Opposition'. He condemned the liquidation of the kulaks and argued that the kolkhozy were not viable and would collapse of their own accord because of their lack of modern machines. According to him the amalgamation of small farms with primitive equipment was equivalent to joining together small boats to make a liner. He did not understand that simple co-operation and the manual division of labour were enough to ensure a higher productivity to the kolkhozy. He argued, therefore, for the dissolution of the kolkhozy and the sovkhozy as unprofitable or even fictional. Thus, even if the bloc of Trotskyists and 'rightists' which Stalin spoke of did not have an organised existence, it is nevertheless true that from then on Trotskyist criticisms coincided with the positions of the Bukharinists in their defence of the rural petty bourgeoisie. Isaac Deutscher writes that 'the differences between the Right and Left Bolsheviks were becoming blurred and obliterated'. (16)

The same Deutscher is struck by this rejection on Trotsky's part of the revolution in the countryside: 'He still thought ... that ... the "transition from capitalism to socialism" should proceed in an essentially peaceful and evolutionary manner. In his approach to domestic Soviet issues the author of "Permanent Revolution" was in a sense a reformist.' (17)

Like all reformisms, Trotsky's was both utopian and reactionary: utopian, because a gradual and peaceful transformation of structures has always proved impossible; reactionary, because by pursuing this utopia one ends up maintaining the 'status quo'.

Trotsky criticised Soviet planning for wanting to go too fast and for aiming at maximal and optimal results. In fact, the rise of fascism, with the threat of war which it involved, obliged accelerated industrialisation. It was necessary to advance by forced marches. It was a matter of the survival of the proletarian power. Stalin spelled it out in a speech in 1931: (18)

No, comrades, this is impossible! It is impossible to reduce the tempo! On the contrary, it is necessary as far as possible to accelerate it. This necessity is dictated by our obligations to the workers and peasants of the USSR. This is dictated by our obligations to the working class of the whole world ... we are 50-100 years behind the advanced countries. We must cover this distance in ten years. Either we do this or they will crush us.

Ten years later, Hitler's armies invaded the USSR.

The political line adopted at the time of the launching of the Five-Year Plans and accelerated collectivisation led to great successes but included some negative aspects, the most pernicious effects of which were not those felt immediately. Let us mention briefly some of the mistakes made in this period:

- The exaggerated importance given to material incentives, illustrated by the Stakhanovite movement. These workers often earned ten or fifteen times as much as their comrades.
- The enormous widening of wage differentials to the advantage of a narrow privileged stratum at the top of the hierarchy, in total contradiction to the Marxist-Leninist principles actually applied until Lenin's death.
- The largely forced character of collectivisation.
- The unilateral emphasis on the technical and material conditions of socialism to the detriment of the political and ideological conditions (economism).

Some of these mistakes were culpable: others were avoidable but were not avoided owing to subjective weaknesses of the Soviet leadership; others were inevitable in the absence of a historical precedent; others, finally, were necessary, in other words imposed by the objective conditions. (19)

Collectivisation, for example, must inevitably have appeared in the eyes of the peasants, even of the non-kulaks, as an externally imposed measure, for historical circumstances had not enabled the

Soviet Communist Party to sink roots among the masses: to quote only
one example, 'a slight misunderstanding with the women collective
farmers ... over the cow', which Stalin mentions, could have been
avoided. (20)   The women peasants who had to hand over their cows to
the kolkhozy thought that they would be left without any milk for
their children.   In the end they should have been allowed to keep
one per household.   In the meantime a large part of their livestock
had been sacrificed.

The mistakes made during this struggle were combated very
energetically by leading echelons of party and state.   Even before
the publication of Stalin's 'Dizzy With Success', urgent orders had
been sent forbidding the imprisonment of poor and middle peasants
for refusing to enter the kolkhozy.   However, although the widespread coercion was the responsibility of local cadres who disobeyed
their instructions, it was true, nevertheless, that they were driven
into a corner, caught between the peasant resistance and the demands
of the centre which had in 1929 fixed a rate of collectivisation too
high to be reached in too short periods. (21)   The end result was
not the one sought, because Stalin's Central Committee did not apply
the mass line in the elaboration of its policy.   Hence it followed
that the orders which it issued underwent a diffraction at the base,
the effect of a concrete situation which had not been taken into
account.   Only the mass line enables this type of error to be
minimised.   Despite their relative efficacy in the struggle against
abuses, the 'selkor' (village correspondents) of the newspapers, the
personal and collective petitions, and the system of reciprocal
surveillance by the representatives of the party and those of the
police services, could not provide a valid substitute for control by
the masses themselves.

Some of Trotsky's criticisms at this time coincide formally with
ours but they are an integral part of his analysis as a whole, which
denounces the Stalinist state as a counter-revolutionary power and
denies the necessary character of certain mistakes deriving from the
unfavourable objective conditions inherited from the preceding
periods.   A comparison will clarify what we mean: in 1922 Lenin
refused the Mensheviks the right to criticise the regime of war
communism although the content of their criticism was the very same
as that put forward by the Bolsheviks themselves.   When the latter
adopted the NEP their enemies gloated: 'What you are saying now we
have been saying all the time, permit us to say it to you again!'
they cried, and Lenin replied: 'Permit us to put you before a firing
squad for saying that.' (22)

Stalin's answer to the Trotskyists in the 1930s was somewhat,
indeed very, similar; for even when they contained a grain of truth
their criticisms from then on became those of anti-communists.

We can be certain, moreover, that had they been in power and
hypothetically chosen the socialist road, not only would they have
made the same mistakes (23) (Trotsky had erected their 'theoretical'
justification in advance), (24) but also would have proved to be
inflexible and ruthless in pushing a pernicious policy to its
logical conclusions, whereas Stalin did know how to stop in time on
a slippery slope because he did not feel compelled, like Trotsky, to
base each change of course in the storms of the class struggle on
eternal principles.   It is interesting to record that the forced

labour camps, the excessive sacrifices demanded of the workers
(Trotsky said that they must give their blood and nerves), the idea
of squeezing the peasants to the limit to extract investment funds:
all this was theorised at the beginning of the 1920s by Trotsky and
his friends under the absurd name of 'primitive socialist
accumulation'.

PRIMITIVE SOCIALIST ACCUMULATION AND PROBLEMS OF THE TRANSITION

Deutscher says of this concept: 'The Marxist historian may indeed
describe and analyse those decades, the Stalinist decades, as the
era of primitive socialist accumulation; and he may do so in terms
borrowed from Trotsky's exposition of the ideas in 1923.' (25)
    Lenin described the expression 'primitive socialist
accumulation', which was coined by Smirnov at the time of war
communism and taken up by Bukharin in 'The Economy of the Transition
Period', as a 'very unfortunate' expression and 'a copy of schoolboy
terms'. It was propagated by Trotsky in a different context from
1922 on. Preobrazhensky theorised it in 'The New Economics',
published in 1925.
    Here is how the latter author justified the petinence of his
analogy: (26)
    Just as the functioning of manufactures and still more of
    factories with machine techniques, so also for enabling the
    complex of state economy to develop all its economic advantages
    and to place itself under a new technical basis, a certain
    minimum of previously accumulated means in the form of natural
    elements of production is needed.
Setting out Trotsky's ideas on the same problem, Isaac Deutscher
defines Marx's view of primitive accumulation as follows: (27)
    The era of primitive accumulation (was) the initial phase in the
    development of modern capitalism when normal accumulation of
    capital had hardly begun or was still too feeble to allow
    industry to expand from its own resources, that is from its own
    profits. The early bourgeoisie shrank from no violent, 'extra-
    economic' method in its striving to concentrate in its whole
    hands the means of production.
In 1922 Trotsky said: 'The proletariat ... is compelled to embark
upon a phase which may be described as that of primitive socialist
accumulation. We cannot content ourselves with using our pre-1914
industrial plant. This has been destroyed and must be reconstructed
step by step by way of a colossal exertion on the part of our labour
force.' And again, the working class 'can approach socialism only
through the greatest sacrifices, by straining all its strength and
giving its blood and nerves'. (28)
    These three quotations demonstrate that there is a theoretical
contradiction underlying the comparison with the primitive
accumulation discussed by Marx. The latter defined it like this:
'The so-called primitive accumulation, therefore, is nothing else
than the historical process of divorcing the producer from the means
of production'. (29) Initially Marx had stressed the fact that 'In
themselves money and commodities are no more capital than are the
means of production and of subsistence. They want transforming into
capital.' (30)

This is an idea which constantly recurs in his 'magnum opus':
'Capital is not a thing but a social relation between persons,
established by the instrumentality of things.' (31)

Marx gave the example of Mr Peel who took with him from England
to Australia means of production worth £50,000 and 3,000 workers.
Once he had reached his destination he was left without a servant to
make his bed or to fetch him a glass of water. 'Unhappy Mr Peel,'
Marx concluded, 'who provided for everything except the export of
English modes of production to Swan River!' (32)

Trotsky, Preobrazhensky and Deutscher make the same mistake.
They do not understand that primitive accumulation is only the
historical process of the creation of capitalist relations of
production and not simply the accumulation of 'the natural elements
of production' (Preobrazhensky) or 'industrial plant' (Trotsky).
For writers who pride themselves on their 'classical Marxism', this
is not without irony.

It is now clear that the historical analogy implied in the
expression 'primitive socialist accumulation' is totally
illegitimate.

Our purpose is not to discuss in detail Preobrazhensky's economic
theory, that is, not the expression, but the concept. It is enough
to point out that Trotsky proved much less consistent than
Preobrazhensky on this question. Preobrazhensky argued that in a
predominantly agricultural country the bulk of investment funds in
the socialist industrial sector would come from the surplus
agricultural product and that accelerated industrialisation could
only be realised by means of a transfer of value from the countryside to the town. It is doubtful whether this form of exploitation
was compatible with the raising of the peasants' standard of living.
Although basically sharing Preobrazhensky's views, Trotsky feared
that he would be accused of advocating the exploitation of the
peasantry and refrained from openly adopting them. The concept of
primitive accumulation was useful to him anew fifteen years later in
'The Revolution Betrayed'.

We have shown that Trotsky's and Preobrazhensky's notion of the
primitive accumulation of capital was not a Marxist one. It is not
surprising to discover that the primitive 'socialist' accumulation
which they talk about is precisely not socialist.

On the one hand, the socialisation of the economy cannot be
likened to the separation of the producers from their means of
production which, on the contrary, they come to own collectively
through their control of state power. Of course, in so far as the
units of production function as enterprises they reproduce the
pattern of the double separation of the immediate producers from
their means of production and of the units from each other.
However, that is a problematic only attained by Charles Bettleheim
in his latest works and one whose existence Trotsky did not even
suspect. Moreover, the latter regarded the tendency to primitive
accumulation as a law of the transition, which the example of China
disproves.

On the other hand, the comparison of the primitive accumulation
of a supposed socialism with that of capitalism is significant and
legitimate in a certain sense. The model of construction of
socialism proposed by Preobrazhensky assumes that it will be

realised mainly starting from the towns thanks to the resources freed by maintaining poverty in the countryside, and by relying on techniques and methods of labour organisation which have given the best results in the advanced countries, and copied as such. This sort of accumulation or expanded reproduction reproduces at the same time relations of production of the capitalist type. Like Preobrazhensky, Stalin thought that it was necessary to levy a 'tribute' on the peasants (cf. his report to the Central Committee in July 1928); just like the Trotskyist theoretician, he identified the construction of socialism purely and simply with the development of a large-scale modern industry based on giant, highly productive units. This 'economistic' idea prevailed for a long time, even to a certain extent in China. Today it is the common heritage of Trotskyists and revisionists as well as the common ground between them and the traditional bourgeois specialists.

Stalin and Trotsky identified the construction of socialism with a mere increase in the productive forces, themselves reduced to machines, the human factor being eliminated. They did not see that after the abolition of the individual ownership of the means of production the essential remains to be done – to revolutionise the relations of production and all the social relations connected to them. They suspected even less the dialectical interaction between these transformations and the development of specifically socialist productive forces. Assembly-line work, the parcellisation of tasks, the conception of the machines, the capitalist organisation of production, presuppose a recalcitrant labour force which submits unwillingly and passively to wage slavery. Taylorism aims to extract the maximum from workers by making them simple appendages of machines devoid of will. The authoritarian relationships in the factory, the type of discipline which rules it, the gulf between intellectual and manual work are equally necessary conditions for exploitation. On the other hand, the productive forces proper to socialism are based on the initiative and creativity of the masses, their enthusiasm, their ingenuity, their self-discipline and their self-education. The Anchan Charter drawn up by Mao in 1960 takes the opposite course to that of Magnitogorsk, which was held up as an example to Soviet industry at the time of the First Five-Year Plan because this latter charter was inspired by capitalist organisation of labour.

The experience of the Great Leap Forward and the cultural revolution enabled the guidelines of a different model to be established. In China the Maoist principle is applied – 'Make the revolution and promote production'. The creation of 'the material basis of socialism' is subordinated there to the destruction of the social relations inherited from capitalism which are replaced by socialist relations. In turn, the socialist relations call forth new productive forces which are proper to socialism. Thanks to the people's communes, the small rural industries, and the principles 'stand on both feet' and 'self-reliance', this process of ideological, political and economic revolutionisation is developing on a very wide basis and transforming the whole country. (33) In their practice, the Chinese workers consciously confirm the thesis already stated by Marx: 'The working class itself is the greatest of all productive forces.'

Chapter 4

A BUREAUCRATIC
ANTI-BUREAUCRATISM

THE QUESTION OF DEMOCRATIC CENTRALISM

Contrary to what is often thought, democratic centralism concerns
questions of elaboration of the party line and leadership more than
questions of organisation. A centralised party is necessary to
unify and co-ordinate all the people's struggles, to centralise and
systematise them after studying the correct ideas of the masses, to
mobilise the masses around slogans corresponding to the tasks of the
moment, to assess constantly the experience gained in the struggles
as a whole, and to educate the masses in the spirit of scientific
socialism so that they can carry through the revolution to the end.
None of these objectives can be achieved if this leadership is not
carried out democratically.

Trotsky's positions on this issue varied considerably during his
life. We see him oscillate from one extreme to another because of
his inability to grasp the dialectical link uniting these pairs of
opposites: the distinction between the party and the class and its
fusion with it; the authority of the centre and its monitoring by
the militants; the need for statutory rules and the fact that they
must be subordinated to 'revolutionary opportunity', as Lenin said.

In an essay written in Siberia in 1901, Trotsky set out his views
on the rigorous centralisation which had to be imposed on a
revolutionary movement: 'If one of the local organisations ...
refuses to acknowledge the full powers of the Central Committee,
(the latter) will cut off its relations with it and will thereby cut
off that organisation from the entire world of revolution.' (1)

At the 2nd Congress of the RSDLP, Trotsky's interventions against
the Economists were so violent that he seemed to be 'Lenin's
cudgel'. The Economists complained about the Iskraists' dictatorial
and Jacobin attitudes. Trotsky declared that the party statutes
should express 'the leadership's organised distrust of the members,
a distrust manifesting itself in vigilant control from above over
the party'. (2)

Trotsky made a 180 degree turn during the Congress and sided with
the Mensheviks. Later he violently attacked Lenin in a number of
his writings.

In the 'Report of the Siberian Delegation', he spoke of his

'disorganising centralism' (op. cit., p.49), his 'egocentralism'
(p. 81), his 'Wille zur Macht' (= will to power, pp. 72 and 82), the
'caricatural Robespierrade' in which he indulged (p. 84), the way in
which he conceived the Central Committee as 'the Warder of
Centralism' (p. 83). In the pamphlet 'Our Political Tasks', he
heaped abuse on Lenin, describing him notably as 'the leader of the
reactionary wing of our Party'. He also aimed other criticisms at
him which Deutscher summarised as follows: (3)

By arguing that ... socialist ideology was brought into the
labour movement from outside, by the revolutionary intelligentsia, Lenin's theory was an 'orthodox theocracy'. His
scheme of organisation was fit for a party which would substitute
itself for the working classes, act as a proxy in their name and
on their behalf, regardless of what the workers felt and thought.

Lenin is 'a hideous caricature of a malevolent and morally repugnant
Robespierre'.

In trying to combine Jacobinism and Marxism, 'Lenin was virtually
abandoning socialism and setting himself up as the leader of a
revolutionary wing of bourgeois democracy'. (4) Trotsky borrowed
this characterisation of Lenin from Axelrod.

Trotsky accused Lenin of wanting to substitute the party for the
proletariat, the Central Committee for the party and finally the
dictator for the Central Committee. The rejection of 'substitutionism' follows in Trotsky's case from his 'sociologism',
namely the idea that social classes can directly lead a political
struggle without their action being mediated by parties. In
'Results and Prospects', he wrote: 'Social Democracy envisages the
conquest of power as the conscious action of the revolutionary
class'. The dictatorship of the proletariat, he argued, at the 2nd
Congress of the RSDLP, would only be possible on the day when the
working class and the party 'became almost identical'. This idea
comes closer to left-wing German social democracy, to the
Luxemburgist current. (5)

Trotsky fought Lenin's democratic centralism right 'to the end';
that is, up to the moment when 'volens nolens', he himself joined
the Bolshevik Party built by Lenin. In it he made a reputation for
himself as an inflexible champion of discipline except when,
outvoted, he himself resorted to the factional methods so often
denounced as such by Lenin. This is one of the paradoxes of
Trotskyism, which attacks bureaucratism in words but does not get
beyond it.

Trotsky in power was considered to be 'the patriarch of the
bureaucrats'. (6) A severe censor of every breach of internal party
discipline, he acted as prosecutor along with Stalin at the 11th
Congress (1922), calling for the expulsion of the leaders of 'the
Workers' Opposition'. Two years before he had campaigned for the
militarisation of the trade unions. In November 1920, he suggested
that state officials should be substituted for the unions' elected
representatives. That is why Lenin criticised Trotsky's tendency to
adopt 'the administrative point of view'. He denounced his dogmatic
formalism, describing it as 'bureaucratic project-hatching'. (7) He
declared that 'his policy is a policy of bureaucratic shake-up of
the trade unions'. (8)

Trotsky's argument on the question of the trade unions amounted

to this: the workers do not need a relatively autonomous
organisation to defend themselves from the Soviet state since it
belongs to them. Lenin replied that they required such an
organisation because they were dealing not with a worker's state but
with a 'worker-peasant' state which was in addition 'bureau-
cratically deformed'. That is why he said of Trotsky's 'pamphlet
programme' 'The Role and Tasks of the Trade Unions': 'From beginning
to end ... it is thoroughly permeated with the spirit of the
"shaking-up-from-above" policy', (9) that is, of administratively
'removing, transferring, appointing, dismissing etc' the union's
elected leaders. Lenin made repeated reference to 'the useless and
harmful bureaucratic excesses of Tsektran' (10) which was headed by
Trotsky. In his 'Testament', Lenin criticised Trotsky for 'the sin
of excessive confidence and an exaggerated infatuation with the
purely administrative side of things'.
     Thus the future enemy of the bureaucracy became that enemy since
he could not be the leading bureaucrat. (11) His concern for
'democracy' dates from the precise moment when he realised that he
was without any power or influence. He remained in the Political
Bureau for several years but in complete isolation. He was defeated
politically (12) by Stalin despite (or because of) his final
unprincipled manoeuvres. An example will illustrate his style of
operation.
     Lenin, who was ill and about to suffer another stroke, had asked
Trotsky to denounce Stalin on the problem of Great-Russian
chauvinism and to defend the small nations, particularly the
Georgians: he had warned him against a 'rotten compromise' with
Stalin. Isaac Deutscher explains his hero's behaviour at the 12th
Congress in terms of his 'magnanimity', 'selflessness', and
'forgiveness', (13) but what did magnanimity and foregiveness have
to do with it when Marxist principles and the fate of communism were
at stake? It may be concluded that Trotsky considered his relations
with the Triumvirate (Stalin, Kamenev and Zinoviev) to be private
relations and his conflict with them to be a personal conflict. So
true is this that Trotsky later explained to his followers his
procrastinations and conciliationist attitude just before and
immediately after Lenin's death as due to the absence of any serious
political differences and to the fact that the attitude of the
leading 'troika' appeared to him as an 'unprincipled conspiracy'
against himself personally. He had to find political pretexts
before launching his great offensive.
     He meant to choose his own ground and so his bargaining with
Stalin was a misconceived, cunning manoeuvre. Trotsky was a poor
tactician because he had understood nothing of Lenin's political
science, the science of 'the conjuncture', and 'the current
situation' which is not empiricism or disregard of principles but
the application of the latter to the concrete analysis of the
concrete situation. As Trotsky did not have a theory of
contradiction he could not have a theory of strategy and tactics.
(14) His sociologism prevented him from conceiving correctly the
nature and role of the party. Lastly, his intellectualism and his
vanity prevented him from judging Stalin at his true worth. (15)
Moreover, he could not reconcile himself to occupying anything less
than first place after Lenin's death.

For a while, Trotsky and his supporters claimed freedom for
tendencies within the party while formally recognising the
prohibition of factions proclaimed by the 10th Congress of the CPSU
with Trotsky's acceptance. In fact, their idea of what a tendency
is (a group with its own leaders and platform) was such that it was
impossible to distinguish it from a faction. (16) This is the
reason why a division into contending factions is a tradition in
Trotskyist organisations. It is one of the causes of their
congenital weakness.

Party unity can survive factional struggle but it cannot be
reconciled to it. The two cannot be conciliated. Lenin thought
that in certain precise circumstances (not always), it was
preferable to reabsorb the malignant tumour constituted by a faction
through principled struggle and on the basis of experience rather
than cut it out, but this never led him to recognise factions and
explicitly accord them rights. In 'Once Again on the Trade Unions',
in which he denounced Trotsky's factionalism, Lenin declared:

> The Party is learning and is becoming steeled in the struggle
> against the new disease (new in the sense that we forgot about it
> after the October Revolution), i.e. factionalism. In essence it
> is an old disease, relapses of which are probably inevitable for
> several years to come, but the cure of which can and should now
> proceed much more quickly and easily.

Trotskyists believe that democratic centralism is the set of rules
which must govern the internal functioning of a Marxist
organisation. They do not see that this can only be a particular
case of the mass line; (17) that politics, not considerations of an
organisational nature, must be put in command. They tend to
consider democracy as an end in itself. Trotsky even came to
consider authority as an end in itself. Hence his oscillations from
militarism to liberalism and vice versa. The source of his
liberalism was a deep, unprincipled desire for conciliation and
unity alternating with an equally unprincipled polemical violence.

The pamphlets in which he inveighed against Lenin fell flat. As
for his manoeuvres as a philistine conciliator, they were destined
to fail. He was never so isolated as when he was at his most
conciliatory.

During the 1930s, Trotsky once more altered his purely
administrative idea of democratic centralism. Henceforth, he
acknowledged the legitimacy of factions and factional struggle in
the party.

During the struggles which rent the American Trotskyist
organisation, he proposed the application of the following
guarantees: '1 No prohibition of factions; 2 No other restrictions
on factional activity than those dictated by the necessity for
common action.' (18)

Given that agreements can be concluded between different parties
to achieve united action it is clear that, according to Trotsky,
factions can act as close but different parties. As a result,
democratic centralism is entirely sacrificed to a bourgeois idea of
democracy. In other words, democratic centralism is reduced to
nothing. The Trotskyists' claim to follow Lenin on this point
proves only that their Leninism is an imposture. In fact, they
still hold to the authorisation of factions which Trotsky finally

accepted. In his pamphlet 'De la bureaucratie', for example,
E. Germain states, 'From the moment factions were forbidden in the
Bolshevik Party, internal democracy could no longer be maintained.'
(19)

It is significant that this principle, intended to avoid splits,
has never prevented them. We can count dozens of splits in
Trotskyist organisations. The latter, usually sects of intellectuals cut off from the masses, have no notion of the 'mass line',
the developed form of democratic centralism. It follows that their
'centralism' is not based on a correct line and that their
'democracy' is only liberalism. Trotsky's attitude to Burnham and
Schachtman shows what aberrations this can lead to. When his two
American disciples stated that the USSR could no longer be
considered a 'Workers' State', Trotsky asked that they be allowed to
act as an organised faction within the SWP (Socialist Workers'
Party): 'If somebody should propose ... to expel comrade Burnham, I
would oppose it energetically.' (20)

When the minority organised its 'National Convention', Trotsky
advised the majority not to use it as a pretext for pronouncing
expulsions. Shortly after, Burnham said: (21)

Of the most important beliefs which have been associated with the
Marxist movement, whether in its reformist, Leninist, Stalinist
or Trotskyist variants, there is virtually none which I would
accept in its traditional form. I regard these beliefs as either
false or obsolete or meaningless.

And he adds, 'For several years I have had no real place in a
Marxist Party'.

Has not liberalism reached its lowest stage of putrefacation when
a self-confessed counter-revolutionary is allowed to exert an
undermining influence in an organisation which styles itself
'revolutionary' and Marxist? If the rejection of such liberalism is
'Stalinist bureaucratism', we can understand the generosity with
which the Trotskyists hand out these epithets, unintentionally
flattering for those on whom they are conferred.

We have just alluded to the mass line, the developed form of
democratic centralism. Here is how Mao Tse-tung defines it: (22)

In all the practical work of our Party, all correct leadership is
necessarily 'from the masses to the masses'. This means: take
the ideas of the masses (scattered and unsystematic ideas) and
concentrate them (through study turn them into concentrated and
systematic ideas), then go to the masses and propagate and
explain these ideas until the masses embrace them as their own,
hold fast to them and translate them into action, and test the
correctness of these ideas in such action ... And so on, and over
and over again in an endless spiral, with the ideas becoming more
correct, more vital and richer each time. Such is the Marxist
theory of knowledge.

It follows from this text and from all the others in which Mao
formulates his idea of the mass line that democratic centralism
presents a dialectical contradictory unity: 'Within the ranks of the
people, democracy is correlative with centralism and freedom with
discipline. They are the two opposites of a single entity.' (23)

The distinction between leaders and led, between those who
elaborate the line and launch the slogans on the one hand, and those

who must assimilate them and apply them on the other, like the discipline of militants in relation to higher instances, constitutes one of the poles of the contradiction; democracy and freedom are its other pole.

Let us now consider the unity of these opposites. The legitimacy and authority of a leadership is not based on its election according to rules but on the correctness of its policy. The latter in turn depends on its ability to establish links with the masses, to learn from them and to systematise their ideas. In order to do this, it must submit to the supervision of the masses, encourage criticism and self-criticism and apply the maxim: 'Hide nothing you know, keep nothing to yourself of what you have to say.' 'No-one is at fault for having spoken, it is for the listener to take advantage.' Thus democracy is at the heart of centralism and vice versa, since it is necessary to centralise the ideas of the masses and to help the latter 'to carry out all their correct ideas in the light of the circumstances'. (24)   In other respects, an individual or a group wanting to make a revolution can only attain their end in the framework of a disciplined activity. This discipline is therefore the concrete form of their freedom. Conversely, if they are not free to formulate criticisms and to give their point of view, this discipline becomes servile and blind submission, it ceases to be revolutionary and is transformed into its opposite. This is why, even in the People's Army, discipline is inseparable from the three democracies (political, economic and military). (25)

Mao Tse-tung's speech to the expanded Central Committee on 30 January 1962 is essentially given over to the question of democratic centralism. We shall quote from it at length because of its interest.

'What is centralism? First of all it is centralising the correct opinions ... (Now) without democracy, opinions will not come from the masses and it will be impossible to decide on the good line.' In this respect:

> When our leading organs decide on a line, guiding principle, policy or method, they are, so to speak, just a processing plant. Everybody knows that if a plant does not have raw materials in the full amount or proper quality, it cannot manufacture a good finished product. If there is no democracy, you don't understand what's going on at the lower levels, the situation is unclear, you don't collect opinions from all sides, you don't let ideas circulate, and you decide questions only on the one-sided or insincere materials of the upper level leading organs, then it will be difficult to avoid subjectivism, impossible to attain unified knowledge and unified action, and impossible to put centralism into effect.

In fact, 'Without democracy there can be no genuine centralism and since everybody's opinion is different, without unified knowledge, centralism cannot be established.'

> Now there are some comrades who are afraid the masses will open up discussions and will offer opinions that do not agree with the leaders of the leading organs. As soon as a problem comes up for discussion they put a damper on the masses' activism and don't let anybody speak. This is a very poor attitude ... Comrades, we are revolutionaries. If we truly make a mistake ... we should

seek the opinions of the masses of the people and of the comrades
and do our own soul-searching. This soul-searching sometimes
requires a number of times. Once won't do. Nobody is satisfied.
Twice, still no satisfaction. Do it three times or until nobody
has any more opinions.

In his speech to the Central Committee on 24 September 1962, Mao
declared:

Don't be afraid to make mistakes. We permit mistakes. Haven't
you already made some! We also allow you to correct mistakes.
If we did not allow mistakes, we could not allow correction of
mistakes ... Last year I said you must also allow me to make my
mistakes and allow me to correct my mistakes, and after I have
corrected them, you will accept me!

In fact, on 30 January, Mao had said:

On 12th June last year ... I talked about my own shortcomings and
mistakes ... The whole Central Committee makes mistakes and it is
my responsibility both directly and indirectly because I am the
Chairman of the Central Committee.

The press has recently said that after Mao's death, China will have
collective leadership. This is presented as a new departure. In
fact, it concerns a principle applicable at all levels and one which
Mao recalled in the speech which we have just quoted: (26)

The Party Committee's leadership is collective leadership and not
the individual say-so of the first secretary ... Take the
Standing Committee or Political Bureau of the Central Committee.
It often happens that not everybody approves of what I say and
regardless of whether I'm right or not, I obey them since they're
the majority.

Democracy on the one hand and centralised leadership on the other,
are the means to an end, which is the elaboration and application of
a correct political line. Mao tells us that 'Democracy sometimes
eems to be an end, but it is in fact only a means'. (27)

Why is it necessary to guarantee to the minority the right to
e press itself, to reserve an opinion and to bring questions out
i o the open? Because, Mao tells us, 'Throughout history, new and
c rect things have often failed at the outset to win recognition
f n the majority of people and have had to develop by twists and
t s in struggle.' (28)

entralism too is a means which must be used because it is
i spensable for all the reasons which we pointed out at the
be nning of the chapter, but also so that the party of the
pr tariat can operate like an army in combat facing an enemy which
als has a centralised leadership. Infringements of party
dis pline, for example, can only be judged in the last instance in
tern of considerations linked to the concrete situation. Mao
Tse- ng was right not to carry out certain instructions of the
Centi l Committee of his party when he was struggling in the
Ching ng Mountains. As far as respect for democracy as well as
that r centralism is concerned, it is politics which, as everywhere, u t be put in command. Lenin expressed this idea by saying
that ' u democracy must be subordinated to revolutionary
opportunit ! (29)

In the s e text, 'Once Again on the Trade Unions', he declared
that, 'fact nal pronouncements' and 'even a split' were justified

'if the disagreements are ... extremely profound and if a wrong
trend in the policy of the party ... cannot be rectified in any
other way'. (30)

BUILDING THE PARTY

As we have already pointed out, in his earlier polemical writings
against Lenin, Trotsky shared the sociological viewpoint of Axelrod,
Parvus and Rosa Luxemburg. (31) He was inclined to think that the
revolutionary party was identical with the conscious elements of the
proletariat and ultimately with the class as such. He thought that
the latter would be led to make the revolution by virtue of the laws
which govern the development of social contradictions. The
conditions of its existence would constrain the proletariat to
pursue its objective interests consciously. Thus the role of the
party would be limited to 'shortening the road and making it
easier', from 'objective fact' to 'its objective consciousness'.
(32) Even so, the vocation of the party was to coincide with the
class. This is why Trotsky, in agreement with the Mensheviks,
thought that one could be a member of the party without militating
in it. Thus he opposed the 'substitutionism' of Lenin who, he
argued, sought to substitute the party for the class, the Central
Committee for the party and the dictator for the Central Committee.
In fact, what he took exception to in Lenin was his distinction
between the party and the class and the accordance of a leading
function to the former. Overestimating 'the spontaneity' or 'self-
activity' of the masses and correspondingly underestimating the role
of leadership, he had no choice but to reject as well Lenin's thesis
that scientific socialism, elaborated by intellectuals who are of
bourgeois origin but have adopted a proletarian class position, is
brought into the proletariat 'from outside the sphere of relations
between workers and employers'. (33) Left to itself, the working
class can neither go beyond the level of economic demands nor
achieve a revolutionary class consciousness.
    Lenin was right, but he laid too much stress on a partial truth.
In the context of his polemic with the Economists he had been led to
'bend the stick' the other way in order to straighten it again. He
acknowledged it himself at the end of the 2nd Party Congress (1903),
thus correcting certain possibly unilateral formulations in 'What is
To Be Done?', particularly the famous quotation from Kautsky. (34)
    In his pamphlet 'Briefly about the Disagreements in the Party',
published in May 1905, Stalin emphasised another aspect of the
reality taken as given in 'What is To Be Done?' He wrote: 'Here is
what Lenin says: The working class spontaneously gravitates towards
socialism, but the more widespread (and continuously revived in its
most diverse forms) bourgeois ideology spontaneously imposes itself
upon the working class still more.' (35) Stalin went even further
since he acknowledged that in the long run the spontaneous movement
of the proletariat would achieve revolution even without social
democracy. (36) Clearly, this is a scholastic hypothesis. In fact,
the existence of a proletarian movement always encourages the
appearance of Marxist intellectuals. Dialectical and historical
materialism would not have been possible without such a movement.

Stalin returned to this question in a vigorously polemical article published on 15 August 1905 in 'Proletariatis Brdzola'. Lenin summed up the central part by noting the author's 'excellent presentation of the celebrated question of the "introduction of consciousness from without"'. Stalin showed that (a) socialist consciousness corresponds to the class position of the proletariat, (b) only social-democratic intellectuals 'possess the necessary means and leisure', for the scientific elaboration of this consciousness, (c) this consciousness is introduced into the working-class movement from without by these intellectuals and the Social-Democratic Party, and (d) when making its propaganda, the party meets with 'an instinctive striving towards socialism' among the proletariat. (37)

In all his later writings in the polemic against the Economists, Lenin constantly emphasised not the (real) spontaneous tendency of the proletariat to submit to the dominant bourgeois ideology when the latter is not fought by revolutionary Marxists, but its (just as real) spontaneous tendency to appropriate socialist theory and to embark on revolutionary action on its own initiative.

As soon as the 1905 revolution broke out, Lenin emphasised 'the amazingly rapid shift of the movement from the purely economic to the political ground ... notwithstanding the fact that conscious Social-Democratic influence is lacking or is but slightly evident'. He exalted the proletarian revolutionary instinct which was breaking through 'all obstacles' such as the 'backwardness of some of the leaders'. (38) He regarded it as highly significant that the Moscow workers in December 1905 were more advanced than 'the conscious element' represented by the social-democrats. They knew by themselves what had to be done. For Lenin: (39)

This is the greatest historic gain in the Russian revolution ... the proletariat sensed sooner than its leaders the change in the objective conditions of the struggle and the need for a transition from the strike to an uprising. As is always the case, practice marched ahead of theory.

At the same time, Lenin went so far as to say that 'The working class is instinctively, spontaneously social-democratic'. (40)

Logically, our ossified Marxist-Leninists who swear only by 'What Is To Be Done?' (of which they remember only the famous quotation from Kautsky) should tax Lenin and Stalin themselves with 'spontaneism'. That would be enjoyable. Unfortunately, they read very little more than a few texts, and always the same ones.

Let us recall that after the May-June 1968 movement in France, the Trotskyists and ossified Marxist-Leninists attacked Mao's mass line and those who wished to apply it in their practice, dubbing the latter with the ridiculous nickname 'Mao-spontex'. They spoke of the inability of the working class, if left by itself, to go beyond trade-union consciousness. According to them, to elaborate the line by gathering the correct ideas of the masses in struggles in which one is a participant before leading them signifies bowing before the necessarily bourgeois (!) spontaneity of the proletariat. It is spontaneism, economism and reformism! As for them, they reckon that communist intellectuals should elaborate the line and programme from books (Marxist classics, collections of statistics, etc) and then call on the masses to follow this self-appointed vanguard.

For forty years the Trotskyist sects (falling into the opposite mistake to that of Trotsky in 1904) have embodied the very essence of this sort of vanguard, the idea of which was so discredited during and after the movement of May-June that Ernest Mandel felt the need to take the precaution against the accusation of conceiving the party in terms of this model. 'There is no self-proclaimed vanguard', he tells us, because 'the vanguard must win recognition as a vanguard'. (41) We would retort, but yes, M. Mandel, there is a self-proclaimed vanguard. In 1939, while he recognised that the Fourth International was not linked to the masses, Trotsky consoled himself, nevertheless, by saying, 'We who are the vanguard of the vanguard'. (42) At any rate, the theoretician of the Fourth International stands on awkward ground. This vanguard must exist before being recognised, otherwise how could it win its recognition? A few pages later Mandel confirms our interpretation of his thought: 'The proletarian army will never reach its historic objectives if the necessary education, schooling and testing of a proletarian vanguard in the working out and agitational application of the revolutionary programme in struggle has not taken place before the outbreak of the broadest mass struggles.' (43)

One could not be clearer. The constitution of the vanguard and the elaboration of the programme must 'take place before' mass struggles and develop outside these struggles. The same applies to the education, training and testing of this curious 'vanguard'. Leaders and programme are thus to be bestowed on the people who would only have 'to recognise' them.

We should have to concede the correctness of Mandel and before him, Trotsky, if it were possible to deduce the laws of the revolution in a given country from general truths about its character (democratic or socialist) and its ultimate end, if it were possible to elaborate strategy and tactics from such deductions – that is, in the end, on the basis of bookish learning – if we could know the conjuncture of the class struggle and answer the question, 'Who are our friends and who are our enemies?' from given statistics based on class being and the mere objective interests of some social category, if we could elaborate, lastly, outside of and in place of the masses, the detailed plan of the transformations to be carried out in all the spheres of social life. (44)

Now 'the concrete analysis of a concrete situation is the living soul, the very essence of Marxism'. The carrying out of this analysis requires consideration of the class position (and not just the class being) of the different social strata, paying particular attention to the attitude of intermediary, wavering elements because victory cannot be won if the Left does not win over the Centre. It must also be based not only on the objective needs of the masses as we conceive them, perhaps wrongly, but also on their wishes, which is impossible without investigation and the latter presupposes links with the masses. If the answer to all these concrete questions about alliances, slogans, etc., could be provided by theory, then programme and line could be elaborated in an armchair. Lenin did not think so. To those who criticised him for not having defined 'a priori' the strategic line and particular tactics, he replied: 'As if one can set out to make a great revolution and know before- hand how it is to be completed! Such knowledge cannot be derived from books and our decision could spring only from the experience of the masses.' (45)

The programme makers would also do well to reflect on the words which Mao Tse-tung spoke to the plenary session of the Central Committee on 30 January 1962: (46)

Until the period of resistance against Japan, we could not determine the general Party line or entire set of specific policies in accordance with the situation. Until the necessary kingdom of the democratic revolution of that time was recognised by us, we could not have freedom'.

Later, Mao related his conversation in 1960 with Edgar Snow: Snow 'wanted me to talk about the long-term plans for China. I said: "I don't know". He said: "You're being too cautious". I said: "It's not caution, I just don't know, I don't have the experience" (of the construction of socialism).' (47)

As Marxists, Lenim and Mao knew that practice comes first, theory after, even if the latter contributes later to illuminate practice. That is why Marx said 'One step of real movement is worth a dozen programmes'. The insurrection of Paris workers in June 1848 and the Paris Commune owed practically nothing to Marxism, whereas the latter owes much to them: to the former, the theory of the uninterrupted revolution and the interpenetration of the democratic stage and the socialist stage; to the latter, the concrete forms of smashing the state apparatus and of the dictatorship of the proletariat. (48)

The Soviets were not inscribed in the programme of the Bolshevik Party and the latter had not launched them as a slogan. This historic initiative came from the masses alone. It was they who invented this form of organisation and power. Lenin declared on this subject: (49)

Had not the popular creative spirit of the Russian revolution ... given rise to the Soviets as early as February 1917, they could not under any circumstances have assumed power in October ... It was the creative spirit of the people, which had passed through the bitter experience of 1905 and had been made wise by it, that gave rise to this form of proletarian power.

We can now understand why in 1921 Lenin considered the translation of 'What Is To Be Done?' as 'undesirable'. He demanded that it should at least be accompanied by 'a good commentary', 'to avoid false applications'. In a new preface as early as 1907 Lenin pointed out that this text of 1902 contained expressions that were 'more or less awkward or imprecise' and that it should not be detached from 'the determined situation which gave birth to it'. (50)

Stalin was a better Leninist than certain of today's anti-spontaneists when he wrote as follows: 'Lenin taught us not only to teach the masses but also to learn from them ... The ordinary people are often far closer to the truth than certain higher echelons.'

Michael Lowy knows this passage from Stalin as well as those we have quoted above but he is careful not to note it. On the other hand, he quotes another one (p. 190) and harps on it with the purpose of setting Stalin against Lenin. It concerns a leaflet in which Stalin wrote 'Let us hold out our hands and gather around the party committees! We must not forget for one instant that only the party committees can provide us with proper leadership, that they alone know how to light up the road to "the promised land", the socialist world.' Whatever Lowy thinks, there is no contradiction here. One can and must insist both on the masses' historical initiative and on the party's leadership. This is what Lenin did, because both are necessary for the victory of the revolution.

True Leninists accept with Mao that correct ideas in politics come from the practice of the masses in struggle illuminated by the beacon of the general principles of Marxism-Leninism borne by the party.

One must study with the problems to be solved in mind. This is a condition for fruitful study. If practice is not combined with study, theory cannot be truly assimilated. The Marxist classics, statistical data from bourgeois economics and sociology are not enough to understand the concrete problems which the class struggle poses on the different fronts in which it proceeds. Books are not useless but practice must be the basis.

'Our principal method is to learn to make war by making it', we are told by Mao Tse-tung, who is adopting a truth already stated by Lenin in his 'Philosophical Notebooks': 'In order to understand, it is necessary to begin empirically, to study, to rise from empiricism to the universal. In order to learn to swim, it is necessary to get into the water.'(51) It is by making the revolution that we succeed in establishing its laws after a great number of mistakes and defeats.

'If you want to know the taste of a pear, you must change the pear by eating it yourself,' Mao teaches us. (52) To know society it is necessary to change it by participating in the revolutionary struggle of the masses. An important moment in this practice is the investigation. In his 'Preface and Postscript to Rural Surveys', Mao declares: 'Investigation is especially necessary for those who know theory but do not know the actual conditions, for otherwise they will not be able to link theory with practice ... No investigation, no right to speak.' (53) It is clear that the investigation in question has nothing in common with the investigations of bourgeois sociology with their vaunted impartiality. The militant is objective to the exact extent of his partiality in favour of the people.

An investigation cannot be undertaken unless one is linked to the masses, in their camp. In order to discover the masses' state of mind one should not make a survey but talk to the well-informed representatives of these masses without hiding one's views - quite the opposite. Mao made anti-religious propaganda while investigating the peasants' attachment to superstitious practices. There is no investigation without practice. Reality is discovered by transforming it. When Mao visited Hunan in January 1927, he was a revolutionary who fearlessly championed the Peasant Leagues despite the reticent, not to say hostile attitude of the leaders of his party. At the same time, he was inspired with the desire to learn from the masses, to become their humble pupil. He knew how to listen and did not set himself up as a giver of lessons. 'It has to be understood that the masses are the real heroes, while we ourselves are often childish and ignorant, and without this understanding it is impossible to acquire even the most rudimentary knowledge.' (54)

The mass line is at once both a method of leadership and a method of knowledge since 'without a really concrete knowledge of the actual conditions of the classes in ... society, there can be no really good leadership'. (55) But only on condition that it is not debased by summing it up in a simplistic formula such as 'correct ideas come from the masses' (they come from practice, particularly that of the class struggle) which certain people take to mean: the ideas of the masses are always correct. Of course, there is always something correct even in the false ideas of the masses, but if one does not make this distinction, if one does not build on what is correct to combat what is false, one will fall into the 'tailism' which Mao denounced in a speech at a conference of cadres in Shansi-Suiyuan. In it he criticised the apparently left-wing policy adopted by Liu Shao-chi during the agrarian reform. Under the pretext of 'Doing everything as the masses want it done', Liu Shao-chi had gone ahead with a strictly egalitarian division of the land and capital goods, forgetting that the sole target of the agrarian reform should be the system of feudal exploitation. Mao reminded him that 'the Party must lead the masses to carry out all their correct ideas in the light of the circumstances and educate them to correct any wrong ideas they may entertain'. (56)

They are falsifying Mao's teaching who claim support from it for a denial of the necessity for a vanguard, or 'leading core of the whole people' in Mao's formula, which seems preferable to us because the core is in the people instead of being ahead and outside of it.

In contrast to what the ossified Marxist-Leninists think, a revolutionary movement can be correctly oriented even if it does not have a Marxist Party at its head. We have cited the example of the rising in June 1848 and of the Commune and we could add that of Cuba. Mao says that 'they (the poor peasants) have never been wrong on the general direction of the revolution'. (57) It is true, nevertheless, that in the absence of a Communist Party, the peasant revolution would have come to a halt in the best of cases in the bourgeois-democratic stage (agrarian reform) and would not have finally suppressed exploitation and oppression in the countryside. Without the leadership of the revolutionary proletarian Communist Party armed with Marxism-Leninism, the thought of Mao Tse-tung, the proletariat will not be able to liberate itself and in so doing the whole of humanity; it will not be able to pursue its struggle in a consistent way; that is, to the end, namely the abolition of classes and the establishment of a communist society.

Those who invoke the example of Cuba to combat this truth proceed from the postulate that that country is a dictatorship of the proletariat which is constructing socialism. Nothing is less certain. According to Bettelheim, the transformation that has taken place in Cuba is not a 'true revolution' any more than those which have occurred in Guinea, Egypt, or Algeria. Neither Cuba nor any of these countries has really escaped imperialist (or social-imperialist) domination. For that, it would have been necessary for the proletariat to have taken power and set off on the socialist road, which it has not done. (58) Let us assume that it has, however, for the sake of the argument. Let us also assume that no involution will occur in the future, that the left of the party leads the masses in their struggle against the bureaucratised leaders who are taking the capitalist road and that the construction of socialism is thus being carried through to the end. In this case, one will be able to conclude that the party in power (whatever its origins and the serious mistakes it has committed) will be transformed through the struggle into a true proletarian communist party. This is almost a tautology.

On 18 September 1968, the 'People's Daily' published an article (59) entitled 'Compass for the victory of the revolutionary people of all countries', on the occasion of the Sixth Anniversary of Chairman Mao's most important inscription for 'Japanese worker friends': 'The Japanese Revolution will undoubtedly be victorious, provided the universal truth of Marxism-Leninism is really integrated with the concrete practice of the Japanese revolution'. The editorial in the 'People's Daily' declared:

> The party of the proletariat in all countries must firmly adhere to the universal truth of Marxism-Leninism and at the same time, proceeding from life itself, maintain close contact with the masses, constantly sum up the experience of mass struggles and independently formulate and carry out policies and tactics suited to the conditions of each country.

For those in Western Europe who quote the thought of Mao Tse-tung as their authority, the problem is posed precisely in these terms: to proceed from reality or from books? To make use of the universal truth of Marxism-Leninism in order to know reality through practice ('the struggle') or to use 'reality' in order to illustrate by examples the truths of Marxism-Leninism and have the illusion of posing concrete problems? There are certain people in France but also in Belgium, Italy and Germany who wish to proceed from 'What Is To Be Done?' and not from reality.

The conclusion to the same article says, 'It is our firm conviction that a truly revolutionary Japanese party armed with Marxism-Leninism is sure to come into being in the flames of revolutionary struggle.'

The party will be born in the flames of the revolutionary struggle, not in the cigarette smoke of a room used for meetings by a few young or not so young petty bourgeois eager to proclaim themselves the party.

We know how the ossified Marxists answer. They answer in an ossified way: the Chinese Communist Party was founded in this way by a dozen intellectuals representing fifty-seven members. This is to forget a 'detail': at that time in China there was neither a bourgeois-'worker's' party nor reformist trade unions misleading the majority of the working class. It will be accepted that this detail is important. In the meantime it is necessary to understand exactly what was this party founded in 1921. Half of the founder members reneged, the anarchist tendency was very strong among them, and of those who did not degenerate Mao said, 'We were just a bunch of eager young men who wanted to make a revolution.' He emphasised, moreover, that these eager young men were 'blind' and remained so 'until the period of the war of resistance to Japan'. 'If somebody says that there was a comrade, for example, any comrade in the Central Committee or I myself, who completely recognised the laws of the Chinese Revolution in the beginning, he would be boasting, don't you believe him for it didn't happen.' (60)

It matters little that there are only a few Maoists at the
beginning. They grow stronger if they actually work to fuse with
the working class, if they participate in its struggles and do not
restrict their activity to setting up and distributing a journal.
On the other hand, it is very important that, in the present
conditions, they do not claim to be the 'true' Communist Party and
do not launch grandiloquent appeals destined to disappear into thin
air when everyone knows that they do not represent anything very
much, otherwise the workers will not take them seriously. Having
been 'had' twice by traditional workers' organisations, the workers
demand that the Maoists prove themselves before giving them their
confidence. In other words, for the Maoist organisation to be able
to present itself as the leading core of the people, it is necessary
for it really to be such, for the conscious workers (especially
they) will not allow themselves to be taken in. This presupposes
that certain conditions are met.
1   proletarianisation of the organisation and its leadership;
2   roots in the working class attested by effective ability to lead
    its struggles;
3   roots in all the other classes and strata of the people with the
    ability to mobilise them and to unify their struggles into a
    revolutionary perspective as a criterion;
4   unification of all proletarian revolutionaries and all true
    Maoists, that is, of all those who can be united.
Such an organisation will be able to lead the united front of all
revolutionary classes and strata. It will have determined on the
basis of practice the character of the present stage, the principal
contradiction, the general political line and the system of
particular lines. It will have helped the masses to elaborate
particular programmes on the different aspects of their condition
(work, security, housing, transport, etc) and will synthesise them
in a programme for a people's regime. It will be capable of
combining legal and illegal, and open and clandestine work. It will
have at its disposal an armed organisation, however embryonic.
    The people will then flex 'the three magic arms' guaranteeing it
victory: the party, the united front, the army. This stage was only
reached in China in 1937.
    It is clear that the building of the party is a continuous
creation, as is the elaboration of the programme, as can be seen
from the constant changes which Lenin made to it. (61) Its official
date of birth is a question of 'revolutionary opportunity' which
must be appraised on the basis of the concrete situation. In
stating the conditions pointed out above we were thinking above all
of France and Italy. The premature birth of the party, in other
words, its emergence as a self-proclaimed vanguard immediately
claiming recognition of its status by fraternal parties and counting
more on their aid than on its own forces, threatens to backfire by
depreciating in the eyes of the masses the idea of a Maoist-Marxist-
Leninist Party and by making more difficult the broad alliance of
all those who appeal to the authority of the thought of Mao
Tse-tung.
    On the other hand, the protracted building of a party presenting
the characteristics we have pointed out sanctions more flexibility
in the choice (or abandonment) of different forms of organisation,

more effectively liberates initiative from below, and ensures the
selection of cadres only on the basis of their success in practice.
By combining legal and illegal methods, by setting when necessary
the violence of the people against the violence of authority, one
educates the militants, attracts the most combative workers and
rejects petty bourgeois individualists and careerists. The
elimination of poisoned blood and the infusion of fresh blood
develop the organisation on a healthy proletarian basis, offering
every guarantee against the dangers of sclerosis, opportunist
degeneration and bureaucratism.

THE TROTSKYIST CRITIQUE OF THE BUREAUCRACY

Reading the pamphlet, 'De la bureaucratie', by E. Germain (alias
Ernest Mandel), we note that, in the chapter deceptively called 'La
théorie trotskyste de la dégénerescence de l'Etat ouvrier
soviétique' (Trotsky's theory of the degeneration of the Soviet
Workers' State), the concepts of 'Thermidor' and 'Bonapartism'
which are nonetheless the foundation of this theory are spirited
away. In their place, we find a definition of the bureaucracy which
can be summarised as follows: an organisation necessitates leaders,
an apparatus and permanent officials and suddenly we have 'budding
bureaucrats'. Such is the genus. The specific difference is this:
of all the leaders, those are thorough-going bureaucrats whom
E. Germain dislikes. Other criteria are vaguely mentioned but this
one is the most certain. Compared with the unstable equilibrium of
Trotsky's theoretical constructions this idea of bureaucracy has
three advantages and one disadvantage: it is simple, pliable and
irrefutable but it serves no purpose - or rather it serves all
purposes, which comes to the same thing.
    It is true, nevertheless, that Germain resurrects an old idea of
Trotsky's which the latter had gone beyond in his own way. This is
the characterisation of the Leninist idea of a party governed by
democratic centralism as 'substitutionist': '(Lenin's) methods ...
lead the Party organisation to substitute itself for the Party (in
the vague and Menshevik sense of the term); then the Central
Committee for the organisation, and finally, a single dictator to
substitute himself for the Central Committee.' (62)
    Trotsky accused Lenin of distrusting the working class. He
reckoned that it was able to intervene as such in the political
arena and could not tolerate the leadership of a united and
centralised party acting as its agent or 'locum tenens'. (63).
    This denunciation of 'substitutionism' (libellous in regard to
Lenin) has had threefold descendents: those who thought that the
proletariat was incapable of becoming the dominant class adopted
theories of the 'new class' of the Burnham or Djilas type; those who
thought the opposite formed certain anarcho-Trotskyist 'workers'-
council' currents; the intermediate position, that of the
Trotskyists, was that bureaucracy is certainly inherent in the
division between leaders and led but that there is a means by which
its effects can be attenuated, namely worker's democracy; that is,
as we have seen, the legitimation of factions which reproduce the
same division! However, Trotsky was not satisfied with such an

elementary analysis of the bureaucratic phenomenon but had attempted to discover its social basis, to explain it in an outwardly Marxist manner in terms of the class struggle. Until Germain came along and turned the 'science' upside-down, Trotskyists described the dictatorship of the proletariat under Stalin as a workers' state led by a Bonapartist bureaucracy. This amounted to a rejection of the Marxist–Leninist point of view according to which bureaucracy always serves and is monitored by the dominant class. Here is how Henri Weber, following Trotsky, justified this position in a pamphlet entitled 'Mouvement ouvrier, Stalinisme et bureaucracie':
'Nevertheless, it can happen that the State bureaucracy rises above classes, erects itself into an autonomous power and temporarily installs its own unmonitored power exercised through the providential intermediary of some all-powerful man.' (64)

At first sight, this thesis is in conformity with Marx's analysis in the 18th Brumaire, in which he says, 'Only under the second Bonaparte does the state seem to have made itself completely independent'. (65) In fact, if the state seems to be independent, that means that it is not so. With regard to 'the bureaucratic caste' which ruled Germany in 1872, Engels tells us in 'The Housing Question' that the state seems to float above classes and to represent the interests of the whole society but that 'In reality, however, the State as it exists in Germany is likewise the necessary product of the social basis out of which it has developed'. (66)

Coming back to the question of Bonapartism in 'The Civil War in France', Marx tells us: (67)

> The State power, apparently soaring high above society, was at the same time itself the greatest scandal of that society ... Imperialism is, at the same time, the most prostitute and ultimate form of the State power ... which fully grown bourgeois society had finally transformed into a means for the enslavement of labour by capital.

It is clear that, for Marx, the function of the Bonapartist state was to exercise the dictatorship of the bourgeoisie and to serve the interests of this class. Whereas, according to Trotsky, although the Stalinist Bonapartist regime is 'the historic weapon of the working class', it oppresses the latter, robs it on behalf of a privileged minority, organises production in the interests of this minority and follows a counter-revolutionary policy on the international plane.

The analogy which Trotsky set up between the 'Stalinist workers' state' and the Empire is artificial and even absurd, moreover, for the nature of the state apparatus varies radically according to the historically determined social formations in which it functions as an instrument for the perpetuation of the social relations, for the domination and repression of one class by another. Marx had already ridiculed this way of masking contemporary realities behind 'superficial historical analogies' which 'forget principles': (68)

> With so complete a difference between the material, economic conditions of the ancient and modern class struggles, the political figures produced by them can likewise have not more in common with one another than the Archbishop of Canterbury and the High Priest Samuel.

Apparently Trotsky was unable to think through current problems except by means of 'superficial historical analogies'.

Even when he applied it to bourgeois regimes, Trotsky used the
term Bonapartism wrongly. In this category he included not only
fascism but also the governments which he called 'proto-fascist',
like those of 'Doumergue and Flandin in France'. (69)

When the Mensheviks called NEP a 'Soviet Thermidor' in 1921, he
acquiesced and even claimed the credit. The comparison is absurd.
Once in power, it is normal for the bourgeoisie to wish to bring the
revolution to a halt in order to enjoy its victories in peace. The
Thermidorians represented the 'nouveaux riches', the speculators and
the acquirers of national wealth who did not want any new upheavals.
The October Revolution, on the contrary, was the revolution of the
proletariat not of the Nepmen and the kulaks. By making temporary
concessions to them the proletariat 'reculait pour mieux sauter'.
NEP was not the consolidation of the gains of a class of exploiters.
It was, quite the contrary, a withdrawal permitting the
consolidation of the power of the proletariat, the most exploited
class, whose emancipation liberates the whole of humanity. Later
and up to 1935, Trotsky ceaselessly warned of the danger of a
Thermidor while denying (against certain of his supporters) that it
had already taken place. Trotsky and his friends analysed the
political struggles throughout this period by drawing on this
analogy. Until 1928 Trotsky saw Bukharin and Rykov as
Thermidorians. In his 'Letter to Friends' in October 1928, he
considered the possibility that the Thermidorian stage could be
skipped. The USSR could pass directly to an 18th Brumaire with
Voroshilov and Budenny in Napoleon's boots! He also considered the
possibility of a restoration of capitalism for which Stalin was
preparing the way: 'The film of the revolution is running backwards
and Stalin's part in it is that of Kerensky in reverse.'

He wrote this just as Stalin was preparing to launch the
collectivisation campaign and the Five-Year Plans. A poor show for
a prophet (armed or not)!

In 1929, in a polemic with some groupuscules claiming his
authority, he defined Thermidor as a counter-revolution
necessitating a civil war. He came to the conclusion that, real as
this danger was, it had not yet materialised. (70) In fact, at this
time, he thought that 'Thermidor ... indicated a transfer of power
to another class'. (71)

A few years later, he had to make a 'painful revision' of all his
past ideas. He then decided that Thermidor had taken place as early
as 1923 when Stalin defeated the left Opposition; Stalin's
government having taken on a Bonapartist character, the Soviet Union
lived under a consulate. Such is the analysis presented in the
pamphlet, 'The Workers' State and the Question of Thermidor and
Bonapartism' in 1935.

Trotsky thus recognised that the USSR had been living under a
Thermidorian regime for twelve years without his noticing it.

These speculations on an inept historical comparison could only
obscure the problems instead of posing them correctly, since they
arose, as we have seen, from a fundamental theoretical mistake. (72)

Later, in his book 'In Defence of Marxism', Trotsky acknowledged
that the notion of caste which he applied to the Soviet
'bureaucracy' did not have a scientific character and was only a
historical analogy (another one!) helping him provisionally to

supply 'the sociology of the present'. The term caste, he said, had
a 'makeshift' character. (73)

Thirty years later, the Trotskyists are still using this
unscientific and provisional 'concept' which designates neither a
class nor an instrument of a class: 'Far from being its servant,
bureaucracy has become mistress of the (entire) society'. They also
describe the apparatuses of the social-democratic and revisionist
parties as bureaucracies, here again without giving this word a
class content; that is, without distinguishing between on the one
hand the bureaucratic nature of these parties which lies in the fact
that they represent bourgeois ideology and interests among the
working class, and on the other hand, the bureaucratic deviations in
a Marxist-Leninist party which reflect the class struggle in the
party in which proletarian ideology must be ceaselessly
consolidated. (74) H. Weber sees in working-class bureaucracy 'a
(privileged) sub-group of the proletariat assuming the leadership
of trade-union and political struggles' (p. 8). In order to speak
of bureaucracy, Weber adopts a functionalist point of view, not the
point of view of Marxist class analysis.

Ultimately bureaucracy would be the product of the division
between leaders and led. Its existence would not therefore be
linked to a determinate class: the bourgeoisie. Taken to its
logical conclusion this line of argument would end up in either the
Rizzi-Burnham school or that of Chaulieu and the anarcho-Trotskyists
of 'Socialisme ou barbarie'.

The degeneration of Burnham and Chaulieu-Cardan illustrates that
it is impossible for the Trotskyists to be rigorous about their
concept of bureaucracy and to continue to invoke Marx and Lenin.

For Lenin, on the contrary, bureaucracy and the tendencies
towards bureaucratism are rooted in capitalism and in the bourgeois
and petty bourgeois mentality. 'There is a petty bourgeois tendency
to transform the members of the Soviets into "parliamentarians" or
else into bureaucrats.' (75)

How can this tendency be fought? 'Those of us who are doomed to
remain at work in the centre will continue the task of improving the
apparatus and purging it of bureaucracy ... the greatest assistance
in this task is coming, and will come, from the localities'. (76)

We see that Lenin talked about purging bureaucracy without
suppressing the apparatus and this by virtue of the link with the
masses: 'The fight against the bureaucratic distortion of the Soviet
form of organisation is assured by the firmness of the connection
between the Soviets and "the people", meaning by that the workers
and the exploited people.' (77)

Bureaucratism has a class nature which had a threefold origin in
Lenin's day:

1 the maintenance of Tsarist bureaucrats in the state
   administration as specialists necessary for their 'administrative
   knowledge';
2 the ideological survivals of capitalism (bureaucratic by nature)
   among the masses and even the leaders, even the revolutionaries;
3 the fact that economic and administrative functions in the first
   stages of the construction of socialism remain tied to the
   heritage of the previous society and induce a corresponding
   ideology, leads to a bureaucratic style of work among cadres.

The struggle against bureaucratism is thus a struggle between proletarian ideology and bourgeois or petty bourgeois ideology. It is a class struggle. To lead it to a successful conclusion, the initiative of the masses must be freed so that they can educate themselves on the political and technical level, so that they can do without bourgeois specialists and so that 'the working class exercises leadership in everything'. 'It is important for us to draw literally all working people into the government of the state. It is a task of tremendous difficulty. But socialism cannot be implemented by a minority, by the party. It can be implemented only by tens of millions when they have learned to do it themselves.' (78)

The process of revisionist degeneration and of the restoration of capitalism, the principal agents of which are the bureaucratic cadres 'who take the capitalist road' has its structural roots in the discrepancy between the possession of power by the working class and its actual ability to exercise it, particularly in the economic and cultural domains. To reduce this discrepancy it is necessary to conduct the class struggle under socialism, the most explosive form of which was the cultural revolution. Like Stalin, Trotsky failed to understand what this class struggle after the expropriation of the propertied classes might have been.

For Trotsky, the danger of the restoration of capitalism came from the contradiction between the forms of property and bourgeois norms of distribution granting extreme privileges to an upper stratum. (79) These norms themselves were caused by poverty and the necessity to resort to material incentives in order to develop industrial production ('primitive accumulation'). Now every inegalitarian distribution necessitates a policeman. 'Such is the starting point of the power of the Soviet bureaucracy. It "knows" who is to get something and who has to wait'. In the eventuality that it would hold on to power, it would not fail to restore private ownership of the means of production for its own benefit.

'It is not enough to be the director of a trust; it is necessary to be a stockholder.' (80)

The preceding is summarised in Figure 1, in which the arrows symbolise relations of cause and effect.

It is true that material privileges contribute to the degeneration of the leaders (it is not the only cause) and to the perpetuation of a bourgeois mentality infected with egoism and careerism, even among the broad masses to whom the cadres give a bad example. Trotsky's mistake was to see in this alone the sole source of the tendencies to the restoration of capitalism, which he defined moreover as a violent revolution conferring on directors the status of stockholders.

In other words, he attributed an exclusive importance to the superstructural legal form of the relations of production, unaware of the problem of their content; he wrote for example, 'The October Revolution has been betrayed by the ruling stratum but not yet overthrown. It has a great power of resistance, coinciding with the established property relations.' (81)

We know today that the development of capitalism (in the USSR for example) is not reducible to a return to individual private owner-ship of the means of production. This may, perhaps, be its final

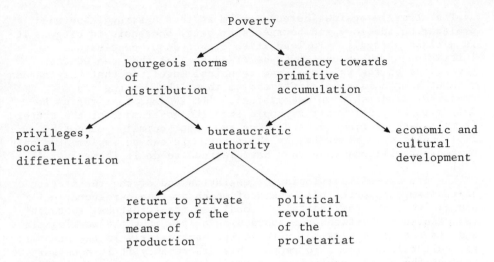

FIGURE 1

result – but it is only an inessential aspect at the moment. On the
contrary, the Trotskyists today who adhere to the words of 'the
master' describe the USSR as a Workers' State. They also use
Trotsky's problematic with regard to China. Everything that Trotsky
said concerning the USSR appears to them to apply 'a fortiori' to
China. As the latter is even poorer than Russia, the tendency to
primitive accumulation and therefore to 'robbing' the masses must be
all the more strongly in evidence there. The same schema thus
unfolds. Not only is this schema not in accordance with the facts
but the concept of 'primitive socialist accumulation' on which it is
based is not Marxist. We showed in Chapter 3 that the analogy thus
established with capitalist primitive accumulation is meaningless
since capital is a relation of production and not a thing, a certain
quantity of money, machines or goods. This analogy helps, moreover,
to falsify the problems and even, paradoxically, to justify certain
of Stalin's mistakes, since he applied, in its essentials,
Preobrazhensky's schema in the construction of the material basis of
'socialism' in the USSR. What the Trotskyists do not understand is
that, to the extent that there is such a thing as 'primitive
accumulation' it is not socialist.

We have seen what were the economic roots of bureaucracy
according to Trotsky. Underdevelopment and scarcity made social
inequalities necessary, all the more so since they engendered a
strong tendency to primitive accumulation. The bureaucrats were
those who knew who was to receive and who was to wait. They
enforced the labour discipline necessary for an accelerated growth
of production and they justified their privileges by exploiting the
country's cultural backwardness.

The bureaucracy's political roots were the revolutionary ebb-tide
in Europe after 1923; the weariness of a Russian working class
decimated and dispersed after the civil war; finally, the specific
corrupting effects of power. (82)

For all these reasons, Trotsky considered that the bureaucratic
phenomenon was unavoidable to a certain extent. It derived, in

fact, from 'the iron necessity to give birth to and support a
privileged minority so long as it is impossible to guarantee genuine
equality'; (83) that is why: (84)

> the tendencies of bureaucratism, which strangle the worker's
> movement in capitalist countries, would everywhere show
> themselves even after a proletarian revolution. But ... the
> poorer the society which issues from a revolution, the sterner
> and more naked would be the expression of this 'law' and the more
> crude would be the forms assumed by bureaucratism.

What would a Marxist Party do if it succeeded in asserting itself?
It 'would shuffle and cleanse the bureaucracy and place it under the
control of the masses'. (85) Hence a few palliatives apart, the
bureaucracy would continue to exist.

Trotsky defined the dictatorship of the proletariat at the
economic, not at the political level: it would reside entirely in
state control of the means of production. For him the construction
of socialism is unrelated to the class struggle; it is solely a
question of economic development. This emerges clearly from this
passage in 'The Revolution Betrayed' among others: 'Soviet forms of
property on a basis of the most modern achievement of American
technique transplanted into all branches of economic life - that
indeed would be the first stage of socialism'. (86)

This idea is based on a confusion between property relations and
the relations of production. (87) The USSR is a 'Workers' State' in
so far as the bureaucracy maintains the collective ownership of the
means of production, 'the dictatorship of the proletariat has found
its distorted but indubitable expression in the dictatorship of the
bureaucracy'. (88) Trotsky accounted for this paradox by means of
the comparison with Bonapartism. In 1929, he still thought (but not
for much longer) that the peasantry would be the social basis of
this Bonapartism as it had been for Napoleon III: 'The enriched
muzhik or the muzhik who only seeks to get rich ... is the natural
agent of Bonapartist tendencies'; (89) and also: 'The problem of
Thermidor and of Bonapartism is in essence the problem of the
kulak'. (90)

But the facts obstinately refuse to comply with his schemas.
Trotsky characterised his own destiny very well when he wrote that
'a petit-bourgeois intellectual - alas! - uses as his "tools"
fleeting observations and superficial generalisations - until major
events club him on the head'. (91)

The expropriation of the kulaks and collectivisation clubbed him
on the head and forced him to modify his analysis of 'Stalinist
Bonapartism', which now became a reaction to the pressure of the
surrounding peasants and the capitalist encirclement: (92)

> The Soviet bureaucracy ... was summoned to regulate the
> antagonism between the proletariat and the peasantry, between
> the workers' state and world imperialism ... Stalin's 'personal
> regime' ... is the product of the living struggle between the
> proletariat and the bourgeoisie in the last instance ... The
> objective function of 'the Saviour' is to safeguard new forms of
> ownership by usurping the political function of the dominant
> class.

Trotsky thus argued that the bureaucracy raised itself above the
people by performing a balancing act between antagonistic classes

'in equilibrium'. Here again, we cannot ask Trotsky to be
consistent. In some of his writings, he said that, faced with the
bourgeois offensive, the proletariat was forced to relinquish power
into the hands of the bureaucracy; in others, he argued that it was
the bureaucracy itself which fostered the rise of the bourgeoisie.
Similarly, Trotsky does not seem to have been sure whether the
bureaucracy manoeuvred in the last instance to serve the proletariat
or the bourgeoisie (there can be no doubt in the case of real
Bonapartism). He acknowledged two 'variants': (93)

> Upon the social foundations of the Soviet state, the economic and
> cultural uplift of the labouring masses must tend to undermine
> the very bases of bureaucratic domination. Clearly, in the light
> of this fortunate historical variant, the bureaucracy turns out
> to be only the instrument - a bad and expensive instrument - of
> the socialist state.

This thesis explains the naïve hopes placed by the Trotskyists of
the Fourth International and by Isaac Deutscher in 'democratisation'
after the 20th Congress. Higher living standards and a higher
cultural level on the basis of 'the socialist relations of
ownership', should surely guarantee the advance towards proletarian
democracy and true socialism? The idea that Soviet culture was not
perhaps completely proletarian, any more than the real relations of
production, did not cross their minds.

In 'The Revolution Betrayed', Trotsky specified the other variant
towards which he leaned more and more at the end of his life: if the
revolutionary interest did not overthrow the bureaucracy then the
counter-revolutionary interest would do it. If neither of them
monopolised power, the bureaucracy itself would restore capitalism
for its own benefit: (94)

> It must inevitably in future stages seek support for itself in
> property relations ... Privileges have only half their worth, if
> they cannot be transmitted to one's children. But the right of
> testament is inseparable from the right of property. It is not
> enough to be the director of a trust; it is necessary to be a
> stockholder.

However, in the same work, Trotsky maintained that the bureaucracy
was 'the instrument of the dictatorship of the proletariat' because
'it is compelled to defend state property as the source of its power
and its income'. (95) Was it or was it not 'compelled'? Complete
mystery remains. Whatever the case, it seems that a new slide in
Trotsky's ideas took place a few years later, since he then declares
that 'the overthrow of the bureaucracy is indispensable for the
preservation of state property in the USSR'. (96)

On the other hand, Trotsky insisted on talking about a
'Bonapartist oligarchy' and simultaneously a 'Stalinist counter-
revolution'. (97) Bonapartism, whether in its classical form
analysed by Marx or in its fascist form, eliminates the parties and
the traditional political personnel of the bourgeoisie but governs
by serving the interests of this class. In 'Stalinist Bonapartism',
on the other hand, although it is 'the historic weapon of the
working class', 'the dominant class' (sic), serves the interests of
imperialism of which it is 'the most valuable agency' (98) and
'transforms the Soviet social order in the interests of a privileged
minority'. (99) Understand who can!

Trotsky's frequent 'volte-faces' on the nature of the Soviet regime and his permanent conceptual wavering are explained by the fact that while he touched on (but did not see) real problems, he proved to be incapable of correctly formulating them in terms of specific contradictions in the transition to socialism. He confused the relations of production with their superstructural legal expression, property relations. Conflating the three instances of social formation (the economic, legal-political and ideological-theoretical levels), he defined the dictatorship of the proletariat by the state ownership of the means of production. In that case, the Asiatic mode of production of the ancient civilisations of Mesopotamia, Egypt, Greece and Peru etc, would have been socialist prototypes; modern Egypt would be a dictatorship of the proletariat. (100) Trotsky did not understand that in a country in which the state disposes of the means of production, the decisive question is to know who holds power. Confronted with the paradox of a 'dictatorship of the proletariat' in which the latter suffers the dictatorship, he extricated himself by resorting either to a medical metaphor which underlined the contingent character of the phenomenon (this dictatorship is 'very sick'!) (101) or to the illegitimate historical analogy with Bonapartism which, on the contrary, linked it to a 'sociological law'.

Now under this latter regime, the state serves the bourgeoisie because it is dominant on the economic level. The proletariat, on the contrary, can only hold economic power on condition that it exercises political power. If it loses the latter, it loses everything.

The perfectly clear meaning of Lenin's texts on this subject has been obscured for half a century by Trotskyist, Stalinist and Khrushchevite ideologies. The Bolshevik leader had emphasised that the only differences between state capitalism in Germany and that set up in Russia in 1918 was that in the latter country, 'the workers hold state power'. According to him, if you combine state capitalism along German lines with 'the proletarian, Soviet state ... you will get all the conditions necessary for socialism'. (102)

The tendencies to bureaucratism which appear within the proletarian state apparatus - that is, the tendencies of certain leaders to cut themselves off from the masses, to behave like despotic overlords, to award themselves privileges - reflects the persistent influence of bourgeois ideology which also tends to deflect the economic, educational and international policy of the socialist state. A struggle develops between the leaders who thus take the capitalist road and the consistent revolutionaries who wish to advance towards socialism, a struggle which is sometimes latent, sometimes overt and sometimes explosive. This struggle between the two lines, between the two roads, is pursued unceasingly throughout the period of the transition to socialism. The elements who, disguised as Marxist-Leninists, are taking the capitalist road may seize power at any moment, that is, deflect the party and the state in a non-proletarian direction. This deviation can become irreversible and lead to the restoration of capitalism. That is why the principal contradiction after the abolition of private ownership of the means of production is the contradiction between the revolutionary masses and the leaders taking the capitalist road.

If, from the principal aspect, the revolutionary masses become the
secondary aspect of this contradiction, the class nature of the
state changes, which entails the usurpation of power by a new
bourgeoisie. The 20th Congress of the CPSU marked such a turning
point, the causes of which obviously go back much further.

The great proletarian cultural revolution made it possible to
resolve in practice and in theory the problem posed by the pursuit
of the class struggle under the dictatorship of the proletariat by
liberating the initiative of the masses through a broad democracy,
so that they could follow affairs of state and overthrow the
reactionary leaders. We know that the slogan of the last stage was
'The working class must exercise leadership in everything', in other
words, not only in the factories (even this is impossible without
struggles) but also in the educational institutions and party and
government bodies.

It is now clear that the analysis of the Soviet regime developed
by Trotsky and based on the concepts of 'bureaucratic centralism',
'Thermidor', and 'Bonapartism', cast no light at all on the struggle
between the two lines and consequently failed to bring out the laws
of development of a social formation in transition to socialism.
Thus all his predictions have been contradicted by events, one after
another. His successors have not been any luckier. They
concentrated the full blast of their criticism on Stalin and put
their hopes in Tito and Krushchev, from whom bitter disappointments
awaited them. They did not understand the cultural revolution in
which the masses have been seen struggling against the bureaucrats,
because it shattered their theoretical moulds into a thousand
pieces.

TROTSKY AND THE USSR

At the beginning of the Second World War, Trotsky gave a long
interview to the 'Saint Louis Post Dispatch' (10, 17 and 24 March
1940) in which he gave the following reply to the question as to
whether the dictatorship of the proletariat would mean the abandonment of the US Bill of Rights: (103)

Socialism would have no value if it did not bring with it not
only the juridical inviolability but also the full safeguarding
of all the interests of the human personality. Mankind would not
tolerate a totalitarian abomination of the Kremlin pattern. The
political regime of the USSR is not a new society but the worst
caricature of the old. With the might and techniques and
organisational methods of the United States; with the high well-
being which planned economy could assure there to all citizens,
the socialist regime in your country would mean from the
beginning the rise of the independence, initiative and creative
power of the human personality.

This was the right kind of language to reassure the most
conservative bourgeois of Saint Louis. It is all a question of 'the
interests of the human personality' (a purely individual category),
or of 'mankind', which mankind, for once unanimous and without any
class distinction, condemns 'the totalitarian abomination', namely,
'the political regime of the USSR'. The latter, he tells us, is not

a new society (a political regime which is not a society!) but 'the worst caricature of the old society'. In other words, the dictatorship of the proletariat constructing socialism is a most abominable caricature of capitalism combined with feudal survivals from Tsarist Russia. Trotsky went further than Sidney and Beatrice Webb, who, in their book 'The Decay of Capitalist Civilisation' (1923), could not even then see a great difference between Bolshevism and Tsarism. At the end of his life, the positions of the father of the Fourth International coincided with those of the most frenetic anti-communists. Abandoning Marxist concepts, he took over their language, the ideological function of which is perfectly clear.

Why did he speak of a 'totalitarian regime' not only in this interview, but also and at length in 'The Revolution Betrayed' (1936)? For the possibility it afforded him to rise above classes and to confound fascist states and communist states in the same virtuous censure as 'symmetrical phenomena' which 'show a deadly similarity in many of their features'. (104) He thus flattered American imperialism, which was opposing both types of state at the time. According to Trotsky, moreover, only 'a planned economy' was lacking in the USA for 'all citizens' to enjoy a greater well-being. Let us note that even non-Marxist authors like Herbert J. Spiro or revisionists like Lucien Goldmann acknowledge the ideological function fulfilled by the notion 'totalitarian regime' particularly in cold-war propaganda after 1945: (105)

> Attempts were made ... to construct the ultimate in self-contradiction, an 'ideology of freedom' ... a whole new conceptual vocabulary was forged ... The key to this vocabulary is the term totalitarianism, which is meant to describe and to explain such diverse political systems as Nazi Germany and the Soviet Union.

At the end of his life, Trotsky went over to this 'ideology of freedom', reaction's war-horse in the post-war period. Even in 1936 the principal objective which he set for the revolution to overthrow 'bureaucratic absolutism' was the restoration of freedoms, especially those of the 'Soviet parties'. (106) His writings contain seeds of the propaganda which amalgamates fascism and communism whose most delirious - because most matter-of-fact - expression is to be found in Lord Radcliffe's report on 'Security Procedures in the Public Service' which states in Chapter 2: 'For the sake of brevity we have followed the common practice of using the phrase "Communist" throughout to include Fascists.' (107)

Of course, Trotsky did not follow his position through to its logical conclusion. He almost identified fascism and communism but without quite taking the leap. The most talented of his followers (Rizzi, Burnham, Schachtmann) did not have this scruple. Nevertheless, it appears from the very article which he wrote to refute Rizzi (108) that Trotsky would have taken over the latter's theory if he had lived on after the Second World War. Here is how Isaac Deutscher summarises the most significant passage in this text: (109)

> The final test for the working class, for socialism, and for Marxism was imminent: it was coming with the Second World War. If the war were not to lead to the proletarian revolution in the

West, then the place of decaying capitalism would indeed be taken
not by socialism, but by a new bureaucratic and totalitarian
system of exploitation. And if the working classes of the West
were to seize power (as in Czechoslovakia) but then were
incapable of holding it and surrender it to a privileged
bureaucracy, as the Russian workers had done, then it would
indeed be necessary to acknowledge that the hopes which Marxism
placed in the proletariat had been false ... Then it would be
necessary (this is Trotsky speaking) to establish in retrospect
that ... the present USSR was the precursor of a new and
universal system of exploitation ... If the world proletariat
should actually prove incapable of accomplishing its mission ...
nothing else would remain but to recognise openly that the
socialist programme, based on the internal contradictions of
capitalist society, had petered out as a Utopia.

It seems to us that this is clear, and it becomes even clearer if it
is noted that throughout this article, Trotsky used the expression
'totalitarian regime' indiscriminately to designate state monopoly
capitalism and 'Stalinist Bonapartism'. In this case one may wonder
why until the very end Trotsky called for the unconditional defence
of the USSR. We must understand what he meant by this ... In a
posthumous article published by the 'Fourth International' (October
1940), he wrote: (110)

Against the imperialist foe we will defend the USSR with all our
might. However, the conquests of the October revolution will
serve the people only if they prove themselves capable of dealing
with the Stalinist bureaucracy as in their day they dealt with
the Tsarist bureaucracy and the bourgeoisie.

Was this not treating the 'bureaucracy' as a class enemy? Was this
not applying to the USSR Lenin's 'revolutionary defeatism' of 1914?
Turning one's weapons not against the enemy without but against
those holding power? Either these words were hot air (they were) or
Trotsky was preparing the ground for the future recruiters of the
Vlassov army. It is in this context that it is appropriate to set
the Hitler-Trotskyist epithet used at that time by communists.

At the time of the 1914-18 war, Lenin issued a call to the
peoples of the world to turn the arms which the ruling classes had
put into their hands for their mutual massacre against the power of
those ruling classes in their own countries. When the Second World
War broke out, Trotsky invited the peoples of the Soviet Union to
'deal with the Stalinist bureaucracy as in their day they dealt with
the Tsarist bureaucracy and the bourgeoisie'. Whatever J.-J. Marie
may think, this is fundamentally the same policy. (111) It seems
that Trotsky wanted to overthrow the bureaucracy with the intention
(praiseworthy, of course, as an intention!) of better defending the
USSR, but to imagine that the accession to power of the 'Bolshevik-
Leninist' Opposition was feasible at that time is lunacy. In so far
as the Trotskyist propaganda had any effect whatever, it could only
incite opposition to Soviet power and weaken its capacity to resist
agression by creating a diversion.

Today, Trotskyists regard the accusation of Hitlero-Trotskyism as
a typical case of Stalinist slander for which they do not have
strong enough words to express their indignation. Now Trotsky's
methods of amalgamation were identical to those of his great enemy.

After Siqueiros's attempt on his life, he wrote a letter to the Mexican attorney-general in which he accused all communist parties of being reserves of spies and murderers in the pay of the GPU. He also added the following detail: (112)

I do not exclude the possibility of the participation of Hitler's Gestapo in the assassination attempt. Up to a certain point the GPU and the Gestapo are connected with each other; it is possible and probable that in special cases the same agents are at the disposal of both ... It is completely possible that these two police forces co-operated in the attempt against me.

Conclusion: It is possible and probable that Siqueiros was a Hitlero-Stalinist agent; it is possible and probable that the Communists who agreed to work for Soviet agencies also put themselves at the disposal of the German agencies!

We said above that Trotsky had nearly identified 'Stalinist totalitarianism' and Nazism, but occasionally the nuance becomes imperceptible. In an article entitled 'The twin star: Hitler-Stalin' (6 December 1939), he claimed to prove that Stalin was Hitler's satellite! A little further on, he asserted that Stalin's aim in Spain had been to 'prove to London and Paris that he was capable of eliminating proletarian revolution from Spain and Europe with much greater efficiency than Franco and his backers' (Hitler and Mussolini). (113)

At a time when the Second World War had already broken out, to make the CPSU led by Stalin the principal enemy was to line up on the side of the counter-revolution. There was no third road. Merleau-Ponty, whose sympathy for Trotsky has never been denied, remarked that when he was killed the moment was approaching at which 'political life would have become impossible for him'. (114) It is to be regretted that the assassin's ice-pick prevented History itself from presenting Trotsky with the verdict on his last bankruptcy.

THE QUESTION OF STALIN

Relatively insecure in their dissertations on 'bureaucracy', Trotskyists are very confident in their denunciation of Stalin. It is more than a war-horse for them; it is a 'raison d'être'. So much so that they need to accuse even the Khrushchevites who betrayed the thought of Lenin's successor and stained his memory of 'Stalinism'. Forced to indulge in perilous feats of pseudo-theoretical tightrope-walking in the matter of the 'Bonapartist caste', they can rely largely on bourgeois specialists when it comes to anti-Stalinist invective. To listen to them, Stalin is (as the English say) the 'skeleton in the Maoists' cupboard': a ball and chain which they drag along, trying to hide it in the folds of their theoretician's toga or in the pocket of their worker's jacket. They dare not discuss him. The Trotskyists may rest easy: the Maoists will discuss him. They are the only ones who can tackle this problem from a proletarian point of view. Above all, they are the only ones who can rely on the thought of Mao Tse-tung and the lessons of the cultural revolution, while the Trotskyists remain - in the best of cases - the prisoners of an ideological horizon which they share

with Stalin. Even when they claim to criticise him they do not
leave the terrain of his problematic, whereas Chinese revolutionary
practice has enabled us to go beyond it on more than one point.
    Stalin was the leader of the international communist movement for
some thirty years. During this period it won great victories and
suffered some defeats but on the whole it emerged from it considerably strengthened. Hence Stalin himself was the target of heinous
attacks on the part of the class enemy, including Trotskyists.
After his death, the Khrushchevite revisionists were only able to
rid themselves of the embarrassing 'dogma' of Marxism-Leninism (i.e.
its revolutionary principles) by mounting a libellous campaign
against him in which his name was almost entirely erased from the
history books and his works were banned. We see in this one more
presumption in his favour. To be attacked by the enemy is not a bad
but a good thing. Does this mean that Stalin did not make mistakes
prejudicial to the construction of socialism and the progress of the
world revolution? Some think that adherence to Maoism implies the
defence of everything that Stalin may have said or done and thus
provides weapons to the Trotskyists and Khrushchevites. Even when
they reluctantly admit that he did make some mistakes, they are more
then discreet as to their nature and, as it were, never talk about
them. Such is not the point of view of the Chinese communists, who
seem to us to be better teachers where Maoism is concerned.
    They have stated unambiguously, 'It is necessary to criticise the
errors Stalin actually committed ... from a correct stand and with
correct methods.' 'While defending Stalin, we do not defend his
mistakes.' What they do not accept is solely the 'complete
negation' of Stalin 'en bloc' which ultimately treated him as an
enemy. They rebel against the gross insults which Khrushchev
heaped on Lenin's comrade-in-arms and successor, describing him as a
'murderer', 'criminal', 'bandit', 'adventurer', 'Ivan the Terrible
type of despot', 'the greatest dictator in Russian history',
'imbecile', 'idiot', etc. (115) They showed that by thus slandering
Stalin, Khrushchev was at the same stroke slandering the CPSU, the
people of the Soviet Union, and the international communist
movement. Moreover, how could one speak of a dictatorship of the
proletariat when an 'Ivan the Terrible type of despot' is ruling?
Besides, it is clear that since Khrushchev had participated in the
leadership of the party and the state in Stalin's time and had been
the particularly zealous satellite and instrument of 'the tyrant',
he should have begun by giving a thorough self-criticism explaining
among other things, his base flunkeyism towards his leader, which
seems especially hypocritical in the light of his 'later about-
face'. (116) Not only did he never make a self-criticism but he
impudently took the credit for some of Stalin's achievements (the
atomic bomb and missiles, for example). As we shall see, Stalin was
not afraid to acknowledge sometimes that he had been mistaken. (117)
    The Communist Party of China has consistently held that Stalin
    did commit errors which had their ideological as well as social
    and historical roots ... Some were errors of principle and some
    were errors made in the course of practical work; some could have
    been avoided and some were scarcely avoidable at a time when the
    dictatorship of the proletariat had no precedent to go by.
'In handling relations with fraternal parties and countries, he made

some mistakes. He also gave some bad counsel in the international
communist movement'. (118)   In the chapters on China and Greece, we
shall give some examples of this. Let us merely recall that,
according to the Chinese, the influence of Stalin's mistakes was
felt in China, 'in the late 1920s, the 1930s and the early and
middle 1940s'. (119)   A long time, practically as long as the
Chinese revolution. They add: (120)

> But since some of the wrong ideas put forward by Stalin were
> accepted and applied by certain Chinese comrades, we Chinese
> should bear the responsibility. In its struggle against 'left'
> and right opportunism, therefore, our party criticised only its
> own erring comrades and never put the blame on Stalin.
>
> We merely asked (them) ... that they should correct their
> mistakes. If they failed to do so, we waited until they were
> gradually awakened by their own practical experience ... we held
> that these were contradictions among the people. (121)

In their own texts devoted to the question of Stalin, the Chinese
have pointed out that he was a revolutionary, not a counter-
revolutionary; that he was a friend, not an enemy. It is a
principled answer which decides the essentials of the problem but
which cannot take the place of a thorough historical investigation.
Only the development of the Soviet people's revolutionary struggles
will create the conditions for such an investigation, without which
one cannot obtain the elements necessary for a final answer. (122)
This is why the Chinese declare: (123)

> The question of Stalin is one of world-wide importance ... It is
> likely that no final verdict can be reached on this question in
> the present century ... But there is virtual agreement among the
> majority of the international working class and of revolutionary
> people, who disapprove of the complete negation of Stalin and
> more and more cherish his memory. This is also true of the
> Soviet Union.

This is a fact which some find astonishing and which should make
them think. Even Western observers have been struck by the applause
which spontaneously erupts in the USSR when, having escaped the
censor's scissors, Stalin's silhouette appears for a fraction of a
second in the showing of old newsreels. (124)   In the conditions
prevailing at present in the USSR these must be regarded as real
political demonstrations which reflect a feeling very widely held in
the Soviet Union, as one may be convinced by talking to men and
women among the people. Their point of view differs greatly from
that prevailing among the bureaucrats, technocrats and the other
privileged members of the intelligentsia, who prefer to mix with
foreign journalists. In Georgia, the population demonstrated
violently against the denunciation of Stalin at the 20th Congress.
As the police made common cause with them, non-Georgian troops had
to be called in for the bloody suppression of the disturbances. An
additional sign that the denunciation of Stalin is unpopular is the
fact that Khrushchev did not publish his secret speech to the 20th
Congress, even though he surreptitiously communicated it to his
friends across the Atlantic.

The advance of revolutionary struggles in the entire world is
accompanied by a renewal of interest in Stalin's writings. Claude
Roy reports that a militant in 'the Black Panthers' replied to one

of his questions by reading to him passages from Stalin's 'Foundations of Leninism' and Mao's 'Little Red Book'. (125)

As we shall see even better later on, the Chinese criticise everything to be criticised in Stalin and emphasise that revolutionaries disapprove not of the criticism but of the complete repudiation of this leader of the international communist movement. Their argument hinges on this idea: Stalin was not an enemy but a great Marxist-Leninist revolutionary who certainly made mistakes but who remained on the side of the people with respect to the fundamental options, the defence of the dictatorship of the proletariat, the elimination of the kulaks and Nepmen, the construction of a powerful socialist economy, support for the world revolution, the defence of Marxism-Leninism. This is why 'A comparison of the two shows that his merits outweighed his faults'. (126)

The question of Stalin is not whether one must condemn or rehabilitate Stalin 'en bloc', the question over which writers in the USSR who are more polemicists than historians confront one another. (127) It is a question of summing up the historical experience of the dictatorship of the proletariat in the USSR and appraising the role of its principal leader on this basis, by proceeding analytically, taking care not to reject everything under the pretext that certain mistakes were serious.

Mao Tse-tung has given us an example of this analytical method which refuses to 'draw simple conclusions which are absolutely affirmative or absolutely negative': (128)

> The question concerning the lien of the central leadership during the period from the Fourth Plenary Session to the Tsunyi meeting, for example, should be analysed from two aspects. It should be pointed out on the one hand that the political tactics and the cadres policy which the central leading body adopted during that period were wrong in their main aspects, but on the other hand that on such fundamental issues as opposing Chiang Kai-shek and carrying on the Agrarian Revolution and the struggle of the Red Army there was no dispute between ourselves and the comrades who committed the errors.

It is clear that long before writing 'On the correct handling of contradictions among the people', Mao did not confuse these with 'contradictions between us and the enemy'. On the contrary, in this point as in all others, the Trotskyist and Khrushchevite critique of Stalin remains a prisoner of the ideological framework which engendered the latter's mistakes.

The Trotskyists reject the Chinese appraisal of Stalin. According to them, one must talk about his 'crimes', not his 'mistakes': the Soviet state which he led was therefore an enemy of the proletariat. But Marxists only know class enemies. Now, the bureaucracy is not a class for the Trotskyists. This embroils them in inextricable contradictions. They become extremely embarrassed when they are forced to acknowledge both the successes of the construction of socialism and the active solidarity which linked the USSR to the world's revolutionary movements in Stalin's time, all of which are, as if by chance, 'Stalinist'. To be sure, as we have said, mistakes were made but the Trotskyists refuse to concede that decisions which had disastrous consequences could have occurred for some other reason than evil intent.

   Such prejudice leads to absurd conclusions. The General Staff of
the Red Army (headed by Tukhachevsky) – three marshall, twenty-seven
generals, twenty thousand officers – were executed or deported for
conspiring with the Hitlerites. We know today that Stalin acted
wholly in good faith. German counter-intelligence had organised a
plot to which President Bénès was an unconscious accessory. It was
he who sent Stalin a dossier compiled by his secret service which
came to the conclusion that the Soviet military were traitors. The
Nazis were at the bottom of this 'information' but the Czechoslovaks
believed it to be authentic. Léon Blum disclosed that he had been
informed of the relations between Tukhachevsky and Hitler's agents
as early as the end of 1936. (129) It seems likely that the French
statesman had drawn on the same sources as Stalin and like him had
put faith in them.
   One cannot see what interest Stalin and the bureaucracy could
have in liquidating, on the eve of the war, the commander of the Red
Army, or in leaving the latter totally unprepared at the moment of
Hitler's aggression. (130) Such examples cannot possibly be
explained from the particular interests of the bureaucracy or
Stalin's will to power. It must be admitted that these were
mistakes, and mistakes acknowledged to a certain extent, besides, by
Stalin himself. At a reception celebrating victory on 24 May 1945,
he stated: (131)

   Our government made not a few errors, we experienced at moments
   a desperate situation in 1941-2, when our army was retreating ...
   A different people could have said to the government: 'You have
   failed to justify our expectations...'. The Russian people,
   however, did not take this path ... Thanks to it, to the Russian
   people, for this confidence.

Some do not understand that it is possible to acknowledge the
seriousness of Stalin's mistakes and argue at the same time that
they are secondary in relation to his merits. To see this more
clearly, let us consider Lenin's attitude to Bebel and Rosa
Luxemburg. The latter had violently attacked Lenin over the
question of democratic centralism, siding with the Mensheviks
against him. After the October revolution she had made incorrect
criticisms of the Bolsheviks' policy of granting the oppressed
nations of the ex-Tsarist empire the right to self-determination and
distributing land to the peasants. She had, moreover, made some
quite serious theoretical errors in her work 'The Accumulation of
Capital'. As for Bebel, he had sometimes revealed a fairly
repugnant opportunism. There are echoes of this in the Marx-Engels
correspondence on the Gotha and Erfurt Programmes. However, Lenin
regarded both Luxemburg and Bebel as 'great communists'. When,
after their death, the revisionists tried to exhalt themselves by
belittling them, Lenin upbraided them in these terms: 'Sometimes
eagles may fly lower than hens, but hens can never rise to the
height of eagles'. (132) In fact, when the proletariat in Berlin
rebelled in January 1919 and the revisionists led the counter-
revolutionary repression, Rosa Luxemburg immediately sided with the
workers. Taken prisoner like Karl Liebknecht, she was assassinated
along with him by the 'soldatesca' on the orders of the Social
Democratic Minister Noske. To say that Rosa Luxemburg's merits
outweighed her mistakes is to argue that she was on the right side

of the barricades in the decisive battles. We must not argue any
differently where Stalin is concerned.

In the USSR the denunciation of Stalin was 'the critique of the
personality cult'. This was only a euphemism to conceal and to bury
away the real problems. It was not the excessive exaltation of a
personality which damaged the USSR and the international communist
movement. It has never been a bad thing to call for the study of
Marx and Lenin, to argue that they were giants of theory; on the
contrary, the opposite is true. It is necessary, in the first
place, to condemn the mistakes made in the construction of
socialism, in the resolution of the contradictions in Soviet society
and in the relations with fraternal parties and countries. The
Khrushchevites were content to criticise violations of socialist
legality and the principle of collegial leadership.
     Even revisionists like Togliatti recognised the limits and the
equivocal charcter of Khrushchev's denunciation of Stalin. He
pointed out: (133)
     As long as we confine ourselves, in substance, to denouncing the
     personal faults of Stalin as the cause of everything we remain
     within the realm of the 'personality cult'. First, all that was
     good was attributed to the superhuman qualities of one man: now
     all that is evil is attributed to his equally exceptional and
     even astonishing faults ... The true problems are evaded ... (the
     ones which concern the causes which led the USSR) to the point of
     degeneration.
While avoiding falling into the reverse cult of personality which
Togliatti denounced, we must guard against the opposite mistake
which might be called economistic or sociologistic - which consists
of seeking the ultimate explanation of Stalin's mistakes, as the
Trotskyists do, in the economic underdevelopment of the USSR at its
birth and in the destruction and partial dispersal of its working
class as a result of the civil war. China was even less developed
than Russia and its working class less numerous. Nor are the
particular interests of the bureaucratic caste enough to explain the
phenomenon. Stalin did struggle in his own way against the
bureaucrats, and the representatives of the bourgeoisie in the
privileged Soviet stratum were only able to usurp all power after
his death. The core of Stalin's mistakes is situated neither at the
legal-political level (the Khrushchevite or Togliattist explanation)
or at the level of the economic base (the Trotskyist explanation),
but at the ideological-theoretical level. After the conquest of
political power and the socialisation of the means of production,
this level becomes the strategic domain in which everything is
decided. It goes without saying that the historical and social
conditions in which Stalin had to act played a role determinant
enough to make certain of his mistakes inevitable, while others were
not, in the sense that a leader like Lenin would not have fallen
into them. As for showing how these effects in the superstructure
were determined in the last analysis by the economic base, this can
only be the work of future studies for which the Trotskyist
schematisations are no substitute. (134)
     Nevertheless, it is possible to give some indications on this

problem. Lenin had deliberately concentrated the Bolshevik forces
in the towns to organise the working class. The latter provided the
bulk of the troops who made the seizure of power possible.
Recruitment in the countryside after the victory was only able to
attract the more educated and ambitious well-off peasants. The
rural implantation of communist cells remained, moreover, very
scattered. So much so that at the time of collectivisation it was
necessary to depend on groups of workers parachuted into the
villages. The party being, for historical reasons, more or less cut
off from the majority of the population (poor and middle peasants),
its leaders were unable correctly to apply democratic centralism,
the mass line, among the people and within the party (one is
impossible without the other). The situation in this respect was
made much worse at the time of collectivisation, which was largely
forced. There can be no correct leadership without the mass line.
It will be remembered that according to Lenin the downfall of the
Bolshevik Party was inevitable if the alliance between the
proletariat and the peasantry was broken (cf. Chapter 2 above, n.
26). The subsequent evolution of the CPSU has shown that Lenin's
fears were only too well founded.

The Chinese have clearly established the immediate causes of
Stalin's mistakes. They say: (135)

> In struggles inside as well as outside the party, on certain
> occasions and on certain questions he confused two types of
> contradictions which are different in nature, contradictions
> between ourselves and the enemy and contradictions among the
> people, and also confused the different methods needed in
> handling them. In the work led by Stalin of suppressing the
> counter-revolution, many counter-revolutionaries deserving
> punishment were duly punished, but at the same time there were
> innocent people who were wrongly convicted; and in 1937 and 1938
> there occurred the error of enlarging the scope of the
> suppression of counter-revolutionaries.

Given that Stalin did, in fact, make numerous and serious mistakes,
it would be truly paradoxical if there were not some genuine
revolutionary militants among those who were sent to the camps or to
their deaths. Could these militants be prevented from expressing
their disagreements? Certainly not, for servile submission is not
the mark of a revolutionary. It is incontestable, moreover, that
no one was able to develop a systematic criticism of Stalin's
mistakes without bringing repression down upon himself.

It even happened that people who were far from being enemies and
who in addition were never opposed to Stalin were oppressed all the
same. There is an example of this in the 'Peking Review' of 24
September 1963 in which Anna Louise Stong recounts her troubles in
the USSR in 1948 when she asked for authorisation to go to China, at
the invitation of Chairman Mao Tse-tung: 'Five months I kept asking
for my Soviet exit visa. Then, just as Chinese friends arrived who
might secure my journey, the Russians arrested me as a "spy" and
sent me out through Poland. Five days in jail I wondered what I had
stepped on. I never knew'. (136)

After summing up the historical experience of the dictatorship of
the proletariat on the basis of the thought of Mao Tse-tung, the
Chinese communists have cast light on the other source of the

mistakes of Stalin, whose failure lay (137)

in not recognising, on the level of theory, that classes and
class struggle exist in society throughout the historical period
of the dictatorship of the proletariat and that the question of
who will win in the revolution has yet to be finally settled; in
other words, if all this is not handled properly, there is the
possibility of a come-back by the bourgeoisie.

Indeed, in his report on the Draft Constitution of the USSR
presented to the 8th Congress of Soviets on 25 November 1936, Stalin
declared that 'all the exploiting classes have ... been eliminated'
and the economic and political contradictions between the working
class, peasant class and intellectuals, 'are declining and becoming
obliterated'. (138)   That is why 'The Draft of the New Constitution
of the USSR proceeds from the fact that there are no longer any
antagonistic classes in society; that society consists of two
mutually friendly classes, the workers and peasants'. (139)

In his report to the 18th Congress of the CP(B) on 10 March 1939,
Stalin was just as categorical: (140)

The feature that distinguishes Soviet society today ... is that
it no longer contains antagonistic, hostile classes ... liberated
from the yoke of exploitation, (it) knows no such contradictions,
is free of class conflicts, and presents a picture of friendly
collaboration between workers, peasants and intellectuals.

In 1952, Stalin seemed to have renounced his conviction that Soviet
society exhibited the image of a stable and perfect harmony.   In
'Economic Problems of Socialism in the USSR', he wrote: (141)

Of course, our present relations of production are in a period
when they fully conform to the growth of the productive forces
... But ... there certainly are, and will be, contradictions,
seeing that the development of the relations of production   lags
and will lag, behind the development of the productive forces.

If these problems were ignored, as they were by Yarashenko, 'our
relations of production might become a serious break on the further
development of the productive forces'.

Unfortunately, such considerations, correct but abstract, and
belated besides, were not enough to dislodge individuals like
Khrushchev who had already usurped power in certain sectors.   The
relations of production which Stalin spoke of here do not
necessarily have a class character, since in the primitive commune
as well as in the future communist society, 'in order to produce,
men enter into definite connections and relations with one another'.
(142)   Thus it is clear from the context that the contradictions to
which Stalin was alluding do not have a class character.

The fact that Stalin was unaware of the contradictions which can
arise among the people and denied the persistence of the class
struggle under socialism did not prevent these two types of
contradiction from existing.   Thus he was confronted by a reality
which he could not think scientifically.   Nevertheless, he had to
tackle the difficulty in one way or another.   The solution which he
came up with necessarily derived from the presuppositions he had
adopted.   As the contradictions were not contradictions between the
people and its class enemies any more than they were non-
antagonistic contradictions among the people, they could not be
inside Soviet society and had to result from the capitalist
encirclement.

In a speech at the Plenum of the Central Committee of the CPSU on 3 March 1937, Stalin stated what seemed to him to be obvious, namely that 'the bourgeois states would send to the rear of the Soviet Union twice and three times as many wreckers, spies, diversionists and murderers than to the rear of any bourgeois state'. (143)

He explained (144) that 'the Zinovievites and Trotskyites ... have turned into a spying and diversive-terrorist agency of the German secret-police': (145)

> Restoration of capitalism, the liquidation of the collective and State farms ... the territorial dismemberment of the Soviet Union, handing the Ukraine to the Germans and the Maritime Province to the Japanese ... wrecking, diversion, individual terror against the leader of the Soviet power, espionage in favour of Japano-German fascist forces - such was the political platform of contemporary Trotskyism ... It is clear the Trotskyists could not but conceal such a platform from the people, from the working class. And they concealed it not only from the Trotskyist rank and file as well, and not only from the Trotskyist rank and file, but even from the upper Trotskyist leadership.

Since practically nobody was 'in the know' it remains to be explained on whom Trotsky could have counted to carry out such a programme. But let us press on, for one paradox more or less does not matter. Further on, Stalin characterised Trotskyists in general as 'an unprincipled band of wreckers devoid of ideas, diversionists, spies, murderers hired by foreign intelligence service organs'. (146)

If these criminals were neither Trotskyist leaders nor members nor even fellow-travellers, in what sense can it be said that they were Trotskyists? The text which we quote leaves us in this quandary.

Stalin acknowledged that the 'Trotskyist saboteurs' were few in number in relation to the Bolsheviks and the masses who supported them. But, he said, 'to build the Dneprostroi requires tens of thousands of workers, but to blow it up requires perhaps a few score people, no more'. Conclusion: 'We must see to it that there shall be none of these Trotskyist wreckers in our ranks'. (147)

As he had emphasised at the beginning of his speech, moreover, that 'the wrecking and diversionist-espionage activity of agents of foreign states, among whom a pretty active role was played by the Trotskyists, has affected in one degree or another nearly all our organisations - economic, administrative and party', (148) his listeners must have taken his speech as an injunction to discover the saboteur or saboteurs, murderers, etc., concealed in their organisation. (149) There was no question, of course, of letting a single one escape with the benefit of the doubt, for it would be too dangerous. Neither was there any question of judging people by their actions. This would be the height of naïvité: 'The real wrecker will show success in his work from time to time', (150) and 'the wreckers usually time their major wrecking work not for the period of peacetime but for the period on the eve of war or of wartime itself'. (151)

In other words, if you showed any success in your work this proved that you were a particularly cunning wrecker and all the more dangerous; best to stop you immediately before you had the time to commit your 'main act of wrecking'.

As the enemy was a common criminal, it was the police who took charge of him and used highly persuasive methods to make him reveal the names of those who had recruited him and those whom he had himself recruited. Through this mathematically simple process, the number of arrests increased exponentially. It was no secret from anyone what 'enlarging the scope of the suppression' meant. Even in Stalin's time, the official Soviet sources contained fairly clear information on the forced labour camps. The English version of 'The forced labour code' was available in London from 1936. In 1949, the official Soviet publications noted 120,000 detainees freed after the completion of the canal from Moscow to the Volga. (152) The coal-mines at Vorkhuta, Karaganda and Tugurska mainly employed this type of labour force. The administrative arbitrariness which presided over its 'recruitment' emerges clearly from the Russian legislative texts themselves. These texts authorised the deportation of Soviet citizens under investigation, without judgment or time limit. (153)

In 1939, Stalin proclaimed in his report to the 18th Congress: (154)

It cannot be said that the purge was not accompanied by grave mistakes. There were undoubtedly more mistakes than might have been expected. Undoubtedly, we shall have no further need of resorting to the method of mass purges.

It is undoubtedly to Stalin's credit that he made a self-criticism in this way, but as well as revealing a tendency to understatement here, he was referring to the purge in the party of 1933-6 and not to the widespread arrests of 1936-8. On this last point, Stalin acknowledged certain mistakes implicitly and by what he did. Yezhov, who had led the purge of 1936-8, was arrested and Beria, his successor, freed many people who had been unjustly imprisoned.

Thus, under Stalin, the different contradictions analysed rigorously by Mao Tse-tung were reduced to a single one: the one between the Soviet people and the spies, wreckers and murderers sent by the capitalist countries. There was also a single method to resolve it: police repression. The rank and file of the party and the broad masses intervened in this struggle only to approve the measures taken. (155)

Nevertheless, in one of his speeches, Stalin did come close to a clear appreciation of the contradictions which faced him: (156)

It cannot be said that the policy of the party may not have come up against contradictions. Not only the backward people who always avoid what is new but also many prominent members of our party have systematically pulled the party backwards and striven in every possible way to put it on the 'normal' capitalist road of development. All these machinations of the Trotskyists and right elements directed against the party, and all their 'activity' to wreck the measures of our government have had only one aim: to nullify the policy of the party and to put a stop to the work of collectivisation and industrialisation.

Stalin acknowledged here that he had to struggle against political opponents and not only against common criminals, but he did not draw any theoretical or practical conclusions from this.

It is true, nonetheless, that 'enlarging the scope of the

suppression' caused a great waste of human resources which makes the French title of one of Stalin's speeches sound rather strange: 'L'Homme, le capital le plus précieux' (Man, the most precious capital). In the Soviet camps, nothing was done to re-educate the internees ideologically. Their function was purely repressive. The common law was used to bully political prisoners, and the most unyielding of them were often executed. In consideration of which, Stalin could proclaim to the 18th Congress, 'the remnants of the exploiting classes have been completely eliminated'. (157)

As a result the state of the dictatorship of the proletariat was only conserved to ensure the defence of the country against the imperialists: (158)

> We have abolished the exploiting classes; there are no longer any hostile classes in the country; there is nobody to suppress ... the role and significance of ... our military, punitive and intelligence organs ... are no longer essential within the country but for the defence of the socialist land from foreign attack.

Consequently we can say that Stalin prepared the way for Khrushchev's theory of the State of the whole people.

This is why the latter was forced to accuse Stalin of exactly the opposite mistake. In his secret report to the 20th Congress, Khrushchev stated: 'Stalin's report at the February-March Central Committee Plenum in 1937 ... contained an attempt at theoretical justification of the mass terror policy under the pretext that as we march forward to socialism, class war must allegedly sharpen'. (159)

In his anti-Chinese book, 'Le Problem chinois', Garaudy invokes once again this legend invented by Khrushchev as a historical truth. He has the effrontery to claim that one of Lin Piao's slogans 'adopts (sic) as its ideological basis the so-called "Stalin Law" according to which the class struggle worsens after the seizure of power and the advent of socialism in proportion to the gains made'. Garaudy quotes Stalin as saying, 'The growth of the power of the Soviet State will intensify the resistance of the last remnants of the dying classes' (in 'Results of the First Five-Year Plan, January 1933), and he denounces 'this false principle which has done so much damage in the party and the state of the Soviet Union'. (160)

Here he makes two mistakes (if we are generous and do not call them 'lies'):

1 The Chinese have never invoked the 'Stalin Law' of which Garaudy speaks as an ideological basis.
2 Stalin did not only say or seem to say that the class struggle worsens after the 'advent of socialism in proportion to the gains made'. He also said the opposite.

The sentence quoted by Garaudy concerns the situation immediately after the expropriation of the kulaks and refers to the last (and all the more violent) convulsions of this dying class. A few years later, the latter had already died, according to Stalin, along with the other exploiting classes.

The report to which Khrushchev alludes is entitled (in French) 'Pour une formation bolchevik', and we have just quoted from it profusely to show that Stalin thought the opposite of what the 'theoretician' of the 20th Congress makes him say. It is true that in it we find the following passage: (161)

The greater our progress, the greater our successes, the more embittered the remnants of the smashed exploiting classes will become, the more quickly they will resort to sharper forms of struggle, the more they will do damage to the Soviet state, the more they will clutch at the most desperate means of struggle as the last resort of the doomed. We must bear in mind that the remnants of the routed classes in the USSR are not alone. They have direct support from our enemies beyond the borders of the USSR.

Must we conclude that Stalin was contradicting himself? I do not think so. This passage is perfectly consistent with all the others I have quoted provided that it is put back carefully into the context of the report which gives it its true meaning.

According to Stalin, the former ruling classes had been liquidated 'as classes', since the economic basis of the exploitation of man by man had been abolished. The individuals who were its agents continued to exist, nevertheless, as 'remnants'. They were supported from without (capitalist encirclement). At the same time, they did not have an autonomous role but constituted one of the 'reserves' of Trotskyist wreckers, murderers and spies (the other reserve being recruited abroad). At the beginning of 1937, Stalin launched an appeal for the elimination of these criminal elements and one year later (as we have just seen) he felt in a position to announce their 'final liquidation'.

Thus one of the principal sources of what we may agree to call Stalin's mistakes was not, as Khrushchev and Garaudy say, a belief in the worsening of the class struggle in proportion to the strengthening of the socialist state, but exactly the opposite: a misrecognition of the class struggle and the concrete forms which it assumes under socialism. This is why Stalin did not see enemies who had to be defeated ideologically and politically by the revolutionary mobilisation of the masses but only spies, murderers and wreckers to be dealt with by the police and the courts. In these conditions he could not prevent true communists being branded as fake saboteurs while false Bolsheviks who were true careerists of the Khrushchev type had access to key posts in the state. (162)

It is now clear why Khrushchev, his acolytes and his successors have been forced to attribute to Stalin erroneous positions which were exactly the opposite to those which he actually held. They could not acknowledge the class struggle under socialism, the possibility that capitalism might be restored if the masses are not mobilised to make the revolution and defend the dictatorship of the proletariat or restore it in all the sectors where power has been usurped by leaders taking the capitalist road. Could they hold out for a single day if a broad democracy was established, if the 240 million people were transformed into 240 million critics? There is nothing the revisionist magnates dread so much as the cultural revolution. The aim of condemning Stalin's methods is to ensure a minimum of security and stability for the leading stratum. At the same time, the latter have to propagate an ideology of the withering away of the class struggle in order to camouflage the dismantling of the dictatorship of the proletariat and the restoration of capitalism that they have achieved. In order to lay a solid basis for its dictatorship, the new bourgeoisie, like the old, needs to claim that its state represents the general interest. In the name of the latter those who revolt can be struck down. The masses are completely disarmed ideologically; Marxism-Leninism loses all practical revolutionary significance and in this way the perpetuity of the system is ensured. Such is the function of that theoretical chimera: 'the state of the whole people'.

The French revisionists should explain to us how it is that the Soviet state of the whole people was able to invade Czechoslovakia. Did not Marx say that a people which oppresses another cannot be free?

When one considers Stalin's mistakes as a whole, one begins to wonder: how were such things possible, even under the dictatorship of the proletariat? The reply to this question conditions the one I shall give to the problem of the degeneration of this power into Khrushchevite despotism, into the dictatorship of a new bourgeoisie.

The Chinese communists have also been very clear on this point. Khrushchevite revisionism, which undertook the restoration of capitalism in the USSR, did not emerge fully armed from the 20th Congress. The terrain had been prepared for it under Stalin:

> After the establishment of socialist relations of production, the Soviet Union failed to carry out a proletarian cultural revolution in earnest. Bourgeois ideology ran rife, corrupting the minds of the people and almost imperceptibly undermining the socialist relations of production. After the death of Stalin, there was a more blatant counter-revolutionary moulding of public opinion by the Khrushchev revisionist group.

The 20th Congress and the elimination of the so-called 'anti-party group' in June 1957 were decisive stages in this process. 'And (Khrushchev's) group soon afterwards staged its "palace" coup to subvert the dictatorship of the proletariat and usurped party, military and government power.' (163)

The cultural revolution which unfolds in the superstructural domain was unthinkable in Stalin's time, among other things because for him it was without an object. In 'Concerning Marxism and Linguistics', he laid it down as a principle of historical materialism that the superstructure disappears with the economic base that engendered it. (164) But he believed that 'in the main we have already achieved the first phase of communism, socialism' in the USSR even before 1936, as he declared in his report on the Draft Constitution. (165)

Since we are granting that Stalin made a number of serious mistakes which helped to prepare the way for Khrushchevite revisionism, must we acknowledge courage and lucidity in those who condemned him publicly in his lifetime? I do not think so at all, for the following reason.

The proletariat needed a revolutionary scientific analysis, not a moralistic denunciation quite within the powers of the bourgeoisie. But Trotsky shared the theoretical premises from which Stalin's mistakes sprang. Both reduced the construction of socialism to the development of the material productive forces; both denied the possibility of a bourgeoisie without private ownership of the means of production; neither recognised the distinction between

antagonistic and non-antagonistic contradictions among the people
and between the people and its enemies. Taking up the same terrain,
posing the same false problems, they differed only in their
solutions. For one, the enemy was the 'Bonapartist bureaucracy';
for the other, 'the agents dispatched by encircling capitalism'.

In 'The Revolution Betrayed', Trotsky invoked a number of
accurate facts relating to the trials, the camps, etc., but the
'facts' do not speak for themselves: otherwise, what need would
there be for a science? Anti-communists pronounced the same
'truths' as Trotsky and for them they were a justification for anti-
communism. Ernest Mandel has argued against us in a debate that the
difference lay in the fact that the bourgeois publicists never
criticised inequality. How naïve! To take only one example, Arthur
Koestler waxes indignant in 'The Yogi and the Commissar' about the
enormous disparities in income in the USSR. The ideological
spokesmen of reaction have always considered it quite fair to attack
revolutionaries for not carrying out their principles in practice.
Isaac Deutscher himself conceded that 'The Revolution Betrayed' has
been a mine of arguments for the '"Sovietologists" and propagandists
of the cold war'. (166) No more than the latter can the Trotskyists
presume on their precocious lucidity vis-à-vis Stalin because they
lacked the first (and indissociable) conditions of a well-founded
critique: revolutionary practice and scientific theory. The same
goes for the other categories of opponents.

Horrified by the violent police repression of all critical
opinion even when it arose from contradictions among the people,
numerous unstable intellectuals and disillusioned cadres denounced
'Stalinism', but in doing so they lapsed into a pre-Marxist
position, adopting an ethical and humanist point of view. (167)
They called for a freedom above classes; hence, in fact, the freedom
for the bourgeoisie to oppress the workers ideologically and
politically. Like Trotsky, Merleau-Ponty jeered at the
'intellectuals in retreat' and the 'league of abandoned hopes' but
he himself demanded of them that they try to 'map out in spite of
everything a path leading to a humanism for all men'. (168) In
fact, only the proletariat can, by liberating itself, liberate all
humanity. It is not by abandoning the outlook of the revolution and
the dictatorship of the proletariat that one will be able to 'map
out a path leading to a humanism for all men'. The interest of 'all
men' remains a hypocritical camouflage for bourgeois interests as
long as classes continue and society has not effected its transition
to the higher stage of communism.

If these intellectuals were traitors, it is by no means for
having criticised some policy or leader but for turning up on the
other side of the barricade, against the people. Not all of them
have become aware of this change in their class position and most
did not wish it. However, it was inevitable not only because there
is no third road but also for another reason that is rarely
suspected: even the best among them, those who had participated in
the revolutionary struggle in responsible positions, were only party
officials; their links with the masses were mediated by the party
apparatus. Once removed from this apparatus, they were cut off from
the masses because in fact they had never been linked to them. It
was possible not to follow Stalin slavishly in his mistakes without

degenerating into a class enemy provided that one remained linked to the masses and learned with them to serve the people and further their fundamental interest, the liberating revolution. Mao Tse-tung and his comrades, who did not always agree with the leadership of their party or with Stalin, did just this. While applying themselves to correcting both the latter's mistakes in practice, they were careful not to make trenchant judgments of them or to make any public condemnation, considering that this could only provoke splits and help the enemy without being of any use to the people.

Nevertheless, it is true that under Stalin the position of intellectuals, even those who strived to assimilate historical materialism, was not exactly an easy one. On the one hand, they more or less confusedly recognised (through their effects) the mistakes of Stalin which we have just discussed. On the other hand, they were more especially sensitive to certain deviations on the level of proletarian policy with respect to science and culture which Stalin, great Marxist-Leninist though he was, had not been able to avoid. (169) I am thinking particularly of the inept criticisms made of relativity theory, cybernetics and classical genetics after 1945. In these cases there was confusion between the scientific theories, not questionable as such, and the philosophical interpretations which were supposedly deduced from them by reactionary scientists or philosophers eager to pass off their idealist rubbish under a guaranteed scientific wrapping. Stalin and Zhdanov fell into the trap that Lenin had revealed in 'Materialism and Empirio-Criticism'. Lysenko, who had the benefit of their support although his ideas were, to say the least, debatable, was able to reduce his critics to silence at the extraordinary session of the Academy of Agricultural Sciences in August 1948 by proclaiming that the Central Committee had 'examined and approved' his report (!). After Stalin's death, Khrushchev came to his aid (particularly in April 1957) and revived the marks of official support which he desperately needed after the costly failure of the attempts to sow winter corn in Siberia in accordance with his ideas.
   Michurin and his disciple Lysenko claimed to be developing Darwin's theory, but in fact their doctrine was an avatar of Lamarckianism. They gave undue prominence to teleological explanations and denied the struggle for existence within the same (particularly vegetable) species. They argued, above all, for the heredity of characteristics acquired through environmental influence, rejecting the distinction between germen and soma. This teaching was not dialectical-materialist and advances in the science were made by a different route. Our steadily growing knowledge of chromosomes and genes, the great discoveries of molecular biology, more especially that of DNA, enable us today to glimpse the concrete possibility of modifying the hereditary patrimony of the species according to our needs. Nature is only governed by obeying it.
   Yet in 1962, Garaudy praised Lysenko for having put forward 'the fruitful idea of transporting transformism onto the experimental level'. (170) In fact, the same relation existed between Lysenko's 'works' and future discoveries in experimental transformism as between the transmutation of elements which the alchemists claimed

to perform and those which take place in an atomic pile or particle accelerator.

As a result of the controversy about Michurinism, communist scientists like Haldane (in England) and Prenant (in France) were estranged from the party and later degenerated more or less.

In China, on the other hand, the Central Committee has never been seen to use its authority to settle a debate between scientists about questions within their sphere of competence and Mao Tse-tung has criticised those of his comrades who 'interfere in certain matters in scientific and cultural work where interference is unwarranted'. (171)

Intervening in the 1947 debate, Zhdanov had correctly emphasised the necessity for a class point of view and the party spirit in philosophy. It may be that, unfortunately, in doing so, he did not sufficiently warn against an immediately political (and therefore simplistic and non-dialectical) reading of contributions to the sciences and arts without consideration of the appropriate scientific or aesthetic criteria. It was at this time that the erroneous idea of distinguishing between a 'bourgeois science' and a 'proletarian science' gained ground - as if it was not obvious that the natural sciences taken in themselves can indiscriminately serve either of the classes, both of which have the same interest in knowing the laws of nature in order to dominate it. In 1950, Stalin put an end to these mistaken ideas by stating vis-à-vis the object of linguistics a truth which can be generalised ('a fortiori') to the objects of the other sciences: (172)

As a means of intercourse between the people of a society, language serves all classes of that society equally, and in this respect plays what may be called an indifference to classes.

But ... the classes are far from being indifferent to language. He also recalled that 'no science can develop and flourish without a battle of opinions, without freedom of criticism', because 'this rule (has been) ignored and flouted in the most unceremonious fashion'. (173)

The Trotskyists and revisionists have enleagued to accuse the Chinese communists of being 'Stalinists', not in the sense in which this is actually true but in order to attribute to them the aim of 'imposing on other parties the order of things, ideology, morals, forms and methods of leadership which were dominant during the period of the personality cult'. (174) But the most radical refutation of these methods is to be found in the practice of the Chinese Communist Party and in Mao's writings, more especially in that entitled 'On the correct handling of contradictions among the people'. There Mao states that the party 'must necessarily let the people take part in political activities', that that is how they can educate themselves, that differences must be resolved 'through criticism or struggle' and that it is permissible to criticise even Marxism. (175) It is clear that on all these points Mao takes an opposite view to the ideas and especially to the practice in force under Stalin. Is not the principle: 'Cure the sickness to save the patient' the opposite to that of curing the sickness by killing the patient which was tacitly applied in Stalin's time as a result of confusion between methods which may be necessary in the struggle against enemies with those which are appropriate for disagreements with comrades or class brothers? When Mao writes, 'Communists must always go into the whys and wherefores of anything, use their own heads and carefully think over whether or not it corresponds to reality and is really well-founded; on no account should they follow blindly and encourage slavishness', (176) he is stating a principle which seems quite new to those who have long been activists in parties trained by Stalin. Just think: to exercise one's critical faculties with regard to the decisions of the party's leading bodies!

In short, Stalin had not ensured the collective participation of the people in political activity. The ease with which the Khrushchevites usurped power has no other explanation.

Mao Tse-tung has always fought attempts to introduce into China Soviet ideas about the army or the party in its internal functioning and its relations with the masses.

The Soviet Red Army knew discipline but not democracy. Exorbitant material privileges were introduced into it to the advantage of the officers and especially the generals. Glittering decorations, gold-laced uniforms, rolling drums and other masquerades contributed to the glorification of the higher ranks, setting them above the simple soldiers. The memory of the strategists of Tsarist feudalism, the Suvarovs and the Kutuzovs were exalted. The factors considered primordial were military, material and technical competence, not proletarian political consciousness. The military hardly ever participated in productive labour; in these conditions, the Red Army was too much like a bourgeois army to correspond to its concept.

For ten years, under Soviet influence, the Chinese People's Liberation Army conformed to this model, but since 1960 it has reverted to the Yenan tradition in order to be a true People's Army. For this it was necessary to turn against the ideas which had prevailed beforehand.

Stalin tended to believe that, in the elaboration of the political line, one had to start from the leaders so as to return to the leaders. Mao's emphasis is quite different: one must start from the masses so as to return to the masses. This means in particular that the party is under the control of the masses and not the opposite.

To strengthen vigilance in the face of the secret machinations of the enemy, Stalin had instituted 'ideological relations' and a whole system of surveillance which, in practice, far from unmasking the careerists, afforded them new possibilities for getting rid of 'intruders' by means of gossip and informing. It was presumably by means of this sort that individuals like Khrushchev succeeded in climbing into the higher echelons of the party. When Liu Shao-chi and his deputy An Tse-wen introduced these Moscow methods into China in the 1940s, Mao opposed them.

With the great proletarian cultural revolution, the novelty of Mao's teaching stood out with the maximum of force and clarity and transformed itself into a hurricane which swept away the old ideas, the old customs, the old fetishes. This unprecedented revolution radiates its liberating ideology throughout the world. It has profoundly changed our image of socialism, which used to bear the imprint of the Russian experience with all its negative aspects uncriticised, and in a sense hitherto uncriticisable.

Chapter 5

REVISIONIST DEGENERATION OR CULTURAL REVOLUTION

THE TROTSKYIST POSITION

Trotsky's disciples wish to remain faithful to him on the question of the nature of the USSR and the other revisionist countries as if nothing had changed since more than thirty years ago. Now, Trotsky's position on this question was always extremely perplexed, confused and contradictory. In 1929 he still thought that the social basis of Thermidor, defined as a 'counter-revolution' and as a 'transfer of power into the hands of another class', was the kulak. 'The problem of Thermidor and of Bonapartism is in essence the problem of the kulak.' According to Trotsky, 'The enriched muzhik or the muzhik who only seeks to get rich ... is the natural agent of Bonapartist tendencies' (cf. Chapter 4, above). When Stalin, whom Trotsky thought was going to lay the basis for the restoration of capitalism ('a Kerensky in reverse'), had expropriated the kulaks against all the predictions of our 'prophet', Trotsky abandoned the Marxist method of analysing a policy by its class content. In fact, in the sense Trotsky understood the term, classes no longer existed in the USSR. To his great perplexity, Bonapartist tendencies continued to assert themselves despite the disappearance of their 'natural agent', the kulak.

In 'The Third International After Lenin', written in 1929, Trotsky still occasionally argued like a Marxist. In it he declared that 'the state apparatus terrorised the proletarian core of the party' and wondered (op. cit. p. 304):

Can this really be the terror of the dictatorship of the proletariat? No, because it is directed against the party, against the interests of the proletariat. Does this mean to say then that this is the pressure and terror of other classes? Obviously it is, for there is no supra-class pressure.

Apparently, for Trotsky after 1929, the rural bourgeoisie (the kulaks), which was terrorising the proletariat by means of the party apparatus, lost power (how, we do not know) and the power was exercised by the bureaucracy as the 'historic arm of the working class' (!) Returning to this problem at the end of his life in 'The Soviet Union and The Fourth International', Trotsky acknowledged that 'the bureaucracy is indissolubly bound up with the role of the ruling economic class'. (1)   It should be added that the bureaucracy always serves the interests of this class. But in that case, what do our present-day Trotskyists have to say about it? Are the Russian workers today 'the ruling economic class'? The question is how, in a country where the means of production are under state control, can the proletariat be 'the ruling economic class' if it is not 'the ruling political class'?

In an interview given just before his death, Trotsky asserted: 'We accuse the leading clique of having transformed itself into a new aristocracy oppressing and robbing the masses ... The immense bureaucracy devours a lion's share of the modest national income.' (2)

The Chinese speak of a 'new bourgeoisie'; why is the expression 'new aristocracy' (feudal?), supposed to be more adequate? How is an industrialised country in which a new bourgeoisie exploits (or 'robs') the masses to be described if not as capitalist? The reply of Trotsky and the Trotskyists is that the bureaucracy does not, properly speaking, exploit the workers but robs them as a parasitic stratum, like the Church, for example. But the latter has always been an integral part of the propertied classes. We know that the Vatican today is a big capitalist power in the same way as in former times it owned more land than the king and the nobles. Even when it owns neither land nor capital the Church exploits the workers by participating in the redistribution of surplus value. We thus come back to the question posed above: who collectively owns the means of production in the USSR? Is it the workers, or else what we call the new bourgeoisie and what the Trotskyists call the bureaucracy? A comparison not being proof, Trotsky cannot be regarded as having solved the problem by comparing the bureaucracy to the Church, a tumour or the 'lumpenproletariat'!

In the same interview, Trotsky argued that 'the liquidation of the private ownership of the means of production is the central historical task of our epoch and will guarantee the birth of a new, more harmonious society'. (3) The least one can say is that he was deceiving himself and that this 'guarantee' was not so certain. Otherwise, how can one explain the Polish workers being forced to rise up against the intensification of their exploitation and the necessity for them to be mown down from tanks and helicopters to make them submit?

Trotsky's wife, Natalia Sedova, finally adopted a clearer and more coherent position than her late husband's dogmatic supporters: she regarded the Soviet Union as 'state capitalism'. (4)

The Trotskyists deny the capitalist character of the countries in eastern Europe and its links with the usurpation of power by a state bourgeoisie which exploits and oppresses the workers. Let us examine their argument as it is developed in the Theses adopted by the 9th Congress of the Fourth International. Taking the example of Yugoslavia, 'since there has clearly never been a social counter-revolution ... since the party in power ... is still the same', the partisans of the thesis according to which capitalism has been restored 'apply ... reformist conceptions in reverse'. (5)

This is the repetition of an old argument of Trotsky's, denying (what he later accepted) that a Thermidor had taken place in the USSR: (6)

> Thermidor does not signify a period of reaction in general ... it indicates a transfer of power into the hands of another class ... Thermidor was a civil war in which the sans-culottes were defeated – can anyone believe ... that power can pass from the hands of the Russian proletariat into those of the bourgeoisie by peaceful means ...? Such a conception of Thermidor is only reformism turned inside out.

A few years later, Trotsky was to prove exactly the opposite, namely, that Thermidor does mean a period of reaction in general ... and so on.

However that may be, it is really strange to argue that the party in power remained the same after repeated, massive and ferocious purges, particularly at the time of the break with the Cominform. Moreover, history offers the example of many parties whose class nature has changed without purges. As for the necessity of a (violent) social counter-revolution, it would undoubtedly have to occur for the old propertied classes to return to power, but not for the formation of new ones.

The Theses of the 9th Congress continue in these terms: 'For Marxists there can be no capitalism without a bourgeois class in power in the economic sense of the term. There can be no bourgeois class without private appropriation of the means of production and the social surplus product.'

First of all, it is wrong to argue that 'there can be no capitalism without a bourgeois class in power'. Capitalism existed under NEP even though the bourgeoisie was not in power. On the other hand, when the Trotskyists say 'in the economic sense of the term' this must be understood as 'in the legal sense' for it is only in this sense that the new Yugoslav bourgeoisie has not appropriated the means of production in a private capacity.

But above all, the Trotskyists are not unaware that besides the state bourgeoisie, there exist in Yugoslavia industrialists who possess enterprises employing up to 500 workers, that capitalism is developing in the countryside, that there is brisk commercial and land speculation (particularly in the tourist areas), that the state monopoly of external trade has been abandoned for the maximum profits of the tycoons; in short, that Yugoslavia is, as one American journalist put it, 'the paradise of free enterprise'.

To embark on an analysis of Yugoslavia's foreign policy would take us too far out of our way. One thing is certain: the US Government knew what it was doing when it gave Yugoslavia aid amounting to several thousand millions of dollars.

An article in 'Le Monde' talks about 'the strange alliance of foreign capital and co-management in Yugoslav enterprises'. (7) Strange indeed, if one takes 'co-management' at face-value. Could capitalist management and worker management make good bedfellows? We are not sufficiently reformist to believe it. In fact, 'co-management' hardly means more than 'participation'. It leaves the workers defenceless before those who hold effective power at the levels of the enterprise and the state, hence the wave of strikes (ultimate weapon) that broke out in 1966 and 1967, as the Theses which we are criticising recognise.

If the workers were masters of the enterprises they would not strike against themselves. If they were masters of the state they would not emigrate and sell themselves as wage slaves in hundreds of thousands on the French and German markets. Only a comprador bourgeoisie could put up its country's wealth for auction by throwing wide the door to imperialist investments which are guaranteed the transfer of their profits and the repatriation of their capital.

We call attention to this magnificent sentence in Paul Yankovitch's article: 'Official circles consider that there is not even any reason to guarantee foreign investors against so-called political risks, since Yugoslav enterprises are already social enterprises and consequently cannot be nationalised.' In other words, now that we have made the revolution, our country offers absolute security to capitalist exploitation. The Yugoslav leaders assert and deny the existence of socialism in their country in the same breath. This same argument which, addressed to foreign investors, constitutes a guileless confession, also serves to deceive the workers. At the least demand our 'officials' apostrophise the workers by asking them what more they want: 'the state belongs to you, the enterprises belong to you'! Trotskyists can be counted on to applaud this mystification. However they should know broadly what they are committing themselves to in the Yugoslav road to socialism, this original, non-Stalinist 'model', etc. It can be characterised as an economy entirely given over to the laws of the market; that is, to capitalist anarchy with its cyclical crises and their accompanying train of bankruptcies and redundancies. There are 300,000 unemployed out of 4 million non-agricultural wage-earners. Speculators are given free reign. The state exports labour and imports capital in order that the people may be doubly exploited by imperialist capital, inside as well as outside the country. Enterprises issue bonds to augment their capital. Banks convert deposits of private individuals into loans to enterprises and pay 7 per cent interest. However, Trotskyists refuse to draw the conclusions obvious facts impose. They repeat, 'the working class has not yet been defeated'. If it has not been defeated then it is in power; how can this be reconciled with what we know about Yugoslav society and Belgrade's policy?

After accusing the Maoists of reformism, the Trotskyists modify their argument a little and accuse them of 'defeatism'. They cry, 'to say that capitalism has already been restored, without massive resistance from the workers, would be to proclaim defeat before the battle; it would demonstrate a defeatism that the recent events have shown to be totally unjustified.' (8)

No doubt it is sad to acknowledge that defeat has come without a battle but, as Renan said, 'The truth may be depressing'. Meanwhile, it is the Trotskyists who propagate a spirit of surrender. They lead the Yugoslav workers away from the struggle for power by assuring them that they have never lost it.

THE SOCIAL BASIS OF THE RESTORATION OF CAPITALISM

The struggle between the capitalist road and the socialist road goes on throughout the period of the transition from capitalism to socialism. At every moment and on every problem the leadership of the party and the state, the subordinate echelons and finally individuals themselves are confronted with the choice between the two roads. The victory of socialism is not assured once and for all; it is the product of an unceasing struggle, a continuous creation. Every relaxation in the vigilance of proletarian revolutionaries leaves the field open to revisionist tendencies and leads to a regression.

The principal contradiction of this whole period is that between the revolutionary masses and leaders who take the capitalist road. It is a class contradiction.

Some cannot conceive of the existence of classes without individual private ownership of the means of production: this is not a Marxist point of view. Marx never identified the relations of production and property relations. The former continue to reproduce themselves after the means of production have been brought under state control. That is why 'Lenin had to remind Bukharin that state control of the means of production was not socialisation'. (9) Division into classes retains its basis in the relations of production for a long period after the seizure of power by the proletariat, for, as was pointed out by 'the founders of scientific socialism, (10)

> the disappearance of capitalism ... does not coincide with the disappearance of private ownership of the means of production but with the disappearance of the wage-earning class.

Meanwhile 'every assertion about classes must also be an assertion about the class struggle'. (11) In other words, the principal criterion for membership of a class is neither class being nor class origin but class position. After the expropriation of the old exploiters, there are surviving 'social elements characterised by their class position' (12) who work for the restoration of capitalism, and new ones are created. These social forces are:

(a)   The former exploiters of whom Lenin said, 'they shall retain, long after the revolution, a whole series of real advantages ... money ... habits of organisation and management, the knowledge of all the "secrets" of administration.'

(b)   The new bourgeois elements engendered by the petty bourgeois environment. Lenin spoke of the 'sea of small production' which threatened to devour the socialist economy before the completion of collectivisation. Even after this, the peasantry long remained attached to individual forms of production. Moreover, the persistence of market relations combined with an inadequate organisation of distribution cause the appearance of new bourgeois elements in the interstices of the socialist system given over to a variety of negotiation and speculation.

(c)   The degenerate leading cadres taking the capitalist road. Most of the cadres in the Communist Party occupy responsible posts in the state apparatus. These officials can become cut off from the masses, feel themselves superior and become authoritarian. They can degenerate by becoming preoccupied with their own advancement, their personal prestige and the material advantages afforded them by their 'role in the social organisation of labour'. The demands and rationality peculiar to their department confronted with particular types of problems and on occasion working for non-proletarian social categories, may make them lose the viewpoint of the whole - the viewpoint which subordinates everything to the march towards socialism, to the revolution.

These authorities repress the creative initiative of the masses in production under the pretext of efficiency and productivity, invoking the necessities of the technical division of labour. They strive to perpetuate the division between brains which think without lifting a finger and brawn which drudges without thinking.

The social forces which we have outlined have allies in the people's minds: traditions, customs, habits, ideas bequeathed by capitalist society. The concentrated expression, the essence of these ideological survivals, is individualism, selfishness, the search for personal gain.

In saying this we are not calling for the 'moral' supplement for which Marx did not hide his contempt. The slogan of the cultural revolution, 'fight self, criticise revisionism', is a slogan of ideological struggle the political significance of which is unquestionable. Selfishness tends to reproduce institutional structures which perpetuate the privileges and the domination of a minority. Before the cultural revolution, many Chinese students imagined that because they were 'literati' they would be appointed to leading posts as a matter of course. They considered their career as the due reward for their university labours and despised those who had not acquired the same bookish knowledge. Thus selfishness and personal ambition breathe new life into ideas inherited from the past which become revisionism when they are decked out as 'Marxist'. The new bourgeoisie being formed relies on this ideology to reorganise society in terms of its interests. We can conclude from this that it is impossible to construct an economy and social relations which are genuinely socialist without the creation of a new man who puts collective interests above everything. The opposite result is obtained if one hopes to stimulate enthusiasm for work by relying on the profit motive and by widening wage differentials excessively as was done in the USSR and which leads to division rather than unity among the workers. As a consequence, bourgeois ideology finds a new social basis. Its underhand progress disaggregates the nascent socialist relations of production.

One cannot struggle against bourgeois ideology solely by resort to administrative and police measures. These make it possible to suppress only its overt expression but in fact leave it to progress beneath the surface in people's minds. The only effective weapon is Marxist-Leninist refutation supported by facts and the participation of the broad masses in ideological struggles. In the USSR, the transformation of the dictatorship of the proletariat into the dictatorship of the bourgeoisie was facilitated by the fact that,

under the pretext of 'dictatorship', the masses were practically
forbidden to involve themselves in politics and to criticise or
overthrow bad leaders.

The people, raised in the ideology of servile submission to the
authorities, overwhelmed by the sense of their helplessness,
diverted from public affairs and from politics into the pursuit of
private interests, nevertheless feel their oppression and passively
resist it, but in the absence of an organised vanguard they cannot
mobilise to fight it in a consistent way. They are a people divided
and atomised like a heap of sand. As revisionist leaders have also
discredited communism in the eyes of the masses, the latter are
defenceless before the reactionary propaganda spread by encircling
capitalism and its internal allies, disguised or not.

The leaders taking the capitalist road who have usurped the
leadership of the party, purge it of militants loyal to the
dictatorship of the proletariat. They turn a blind eye to the
misappropriation of public funds for speculative ends, while
intensifying the exploitation of the mass of workers for the benefit
of a narrow privileged stratum. They encourage the accumulation of
savings by offering high interest rates (therefore unearned incomes)
(13) and launch economic reforms which restore the free functioning
of the market, the authority and autonomy of the managers of
enterprises, etc.

In the forms which the restoration of capitalism took in
Yugoslavia, only the principal means of production remain state-
owned but the laws of the functioning of the economy are now simply
the laws of the capitalist mode of production as they were extracted
by Marx, Engels and Lenin:
- the market as the regulator of the whole economy;
- the prices of production law of a free circulation of capitals
(free buying and selling of the means of production by enterprises);
- the law of profit as the motor of production;
- the existence of an industrial reserve army (unemployment);
- economic crises, spontaneous movements of investments.

In particular, the appearance of unemployment (the suppression of
the right to labour) is the undeniable proof that the means of
production are separated from the producers, that the proletarian,
or rather his labour-power, has reverted to the state of a
commodity, a plaything of market fluctuations enriching those who
control it ('alienation'). Meanwhile, the dictatorship of the
proletariat has given way to 'the state of the whole people', the
transparent mask of a new class oppression. The bourgeoisie has
always presented its reign as that of universal reason and the
general interest. The new bourgeoisie in the revisionist countries
is no exception.

Charles Bettelheim promises a book on the restoration of the
power of the bourgeoisie in the USSR, but we are already indebted to
him for precise and illuminating indications on this subject which
we think it would be useful to present in an abridged form.

The conquest of political power by the proletariat only opens the
way to the elimination of capitalist relations of production, which
continue to reproduce themselves even in the enterprises under state
control. In fact, the 'enterprise' necessarily has a capitalist
character owing to the fact that (14)

its structure has the form of a double separation, the separation
of the labourers from their means of production (the counterpart
of which is the possession of these means by the enterprises,
that is to say, by their directors) and the separation of the
enterprises from one another.
This is an obstacle to their effective socialisation. The directors
of the enterprises buy the labour-power 'necessary for the
conversion into value' of the means of production. They can dismiss
the workers whose relations with the enterprise remain on a wage
basis. The reproduction of the separation of the labourers from
their means of production is accomplished, moreover
through specific ideological relations: management 'authority',
the internal hierarchical organisation of the enterprise, the
social division of labour which connects the labour of management
and 'intellectual' labour on the one hand and the practical and
manual labour on the other hand.
The ideological institutions (the school, etc.) which prepare the
workers for life in the 'enterprises' also reproduce these
ideological relations and 'Subordinate the technical division of
labour to the social division of labour'. Finally: (15)
the reproduction of the separation of the labourers from their
means of production is also ensured by the political relations
within the enterprises: legal authority of the management which
can call on the means of repression, supervision exerted 'from
top to bottom', and the application of sanctions in the same way.
The presence of such capitalist social relations and therefore of
the supports of these relations characterises the whole transition
from capitalism to socialism. It provides the social basis for the
restoration of capitalism: (16)
The real importance of state ownership depends on the relations
existing between the mass of labourers and the state apparatus.
If the latter is truly and concretely dominated by the labourers
(instead of being set above them and dominating them), state
property is the legal form of the labourers' social property; on
the other hand, if ... the state apparatus ... is dominated by a
body of officials and administrators ... this body becomes the
effective owner (in the sense of a relation of production) of the
means of production. This body then forms a social class (a
state bourgeoisie) on account of the relation existing between
itself and the means of production on the one hand and the
labourers on the other.
During the transition to socialism, the dominance of socialist
relations of production and the transformation thanks to this
dominance of the relations of real appropriation (essentially
those which are reproduced within economic units) depends on the
intervention of the other (ideological and political) instances
of the social formation in the economic instance. (17)
The transition to socialism (18)
demands a constant struggle against the tendency to the
separation between functions of control, management and
execution. This tendency is itself inscribed in the ideological
relations which are reproduced by the (economic, ideological and
even political) institutions inherited from societies dominated
by non-labourers because these institutions are not and cannot

generally be immediately 'revolutionised' and managed by the workers.

However, reproduction of the old bourgeois (social) relations (at the level of the enterprises) and of the different political and ideological apparatuses signifies that the agents of the reproduction of these relationships, which constitute bourgeois social forces, are still present under the dictatorship of the proletariat and in spite of the nationalisation of the means of production. It is this which makes the dictatorship of the proletariat necessary, for the class struggle goes on. One of the possible results of this struggle is the return to power, under forms which are not readily detectable, of bourgeois social forces. This happens when the representatives of these forces take over the leadership of the state and the ruling party; from that time, the class character of the state, of nationalised property, and of planning is no longer proletarian but bourgeois. In this situation, domination by the producers over their conditions of existence, which, at the moment of the proletariat's seizure of power is first assured by the state apparatus - pending being so in other forms which are not immediately realisable because they demand a profound trans-formation of the economic, political and ideological relations - ceases altogether and is replaced by that of an exploiting class. On the basis of the existing economic, political and ideological relations, this class can be nothing but a bourgeoisie. The latter appears as a state bourgeoisie. (19)

ERNEST MANDEL'S NEW THESES

In no. 45 of the 'Quatrième Internationale', E. Mandel has tried to found the old Trotskyist theories about the nature of the Soviet state on new bases, so that they take into account the intervening changes in the USSR on the one hand and the analysis made by the Chinese and Charles Bettelheim on the other.

According to Ernest Mandel, it is the orientation of investments which distinguishes nationalised property from private property.

In the first case, they are decided at the national level; in the second, at the level of the firm. And he adds, 'everything else follows from this'. After establishing this difference, he submits that 'planning ... is ... an ensemble of human relations of production'. Is this a truism? No, for these are 'human' relations in order not to be 'class' relations. Everything else follows rather from this. Humanism is never innocent. Having grasped this link Mandel pulls the whole chain to him. He forges two new 'Marxist' (?) concepts with these 'human relations of production': (a) 'relations of planning'; (b) 'the socialist and planned mode of production'.

Mandel also describes this mode of production invented 'ad hoc' as 'non-capitalist'. We know that for the 'newly independent countries' (in reality those dominated by imperialism and social-imperialism) the Soviet publicists advocate a 'non-capitalist road', the most developed examples of which are supposed to be Egypt and Burma since in them the state possesses most of the means of production. (20)

Like them, Mandel implies that this new 'mode of production' is the one which predominates in a 'society in transition from capitalism to socialism'. Vis-à-vis the USSR he talks about 'socialist planning' without explaining how this planning is socialist, and about 'collective ownership' while being careful not to specify that it is collective ownership of the state bourgeoisie.

Mandel acknowledges, of course, that the 'bureaucracy' appropriates a part of the social surplus product but refuses to call this 'bourgeois exploitation'. Presumably if driven into a corner he would concede the existence of exploitation in the USSR and reject only the epithet 'bourgeois'. (21) In his article he invokes the (real) differences between the way in which, for example, the American economy and the Soviet economy function and develop. But he does not even try to demonstrate that, in order to determine the nature of the Soviet state, these differences are essential from a class point of view, a point of view which he renounces when he talks about the mode of production. It is not enough that the orientation of investments be decided at the level of the state; this orientation must also conform to the interests of the working class and the economic policy as a whole must conform to the immediate and long-term interests of the proletariat – this is 'putting politics in command'. Failing which, one cannot speak of the transition to socialism.

Mandel's whole argument is based on the opposition between a supposedly planned mode of production and a supposedly commodity mode of production co-existing in the USSR. According to him, the struggle between the dynamic of one and the dynamic of the other will necessarily end either in the Trotskyist 'political revolution' or in a counter-revolution which will have to overcome 'the fierce resistance of the Soviet proletariat'. We thus find, hardly rejuvenated, the traditional Trotskyist theses which we have already criticised. Mandel's attempt to bring them up to date collapses in its turn once one refuses to accept the 'modes of production' which he has invented for the purpose. The introduction of a plan is not enough either to eliminate social classes or to found different class relations. But the relations of production are class relations. (22) This is enough to rule out talk of a planned mode of production.

In his second letter to Sweezy, Bettelheim had already pointed out that 'bourgeois "plans" and "planning" are possible' and that

the real contradiction (the contradiction which the expression 'plan/market contradiction' designates in the ideological modes the one whose existence it signals while masking it), is that of the domination or non-domination by the producers over the conditions and results of their activity.

It follows that 'the fundamental question is not whether the "market" or the "plan" (therefore also the "state") dominates the economy but the nature of the class which holds power'. (23)

Mandel thinks that he is posing a very awkward question by asking 'what changes in the relations of production or the mode of production manifest this restoration of capitalism, this counter-revolution (in the USSR)?' Bettelheim's analyses which we have just summarised suggest a perfectly clear answer. The nationalisation of the principal means of production by the proletariat in power is a first step, necessary but by no means sufficient to install the socialist relations of production. The old relations of production therefore continue to reproduce themselves at the level of the enterprises as long as these are not revolutionised. The 'installation' having been realised at the level of the juridico-political superstructure, 'restoration' has been possible by the 'road' of a 'usurpation' of the political power conquered in 1917 by the vanguard of the proletariat.

SOME FACTS TO ILLUSTRATE THE RESTORATION OF CAPITALISM IN THE USSR

Legal exploitation and speculation

For many years, speculation in the commercial domain has assumed vast proportions and this has sometimes been echoed in the Soviet press when there have been particularly scandalous cases which have aroused public indignation. The managers of the state enterprises often buy machines with their own money, make workers labour for them and sell the product for their own profit. They are individual capitalists in the classical sense of the term. 'Private' economy is also developing in the Russian countryside. In 1963, the family plots of the Kolkhozniks and Sovkhozniks of Kazakhstan produced 874,000 metric tons of potatoes while the 'public economy' of the kolkhozy and sovkhozy produced only 254,000 metric tons. The same year, the yield in vegetables from private plots was nearly three times as much as that from 'collective farms'. It is not surprising, therefore, if the peasants devote only 180 days per year to the collective land in the Ukraine and only 135 in Georgia in order to work the rest of the time on their individual allotments. (24) The Soviet press has revealed that hundreds of kolkhozniks devote themselves daily to trade on the free markets. Among them, certain speculators 'with long experience' are capable of clearing enormous profits. They rent whole trains to carry fruit, for example, from the Caucasus or Central Asia, to resell for their weight in gold in Moscow.

The principal agents of the restoration of capitalism are not, however, the speculators, a marginal (and secondary) phenomenon in a country in which the means of production are mainly state-owned, but 'the collective owners of the state', the ensemble of those who have leading posts in the apparatus, the 'bureaucratic bourgeoisie', (25) the 'state bourgeoisie', (26) who profit from their power to enrich themselves at the workers' expense. (27)

> As was disclosed in the book entitled 'Lawful Remuneration on the Collective Farm' by Shabakov, among the 27 collective farms which had been investigated in Kazkhstan, chairmen of 11 collective farms drew wages 15, and even 19 times that of an ordinary member. In 1965, the chairman of the Baku Worker Collective Farm in the Azerbaijan Republic received an average monthly pay of 1,076 roubles; the chief accountant, 756 roubles. By contrast, an average farm member received less than 38 roubles ... The leading staff and 'experts' of the state farms receive full pay no matter whether the crops are good or bad and their annual bonuses are as much as 5 or 6 times their monthly pay.

A leader at the Paris Commune Members' Collective Farm in the Ivanovo Region of the Russian SFSR embezzled at one time enough money to 'fully pay the monthly wages of all farm members'. (28)

Economic reform

Since 1962 the economists Lieberman and Trapeznikov have made recommendations for an economic reform conferring greater autonomy on the enterprises at the expense of planning, largely restoring the free functioning of the market, making profit the criterion of the success of the enterprise and lastly, involving management and staff. The reform was adopted in September 1965, put into effect from 1 January 1966 and became general during 1969.

Here is what we read in 'L'Express' of 28 August 1967:

The Soviet authorities have decided to arouse enthusiasm for economic reform the other week by authorising the publication of a book which praises 'American efficiency'. Such is its title. The author, Nicolas N. Smeliakov, an engineer and Deputy Minister of Foreign Trade, lived in the USA as head of a permanent trade mission.

It is easy to understand that Soviet citizens do not abound with enthusiasm for economic reform when one considers its consequences:

- reform gives the managers of enterprises the right to alter wage scales, to fix the proportion of profits allotted to bonuses and the distribution of the latter, and therefore to favour some people – starting with themselves – at the expense of others;

- in order to get the maximum profit, the managers of enterprises increase productivity, particularly by speed-up;

- they gain the right to lay off workers from their factories, who thus become superfluous;

- to palliate the resulting 'structural' unemployment, the state creates an employment agency called the 'Administrative Bureau for the Utilisation of Manpower'.

For the labourers, the reform signifies misery and unemployment (or at the very least uncertain employment). Only a privileged minority will be made rich. In this way the income differential which was already excessively wide will grow even wider. Such, in fact, is the policy consciously pursued since 1964. (29) The Soviet leaders do not hide it and even go so far as to find 'theoretical justification' for their anti-working class policy. The Central Committee proclaimed in its Theses on the Fiftieth Anniversary of the October Revolution:

Egalitarianism would cut the ground from under the relationship between the workers' material incentives and the product of their labour and would sap their urge for vocational and cultural improvement. The socialist system of society offers people moral and material incentives for increasing the productivity of labour and developing their capacities and endowments. (30)

According to 'Izvestia' on 4 March 1966, wage differentiation alone guarantees increases in productivity and therefore becomes a fundamental element in the construction of communism! (31)

In other words, the greater the inequalities and the more people act in terms of their individual interest, the closer we get to communism!

Finally, the reform will lead to rising prices and an increasing
dependency on the capitalist world. Here is what one Western
observer has said: (32)

The price of the reform's success remains to be paid: the
acceptance of a certain amount of inflation and a noticeable
deterioration in the terms of trade with the outside world.
Perhaps the Soviet leaders will judge that this price is not too
high when it involves stabilising economic relations with the
West in a period when the threat from the East is growing.

It will be remembered that at the time when these lines were
written, the correspondent of the Soviet Agency Novostni stated in
'Le Monde' that the USSR was defending Western civilisation on the
Amur and the Ussuri.

Today the restoration of capitalism in the USSR is visible to the
naked eye. Even the ideologists of the bourgeoisie are aware of it
in their own way and congratulate themselves on it. (33)

The general orientation of the reforms, contain measures which go
along with them and especially the climate in which they are
carried out allow us to think that they constitute only a first
step on the road to more profound changes ... In the present
stage of development of industrial societies, the system of a
market and a plan constitutes the only formula in the East as
well as in the West.

We can trust the specialised dispensary of anti-communism which
publishes 'Est-Ouest' to discern what is as good for the capitalist
East as well as for the capitalist West.

The repression of the people

'Man is made in such a way that in general he does not permit
himself to be exploited at will; this is why he must be coerced and
oppressed.' (34)

In order to maintain their power and supervision over the means
of production, the new bourgeois exploiters led by the Brezhnev-
Kosygin clique are forced to resort to repression whenever deception
proves inadequate. That is why they set up a 'USSR Ministry of
Public Order' in July 1966. In December of the same year, they
adopted a 'resolution for the strengthening of labour discipline'
which affirms the necessity for a full use of the 'administrative
measures foreseen by the law' and extends the role 'of the Public
Prosecutor and the Supreme Court of the USSR'. In other words,
labourers who revolt against 'labour discipline' - that is, against
the exploitation they suffer - are beaten down legally or even
administratively.

At the beginning of 1967 new amendments were added to Soviet laws
which stipulated that 'anyone who infringes Soviet political and
social order' and 'spreads anti-Soviet slanders' is liable to three
years' imprisonment. In January 1967 a group of Soviet youth
demonstrated against the introduction of these new clauses. Two of
them were sentenced to three years' imprisonment on a charge of
'Violation of public order'. (35) It is well-known that those
citizens who protested against the invasion of Czechoslovakia in
August 1968 received heavy prison sentences.

Political opponents are usually imprisoned in labour camps with common rights but it is very common to intern them in mental hospitals, where they are forcibly administered stupefying drugs. Not to regard the Soviet system as the best possible is proof that one is not 'adjusted' and therefore not sane.

Ideological degeneration

The analysis of Soviet society contained in the notes sketched at the end of his life by the well-known economist Eugène Varga does not go beyond a surface description of phenomena and bring out their causes. In fact, his attempts at explanation based on the interruption of Russian capitalist development at its beginnings or the necessity for the USSR to set aside an enormous budget for defence do not seem convincing. Nevertheless, there are many observations in these notes which coincide with other accounts such as those which four Japanese students published in the Belgian Marxist-Leninist journal 'Clarté' (no. 110) and which confirm our own picture of revisionist degeneration. Here is what Varga writes:

Moreover, material relations in Soviet society are often conducive to immoral survivals and actions. On the one hand, the lavish conditions enjoyed by the leading groups of the Party bureaucracy ... lead to complacency and arrogance, often also to perversion. They are driven to seek even greater personal prosperity, appropriating and squandering the property of the state, to demoralisation and sometimes to outright crime.

Varga deplores in 'the middle sections' (36)

The absence of a truly democratic content and of the civic sense to which it should give rise. The lack of these makes the members of Soviet society concentrate on satisfying personal family matters and leading a petty bourgeois existence. Apart from matters connected with his employment, the ordinary Soviet citizen thinks mainly about acquiring personal property, a good flat, a dacha with a garden, a television set, clothes, etc; he saves up for this, boasts about it to his relations and neighbours ... On the whole the citizens of the USSR have not had the slightest idea of what a true Soviet democracy would be like, or the social relations that would result from it ... This society is ... based on the cult of officialdom ... Today, as before, the power of the state is concentrated in the hands of the top leaders of the party bureaucracy. Political conditions are still being concealed from the working people.

We could multiply the examples showing that bourgeois common sense passes for good sense as such in the pro-Soviet bloc. The author once happened to argue with a young Hungarian architect working in France, where she stayed for two years. She was a party member and regarded herself as a faithful communist. Speaking of her experience of French building-sites, she said that she was shocked by the workers' unwillingness. To our suggestion that perhaps this was a form of resistance to capitalist exploitation and therefore laudable from a proletarian point of view, she replied that it was just laziness, the mother and father of all vices - no matter whether in France or in the socialist countries.

Those who have travelled in the USSR have been able to observe many things, all of which lead to the same conclusion: the dominant ideology there is that of the ruling class, the state bourgeoisie. K. S. Karol has summarised certain features of this ideology fairly well: (37)

> The values of the leading Soviet class are hardly distinguishable from those which predominate among the Western bourgeoisie. The power elite in the USSR believes firmly in the necessity for a social division of labour, in hierarchical methods in the economic and political sector and in all dogmas of 'promotion by merit'.

Of course, the Soviet leaders make a great show of their supposedly intransigent fidelity to Marxism-Leninism, but it becomes more and more difficult for them to reconcile their real, deeply conservative practice and ideology with the exaltation of Lenin and the revolutionary origins of their state. They are shown up in a truly laughable way when they attribute to Lenin Otto Bauer's 'theory' of five 'social factors of force', described by Lenin as a petty-bourgeois degradation of Marxism. This 'mistake' made in point 14 of the 'Theses for the hundredth anniversary of the birth of V. I. Lenin', published on 23 December 1969 by the Central Committee of the CPSU, should rather be called 'an exceptionally candid disclosure'.

The Austrian social democrat Otto Bauer published a pamphlet in 1920 in which he accused the 'tyrannical socialism' of the Bolsheviks of doing 'violence against the social factors of force'. Speaking of this absurd theory, Lenin declared before the Second Congress of the International:

> A German variety of philistinism is required, and you get the 'theory' that the 'social factors of force' are: number; the degree of organisation; the place held in the process of production and distribution; activity and education. If a rural agricultural labourer or an urban working man practises revolutionary violence against a landowner or a capitalist, that is no dictatorship of the proletariat ... That is 'violence against the social factors of force'.

A little earlier, Lenin had commented: (38)

> Bauer's book will be a useful if peculiar supplement to the textbooks on communism. Take any paragraph, any argument in Otto Bauer's book and indicate the Menshevism in it, where the roots lie of views that lead up to the actions of the traitors to socialism ... this is a question that could be very usefully and successfully set in 'examinations' designed to test whether communism has been properly assimilated. If you cannot answer this question, you are not yet a communist, and should not join the Communist Party.

Thus we see that the Soviet leaders' 'mistakes' cannot be put down to a gap in their learning. Lenin had already explained that it was a question of whether or not one is a communist. By confusing the elucubrations of an Otto Bauer with the thought of Lenin, they themselves have proved that they are incapable of distinguishing between the idea of a 'social traitor' and a Leninist idea. This is indicative of the limits of their duplicity. They have vainly endeavoured to camouflage their real ideology beneath the pomp of a bookish Marxism-Leninism. Their ideology has played a mean trick on them which is more revealing than a Freudian slip and precisely in a text meant to present them as the worthy heirs of Lenin.

The Bolshevik leader described the Social-Democratic Parties as bourgeois workers' parties - workers' through their recruitment and electoral influence, bourgeois through their leadership and policy. Mao Tse-tung is therefore directly in the line of Leninism when he says 'Revisionism in power is the bourgeoisie in power'.

THE CULTURAL REVOLUTION

The revisionist degeneration which long ago affected the Soviet 'elites' in cultural and political areas came officially into the open after the 20th Congress (February 1956); first on the ideological front, with the abandonment of essential Marxist-Leninist principles (parliamentary and peaceful transition to socialism, condemnation of war in general, humanism above classes, the proclamation in 1961 of the Soviet state as no longer a dictatorship of the proletariat but as a 'state of the whole people', etc); then in the domain of international policy ('the Camp David spirit' in 1959, the withdrawal of Soviet experts from China in the summer of 1960, etc); lastly on the economic plane with the economic reform in 1965. In 1963, many years of effort exerted by the Soviet clique to convince the Americans that they were no longer a revolutionary power were finally crowned with success. By breaking with China they made the right pledge to win the confidence of their imperialist interlocutors, hence the Moscow Treaty. (39) These were the alarm signals which aroused the Chinese very early on. A dispute ensued which ended in the public split over differences in December 1962. (40) The class significance of the political turn taken by the USSR during this period was unmistakable, but it was more difficult to elucidate its causes and to grasp quickly all its political importance.

However, as early as 1962, Chairman Mao had penetratingly characterised the fundamental problems of the transition to communism:

Socialist society covers a considerably long historical period. In the historical period of socialism, there are still classes, class contradictions and class struggle, there is the struggle between the socialist road and the capitalist road, and there is the danger of capitalist restoration.

How can a catastrophe such as the one which has already occurred in the USSR be prevented? In his Report to the 9th Congress, Lin Piao quotes Mao's proposals in an interview in February 1967: (41)

In the past we waged struggles in rural areas, in factories, in the cultural field, and we carried out the socialist education movement. But all this failed to solve the problem because we did not find a form, a method, to arouse the broad masses to expose our dark aspect openly, in an all-round way and from below.

And Lin Piao adds, 'now we have found this form - it is the Great Proletarian Cultural Revolution'.

Mao defined the latter as necessary for 'consolidating the

dictatorship of the proletariat, preventing capitalist restoration
and building socialism'. (42)

The targets are 'those persons in authority who are taking the
capitalist road' and also certain 'academic "authorities"' who
propagate bourgeois ideology. (43)

The methods are:

- mobilisation of the masses, it being understood that 'the only
method is for the masses to liberate themselves, and any method of
doing things in their stead must not be used'; (44)

- criticism by argument, supported by facts, in conditions of
'broad democracy', thanks to the real possibility given to everyone
to express themselves individually or collectively by posters,
journals, pamphlets and verbally in meetings and debates.

The struggle is mainly ideological. The masses participate in it
by using the weapons of criticism and not the criticism of weapons.
This is possible through the fact that the revolution unfolds under
the dictatorship of the proletariat.

Its immediate stakes are the institutions, organisms and
different apparatuses usurped by leaders who have embarked on the
capitalist road. It is a revolution in the superstructure, that is,
its terrain is constituted by the legal-political instance and the
instance of ideology. In fact, in order to carry through a lasting
victory over bougeois ideology, it is necessary to wrest the
schools, the press and the other state ideological apparatuses
(forms in which ideology is realised) from the domination of
bourgeois intellectuals. (45)

By transforming the superstructure, the cultural revolution puts
it at the service of the construction of a socialist economic base.
It creates the conditions for revolutionising enterprises. As a
result, relations of production of a capitalist type give way to
socialist relations of production. The productive forces proper to
socialism, based on the initiative, creativity and ingenuity of the
masses are liberated and set in motion. Such is the meaning of the
slogan 'Grasp revolution, promote production'.

The cultural revolution effects a profound upheaval of the social
totality in all its determinations, levels and instances. In
particular, it demolishes the mechanisms which reproduce the old
social relations at the level of the ideological state apparatuses -
educational, familial, cultural and informational - replacing them
by other mechanisms reproducing socialist relations. It thus
transforms the moral physiognomy of the country and, finally, thanks
to the reciprocal action of the superstructure, it transforms the
modes of production itself which does not become socialist by
nationalisation alone, for 'capitalist relations of production
continue to reproduce themselves in the enterprises' (Bettelheim).

The most prominent leaders taking the capitalist road, like Liu
Shao-chi, relied on the agents of the reproduction of bourgeois
social relations at the level of the enterprises and the political
and ideological apparatuses. Seizing on a favourable conjuncture,
they would have taken hold of central power, and this would have
amounted to the restoration of capitalism in a new form. To guard
against this danger, to sweep aside the obstacles which these
bourgeois elements placed on the socialist road, it was necessary
for the masses to revolt against them, to tear from them the power

which they had usurped, to criticise them and to destroy their prestige and moral authority.

In the course of this struggle, the masses have educated themselves, they have raised the level of their political consciousness, and learned to outmanoeuvre the enemies concealed amongst them. In doing so, they have assimilated the thought of Mao Tse-tung and mastered its living application. Thus the conditions have been created for translating into reality Mao's slogan 'The working class must exercise its leadership in everything'.

Three stages can be distinguished in the cultural revolution, so long as they are not seen as strictly chronologically separate and the more or less contingent vicissitudes of its real historical development are ignored:
- the mobilisation and revolt of the masses;
- seizure of power, the 'Great Alliance', the 'Triple Combination';
- 'struggle-criticism-transformation' during which take place the transformation of the system of management of the enterprises, the entry of the working class into the apparatuses and institutions of the superstructure, and the consolidation-construction of the party by the expulsion of what has been corrupted and an influx of new blood carried out 'in the open': under the supervision of the masses.

In fact Mao unleashed the cultural revolution because he had realised that the contradiction between the proletarian line and the bourgeois line could not and should not be resolved in the confines of the party and by struggles in the apparatus but only by encouraging the intervention of the broad masses.

Thus the latter were called on to settle a political debate inside the party; this was contrary to tradition and clashed with the habits of thought of cadres bogged down in these traditions. The masses could only liberate themselves if it was clear that the organisms of the party and their hierarchy were not untouchable. This is why the 'Decision in 16 Points' proclaims: (46)

In certain schools, units and work teams of the Cultural Revolution, some of the persons in charge have organised counter-attacks against the masses who put up big-character posters criticising them. These people have even advanced such slogans as: Opposition to the leaders of a unit or work team means opposition to the Central Committee of the party, means opposition to the Party and socialism, means counter-revolution ... This is an error in matters of orientation, an error of line, and is absolutely impermissible.

The 'Decision in 16 Points' clearly implies that the leaders of the party and state organisations draw their authority solely from their link with the masses, a link which in this case shows itself by the fact that they 'stand in the van of movement and dare arouse the masses boldly', and encourage them 'to expose every kind of ghost and monster and also to criticise the shortcomings and errors in the work of the persons in charge'. (47) Like a marvellous litmus paper, the mass movement has revealed the true class position of cadres by forcing them to take sides.

At the level of the economic base, the cultural revolution has allowed the real and concrete application of Mao's ideas, which Liu

Shao-chi and Po Yi-po, the director of the economy, had suppressed in the preceding period. These ideas were already clearly inscribed in the famous Constitution of the Anshan Iron and Steel Company drawn up by Mao in 1960: (48)

1   Keep politics firmly in command.
2   Strengthen Party leadership.
3   Launch vigorous mass movements.
4   Institute the system of cadre participation in productive labour and worker participation in management, of reform of irrational and outdated rules and regulations, and of close co-operation among workers, cadres and technicians.
5   Go full steam ahead with the technical innovations and technical revolution.

Po Yi-po opposed this programme point by point. Not putting proletarian politics in command, he inevitably allowed bourgeois politics to prevail in the end. For him, profit had to be the criterion of success and workers' effort had to be governed by material incentives. He declared that power of decision reverted to one leader (to the manager) and advocated the management of enterprises by experts. The latter often used their 'knowledge' to impose on the workers and did not liberate the latter's initiative by appealing to their practical experience and ingenuity to promote the technical revolution. They themselves tended to copy foreign methods. The supporters of this policy justified it by invoking the imperatives of 'production before everything'. The Shanghai tool-machine factory provides an example of revolutionarisation in conformity with the principles stated by Chairman Mao.

With the cultural revolution
the proletarian revolutionaries have truly taken into their hands the leadership in the factory, including power over technical matters. The bourgeois technical 'authorities' ... have been overthrown'. They have broken 'with the model of individual advancement (to rise in the hierarchy, to join the body of 'experts', to struggle to become an engineer) to the profit of collective research and advancement.

The relations between workers and technicians have been transformed. They used to be based on the model of the division of labour between conception and performance. This meant that

'the engineer gives the word and the worker does the job' or 'the engineer has the idea and the worker carries it out'. This was still the old nonsense of 'those who do mental work rule, while those who work with their hands are ruled' ... The rank and file workers now take part in designing and the technicians go to operate machines in the first line of production.

Among the young technicians, 350 were college graduates and around 250 were promoted from among the workers: (49)

The facts show that the latter are better than the former ... The chief designers of six of the ten new precision grinding machines successfully trial-produced in the first half of this year are technical personnel of worker origin ... Many technicians of worker origin, free from the spiritual fetters of working for personal fame or gain and rich in practical experience, dare to do away with fetishes and superstitions and break through all unnecessary restrictions and are the least conservative in their thinking.

Journalists and other Western Sinologists feel obliged to choose
between two interpretations of the cultural revolution: it is either
supposed to be quite spontaneous or else completely manipulated.
Mao Tse-tung is either a 'sorcerer's apprentice' or else the
Machiavellian 'secret conductor of the orchestra'. The two terms of
the alternative are false. The cultural revolution was unleashed
and led by Mao in accordance with his 'Great Strategic Plan'. At
the same time, it was a movement from the base responding to the
profound aspirations of the masses and obeying a dynamic of its own.
Mao Tse-tung made it possible:

- by guaranteeing his control of the army from 1960 by
revolutionising it, the pillar of the dictatorship of the
proletariat and by purging it of doubtful elements such as Lo
Jui-ching (at the beginning of 1966);

- by encouraging Yao Wen-yuan to criticise Wu Han's 'historical
play', in other words to attack the 'black gang' which controlled
the municipality and press of Peking (10 November 1965);

- by publishing the circular of 16 May 1966 which, through Peng
Chen, the Mayor of Peking, was aimed at all the 'other individuals
of the Khrushchev type'.

As a result, the masses were the driving force of the movement
and the role of the 'proletarian headquarters' was:

1   to give the greatest publicity to the exemplary initiatives of
    the base, such as the 'first national Marxist-Leninist big
    character poster' displayed on 25 May 1966 criticising the Vice-
    Chancellor of Peking University;
2   to systematise the lessons of the experience of the mass movement
    in the form of general political directives.

Most often the central authorities refrained from intervening in the
local conflicts which had to be settled by the masses (except in
specific cases like that of Wuhan). This was the reason why nearly
three years were necessary for revolutionary committees to take
power in all provinces, with all that this implied in the way of
troubles and disorders. Nevertheless, throughout the cultural
revolution and its preliminary stages, Mao Tse-tung knew how to
manoeuvre with the ability and consumate clearsightedness of the
great strategist and great tactician which he has always been.

In short, the cultural revolution was a directed movement but
directed in accordance with the principles of the 'mass line'.

The 'broad democracy' which characterised it was real, and such
as no people in the world has ever known. The organisations and
groups of Red guards and revolutionary rebels who proliferated from
the start had the free use of premises and the necessary equipment
for the diffusion of their ideas: paper, ink, photo-copying
machines, loud-hailers and even walkie-talkies, useful for
co-ordinating the development of demonstrations.

In the first stage of the revolution, the groups even abused
their freedom since they did not always respect the order to abstain
from any resort to violence. The police refrained from intervening
even when certain leading organs called for their help.

All the leaders were criticised: not only Liu Shao-chi, the
President of the Republic, Teng Hsiao-p'ing, the General Secretary
of the Central Committee, and Tao Chu, the head of propaganda, but
also the Minister for Foreign Affairs, Ch'en Yi, Mao's wife, Kiang

Sing, Chou En-lai, the Prime Minister, and even Lin Piao and Mao
Tse-tung himself.

The Trotskyists have claimed that the 9th Congress was
prefabricated. How then explain that the discussion on the choice
of candidates to the Central Committee alone took all of nine days
if Mao was able to dictate to the delegates the list which suited
him?

The Chinese Communist Party has never been monolithic. A party
without contradictions is a dead party.

The broad democracy we have discussed was based on a set of
political principles formulated long ago by Mao Tse-tung and still
valid. They have been explicitly incorporated into the new statutes
of the party.

The 'Decision in 16 Points' states:

It is normal for the masses to hold different views. Contention
between different views is unavoidable, necessary and beneficial
... Any method of forcing a minority holding different views to
submit is impermissible. The minority should be protected,
because sometimes the truth is with the minority. Even if the
minority is wrong, they should still be allowed to argue their
case and reserve their views.

With regard to the resolution of contradictions among the people,
Lin Piao recalled in his report what 'Chairman Mao has taught us
many times': 'Help more people by educating them and narrow the
target of the attack', and 'Carry out Marx's teaching that only by
emancipating all mankind can the proletariat achieve its own final
emancipation'. In the struggle against the enemy, said Lin Piao,
quoting Mao, 'Stress should be laid on the weight of evidence and on
investigation and study, and it is strictly forbidden to obtain
confessions by compulsion and to give them credence.' And Lin Piao
added, 'To handle this part of the contradictions between ourselves
and the enemy in the manner of handling contradictions among the
people is beneficial to the consolidation of the dictatorship of the
proletariat and to the disintegration of the enemy ranks'. (50)

According to the Trotskyists, 'the Liu grouping took control of
the party apparatus and pushed Mao to one side'. (51) The latter
had mobilised the students 'as the instrument to re-establish his
control over the country'. (52) This interpretation, borrowed from
the bourgeois press, has been refuted by Jean Daubier who, among
other things, asks: how, deprived of power, was Mao able to have Liu
Shao-chi's line condemned as a right deviation in September 1962,
and again in 1964 the one which he had applied 'to Tao Yuan, and to
publish the twenty-three articles which concretised this condemnation'? (53) It is only true that Mao, with a small majority on
the Central Committee, saw the application of his policy thwarted by
the representatives of the reactionary line and the conservative
elements.

The Trotskyists have not gone as far as the revisionists in the
deceitful exploitation of the army's intervention in the cultural
revolution. Livio Maitan's report, which we have already quoted,
only notes with regard to the role played by the military in the
'revolutionary committees' that 'the structure of any army - even

the most democratic', cannot 'be considered a model of proletarian democracy for society as a whole'. (54)   This gibberish does not mean anything:

1   The Chinese have never said that the structure of their army was a model of democracy for society as a whole.
2   Democracy is not a matter of 'structure' but of function.   It concerns the way in which the decisions are taken and relations between the leaders and the masses.   Democracy exists when the leaders consult and listen to the masses and when their decisions correspond to the needs and wishes of the masses.
3   It is meaningless to talk of 'any army – even the most democratic'.   The difference between the People's Liberation Army and the bourgeois armies is one not of degree but of kind.   The People's Liberation Army is not an army in the usual sense of the word precisely because it is a people's army.   The word 'army' must be understood in a figurative sense.   It is a metaphor.

An army 'stricto sensu' is an instrument which guarantees the subjection of the vast majority to a small minority.   It is a parasitic organisation apart from the people in which a blind and as it were mechanical discipline prevails.   Drill is the extreme form of the methods by which recuits are transformed into robots. Although adults, the soldiers, and even the pupils of certain training schools dependent on the War Ministry do not have the same political rights as other citizens.

Such is the case because if need be it must be possible for such an army to be used to massacre the people (cf. the Paris Commune, the 1927 massacres in China, those in 1965 in Indonesia).

The Chinese Army is quite different.   It is closely bound to the people.   Far from being parasitic, it produces everything which it needs, sets up pilot farms and leads vanguard industrial enter- prises.   It is an elite body not only on the military, but also on the political level.   To be accepted in it is an honour sought by everyone and granted to the best.   Discipline is all the stronger in this army, for it is based on the 'three democracies', namely: (55)

1   Political democracy: the right and the duty of the soldiers to criticise the officers, for political discussion, criticism and self-criticism must unfold without regard for hierarchy.
2   Economic democracy; in which 'the representatives elected by the soldiers must be ensured the right to assist (but not to bypass) the company leadership in managing the company's supplies and mess' and in which the officers share the same living conditions as the soldiers.
3   Military democracy: in which 'in periods of training there must be mutual instruction as between officers and soldiers ... and in periods of fighting' there should be discussions by the soldiers in big and small meetings on 'how to attack and capture enemy positions'.

The officers share the life of the soldiers and do not benefit from any privilege.   Since 1964 when visible signs of rank were suppressed, it can and does frequently happen that senior officers are taken for private soldiers.   They are not supposed to enlighten 'the culprit' under any circumstances unless this is necessary for performing duties.

In January 1967 Mao issued a call for the army to support the

left. This is what it did at Harbin, especially at the time of the
seizure of power by the proletarian revolutionaries. But its
intervention in the cultural revolution consisted primarily of
sending small groups of unarmed soldiers to places where revolutionary rebels were divided into rival organisations in order to
help the militants to study the thought of Mao Tse-tung while
keeping in mind the problems to be resolved. In spite of their
political prestige the soldiers did not play much of an arbitrating
role. They contributed above all to a raising of consciousness by
organising discussion and study on a principled basis so as to
overcome the closed-circle mentality. The end thus aimed at was to
effect the 'Great Alliance' between all the revolutionary
organisations, the indispensable condition for working out a
'revolutionary committee' based on the 'Triple Combination', that
is, bringing together authorities springing from: (a) rebel
organisations; (b) revolutionary cadres; and (c) the army (or
people's militia). The first two categories of authorities as well
as the militia men were elected in secret ballots by the masses and
were subject to recall at any time.

The Trotskyists - too - try to exorcise Maoism by representing it
as an avatar of Stalinism. This is not easy; thus, they have to
concede that 'those who view Mao's present position as nothing but a
replica of Stalin's tyrannical personal dictatorship ... (are) in
error'. Having thus proved their 'objectivity', they feel all the
happier to denounce 'the outrageous cult of Mao' by playing, just
like the revisionists, on the equivocation: cult of personality =
Stalinism. (56)

Yet they themselves are far from underestimating the role of
leaders in history, as is attested in the texts of Trotsky's in
which he demonstrates that without Lenin there would have been no
1917 revolution. The Chinese people who know the history of their
revolution, know that Mao has led them from victory to victory for
fifty years. It is natural that they should feel a deep affection
and veneration for him. Indeed, the expressions of these sentiments
sometimes assumes forms which are a little excessive and folkloric,
but this is characteristic of popular infatuations. Moreover, China
has behind it several thousand years of the cult of the 'Son of
Heaven'. Traces of it remain. Mao complained about this to Edgar
Snow in December 1970. During the cultural revolution he had
intervened several times to proscribe excessive or incorrect
formulae on the theoretical level. He is no longer described as
'the great leader, great commander, great educator and great
helmsman'. His thought is no longer hailed as 'the summit of
Marxism-Leninism', an image possibly implying the idea of a future
decline. Lastly, people are no longer urged to place themselves
'under the absolute authority' of his thought, for as Mao had
observed, 'there is no absolute authority but only relative
authorities'.

These excesses were generally the ultra-left's doing. The
attacks on this current in 1971 were followed by a reduction in the
number of portraits of Mao in Chinese towns.

It is interesting to find in the article in which Edgar Snow
relates his conversation with Mao in 1965, alongside Mao's critical
remarks on the 'cult of personality', the sort of statement on which

this cult thrived. Edgar Snow told his host that he was the
greatest Chinese statesman and in addition, a great strategist, poet
and philosopher. Mao's reply is characteristic of the man. He did
not stoop to the false modesty of rejecting his interviewer's
flattering formulae. He explained to him only that he would no
doubt have become a simple schoolmaster had it not been for the
exploitation and oppression of the Chinese people, in the face of
which he was unable to remain passive. In other words, the
revolution made Mao as much as Mao made the revolution.

MAOISM, THE SCIENCE OF THE REVOLUTION AND THE THIRD STAGE OF MARXISM

Throughout this book we have used the term 'Maoism' as a synonym for
'the thought of Mao Tse-tung', an expression only naturalised in
China. Why is this and what are our reasons for considering the
first term just as correct?

We base our view on the fact that the relation between the
thought of Mao Tse-tung and Marxism-Leninism is exactly the same in
nature as that between the thought of Lenin and that of Marx. By
summing up the revolutionary practice of his age, an age in which he
was one of the principal actors, Lenin developed Marxism while
remaining faithful to its universal truth. Mao has done the same in
our era. Like all sciences, Marxism progresses and enriches itself
without the new knowledges destroying what has been acquired in the
preceding period which they integrate into a wider synthesis. (57)
This history is at one and the same time continuous and
discontinuous.

In a series of articles celebrating the 90th Anniversary of the
Paris Commune in 1961, the Chinese communists put forward a thesis
which they support more than ever today: that of the three stages of
Marxism. The first, placed under the sign of Marx and Engels, had
been marked by the Commune; the second, that of Leninism, had
culminated in the October revolution; the third was that of the
thought of Mao Tse-tung and of the Chinese revolution.

Just as Leninism is the Marxism of the epoch of wars and
revolutions which opened in 1914, the thought of Mao Tse-tung is the
Marxism-Leninism of our era, in which imperialism will meet its
final end and in which socialism marches towards victory throughout
the world. Mao Tse-tung has led the Chinese revolution; he has
summed up the international revolutionary experience for half a
century; he has drawn the lessons from revisionist degeneration,
particularly in the USSR; he has unleashed and led the cultural
revolution so that China would avoid a similar fate. In doing so,
he has solved a whole series of problems, concerning particularly
the theory of (dialectical) contradiction, the theory of the united
front, that of the people's war, that of class struggle in the
transition to socialism and of contradictions among the people. Mao
has thus carried Marxism to a higher level.

If the Chinese do not use the term Maoism, in our opinion it is
for three reasons: (a) out of a concern not to emphasise the novelty
of the thought of Mao Tse-tung in relation to Marxism-Leninism so as
not to provide ammunition for revisionist propaganda; (b) because
Mao is alive and modesty forbids him to talk of Maoism himself and

because he and his comrades prefer to leave the adoption of the term
to posterity; (c) because certain allies in the international
communist movement who are disposed to respect the thought of Mao
Tse-tung and occasionally make it their inspiration may be reluctant
for the moment to proclaim their adherence to Maoism; that is, to
recognise it as the Marxism-Leninism of our era. General reference
to Marxism-Leninism without further detail provides a wider common
ground and makes it easier to isolate the revisionists on a world
scale and within each Communist Party.

The latter are purely tactical reasons. In no respect do they
invalidate the theoretical arguments which we have just presented.
It so happens that not only do we not have the same tactical motives
for adopting the Chinese usage but, on the contrary, the conjuncture
of the struggle between the two roads among the movements which lay
claim to the thought of Mao Tse-tung requires that one should
differentiate oneself from the ossified Marxist-Leninists who have
understood nothing of Mao Tse-tung's original contribution and who
only verbally recognise its universal validity, and hence its
applicability in Europe, and who reject the term Maoism because of
this. This is why in France the latter was adopted by the 'Gauche
prolétarienne' at its birth. (58)

We do not claim by any means that there are ready-made recipes
for revolution in any country whatever in the works of Mao. Maoism
should be regarded in exactly the same way as Mao regarded Marxism-
Leninism, as a foreign doctrine which he was able to acclimatise to
China. One must 'assimilate it and know how to apply it and
assimilate it with the single aim of applying it'. This is
impossible if one is content to repeat stereotyped formulae instead
of using one's brains. Like all sciences, the thought of Mao is the
systematisation of acquired knowledge (in this case that of the
revolutionary experience of the peoples). The assimilation of this
acquisition and its living applications are the precondition for a
correct solution to the new problems posed and hence the precondition for a further development of the theory.

How can one define the unity of the organic development and the
invariance of Marxism? Marxist theory aims to know the world in
order to transform it; it succeeds in knowing it through and by
means of its transformation. By penetrating the masses, by becoming
a material force, it transforms the world and transforms itself in
the process. Theory can only be assimilated by putting it into
practice. That is why the Marxologists understand nothing about
Marxism. Like the party, theory is only a means to free the people.
To make it an end in itself is to harden it into a dogma, into
scholastic speculation. Theory can only be developed by really
applying it, i.e., successfully applying it. It is true, of course,
that we can learn many lessons from the analysis of a defeat;
communists constantly sum up their experience including their
defeats - but only victorious exemplary applications permit the
verification of the validity of a theoretical innovation, that is, a
new solution to the ever-new problems raised by practice. To go
beyond the Marxism of a certain stage, to make it progress, it must
have previously been assimilated through its application in the
revolution. This is what Lenin and Mao did. On the contrary,
Bernstein, Kautsky, Khrushchev, Togliatti and other Dubceks revise

the acquisitions of the theory as a result of their refusal to apply it to make the revolution. Their policy is the effect of the pressure of bourgeois ideology which exists deep down in every one of us. For the Trotskyists, dogmatism - the tendency to deduce from a few general truths the response to all problems - happily co-exists with the crudest empiricism and a straight-forward surrender to all the fetishes of bourgeois ideology: individualism, liberalism, the cult of knowledge and technique, etc.

Every chapter of this book contains elements of a reply to the question - What is Maoism? In what follows we shall emphasise only its democratic, undogmatic and non-repressive character.

The thought of Mao Tse-tung brings to the masses the conceptual instruments which enable them to intervene actively in politics and to take their destiny into their own hands. The very vigorous ideological struggles between different currents and organisations during the cultural revolution in China and the fact that the 9th Congress required all of three weeks of discussions, show that a general reference to Mao's thought by no means signifies some kind of standardisation of the Chinese, who are sometimes presented by the Pekinologists as a society of ants and not of human 'subjects'. (59) If one is to believe them, only one man has the right 'to think' in China. As if Mao were not the theoretician of the contradictions among the people, that is, of the legitimacy of differences of opinion among men pursuing the same ultimate ends. In fact, far from exempting its adherents from having to think for themselves, Maoism, on the contrary, enables them to do it in a rigorous way. It does not provide them with a set of recipes valid for all situations but demands of them that they 'set the machine (the brain) to work', that they 'dissect one of several sparrows' (that they analyse problems concretely after investigation); in short, that they dare to think, to talk, to act. Mao says: (60)

Communists must always go into the whys and wherefores of anything, use their own heads and carefully think over whether or not (what they are told) corresponds to reality and is really well founded; on no account should they follow blindly and encourage slavishness.

In contrast, in the capitalist countries civil responsibility is synonymous with passivity and slavishness. Governments appeal to 'the silent majority' and ... speak for it. They do all that they can so that it will remain silent through a sense of impotence and resignation. They use police terror when necessary to prevent it from having its say and occupying the forestage of history. Just think, that would be the revolution! Before inventing participation, De Gaulle compared the head of state to the captain of a ship. The citizens were the passengers, expected to stay in their cabins, the understanding being that they had nothing to say on the subject of running the ship. Even in daily life, the ordinary man has to obey his superiors, officials, police, everyone who is invested with any authority whatsoever, without dispute, without 'going into the whys and wherefores of anything'. A recurrent phrase in popular speech is 'Don't even try to understand'.

Well, Mao invites the people not only to search for understanding but also to reject what is unreasonable. 'It is right to rebel' he has proclaimed, and this holds true not only for the capitalist countries, but also for China, whose leaders or cadres may degenerate and cease to serve the people. For the latter, to seize Marxist-Leninist science (the thought of Mao Tse-tung) is to reject all other authority, to win the right to criticise all authority from a proletarian viewpoint, to master politics, the conduct of the class struggle, the laws of uninterrupted revolution. It is to make history consciously instead of submitting to it. It thus appears that far from being 'repressive' as certain distressed spirits among 'anti-authoritarian' intellectuals claim, the thought of Mao Tse-tung is, in fact, liberating by the same right as all forms of rationality.

Undoubtedly it is permissible to deny the scientific status of Marxism in general as well as Maoism in particular. In this case refutations are necessary on a theoretical and practical level. Lenin refuted Menshevism in a series of writings. Furthermore, like Socrates who demonstrated movement by walking, Lenin demonstrated the legitimacy of socialist revolution in Russia by making it.

Raymond Aron asserts that 'the theory according to which social contradictions by themselves lead to a classless society and a mathematical or physical proposition have nothing in common'. (61) He takes good care not to explain that for a Marxist the concept of 'social contradictions' refers to social reality in its totality, whose motor force they are. Once this is known it becomes clear that if social contradictions do lead to a classless society they must lead there 'by themselves', unless we admit to the intervention of a God. Left in ignorance of this explanation the reader is led by this procedure, as infallible as it is surreptitious, to believe that, according to Marxists, the revolution will be made all by itself and that society will go over to communism without our having any hand in it. How could Marxism claim to be scientific if it were a fatalism and therefore the most elementary of superstitions?

While suggesting this conclusion with his usual dexterity, Aron avoids compromising himself by making it explicit; he is content to state that 'a mathematical or physical proposition' has 'nothing in common' with a Marxist proposition, that Marxism 'does not represent a science in the sense of a natural science such as mathematics or physics'. Maybe yes, maybe no. What are we to understand by 'in common', 'in the sense of'? What Aron is putting forward is obvious (with the obviousness of a truism) or false, according to whether the formulations are taken 'sensu stricto' or 'lato'. Thanks to this semantic fog he can pass off as self-evident an assertion which is at the very least questionable.

All the sciences differ among themselves by their object, their concepts and their methods, but they all possess certain common features. We shall enumerate those which historical materialism shares with the other sciences:

(a) It states in a rigorous way an ensemble of general truths (laws).
(b) The known facts do not contradict these laws.
(c) The latter make it possible to explain the facts by their causes.

(d)   They make it possible to work out predictions and therefore
          to put hypotheses about new facts to the test of practice.
It follows from the last characteristic that politics (the conduct
of the class struggle, history in the present) is a true
experimental science.

In the domain of the natural sciences all men are interested in
knowing the objective truth whatever their class membership. This
is not true in the case of the 'social sciences'. Here the same
consensus cannot be attained because interests are opposed. In
order to survive, the bourgeoisie has to achieve a real 'repression'
of the truths which condemn it. It cannot admit, for example, that
its reign is not eternal, that the bosses need the workers but the
workers do not need the bosses. As for the proletariat, it has no
particular interests to defend. In liberating itself it liberates
the whole of humanity. In this sense it is the 'universal class'.
Only intellectuals who side with the proletariat could discover the
universal laws of historical development which reveal to the
proletariat the way to its victory. In short, the working class and
the revolutionary intellectuals who have joined its fight have an
interest in knowing and publishing the truth while the bourgeoisie
have an interest in masking it by masking it from themselves.

Two points in conclusion.

As in the other sciences, the assimilation of the acquisitions of
historical materialism is necessary in order to go further, but does
not carry a guarantee of success. The truth is always concrete.

On the other hand, the failure of a political line does not bring
into question the validity of historical materialism, but only that
line. It is still necessary to analyse, setting out from the
lessons of this failure, in what respects the line was wrong, for
certain setbacks are inevitable by virtue of the balance of forces.

Chapter 6

STALIN AND TROTSKY ON THE CHINESE REVOLUTION

INTRODUCTION

In using two examples, China and Greece, to criticise the Trotskyist version of history, we have no intention of justifying Stalin's international policy. Stalin made many mistakes, some of them serious, on this level. But in their political vehemence the Trotskyists go further. Their argument proceeds from postulates (presented as conclusions) which constitute a total falsification of history and which, furthermore, are anti-Marxist from the point of view of method. Put briefly, these are:

  (a) All the Communist Parties in the world were manipulated by Stalin as mere puppets, deprived of any will of their own.
  (b) Stalin deliberately and systematically imposed on them a line which led to their defeat and even to their destruction. He was the 'organiser of defeats'.
  (c) Stalin acted in this way to safeguard the existence of the USSR and because the interests of the Soviet bureaucracy were the only ones that mattered to him.

This last explanation is really absurd. The security of the USSR was best guaranteed by the strengthening of the revolutionary movements undermining the imperialist rear. It is hard to see how a victory of the revolution in China, Germany, Spain or Greece could have endangered the USSR. In Stalin's time the USSR inspired fear and hatred in reactionaries precisely because they had good reason to see it as the Red base of the world revolution. At present this is no longer the case and the anti-communists who used to write on the walls 'Send the commies to Moscow' today write 'Send the commies to Mao'. The mythical, secret puppet-master has changed his lair.

As for the first two points, they are needed to lay the blame for all the defeats on to Stalin, but the Trotskyists have never provided the least proof of this. Moreover, research which is in any way serious reveals a multitude of facts that invalidate the Trotskyist theses. For example, how can Stalin be held responsible for the mistakes made by the CCP in the period 1928-35 when we know:

1 that an exchange of messages between the Kiangsi bases and Moscow required six to eight months;
2 that, whenever he had knowledge of them, Stalin upheld the

positions of Mao Tse-tung and not those of the CCP leadership
which he is supposed to have put in the saddle.
3   that the latter carried out the Comintern's instructions only
when it suited it to do so.

We have anticipated a little to show that our aim is to recall the
little-known or misunderstood facts which will help us to arrive at
a more accurate and nuanced idea of history than the one provided by
writings oriented by a pre-occupation with anti-Stalinist polemic.

It is only after sweeping away the hotch-potch accumulated by
forty years of falsification that one can begin to tackle the really
interesting questions such as the historically real content of the
concept of Stalinism; the contribution of the International, based
in Moscow, to the education and ideological unification of the
international communist movement; the historical roots of the
opportunist degeneration of this movement, etc.

In his book 'Fascisme et dictature', Poulantzas argues that the
relation between the Comintern policy and the USSR was channelled
through a line characterised by 'economism, the absence of a mass
line and the abandonment of proletarian internationalism'. (1) He
specifies, moreover, that the last trait 'appears principally ... in
the theses and concrete policy regarding "the national question" and
"the colonial question"'. (2)

Let us note in passing that it is precisely the Chinese,
Yugoslavian, Albanian and Vietnamese Communist Parties concerned by
these theses and this policy which seem to have been the least
troubled by them since they were victorious. We shall see in what
follows that an investigation of the relations between the Comintern
and the Chinese Communist Party by no means corroborates
Poulantzas's thesis. Of course it may be presumed, for example,
that the line of unprincipled unity in the anti-Japanese front
favoured by Wang Ming had been encouraged by Stalin; there is also
the fact that the Moscow press condemned Chiang Kai-shek's arrest in
Siam as a Japanese-inspired plot; (3) but all this is not enough to
lead one to deduce an 'abandonment of proletarian internationalism'.
It is not what the Chinese think, and they are in a better position
than anyone to know. We still do not have means to determine the
periodisation of the class struggle in the USSR on the basis of its
internal factors, but we do know its effects at the level of its
international policy. It emerges from this that 'the process of the
reconstitution of the Soviet bourgeoisie' already in action in
Stalin's time could only end in the usurpation of state power after
his death.

The chapter which follows has extremely restricted aims. It
should not be looked to for a systematic study of the history of the
Chinese Communist Party at the time of the First and Second
Revolutionary Civil Wars. By taking the example of the defeats
suffered by the Chinese revolution from 1927 to 1935, we propose to
establish the following points:
1   that Trotsky's positions on China were wrong;
2   that the Trotskyists falsify the history of this period in the
framework of their propaganda with a view to canonising Trotsky
and presenting Stalin as the source of all the evils which have
befallen the communist movement;
3   that, independently of the specific cases of falsification which

we shall demonstrate with supporting documents, their interpretation of history proceeds from the fundamental theoretical mistakes which were brought to light in the preceding chapters.

CHRONOLOGY: LANDMARKS (1926-7)

On 1 July 1926 the Northern Expedition was launched. The Canton armies advanced rapidly, taking Changsha on 12 July, completing the conquest of the triple city of Wuhan on 7 October and seizing Nanchang on 8 November.

The victorious advance of the Nationalist armies was made easier by the revolutionary agitation organised by the communists in the enemy's rear. Everywhere the peasant leagues and unions arose and seized power. In Hunan alone, where Mao Tse-tung was active, the peasant leagues had 1 million members in November 1926, 2 million in January 1927, and 5 million in April of that year. (4)

The victory of the revolution in the Yangtze Valley led to clashes with the imperialists. On 7 September, British gunboats bombarded the unarmed population of Wansien and their troops fired on demonstrators in Hankow. As a result of these incidents the workers in Hankow occupied the British concession (January 1927). American and British warships bombarded Nanking on 24 March, some foreigners having been killed when the town was seized.

Shanghai was liberated at this time (23 March) following a workers' rising led by the communists, notably Chou En-lai.

On 10 March, Chiang Kai-shek had made a speech violently attacking the Kuomintang Government that had been set up at Wuhan and containing veiled threats against the communists. Wuhan replied by withdrawing from Chiang nearly all his special powers. The communists received a seat in the Presidium of the Political Council and two Ministries.

Terrified by the setting up of a municipality dominated by the representatives of the toiling masses and depending on the support of 2,700 armed workers, the bankers and compradors of Shanghai called Chiang Kai-shek to their assistance. The latter needed money: they handed over 45 million yuan. With the agreement of the authorities of the French and Anglo-American concessions 5,000 rifles and trucks were supplied to the members of the green and red gangs who, moreover, were authorised to traverse the concessions to massacre the workers and revolutionary intellectuals. Chiang's troops organised similar massacres in Canton and Nanking (12 April). (5)

The Wuhan government immediately dismissed Chiang Kai-shek from all his posts and expelled him from the Kuomintang (17 April). But on the following day he set up his own government at Nanking.

On 17 May, General Hsia Tiu-yin rebelled against the Wuhan government and declared himself for that of Nanking. He tried to seize Wuhan and was defeated by the mobilisation of the people in the capital of Hupeh and by the arrival of the troops of the pro-communist General Yeh-T'ing. On 21 May, a general of the Wuhan Government launched a bloody repression of communists and militant workers and peasants in Changsha. Later, arrests and massacres of the communists were multiplied in the regions controlled by Wuhan. The final break between the 'left' Kuomintang and the communists occurred on 16 July. Borodin left on 27 July and the hunted communists went underground. (6)

At Nanchang on 1 August, there was a rising of the left Kuomintang garrison, commanded by communists (Chu Teh, Ho Lung, Yeh T'ing). These troops (30,000 men) headed south but were dispersed following heavy fighting in the Swatow region (27-30 September). Only a few thousand soldiers under Chu Teh escaped. In April 1928, they joined the forces which Mao Tse-tung had led into the Ching Kang mountains after the defeat of the Autumn Harvest Movement. (7)

Other risings led to the creation of more or less durable 'soviet' Red bases in the provinces of Kwantung, Hupeh, Shensi, etc.

On 11 December, the Canton insurrection was unleashed under the leadership of Yeh T'ing. The insurrection had the advantage of the complicity of Yeh Chien-ying (future Field-marshal of the People's Liberation Army) who commanded the training regiment and also from a situation which was momentarily very favourable since conflicts between two nationalist generals had led one of them to deploy his troops outside the town, leaving the latter ungarrisoned. The forces which took part in the action were 2,000 Red guards, 200 men from the training regiment and some 8,000 workers and peasants armed with rifles captured in the military depots, of whom 2,000 were communist workers freed from prisons. They were crushed two days later by the 50,000 Kuomintang who intervened immediately; 1,000 insurgents escaped and reached the sovietised zones of Haifeng and Lufeng while others were the germ of the guerillas of the Yu Kiang River. (8)

According to the Trotskyists, the 'Canton Commune' was a 'suicidal insurrection decided in Moscow' by Stalin, who desired a victorious announcement for the 15th Congress. No proof is ever forthcoming to support these allegations. It is clear, anyway, that for reasons of distance, Moscow could not decide particular operations and had to be content with transmitting general guidelines. So far as the substance of the problem is concerned, it must be seen that even risings destined to be defeated may be worth more than surrender without a fight. The Autumn Harvest insurrection was also a defeat but it was the beginning of the long march of the Chinese Communist Party to victory. Nevertheless, it does seem that the price paid in Canton was too high. In any case, risings in the towns stemmed from an erroneous strategy, striking the enemy at his strong point when his weak point was in the countryside. The Trotskyists cannot make this criticism - the only correct one - for they also thought that China had to be liberated in the towns first of all.

It was by rejecting this mistake on the basis of its experience, without listening to the Trotskyists, that the Chinese Communist Party regained the lost terrain in the following period. The communists were 'neither cowed nor conquered nor exterminated. They picked themselves up, wiped off the blood, buried their fallen comrades and went into battle again'. (9) Far from stopping the course of history, the reverse in 1927 planted the seeds of future victories.

As Mao Tse-tung has said, 'Struggle, defeat, new struggle, new defeat, once more new struggle, and so on till victory - such is the people's logic.'

HOW ISAAC DEUTSCHER WRITES HISTORY

We read in Isaac Deutscher's 'The Prophet Unarmed' (p. 317):
>   Only in 1921 did the Chinese Communist Party, based on small
>   propagandist circles, hold its first congress. But no sooner had
>   it done so and set out to formulate its programme and shape its
>   organisation than Moscow began to urge it to seek a rapprochement
>   with the Kuomintang.

And on p. 319 of the same work, that in 1922 Maring
>   told Ch'en Tu-hsiu and his comrades that the Communist
>   International firmly instructed them to join the Kuomintang,
>   regardless of terms. Ch'en Tu-hsiu was reluctant to act on this
>   instruction, but when Maring invoked the principle of
>   international communist discipline, he and his comrades
>   submitted.

Astonishing as this may appear, the sources (even the Trotskyist ones!) totally contradict this version of the facts. Maring (alias Sneevliet), the Comintern representative, who became a Trotskyist in the 1930s, told the Trotskyist historian Harold Isaacs that the majority of the Central Committee, including Ch'en Tu-hsiu, agreed with his views and that those who opposed him, in particular the then 'ultra-leftist' and later turncoat Chang Kuo-tao, had not done so for reasons of principle, but because they did not believe at the time that the Kuomintang could become a mass movement in which it would be useful to militate. He insisted on the fact that he did not have precise instructions at that time. (10) His account is confirmed by Pavel Mif, a member of the Far-Eastern Bureau of the Comintern, according to whom the first instructions regarding 'the co-ordination of the activities of the Kuomintang and the young Chinese Communist Party' were issued by the Executive Committee of the Comintern in a special communication dated 12 January 1923. (11)

Let us note that the strategy of penetrating a non-proletarian but progressive mass-movement had been tried with great success by Sneevliet himself in the Dutch East Indies, where the communists had set up cells in the peasant organisation Sarekat Islam. It was this experience which inspired the tactic of the united front with the revolutionary nationalist movements of the colonial and semi-colonial countries adopted by the 2nd Congress of the Communist International. It was Lenin who first sent Sneevliet to China (1920). Moreover, the latter attached great importance to the CCP's maintenance of political and organisational independence.

Now, in a text dating from the period when he was striving to justify himself against the criticism directed at him by the CCP leadership, Ch'en Tu-hsiu tells us that Maring had urged the Chinese communists to enter the Kuomintang because (12)
>   it was not a party of the bourgeoisie but a party common to
>   various classes ... the five members of the Central Committee of
>   the CCP unanimously opposed this suggestion because entry into
>   the Kuomintang would have introduced confusion into the class
>   organisation and fettered our independent policy. Finally, the

Third International delegate asked categorically whether the
Chinese Communist Party would conform to the decision of the
International.

It is now clear where Deutscher got his information. He passed over
the sources (even the Trotskyist ones) which did not have sufficient
grist for his mill and chose an interested party whose 'pro domo'
plea was intended to shift the blame for his own faults on to
Stalin. Throughout an exposition covering several pages Deutscher
takes Ch'en's account for Gospel truth, all the more so as he
considers him to be a greater theoretician than Mao Tse-tung. (13)

He also said of Ch'en: 'At every stage he frankly stated his
objections to Moscow's policy; but he did not stick to them. When
overruled, he submitted to the Comintern's authority, and against
his better knowledge carried out Moscow's policy.' Poor Ch'en! He
could say with the Latin poet 'Video meliora proboque, deteriora
sequor' ('I know the right, approve it, and yet the wrong pursue.')

Historical reality is infinitely more complex than this
apologetic thesis which the Trotskyists hand down from one
generation to another, simplifying and deforming it as they go.
This degradation from history to mythology can be traced by
comparing Harold Isaacs to Deutscher and the latter to Broué.
Fernando Claudin, too, slavishly takes up this legend, referring to
Ch'en Tu-hsiu's 'Letter to Comrades' which he says 'has great
interest, both human and historical'! (14)

Dov Bing, a more serious and less naïve investigator (though even
more anti-Stalinist), has unearthed more than one falsehood in this
account, which should be treated with great caution given its
interested character.

There is no documentary evidence (before 1929) that Ch'en Tu-hsiu
had only reluctantly agreed to join the Kuomintang. Even if this
was so, it cannot be seen as the sign of a left-wing position. In
their 'Shanghai Letter', the three members of the Comintern mission
showed that opportunism made Voitinsky and the right of the CCP want
the Communists not to enter the Canton government; more precisely,
so that they would not have to struggle against the right-wing of
the Kuomintang. (15) Likewise, it was a 'defeatist mentality' that
made the Comintern executive representative (in agreement with
Borodin) propose after the coup on 20 March 1926 that the communists
should leave the Kuomintang as Chiang Kai-shek wanted. (16) The
most right-wing leader in the party, T'an P'ing-shan, had criticised
the policy of integration into the Kuomintang at the Comintern
Plenum of November 1926. As Minister of Agriculture in the Wuhan
Government he was, however, most zealous in holding back the peasant
movement against certain instructions of the Comintern.

The policy of working within the Kuomintang was, after all,
perfectly correct in the framework of the struggle against
imperialism and the militarists. It gave a colossal impetus to the
mass movement in the towns and the countryside. Li Ta-chao and Mao
Tse-tung had carried out this policy enthusiastically for reasons
quite independent of Comintern instructions. Mao seems even to have
been subjected to sharp criticisms from some of his comrades such as
Li Li-san, who attacked him for putting too much emphasis on
co-operation with the Kuomintang. (17)

As early as 1923, Ch'en Tu-hsiu denied that the Chinese

peasantry - half of whom according to him were small proprietors -
could accept communism and be anything more than a vacillating ally
tending to compromise with reaction. As Stuart Schramm says, 'this
disdain for the peasantry was not characteristic of the Comintern
line in the same period'. (18) In fact the thirteen-point directive
presented to the 3rd Congress of the CCP in May 1923 and drawn up
under Bukharin's guidance, argued that the peasant problem should
occupy a central position in the policy of the party.
    We shall see later that Ch'en's distrust of the peasant movement
and his refusal to support it or to accept its arming, were
diametrically opposed to other specific resolutions adopted by the
Comintern. The right opportunists of the CCP verbally accepted the
International's recommendations and then acted in the opposite
sense, as they were encouraged to do by Voitinsky and Borodin. (19)
To present them as consistent and lucid revolutionaries obeying,
nevertheless, 'perinde ac cadaver', is a fable which does not stand
up to examination.

TROTSKY AND THE CHINESE REVOLUTION (1923-7)

Deutscher himself disputed the truth of 'one of the legends of
vulgar Trotskyism which maintains that the Opposition had from the
beginning unremittingly resisted Stalin's and Bukharin's "betrayal
of the Chinese Revolution"'. (20) He showed that up until 31 March
1927 Trotsky had only criticised (incidentally and in passing, so to
speak) the Comintern's China policy on a single point: the CCP
joining the Kuomintang. Furthermore, he did it only within the
secrecy of the Political Bureau.

Principle alone cannot decide whether Trotsky was right on this
question. It is necessary to study the facts and to endeavour to
study thoroughly the specificity of the Chinese situation at that
time. Between 1922 and 1927, the number of members of the CCP
increased from 300 to nearly 70,000 and the unions which they
controlled reached 3 million members. They penetrated the
Kuomintang apparatus from top to bottom. Chou En-lai carried on the
functions of Assistant Political Director of the Whampoa Military
Academy, (21) Mao Tse-tung was a member of the Central Committee of
the Kuomintang and Director of the Peasant Movement Training
Institute (cadre school). Ch'en Tu-hsiu and Borodin were the
lieutenants of Sun Yat-sen and then of Wang Ching-wei. Other
Kuomintang leaders were very close to them, such as Liao Chung-k'ai
who, for this reason, was assassinated by the rightists. The
communists and the left Kuomintang controlled 90 per cent of the
Kuomintang committees at the base and intermediary levels. At the
same time, the communists retained in practice the autonomy of their
organisation and made propaganda quite freely. In fact, until
Chiang Kai-shek's about-turn, the middle or national bourgeoisie
played an objectively revolutionary role, while remaining hesitant
and vacillating. Concern for its interests induced it to fight
imperialism and its allies - the warlords and the comprador
bourgeoisie. Semi-feudal relations in the countryside and wars

between militarists restricted the domestic market. The imperialist ascendancy helped to bar any possibility of expansion to it. This is why the Chinese industrialists and merchants of Canton and Shanghai came to finance the Hong Kong strike committees! Thus the Kuomintang-CP united front was at one and the same time possible, necessary and enormously profitable to the revolutionary movement and to the Communist Party. This does not mean that it had to be prolonged for as long as it was, at the expense of consistent revolutionary action in the countryside; we shall talk about this question later in this chapter. For the moment, we can conclude that Trotsky was wrong to condemn the alliance with the Kuomintang as early as the beginning of 1924. In doing so, moreover, he came into contradiction with the positions sustained by Lenin at the 2nd Congress of the Communist International: (22)

> There is not the slightest doubt that every nationalist movement can only be a bourgeois-democratic movement ... the Communist International must enter into temporary arrangements, even alliances, with the bourgeois democrats in the colonies and backward countries, but should not merge with them, and should maintain at all costs the independence of the proletarian movement even in its most embryonic form.

Trotsky's argument condemning the entry of the communists into the Kuomintang was that in doing so they were sacrificing their political independence. For him, the criterion of this independence was the fact of possessing a daily newspaper. The CCP did not have a daily, but it did have several periodicals. The independence of these was such that in September 1926 the party journal 'Hsiang-tao' stated that the Northern Expedition was not propelled by the masses and that the Kuomintang government did not represent the people but was merely 'the special organ', of a cabal of generals to serve their 'personal ends'. (23)

In May 1927, that is, after the break with Chiang Kai-shek, Trotsky, making a complete 'volte-face' at the 8th Plenum of the International, denied advocating the withdrawal of the communists from the Kuomintang. (24) This is a fact little known to Trotskyists - and Deutscher passed it over in silence.

It was in April 1927 that Trotsky seized upon the Chinese question as a warhorse in the struggle he was then conducting along with Zinoviev and Kamenev against the Political Bureau. Until then he had only concerned himself with the question from the point of view of the state interests of the USSR. In 1926, he had chaired a commission whose task was to elaborate recommendations for the Political Bureau regarding the line of Soviet diplomacy in China. He submitted the report on 25 March. Here is what Deutscher said about it: (25)

> Trotsky's commission reckoned with China's continued division; and its recommendations were as if calculated to prolong it ... (It) did not seek to promote revolution but to secure every possible advantage for the Soviet government. Thus the commission suggested that Soviet diplomatic agencies should seek a 'modus vivendi' and a division of spheres between Chiang Kai-shek's government in the south and Chang Tso-lin's in the north ... The commission urged Soviet envoys to prepare public opinion 'carefully and tactfully' for this arrangement, which was likely to hurt patriotic feelings in China.

We shall refrain from any comment on this report. Everyone knows what the Trotskyists would say about it if it was not signed by Trotsky but only by Stalin. Let us simply point out that it was easy for the former to criticise others once he himself no longer had any responsibility. There being no risk that his proposals would be put to the test of adversity he could always exclaim, 'Ah, if only you had listened to me!' What can be discussed, on the other hand, is his analysis of the class contradictions in China and his appraisal of the motor forces of revolution in that country.

Trotsky clearly underestimated the revolutionary potential of the peasant class in China. He says that 'there is almost no estate of landlords in China' (sic), and he adds that 'the specific weight of the agrarian question in China is therefore much lighter than in Tsarist Russia'. (26) In the same work, which as we know dates from November 1929, he quoted one of his old speeches, 'The town is the hegemon of modern society and only the town is capable of assuming the role of hegemon in the bourgeois revolution,' and he added in a note, 'Do the belated critics of the permanent revolution agree with this? Are they prepared to extend this elementary proposition to the countries of the East, China, India, etc.? Yes or no?' (27)

No, Mr Trotsky! Of course the proletarian party secures the hegemony in the revolutionary movement at the level of ideological and political leadership, but its most numerous troops and also some of its leaders come to it from the peasantry. Its most promising field of action is the countryside, for 'the revolution is always strongest where the counter-revolution is weakest' (Mao). It was by encircling the towns from the countryside that it was eventually able to liberate China. The poor peasants were the principal motive of the Chinese revolution. Trotsky's prognosis was exactly the opposite. In July 1928, he wrote, 'It is only with a new rising wave of the proletarian movement that one will be able to speak seriously about the perspective of an agrarian revolution.' (28)

Causes of the opportunist errors of the CCP leadership

We have shown that the alliance with the Kuomintang corresponded to a correct policy up to and including the Northern Expedition. Before the success of this campaign, neither the communists nor the reactionary element of the Kuomintang were ready for the trial of strength which they jointly foresaw but deferred in order not to harm the anti-imperialist struggle and because at that time the right-wing of the middle bourgeoisie had not yet switched to the side of reaction, for objective reasons. To demand, as Trotsky did in April 1926, a communist withdrawal from the Kuomintang, was senseless and would have had disastrous consequences.

Once victory had been won in the Yangste Valley, the Nationalist leaders and officers in their army became uneasy about the swelling movement of the popular masses in as much as it was undermining the bases of the quasi-feudal relations in the countryside and strengthening the workers too much for the normal pursuit of capitalist exploitation in the towns. They immediately began to take repressive measures against the people. In a sense we can say that the (military) victory of the revolution led to its (political) defeat. In fact, seeing the way the wind was blowing, the Toukiens (militarists of the northern clique) changed camps and went over to the Kuomintang. Of the fifty-six generals who thus rallied, fifty-one were feudal landowners.

At this moment, the CCP was confronted with following dilemma:

- whether to maintain its alliance with the Kuomintang at any price, by restraining, if necessary, the revolutionary movement of the masses;

- or, realising that a new stage in the revolutionary process had irrevocably been reached and that the principal contradiction had shifted, leaving the right-wing of the national bourgeoisie on the side of imperialism and feudalism, to stand resolutely at the head of the exploited masses in revolt. (29)

The Chinese communist leaders (and to much lesser degree the Comintern) refused to see that a choice had to be made. In practice they chose the first path more often than not, while the Comintern instructions would rather have suggested to them to choose the second. The alliance with the Kuomintang had succeeded too well for them not to be tempted to prolong it as long as possible. Taking their hopes for realities and the 'revolutionary' phraseology of certain left Kuomintang leaders seriously, they thought they could play both games at once, eventually isolating the new right which had formed around Chiang Kai-shek. They counted on the 'dynamic' of the revolution to achieve this result. They believed in this all the more since in actual fact the right had been isolated and defeated in the preceeding period. (30) They realised, of course, that in such a perspective they would have to hold back the agrarian revolution. But they thought that this would only be a pleasure deferred. Besides, they were genuinely shocked by the stories that were circulating regarding 'excesses' committed by the peasants. As Mao said, 'Even quite revolutionary minded people became down-hearted as they pictured the events in the countryside in their mind's eye; and they were unable to deny the word "terrible".' (31)

It was against them and not Stalin that Mao wrote his report on the peasant movement in Hunan Province, in which he demonstrated that, from a revolutionary point of view, things were, on the contrary, going 'fine'. Almost all the communist leaders believed the stories about the 'excesses' of the peasants and declared that the most effective method of combating counter-revolution would be to check them. (32) There were even landlords and sons of landlords among the party leaders.

Chu Teh told Agnes Smedley how the communist leaders in the Tungku region set up another 'Communist' Party because 'these "intellectuals" ... had done everything for the revolution - except to divide their own land among their tenants'. (33) The 'Shanghai Letter' sent by three members of the mission of the Communist International on 17 March 1927, emphasised that 'the leading bodies of the CCP are not linked to the masses', and that they look down on the workers and peasants and 'deny their revolutionary aspirations'. (34)

To explain the mistakes made by the CCP leadership in this period requires above all a study of the development of the contradictions in China, in the Kuomintang and in the CCP itself. It is only on this basis that one can isolate the influence of the Comintern representatives in China and of Stalin's counsels. The latter were moreover far from being as opportunist as the policy pursued by the CCP.

DID STALIN DELIBERATELY BETRAY THE CHINESE REVOLUTION?

Deutscher says straight out: 'Stalin and Bukharin considered themselves entitled to sacrifice the Chinese Revolution in what they believed to be the best interests of the consolidation of the Soviet Union.' (35)

This thesis has been taken up by bourgeois historians so that it currently figures as a 'historical truth'.

Of course Stalin made mistakes, for he could not know the concrete situation better than the Comintern representatives in China or the Chinese communist leaders who were on the spot. Mao Tse-tung was the only one among them in this period to analyse correctly the class contradictions in China, to show the enormous importance of the revolution in the countryside and to advocate resolute revolutionary action. It is true none the less that correct instructions from the Comintern and from Stalin on important points were not carried out by the leadership of the Chinese Communist Party.

In November 1926, the 7th Plenum of the Executive Committee of the Comintern adopted a resolution on China which put the emphasis on the peasant revolution while asserting that it was necessary to support the Kuomintang. In particular, it declared that: (36)

The proletariat must choose between the prospect of a bloc with large sections of the bourgeoisie and the prospect of the continued consolidation of its alliance with the peasantry. If it does not put forward a radical programme, the proletariat will be unable to draw the peasantry into the revolutionary struggle and will forfeit its hegemony in the national liberation movement.

This resolution had been adopted on the basis of a series of 'theses' which M. N. Roy (the Indian communist leader) had submitted to Stalin. (37)

In those days Stalin listened carefully when someone dealt with a subject about which he knew nothing, and when he had heard a fair presentation, he accepted it quickly and without equivocation.

Here are a few passages from a speech which Stalin gave before the Chinese Commission of the International which elaborated the above resolution: (38)

I know that there are certain people among the members of the Kuomintang, and even among the Chinese communists, who do not consider it possible to unleash the revolution in the country-side, because they fear that if the peasantry is drawn into the revolution, the united anti-imperialist front will be undermined. This is a profound mistake, comrades. The anti-imperialist front in China will be the stronger and more powerful the sooner and more solidly the Chinese peasantry is drawn into the revolution.

Speaking at the same 7th Plenum, Stalin had warned against a strengthening of the right-wing in the army to the extent that the victories of the Northern Expedition brought about the surrender of the enemy. (39) At the same session, Petroff, the Russian delegate, stated, 'It is possible that after the victory of the Canton government has strengthened its right-wing, the bourgeoisie there will play a greater role and will reach an agreement with the imperialists.' (40) As early as 1925, a high-powered Comintern functionary had contended that the Chinese bourgeoisie would probably 'establish a ... military dictatorship' in order to 'prevent the development of the revolutionary struggle of the proletariat, the peasantry and the urban poor'. (41)

In another connection Stalin quoted a document of the International drawn up a year and a half before Chiang Kai-shek's 'coup d'état' in which it was said: (42)

Our course must be steered towards the arming of the workers and peasants, the transformation of the peasants' committees in the localities into the actual organs of power, accompanied by armed self-defence, etc. The Communist Party must everywhere come out as such; a policy of voluntary semi-legality is impermissible; the Communist Party must not act as a brake on the mass movement.

We must stop here to make four remarks:
1 Stalin did not realise clearly that, if led by the communists, the deepening of the peasant revolt would be fatal to the alliance with the Kuomintang leadership. Preparations therefore had to be made and the most favourable moment chosen for this break.
2 Stalin formed a view on the basis of reports which reached him from very different sources. As the Oppositionists in the CCP were often consigned to Moscow, they were in a position to wield a certain influence there and sometimes took the floor before the Executive Committee of the International. In general, the influence of the Chinese leaders on the Comintern line in China was much greater than the influence of the Comintern on the policy of the CCP. (43)
3 The CCP leadership's freedom of choice was all the greater as:
   (a) the International's instructions entailed contradictory demands like those quoted above, namely they were to remain in the Kuomintang while arming the workers and peasants and urging them to seize power;
   (b) the Comintern representatives in China - Borodin, Voitinsky and then Roy - each had very different views on the application of these instructions.
4 The Comintern had warned against the strengthening of the right and the danger of a military coup d'état while pointing out the only possible defence: the arming of the workers and peasants.
The 'Report on an Investigation of the Peasant Movement in Hunan', ('Selected Works', Volume 1) became known in Moscow in May 1927 and produced a strong impression. (44) There is an echo of this in 'Memoirs of a Revolutionary' by Victor Serge who says in particular: 'The future military leader of Soviet China was very close to us (in the 'left Opposition') in his ideas; but he stayed within the party line in order to keep his supplies of weapons and munitions.' (45) Serge does not explain exactly to what use these arms could have

been put. Certainly not to make the revolution, since Stalin was
against it and wanted at any price to strangle it! Anyway, it is
quite simply absurd to speak of the USSR sending military equipment
to the Chingkang Mountains when it took six months for a mere letter
to get there by underground routes. (46)

In the Foreword to his collection of documents on the Chinese
question, Broué quotes an article published in 'Clarté' in Paris on
15 August 1927, in which Victor Serge commented on the 'Report on an
Investigation of the Peasant Movement in Hunan'. Broué gives the
Trotskyists credit for distinguishing Mao Tse-tung from the other
Chinese leaders. To present things in this way and to imply that in
this respect the Opposition was particularly clear-sighted, borders
on deception. During the 8th Plenum of the Executive of the
International in May 1927, it was the defenders of Stalin's
'theses', namely Bukharin and Togliatti (Ercoli), who quoted Mao's
report at length while Trotsky and Vuevich did not mention it. (47)
This was no accident. Stalin, who also took Mao's information and
analyses as his basis, held that after Chiang Kai-shek's 'volte-
face', the struggle of the Chinese people had entered a new phase of
anti-feudal and anti-imperialist agrarian revolution. This
appraisal was rejected by the Trotsky-Zinovievites, whereas it was
adopted by the Chinese communists.

During the 8th Plenum, Trotsky protested that the Opposition was
by no means proposing a withdrawal of the communists from the
Kuomintang. Now his supporters attribute the defeat suffered by the
Chinese Revolution in 1927 to the fact that the CCP had entered it
and did not withdraw from it in time. The line which Trotsky
advocated in the sessions on 23-6 May in that year itself deserves
some explanation from them. They prefer to maintain a prudent
silence.

Zinoviev's 'theses', which Trotsky defended, even went so far as
to proclaim that, 'It is necessary to give the most energetic aid in
all respects to Hankow (capital of the left Kuomintang) and to
organise from there the defence against the Cavaignacs.'

The differences at the 8th Plenum turned on the question of
whether or not the communists should issue an appeal for the
formation of workers', peasants' and soldiers' soviets. Stalin
showed that this was incorrect at this stage, for it would have
meant the creation of a dual power and the setting up of a counter-
government with the aim of overthrowing that of the left Kuomintang
in which the communists had a place. These consequences, which
necessarily followed from such a slogan, were, moreover, totally
incompatible with the line of strengthening the left Kuomintang
which Trotsky and Zinoviev recommended at the same time, sublimely
unaware of the contradictions in which they were embroiling
themselves.

The resolution as it was amended in the commission emphasised
that 'new breaks in the national revolutionary front are not only
possible but inevitable ... There will be new betrayals and new
partial defeats'. (48)

The only (relative) guarantee against such defeats lay in the
following 'fundamental directive': 'to unleash the mass movement of
peasants and workers'. (49) It was necessary, moreover, to create
'reliable armed units' as well as 'units made up of revolutionary
workers and peasants.' (50)

In May 1927, a great controversy broke out in the heart of the CCP over the question of whether or not the Wuhan (Hankow) government should be supported in its plans to launch a military campaign against Nanking (Chiang Kai-shek's location) and Peking. Roy, who had represented the Comintern since the 7th Plenum, suggested retaking the territories of southern China, controlled at that time by the leaders of the right-wing of the Kuomintang. Once this goal was attained, it would be possible to encircle Nanking and Shanghai and to defeat Chiang Kai-shek and international imperialism. But, he said, (51)

> The Communist leaders would not accept the alternative plan of action. They argued that refusal to support the second Northern Expedition would amount to a break with the left Kuomintang (52) ... I referred the disputed question to Moscow. The answer was ambiguous. It was in favour of doing both the things simultaneously: to carry on the military plan (the Northern Expedition), and develop the revolution in the territories of the Wuhan government.

Already in mid-April the most representative members of the Chinese Communist Party had greeted the theses of the Communist International, presented to them by Roy, without enthusiasm. (53)

Here we see once more that, when they wanted to, the CCP leaders could stand up to the representatives of the Executive Committee of the Communist International. As for Stalin's instructions, they always remained a dead letter when they were not in tune with the right opportunism of the Chinese leaders.

On 1 June 1927, Stalin sent a telegram to Hankow in which he said, among other things: (54)

> We are decidedly in favour of the land actually being seized by the masses from below ... You must not sever yourselves from the worker and peasant movement, but must assist it in every possible way. Otherwise you will ruin the cause ... A large number of new peasant and working class leaders from the ranks must be drawn into the Central Committee of the Kuomintang. Their bold voice will stiffen the backs of the old leaders or throw them out on the dust-heap ... Organise your own reliable army before it is not too late. Otherwise there can be no guarantees against failures.

After receiving this telegram, Roy acted incredibly rashly: he went and showed it to Wang Ching-wei, bringing about an immediate break between the Wuhan government and the CCP despite an ultra-defeatist eleven-point statement published by the leadership of the latter in a fit of panic. Roy's calculations are most satisfactorily explained by an author who belonged to the left Kuomintang: (55)

> Roy's idea was that the left Kuomintang could only survive when in alliance with the Communists, as otherwise they would be crushed by the Rightists. They should, therefore, be informed of Stalin's cable. Borodin, however, realised that the left Kuomintang ... would at once sever their relations with the Communists if they saw the resolution ... A majority of the Chinese Communists sided with Borodin, being also of the opinion that the time for overt action had not yet come.

Thus Stalin's envoy, the 'leftist' Roy, (56) precipitated the break between the left Kuomintang and the CCP at a time when the latter

was defenceless because of the defeatist policy of its leadership
in the previous period. Let us now re-read Deutscher's account to
see if it agrees with the facts and documents we have just quoted.
We must also be careful to guard against the very special 'literary'
methods according to which it is constructed, for the author not
only leaves out all the facts which are awkward for his thesis – he
somewhat confuses the chronology so as to present events in the way
most favourable to Trotsky's analyses.

   We have said that Deutscher brushed aside 'nearly' all the facts
which contradict the Trotskyist 'schema'. It is precisely because
of this 'nearly' that he is not in too good an odour with his
co-religionists.

   A thorough, scientific, historical study of this period remains
to be carried out.

THE COMINTERN AND THE CCP FROM 1928 TO 1935

The Resolution of the 9th Plenum of the Comintern (February 1928)
advised the CCP to set as its objective the 'initial victory in one
or several provinces' (where the peasant movement was strong), as
the uneven development of the revolution made it impossible for the
moment to envisage victory throughout the country. The 6th Congress
which met in the summer of 1928 came to the same conclusions.
However, after Li Li-san's return to China, the CCP leadership he
headed adopted positions diametrically opposed to the Comintern's
analyses. In an article published in 1930, Li Li-san argued that it
was 'impossible to achieve victory in one or more provinces without
connecting it with the whole country'. (57) In the same way,
according to the Political Bureau's letter dated 11 June 1930, given
that the 'fundamental political crisis in China is equally sharp in
every part of the country, a great workers' uprising in any city
will develop into a nation-wide revolutionary high-tide' which would
spread throughout the world and without which the revolution in
China was doomed to defeat. (58) In fact, Li Li-san had never
accepted the idea of the uneven development of the revolution, any
more than that of a process passing through determinate stages. In
the article of 1 April 1930 mentioned above, Li Li-san maintained
that it was 'a mistake to grant that the revolution can begin to be
transformed into a socialist revolution only after its victory in
the whole of China'. He thought that this was possible
'immediately'. (59) That is why he was condemned after the 4th
Plenum of the Central Committee (January 1931) for advocating the
organisation of collective farms and other 'premature socialist
measures'. Finally Li Li-san subordinated victory in 'one or
several provinces' to the success of workers' insurrections in the
main cities.

   The positions of Li and Trotsky are manifestly similar on all
these points. However, Trotsky constantly denounced the CCP
leadership as made up of mere functionaries obedient to Stalin's
every gesture. (60)

   In some letters addressed to the Central Committee of the CCP at
the end of 1928 and the beginning of 1929, Mao Tse-tung expressed
certain disagreements with the political line of the leadership.

The latter passed these documents, together with their own replies, to the Executive Committee of the International in Moscow, counting on its approval. Its expectations were disappointed, for the Comintern reply dated 7 June 1929 supported the positions put forward by Mao in his letter of 25 November 1928, and the reply of 26 October 1929 adopted Mao's positions in his letter of 5 April. To be more precise, in the first of these missives the Comintern accepted practically everything that Mao had written on the problem of the rich peasants. Li Li-san advocated an alliance with the latter, for in attacking them there was a danger of cutting oneself off from the middle peasants. He also considered it absurd to start by dividing the land when one was going to collectivise it later. Envisaging rapid victory on a countrywide scale in China, he wanted immediate propaganda in favour of collective farms in the expectation in the meantime of drawing the rich peasants into the struggle against the warlords and the imperialists. In its letter to Mao, the Comintern unequivocally condemned any idea of an alliance with the rich peasants and accused the Chinese leadership of making mistakes. Mao later nuanced his position, making a finer distinction between the well-off peasants (cultivating their land themselves) and semi-feudal, small landlords. He was disposed to leave the former in peace. On the other hand, Li Li-san's attitude to all those who employed labour on their land hardened considerably. After 1931, Mao came into conflict with the new leadership, for he opposed the policy of eliminating the well-off peasants. This is what explains the errors of certain American Sinologists who believe that the Comintern letter alluded to Mao's line. Lucien Bianco has misguidedly copied them without checking their sources. He writes: (61)

> One of the first references to Mao which appears in the Comintern documents is a letter of June 1929 from the Executive Committee of the International addressed to the CC of the Chinese Party. It criticises fairly sharply his policy which was excessively moderate with regard to the rich peasants; in short, a Mao suspected of kulakophilic tendencies.

In fact Mao's name does not appear in the Comintern document and the latter is attacking the line of the CCP leadership, which is also condemned in other matters.

Li Li-san did not want the peasant movement to develop to the point of becoming the principal force of the Chinese revolution. In one of his articles he stated that 'Without the strike-waves of the working class, without armed insurrection in the key towns, there will be no success in one or several provinces. It is a seriously wrong idea which foresees "using the villages to surround the towns", and which counts on the Red Army alone to occupy the towns.' (62) Aiming for victory on a national scale, he considered that it was necessary first to win over the people as a whole. This was why he advocated abandoning the Red bases and dissolving the Red Army, whose men were to be divided into mobile detachments making propaganda in the villages.

The Comintern firmly pointed out to the CCP leadership that it should consolidate the guerilla struggle and extend it at once while combating the suspicious attitude to the peasant movement manifested within the party. Declaring Mao to be correct, it pronounced

against dispersing soldiers to act as 'roving guerilla bands'. The
Red Army should be strengthened in such a way that 'in the future,
according to the political or military circumstances, one or several
political or industrial centres can be occupied'. (63)

Thus we see that the Comintern adopted Mao's theses on protracted
war and encircling the cities from the countryside. At this time,
moreover, Mao was held in very high esteem in Moscow. The obituary
notice to him in the 'International Press Correspondence' in March
1930 as a result of a false report is very significant in this
respect. The eulogies lavished on him in that text implicitly
placed him above all the Chinese leaders. His fame is also attested
to by a short poem by Bertold Brecht inspired by an episode in the
Chinese Civil War - 'Die Andere Seite' - moving in its simplicity
and its wholly Chinese precision.

Later, when the new CCP leadership was set up in the Kiangsi Red
Base and took the political command of the army away from Mao, in
October 1932, the latter's preponderant influence in the base
organisations was undermined by an insidious campaign aimed at him
although it took as its target Lo Mai and his so-called 'League of
Big Peasants'. Mao counter-attacked and an extract from the speech
in which he attacked 'the leftists' (the party leadership) for
underestimating the strength of the Kuomintang, appeared in
'International Press Correspondence' on 17 November 1933. (64)

A former communist turned Trotskyist, Li An, called the Po
Ku-Wang Ming leadership 'the returned students' because of their
youth and because they had studied in Moscow and only returned to
China in 1930. According to Li An and most American Sinologists,
these 'twenty-eight Bolsheviks' had been set in the saddle
('appointed', says R. C. North) by Moscow and acted in accordance
with Comintern instructions. Reality is less simple. This group
had acceded to the leadership at the session of January 1931 thanks
to an alliance with the much-criticised Li Li-san group. Besides,
it is untrue that the new leaders acted as a bloc and did not have
a policy of their own. In 1933, one of them, Lo Fu, who was
acknowledged to be a leading theoretician, expressed differences
with the others on the question of the well-off peasants and of the
problem of the relations with small capital. As the revolution was
in its bourgeois democratic stage, he was opposed to the struggle
against these two classes. Lastly, the facts prove that in this
period as in the preceding one, the CCP line did not always
correspond to the views of Moscow. In fact, after the first battle
of Shanghai in February 1932, the Comintern was again at issue with
the CCP line. On 15 March and 1 April 1932, its journal, 'The
Communist International', published two articles on the war in
China. In the first it criticised the point of view of a number of
Communist Parties (among them the Chinese Communist Party),
according to which Japanese aggression aimed to destroy Soviet China
as a first step prior to an invasion of the USSR. 'Their slogan
regarding the Japanese attack was not the slogan for the defence of
the Chinese people from the imperialists, nor the slogan "Hands off
China", but almost exclusively "Defend the Soviet Union".' (65) In
the second, the Comintern journal attacked the CCP more
particularly. It stated that the latter 'must fan the flame of war
to develop it into a national liberation war of the toiling masses

... against the imperialist plunders and first and foremost against Japanese imperialism'. (66)   It is evident that the Comintern once more sided with Mao.   He also considered from now on that the principal enemy was Japan.   In conclusion we can assert:

1   that the political line of the CCP from 1928 to 1935 was not elaborated and decided in Moscow and it was even the case that the Comintern's counsels were implicitly rejected in practice;

2   that such important decisions as those not to co-operate with the rebel generals in Fukien in November 1933 and to adopt a static defence against the 5th Encirclement Campaign were taken without consulting Moscow. (67)   Such consultation was, besides, impossible at short enough intervals, given the isolation of the Kiangsi Red Base;

3   that the Comintern's positions depended on the theses of the Chinese leader whose analyses appeared most convincing; the International's Bureau had no other source of information;

4   that the Comintern, in which Stalin's influence was preponderant, gave proof of a surer judgment of the situation in China than the Chinese leaders, with the exception of Mao.

At the time of the dissolution of the Third International, Mao Tse-tung explained that (68)

> Since the 7th World Congress of the Communist International in 1935, the Communist International has not intervened in the internal affairs of the Chinese Communist Party.   And yet, the Chinese Communist Party has done its work very well, throughout the whole Anti-Japanese War of National Liberation.

This obviously does not mean that the USSR did not have a Chinese policy.   We suggested above that Wang Ming's line after 1937, of subordinating the Communist Party to Chiang Kai-shek's authority under the pretext of a united front, was in all probability favoured by Stalin.   Since, besides, in the heat of the polemic against Trotskyism, certain Marxist-Leninists go so far as to say that the communist offensive in 1947 came after 'twenty years ... of political work developing the line established by Stalin and the Communist International', it is useful to quote what Mao himself said on this subject on 30 January 1962 to an expanded meeting of the Central Committee (7,000 participants): (69)

> These comrades of the Comintern (who were concerned with Chinese affairs) did not understand or said they did not understand the Chinese society, nation or revolution.   For a long time we ourselves could not recognise clearly the objective world of China, let alone the foreign comrades.

In another speech delivered to the Central Committee on 24 September 1962, Mao declared: (70)

> In 1945, Stalin blocked the Chinese revolution.   He said that we could not fight a civil war but should co-operate with Chiang Kai-shek, otherwise the Chinese nation would perish ... after the victory of the revolution, he suspected that China would be a Yugoslavia and I would become a Tito.   Afterwards when I went to Moscow to sign the Sino-Soviet alliance and mutual aid treaty, there was some struggle there too.   He didn't want to sign but after a couple of months of negotiations he finally agreed.   When did Stalin begin to believe us?   Since the resist-America aid-Korea campaign, the winter of 1950, he believed we were not a Tito, not a Yugoslavia.

According to the Chinese, Stalin gave them erroneous advice
throughout their revolution (cf. Chapter 4, above) but they have
only given a very few indications on this subject. While waiting
for them to provide more we must hold to the facts established by
documentary proofs and not supplement them by imagination or
interpretation.

The correct strategy - the encirclement of the towns by the
countryside and the liberation of China as the result of a
protracted war conducted by armies recruited mainly from among the
peasantry - was elaborated by Mao Tse-tung and not Stalin. While
the latter, unlike Trotsky, accorded great importance to the peasant
movement, like his brother enemy he subordinated this movement to
the development of the revolution in the towns. On 30 November
1926, he stated: 'One cannot build Soviets in the countryside and
avoid the industrial centres of China.' (71) We observe once again
that Stalin and Trotsky opposed each other but on the basis of
common assumptions which they believed to be principles when they
were really prejudices. However, Stalin did not share Trotsky's
sociologisms and believed that it was possible for the proletariat
to exercise its leadership over predominantly peasant forces. This
is why Trotsky and not Stalin became the enemy of the Chinese
revolution, as we shall see.

TROTSKY AND THE CHINESE REVOLUTION AFTER 1927

Reading Trotsky's polemical writings on the Chinese Revolution fills
one with astonishment and admiration. The aplomb with which he held
forth on this distant country and his audacity in setting himself up
as the spokesman of History, thundering forth anathemas against
those who did not share his opinions, are impressive, even
deceptive. It appears that this man knew no doubt; for him
everything was simple and clear, neither future nor past held any
secrets. How can we argue with a 'theoretician' who, not satisfied
with mastering the 'telescopes' and 'microscopes' of Marxist
science, claimed to possess powers amounting to extra-sensory
perception? At the Plenum of the Executive Committee of the
Communist International in May 1927, he was proud to have pointed
out that 'the adventurist risings of Ho Lung and Yeh T'ing were
inevitably doomed to defeat'. (72)

Now in May 1927, Ho Yung and Yeh T'ing would themselves have been
greatly astonished if they had been told that in three months' time
they would be leading a military rising! A few pages earlier,
Trotsky plays the condescending pedant: one is told to 'Remember
that Shanghai and Canton are part of the province of Kiangsu'. (73)
One can, of course, be a good communist and never have looked at a
map of China in one's life (although this is a serious handicap, if
only for understanding news bulletins) but Trotsky claimed the right
to give lessons to the international communist movement and to
dictate their political line to the Chinese communists while in
complete ignorance of their country. In his writings on China he
wrestled above all with his familiar demons. Everything is a matter
of the Mensheviks, of Kerensky, of different phases of the 1917
revolution. In his customary categorical and peremptory tone, he
said, for example: (74)

The Executive Committee of the Communist International determined
in advance the victory of Chinese Kerenskyism over Bolshevism, of
the Chinese Miliukovs over the Kerenskys, and of Japanese and
British imperialists over the Chinese Miliukovs. In this and
only in this lies the meaning of what happened in China in the
course of 1925-7.

In this passage the logic (if it can be so called) of Trotsky's
argument is patently visible. His sole concern was to lay exclusive
responsibility for the defeats in 1927 on Stalin and Bukharin who,
according to him, were guilty of deliberate betrayal. To confer a
certain plausibility on his indictment he concocted a schema based
on historical recollections and without any relation to the class
struggle in China. Trotsky did not even begin to analyse the
concrete situation in that country to which, in fact, he denied any
differences of detail from Russia in 1917. In so far as he conceded
some differences, here is what he said: (75)

The Third Chinese Revolution ... will not have a 'democratic'
period, be it even for six months, as was the case in the October
Revolution ... it will be compelled from the very beginning to
effect the most decisive shake-up and abolition of bourgeois
property in town and country.

According to the Chinese communists, the new-democratic stage of the
revolution came to an end in 1949 with the liberation of the whole
of China. Although the power established at this time was based on
a class alliance, it exercised in its essence the dictatorship of
the proletariat. As for the period of democratic reforms, it lasted
(in the liberated areas) from 1948 to 1952. At this stage only
bureaucratic and comprador capital was nationalised, which enabled
the state to occupy 'the dominant heights of the economy'. The
socialist transformation of the whole economy only started in 1952.

In November 1929, Trotsky criticised telegrams published in
'Pravda' noting the operations of an armed communist detachment of
22,000 men led by Chu Teh. This new development disturbed him for
it hardly fitted in with his little armchair schemes. Hence he
asked some questions but not in order to extend his knowledge for he
immediately suggested a range of replies, all of which conveniently
condemned the Communist International and its 'local functionaries'
in the Chinese Communist Party. Trotsky began by appearing naïve:
'Has the general strike pushed the proletariat to the insurrection?
If such is the case, then everything is clear and in order (sic!).'
(76)

He knew very well that this was not the case and that nothing was
therefore 'in order'. In other words the peasants are forbidden to
revolt if there is no general strike in the towns: 'Does this
insurrection spring from the situation in China ...? Hardly had
this very sensible idea crossed his mind than he dismissed it, for
the quarrel was with Stalin and not with the Chinese communist
leaders: (77)

or rather from the instructions concerning the 'third period'?
... The rebellion of Chu Teh appears to be a reproduction of the
adventurist campaigns of Ho Lung and Yeh T'ing in 1927 and the
Canton uprising timed for the moment of the expulsion of the
Opposition from the Russian Communist Party ... Have the Chinese
communists risen in rebellion because of Chiang Kai-shek's

seizure of the Chinese Eastern Railway? ... If that is what it
is, we ask who has given such counsel to the Chinese communists?
Who bears the political responsibility for their passing over to
guerilla warfare?

Trotsky did not make an accusation (he did not have a shred of
evidence) but he made a treacherous insinuation (which is as
effective as a slander) inviting his readers to discover the culprit
by following his gaze. Considering its consequences, his crime was
black indeed: (78)

But what is the perspective opened up by this uprising of the
today isolated Chinese communists in the absence of war or
revolution? The perspective of a terrible debacle and of an
adventurist degeneration of the remnants of the Communist Party.
In the meantime it must be said openly: calculations based on
guerilla adventure correspond entirely to the general nature of
Stalinist policy.

If the line followed by the Chinese communists, namely protracted
armed struggle based in the countryside, was Stalinist adventurism,
what is more natural than for them to regard Stalin as their friend
and the Trotskyists as their enemies? Did not the latter describe
the Red Army as 'a movement of roving rebels'? (79)

Stalin having said at the 16th Congress that the Chinese workers
and peasants had created a Red Army and a Soviet government, Trotsky
declared that perhaps it was 'pardonable' for the Chinese peasantry
to call their movement Soviet and their partisan bands 'Red Armies'
but not for Stalin to confine himself 'to a cowardly and ambiguous
generalisation of the illusions of the Chinese peasantry'. (80)

The creation of the first Red Bases, the first fruits of the
communists' victory in China, reduced to a negligible illusion of
backward peasants! (Of whom Mao Tse-tung was one!) For Trotsky
there could be no doubt: (81)

The appearance of the Soviet government under these circumstances
is absolutely impossible. Not only the Bolsheviks but even the
Tseretli government or half-government of the Soviets could make
its appearance on the basis of the cities.

The central Base at Kiangsi where Mao Tse-tung had actually
established a Soviet government, then covered 30,000 km.^{2} and had a
population of 5 or 6 million inhabitants. There were, moreover,
some fifteen smaller bases. The Red Army troops defending them
numbered 60,000 to 70,000 men by 1930. (82)

All this, according to Trotsky, was 'absolutely impossible'. As
the (Trotskyist) 'Provisional International Secretariat of the
Communist Opposition' stated shortly afterwards: (83)

only the hegemony of the proletariat in the decisive political
and industrial centres of the country creates the indispensable
conditions as much for the establishment of the Red Army as for
the establishment of the Soviet system in the countryside.
Revolution is a closed book to anyone who does not realise this
... (The task of the Chinese communists) is not to throw their
forces into the scattered foci of the peasant rising, since their
party, which is few in number and weak, will in no way be able to
embrace it ... but to concentrate their forces in the factories
... to organise (the workers) in the struggle for economic
demands, for the slogans of democracy and agrarian revolution.

According to the same text, 'the independent landlord class does not exist at all in China'. More, 'the middle peasantry is non-existent in China'. It follows that the class struggle in the countryside was a struggle between the poor peasants and the bourgeoisie! (84)

In his 'Speech at a Conference of Cadres in the Shansi-Suiyan Liberated Area' (1 April 1948), Mao estimated the proportion of middle peasants at about 20 per cent. (85) More recent estimates bearing on the whole of China fix this proportion at 30 per cent. (86) In the speech we have just cited, Mao emphasised that 'the poor peasants and the farm labourers must form a solid united front with the middle peasants', taking in 92 per cent of families in the rural population. He specified: (87)

> The target of the land reform is only and must be the system of feudal exploitation by the landlord class and by the old-type rich peasants, and there should be no encroachment either upon the national bourgeoisie or upon the industrial and commercial enterprises run by the landlords and the rich peasants.

William Hinton, author of the famous 'Fanshen', has clearly showed how Liu Shao-chi's so-called 'poor peasants and agricultural labourers' line which at the time of the agrarian reform had aimed at a rigorously egalitarian division of the land and the expropriation of the agricultural equipment and in general the capital of the landlords and the rich peasants, was 'left' in appearance but right in reality. This utopian and reactionary line might have led to a disaster if it had not been corrected in time by Mao Tse-tung. (88) It is precisely because the Chinese communists have been able to distinguish the stages of the revolution that they pursued it without interruption. A Trotskyist line would have led them directly to defeat, for the very simple reason that it was based on a radically incorrect analysis of the class struggle in China, one therefore incapable of answering the fundamental question: who are our friends and who are our enemies?

The Chinese communists have verified it experimentally so to speak. After the defeat of the First Revolutionary Civil War 1925-7, three leftist lines were applied by their leadership, led first by Ch'u Ch'iu-pai, then by Li Li-san and finally by Wang Ming. The line enforced by the last had the most harmful consequences (loss of the central Red Base at Kiangsi-Fukien and 90 per cent of the forces amassed by the communists). Although these leaders were hostile to the Trotskyists, their political ideas very often started from assumptions of a Trotskyist character. Let the reader judge.

The putschists of the first 'leftist' line argued that the Chinese revolution was 'permanent'; that is, they confused the democratic and the socialist revolution. Although most of the tasks set by the different 'leftist' lines had a democratic character, their champions did not clearly distinguish the two stages of the revolution and were impatient to go beyond the democratic stage. They advocated struggle against the bourgeoisie as a whole, including the upper stratum of the petty bourgeoisie and emphasised the struggle against the well-off peasants. They were reluctant to acknowledge that the Red Army movement was a peasant movement led by the proletariat. Their gaze was fixed permanently on the towns and their primary objective was to seize these towns. They subordinated work in the countryside to work in the urban centres, instead of the

opposite. As a result the failure of the latter also to a great
extent wrecked the former. Not understanding that the revolution
was developing unevenly in China as in the rest of the world, Li
Li-san thought that the principal towns should lead the movement and
become the centre of a revolutionary high tide on a national scale
which in turn would spread throughout the world, otherwise the
revolution in China was doomed to defeat. When it became clear in
consequence of Japanese aggression that the attitude of the
intermediate strata and of some local groups of landlords, big
bourgeoisie and military leaders was changing, making them potential
allies in the struggle against Japan, Wang Ming and the party
leadership refused to recognise this development and maintained a
sectarian 'closed door' attitude.

On all these points, Mao took the opposite view to the 'leftist'
lines, which he fought as far as he could. As early as the First
Revolutionary War he had pointed out - as had Stalin, too - that the
task of the Chinese revolution at this stage was to fight
imperialism and feudalism; the peasants' struggle for the land was
the fundamental content of the fight. (89) He insisted on the need
to unite all forces capable of being united, particularly the
intermediate strata (middle peasants, petty bourgeoisie) but also a
fraction of the national bourgeoisie and even certain patriotic
gentry, after the Japanese aggression. He showed that the
revolutionary forces had to create red bases in the countryside
where the reactionary power was weakest. For this they had to rely
on peasant guerillas, to avoid decisive battles, 'to turn the
backward villages into advanced, consolidated base areas, into great
military, political, economic and cultural bastions of the
revolution' and in this way gradually to 'achieve the complete
victory of the revolution in China through protracted fighting'.
(90)

At the Tsunyi Conference (January 1935) Mao Tse-tung's correct
political line was adopted and he himself was swept to the head of
the party. From then on the party was always victorious.

At the beginning of the same period (1929-35) the defeatist group
of the former period, represented by Ch'en Tu-hsiu in particular,
moved to the same position as the Trotskyists. Like them, he argued
that after 1927, the bourgeoisie had won victory over imperialism
and feudalism and the bourgeois democratic revolution was thus
complete. The Chinese proletariat should prepare itself for the
socialist revolution to come and in the meanwhile restrict itself to
a legal struggle centred on the slogan 'For a Constituent Assembly'.

They professed the greatest contempt for the Red Army and for
guerilla struggle in general. The Trotskyist International
Secretariat had stated in September 1930 that the peasant detachments were 'necessarily restricted to a determined province and
incapable of realising extensive centralised strategic operations'.
A glaring contradiction was inflicted on them a few years later by
the Long March of 10,000 km. during which four armies of partisans
crossed a dozen provinces half the size of France, fighting again
and again until they finally came back together in Shensi.

Speaking of the Red Army in 1932, Trotsky formulated the
prognosis that its eventual victory 'would signify a new defeat for
the workers' and would give 'power to a new bourgeois clique' just

as 'in the old China, the victory of the peasant revolution ended in the creation of a new dynasty'. His criticism of the Red Army was that it was composed mainly of peasants and operated mainly from the countryside. His sociologism prevented his conceiving that the Chinese Communist Party might provide a proletarian leadership for a peasant movement. (91)

After 1933, Trotsky and his Chinese supporters denounced the calls for a united anti-Japanese Front issued by the CCP and refused to oppose the steady conquest of China by Japan.

In an article published in February 1933 in the journal 'La Lutte des classes', Trotsky attacked the Chinese Communist Party for its slogan of national revolutionary war against Japanese imperialism. (92) In his opinion such a slogan could only serve the interests of the Anglo-Franco-American imperialists. The communists should therefore have abstained from participation in the resistance against the Japanese invaders unless the latter also attacked the USSR.

Trotsky did not understand that the difference between great imperialist powers and small nations gives the latter the right to exploit the contradictions between imperialisms in order to escape direct subjugation and oppression. On the contrary, Lenin, who denounced the two imperialist camps in the First World War as international robbers with conquest as their aim, at the same time justified the resistance of Serbia against whom the 'German bourgeoisie has carried out a rapacious war ... to subjugate it and to stifle the national revolution of the Southern Slavs'. (93)

In 1912, Lenin had acclaimed the victory of the Balkan countries over the Turkish Empire which made possible the national emancipation of many peoples, despite the fact that the conflicting parties were monarchies more or less in fief to the different imperialisms. (94)

If this defence of national self-determination was justified before 1914, how much more must it have been in China when a powerful Communist Party could take the leadership of the war of resistance against Japan. (95) Trotsky did not understand that in certain conditions a secondary contradiction in principle can become a principal one in fact and relegate to a secondary level the principal contradiction of the previous stage. Thus in China during the Agrarian Revolutionary War from 1927 to 1936 the principal contradiction was between feudalism and the popular masses. In the following period the contradictions shifted as a result of Japan's invasion of China. Japanese imperialism and its Chinese allies came to constitute one of the poles of the principal contradiction, while the popular masses occupied the other. The contradictions between the classes in the Chinese nation then passed temporarily into a subordinate position, as did those between the Chinese people and the Anglo-American imperialists. (96)

In a letter which the Trotskyists sent to the great writer Lu Hsun in order to win him over to their views, they wrote on 3 June 1936:

> Now the Reds' movement to conquer the country has failed. But the Chinese Communists who blindly take orders from the Moscow bureaucrats have adopted a 'New Policy'. They have made a 'volte-face', abandoned their class stand, issued declarations

and sent representatives to negotiate with the bureaucrats,
politicians and warlords including those who slaughtered the
masses, in order to form a 'united front' with them. They have
put away their own banner and confused the people's minds, making
the masses believe that all those bureaucrats, politicians and
executioners are national revolutionaries who will resist Japan
too. The result can only be to deliver the revolutionary masses
into the hands of those executioners for further slaughter.
These shameless acts of betrayal on the part of the Stalinists
make all Chinese revolutionaries blush for shame.

Lu Hsun replied in an open letter - this amongst other things: (97)
Your 'theory' is certainly much loftier than that of Mao
Tse-tung, yours is high in the sky while his is down to earth.
But admirable as is such loftiness, it will unfortunately be just
the thing welcomed by the Japanese aggressors. Hence I fear that
when it drops down from the sky it will land on the filthiest
place on earth.

The testimony of Ch'en Tu-hsiu himself coincides with that of Lu
Hsun. In 1938 he wrote an essay, a copy of which he sent to
Trotsky. In it he stated: 'By their sectarian arrogance, their
purely negative attitude towards Maoism and their insensitivity to
the needs of the war against Japan, the Trotskyists were cutting
themselves off from political realities.' (98)

In 'Transitional programme' Trotsky declared that 'at the
beginning of the Sino-Japanese War the Kremlin once again made the
Communist Party the slave of Chiang Kai-shek, stifling in its cradle
the revolutionary initiative of the Chinese proletariat'.

In 1949, in the journal of the Fourth International, a leader of
the Chinese section called for a fight against Mao Tse-tung, who
would try to compromise with the bourgeoisie. On the same occasion,
he announced the imminent triumph of Trotskyism in China. (99)

One would have thought that, demonstrating the minimum of base-
level empiricist realism of which they are capable, the Trotskyists
would have tried to draw some lessons from their total failure on
the theoretical and practical level in China. One might have hoped
that they would revise their assessments, so often contradicted by
the facts. But no. In his last work, 'The Unfinished Revolution',
(100) Deutscher wonders (p. 85) whether the strategy of encirclement
of the towns by the countryside was a stroke of genius:
Or was it, perhaps, an adventurer's desperate gamble? Its
eventual success makes it appear to have been the former. But
... in truth, Mao's strategy needed for its success an extraordinary combination or coincidence of circumstances, such as he
neither foresaw nor could have foreseen ... Normally, in our
epoch - and this has been so even in undeveloped China - the town
dominates the country economically, administratively and
militarily to such an extent that attempts to carry the
revolution from country to town are doomed beforehand.

Thus, all the experience of the world revolutionary movement for the
last forty years is declared null and void for reasons of principle!
For the revolution does not triumph 'normally'. Lenin showed that
for it to do so there had to be a combination of exceptional
circumstances and Mao has done the same in explaining why the Red
Bases were able to hold out in China. The role of the revolutionary

leadership consists precisely of isolating the laws which govern
this 'exception'.

The disdain which he displays for the Maoists did not prevent
Deutscher from regarding the transition to socialism in China as one
of 'Trotsky's posthumous triumphs'. (101) But given Trotsky's firm
condemnation of Maoism as a peasant perversion of Marxism, 'to give
the impression that he would have saluted Mao's victory as a
confirmation of his prognosis, is to accord to him prophetic
triumphs at the expense of his intellectual integrity'. (102)

THE INFLUENCE OF THE TROTSKYIST INTERPRETATIONS

The Trotskyists' theses on the Chinese revolution, having been taken
up admiringly by bourgeois journalists and historians figure as
historical truths by dint of repetition. So much and so well that
no one any longer dreams of asking for proof from these zealous
propagandists who disguise an elementary and visceral anti-communism
beneath the appearance of a dubious historical erudition.

Hélène Carrère d'Encausse and Stuart Schram assure us that Stalin
'sacrificed the Chinese revolution to the security of Russia's
frontiers', (103) which is precisely the Trotskyist interpretation.
These two historians are not content to analyse verifiable facts but
indulge in a strange psychoanalysis of Stalin, imputing to him
hidden motives and counter-revolutionary intentions which they would
be at a loss to support with documentary proof. They elevate
intention into a method of historical investigation. They write:
(104)

> In Asia, the policy adopted by Moscow beginning in 1947 was a
> policy of armed uprising by the workers and peasants, directed
> not only against the colonial powers, but also against the local
> bourgeoisie. Such a line, by which the Communist Parties and the
> numerically small groups under their influence cut themselves off
> from the struggles of the Asian peoples for their independence,
> could only lead to failure. It thus had the great advantage for
> Stalin of allowing him to be revolutionary and intransigent in
> words, without running any great risks of fostering a situation
> in Asia that might disturb his own tranquillity.

The authors go in for speculative psychology while presenting a
simplistic version of history. The Telengana uprising, for example,
was not by any means aimed at the Indian bourgeoisie but at a caste
of landlords.

It will have been noticed that they affect to criticise Stalin
from the point of view of the interests of the world revolution.
Coming from them, such an argument might arouse ironic reactions,
but it is cunning. An instigator of revolution, Stalin is at the
same time a counter-revolutionary. Whatever he does he is wrong.
If he gives 'counsels of prudence' he is accused of trying 'to halt'
the revolution. (105) If he calls for an uprising he is sending
communists to their deaths. If he says nothing he is indifferent to
the movement. Nothing could invalidate this 'hermeneutic reading'
of history in which the 'a priori' interpretation not only assigns a
meaning to certain facts but produces that of others (Stalin's
motives). We owe it to ourselves, however, to call attention to

this strange method which a little later leads the authors to accuse
the Chinese of racism because they condemned the American intervention in the Lebanon in 1958. (106)

When such eminent specialists write this kind of history we are
tempted to be indulgent towards the thoughtlessness of certain
Trotskyite theoreticians who, confident in their prefabricated
schemata, easily give way to the temptation to write 'de omni re
scibili'. We extract a passage from an article by Pierre Naville
(who has also devoted a whole book to China) which might have been
written especially for us: (107)

> Until 1945, Chiang Kai-shek operated from his bases in Yunan
> (Chungking) ... Mao and the Communists restricted themselves to
> protecting the shifting frontiers of their north-western bases.
> Their material weaknesses made major offensive operations against
> Manchuria and Peking impossible ... On the other hand, the USSR
> needed the neutrality of Japan to hold the Western Front against
> Germany; Mao was dissuaded from anything which might unleash
> operations which would have brought the Japanese forces as far as
> Lake Baïkal.

Such a text presents us with an 'embarras de richesses', as Marx
said. Chungking is the capital of Szechwan and not of Yunan. Mao
and the Communists did not restrict themselves to protecting the
frontiers of their bases in the north-west. They liberated vast
regions with a population of 86 million. At the end of the war, the
Japanese in northern China controlled only the towns and the main
lines of communication. Communist armies numbering 900,000 men were
operating in their rear and inflicting considerable losses. Lastly,
thanks to Sorge, the famous spy, the USSR knew from the beginning of
the war that it had nothing to fear from Japan whose hands were kept
full by the Chinese communists and who were confronting a formidable
enemy in the Pacific. The automatism which sees Stalin's hand
everywhere sacrificing the revolution to the security of the USSR
here appears as a real tic. For a less prejudiced mind the Japanese
would have been all the less inclined to open a new front in Siberia
in that their rear would be all the more under attack from the
Chinese communists, but the Trotskyists have reasons that reason does
not know. And why did Stalin need to dissuade Mao from an enterprise for which he did not have sufficient strength? Naville would
find it very difficult to provide the slightest indication (not to
speak of proof) to support his assertion that the USSR 'dissuaded
Mao' from launching an offensive. It is not a known fact but a
deduced 'fact'. Stalin must have acted so to conform to Naville's
idea of him. We can apply to Naville, as to all Trotskyists,
Voltaire's ironic addition to Pico della Mirandola's motto: 'de omni
re scibili, et quibusdam aliis.' They can hold forth on all things
that are knowable and several others besides.

When composing the first version of this work, we thought that it
was superfluous to comment, even ironically, on Dominique Desanti's
'L'Internationale communiste' (Payot, 1970). We thought that
enlightened critics would speedily expose this collection of
contrived anecdotes drawn from who knows where. Wrong! Supposedly
serious journals have spoken well of it and experience proves, alas,
that pretentious ignorance can deceive, especially if it is helped
by a lively pen and cunning advertising.

Mme Desanti's anti-Stalinist passion plus her dislike of patient historical investigation have made her a willing dupe of the Trotskyist schemas. Without wishing to harp on her ignorance it does not take us too far out of our way to present a few of the finest pearls curiously passed over in silence by the specialist scholars of the bourgeois press.

Our Clio does not perhaps take Piraeus for a man like La Fontaine's ape, but she does take Wuhan for a province (p. 149) and the Fourth of May Movement (1919) for an organisation. The latter is supposed to have controlled a journal called 'New Youth', 'created', it seems, on the same day (p. 133). Actually this journal had appeared since 1915 and had contributed to the penetration of revolutionary ideas among the student youth whose anti-imperialist demonstrations launched what has been called the 'Fourth of May Movement', analogous in certain respects to the movement of May-June 1968.

Further on Mme Desanti tells us that 'as early as 1919, the Chinese emigrés in France ... had formed a Communist Party ... Chou En-lai and Chu Teh were among the founders of the Party in exile.' (p. 134) The truth is a little different. The 'Chinese Socialist Youth Group' was constituted in Paris in 1921. In the following year it became the 'French branch of the Chinese Communist Party'. As for Chu Teh, he joined the CCP in Berlin in 1922. He was not a founder-member.

According to Mme Desanti, 'Li Tao-chao' (sic) was 'strangled by a brigand leader the Kuomintang was not to disown' (pp. 134-44). In fact, Li Ta-chao was arrested in the Soviet embassy in Peking after a search ordered by Marshall Chang Tso-lin, the master of Manchuria since 1911 and in 1927 of Peking. The Marshall was by no means dependent on the Kuomintang and was more of a statesman than a brigand leader.

These are, so to speak, disinterested mistakes. There are others which are less innocent. The latter show the influence of the Trotskyists, the main purveyors of anti-Stalinist slanders for forty-five years. Mme Desanti writes, for example: 'At the 7th Plenum of the Communist International, T'an P'ing-shan, the instigator of the Chinese agrarian revolts, proposed that the Chinese Party should continue to support the insurrectionary peasants. A telegram from Stalin decided the opposite' (p. 150). It is strange that Stalin should telegraph from Moscow to a Plenum which was meeting in Moscow and in which he took part! Anyway, not only was T'an P'ing-shan a notorious rightist, not the 'instigator of the agrarian revolts' but as Wang Ching-wei's Minister of Agriculture he intervened after the bloody incident at Changsha on 21 May 1927 to dissuade the peasant militia from responding. Mme Desanti summarises a point from Trotsky's intervention before the 8th Plenum of the Executive Committee of the Communist International in the following terms: 'The Chinese Communist Party should be made to leave the Kuomintang immediately! What can one hope for from Chiang?' (p. 151). If our historian had taken the trouble to read Trotsky's speech, she would have seen that he denied having called for the withdrawal of the communists from the Kuomintang (cf. Chapter 5, above, and n. 41 in that Chapter). 'One must have a good memory after one has lied' (Corneille). Let down by hers, Mme

Desanti muddles up her chronology. At the end of May 1927, there
could have been no question of an alliance except with the left
Kuomintang which was hostile to Chiang.   \

Although Mme Desanti faithfully echoes Trotsky's falsifications,
we cannot deny her a certain originality, for she ornaments them
with blunders of her own making. Consider this one for example:
(p. 156)

> The International which, through Neumann, Stalin's special envoy,
> had unleashed the (Canton) insurrection against the advice of the
> Chinese communists, then made the Chinese responsible for the
> insurrection. Ch'en Tu-hsiu, the Chairman of the Party, served
> as a scapegoat. When he defended himself he was expelled.

Not only can our author not provide the least indication that the
Canton insurrection was decided against the advice of the Chinese
communists (we defy her to), but she is also grossly mistaken about
the facts. Ch'en Tu-hsiu was not relieved of his functions as
General Secretary of the Party (he was not its chairman) and
expelled from the Central Committee after 11 December 1927, but at
the session of the Central Committee held on 7 August 1927,
therefore four months before the Canton Commune. He could not be
held responsible for its defeat and never has been.

One of the most extravagant pronouncements in Mme Desanti's book
concerns Mao. He 'elaborated a totally new action without ever
theorising it: the theory was only established after victory' (p.
156). Let us simply point out that the four volumes of the
'Selected Works', where the results of his effort at theoretical
systematisation are recorded, do not start in 1949 but come to an
end at that date!

The fact that the critics have not noticed such enormous blunders
speaks volumes for the favourable bias they have towards those who
attack Stalin.

The case which we are now going to examine must be dealt with
separately, for it concerns an honest journalist who has been all
the more easily taken in by the Trotskyist version of history since
the latter has never been seriously refuted.

According to Trotsky, 'the Central Committee of the Chinese
Communist Party only served as a mechanism fated to transmit the
instructions' of the International. (108) In 'China. The Other
Communism', K. S. Karol informs us that 'several Western historians
have tried to establish more accurately to what degree even
secondary decisions were dictated by Moscow'. (109)

The author does not seem at all suspicious that these historians
(like Trotsky) might not have been prompted solely by the love of
the truth. He himself has the merit of frankness if not of discern-
ment. He does not hide from us that, according to him, 'the most
impartial account of the part played by the Chinese affair in the
duel between the Stalinists and the Trotskyists is provided by
Deutscher ... (who) ... avoids glorifying the insight of either of
the protagonists'. (110)

Let us open 'The Prophet Unarmed' at p. 330. There we read the
following judgment of Trotsky's interventions in the polemics on
China: 'His analyses of the situation were of crystalline clarity;

his prognostications were faultless; and his warnings were like
mighty alarm-bells.'

While one of the protagonists is thus dithyrambically glorified,
correlatively the other is literally dragged in the mud in this
highly 'impartial' account, which relies, in fact, solely on
'Trotskyist sources' (Trotsky, Ch'en Tu-hsiu, Harold Isaacs),
without the slightest attempt at an historical critique.

Karol offers us a rehash of this hotch-potch of old polemics,
embellished, it is true, by an original and fairly surprising
summary of Stalin's positions. We shall refrain from discussing
this last point, for although we must take into account his
influence as a journalist, we do not have to take him seriously as a
theoretician.

Karol asserts that the Chinese falsify their own history like the
Soviet Union is supposed to have done in Stalin's time. Therefore
he enquires into the effects which de-Maoisation will inevitably
produce after Mao's death when the Chinese discover their true past.
At first sight, Karol provides many proofs of this falsification but
it is advisable to look into them more closely.

For example, he dedicates a chapter to suggesting the idea that
Ch'ü Ch'iu-pai, whom he presents as a crypto-Trotskyist, fundamentally disagreed with the Maoist strategy of the encirclement of
the towns by the countryside and that this was the reason why he did
not follow the Red Army at the time of the Long March but withdrew
to Shanghai where, side by side with Lu Hsun, he returned to a
purely cultural struggle. All this is in order to explain why the
Chinese Communist Party 'simply decided that he should be handed
down to posterity in his character of Marxist literary critic,
friend of Lu Hsun and victim of the Kuomintang'. (111) According to
Karol, the Chinese communists deliberately hide from the masses that
Ch'ü Ch'iu-pai had been a party leader and even its General
Secretary for nearly a year. They have 'officially confined him to
the literary domain'. (112)

This is entirely false. What Karol says does not correspond to
history as it is taught in China. (113) Furthermore, he who claims
to teach the truth to the Chinese is wrong with regard to Ch'ü
Ch'iu-pai's biography. To demonstrate this, we cannot do better
than to reproduce the note which is dedicated to the latter in
'Resolution on questions of party history', published as an appendix
to 'Our Study and the Current Situation' by Mao Tse-tung in the 1961
English edition of his 'Selected Works': (114)

Comrade Ch'ü Ch'iu-pai, one of the earliest members and leaders
of the Chinese Communist Party, was elected to the Central
Committee at the 3rd, 4th, 5th and 6th National Congresses of the
Party in the years 1923-8. During the First Revolutionary Civil
War he actively fought against the anti-Communist, anti-popular
'Tai Ch'i-tao doctrine' of the Kuomintang's right-wing and
against the right opportunism represented by Ch'en Tu-hsiu in the
Chinese Communist Party. After the Kuomintang's betrayal of the
revolution in 1927, he called the emergency meeting of the
Central Committee of the Party on 7 August which ended the
domination of Ch'en Tu Hsiuism in the Party. But from the winter
of 1927 to the spring of 1928, while directing the work of the
Central leading body, he committed the 'left' error of putschism.

In September 1930 he conducted the 3rd Plenary Session of the 6th Central Committee of the party, which put an end to the Li Li-san line that was harming the party. However, at the 4th Plenary Session of the 6th Central Committee in January 1931, he was attacked by the 'left' dogmatists and factionalists and was pushed out of the central leading body. From that time to 1933 he worked in the revolutionary cultural movement in Shanghai in co-operation with Lu Hsun. In 1933 he arrived in the Red base area in Kiangsi and was made Commissioner of People's Education in the Workers' and Peasants' Democratic Central Government. When the main forces of the Red Army embarked on the Long March, he was asked to stay behind in the Kiangsi base area. In March 1935 Comrade Ch'ü Ch'iu-pai was arrested by the Chiang Kai-shek gang in the Fukien guerilla area and on 18 June he died a martyr's death in Changking, Fukien Province.

We see to what extent Karol's speculations and insinuations are gratuitous – he did not take the trouble to carry out the necessary checks before imputing to the Chinese communists the decision to transform a slightly 'leftist' leader of the Chinese Communist Party into a mere literary critic.

Our journalist has written a book of 480 pages, 110 of which are on 'Their history as they (the Chinese) see it today', to which he opposes True History. We have shown his ignorance of both. The absorption of uncriticised Trotskyist schemas makes one inapt for study, as it engenders the euphoric illusion that one can do without it.

According to Karol, 'the great weakness of the Chinese system of history lies in its attachment to falsifications of the history of the workers' movement imposed by Stalin.' (115) We ask: how can those who reproduce Trotskyist falsifications be qualified to denounce Stalin's falsifications?

One point in conclusion. We have just criticised one chapter of one book of Karol's. This author is not inspired by a systematically anti-Maoist 'parti pris', as is shown by his brilliant exposition of Chinese international policy in 'Le Nouvel observateur' on 28 September 1970 and by the conclusion to his last book on Cuba. The tone of this refutation may thus seem violent.

Let us make ourselves clear: wishing to illustrate the insidious influence of Trotskyist historiography in general, we could not find a more conclusive example of the damage it does than that of a journalist whose independence of judgment and progressive attitude are beyond doubt. Deceived himself, he contributes to the deception of others. We cannot treat this as a crime of Karol's when genuine revolutionaries linked to the masses like those who publish 'Lotta Continua' convey the same falsifications in an article entitled 'La Cina venti anni doppo' (15 October 1970) in which, however, they do not hide their enthusiasm for the cultural revolution, the universal lessons of which they emphasise. Karol can consider himself in good company politically, all the more in that Jean Baby, too, adopted the Trotskyist version of history in his book on the Sino-Soviet dispute (pp. 251-2), but he had admitted his mistake in a conversation with the author of this text.

Chapter 7

THE DEFEAT OF
THE GREEK COMMUNISTS

The history of the Greek communist movement over the last thirty years shows strikingly how true it is that it is necessary to investigate the internal factors which determined the constant predominance of opportunist tendencies in the leadership rather than to fall back on the explanatory master-key - Stalin. The 'internal' Greek Communist Party no longer acknowledges the authority of the CPSU and has condemned the intervention in Czechoslovakia. It is clear that in daring to preach the peaceful road to socialism and opposing armed struggle, putting it off until that blue moon, the 'last resort', as if the hour of the last resort had not struck long ago, Mr Theodorakis has no need to receive orders from the Kremlin or to come under its influence to be an opportunist.

The following text consists of selections from a work in preparation on Greece. We begin with the British intervention in 1944.

THE GREEK COMMUNISTS IN THE RESISTANCE

In three years (1941-5) the Greek communists, already few in number, hunted and exterminated before the war by the fascist Metaxas regime, had successfully established a formidable military force (the ELAS) and liberated large areas. When the occupying forces withdrew from the country power lay within their reach. They did not seize it. Intimidated by the power of Britain, anxious to avoid a trial of strength, deluded about the democratic professions of faith of the English, and aware of the immense popularity of the 'National Liberation Front' (EAM) which they led, they hoped to accede to power by the 'normal' wide and level road and to economise on the 'Long March' via the precipitous maths of protracted war; the wide road led them to the precipice. That is why they signed the Lebanon agreement, the terms of which gave some EAM personalities unimportant portfolios in the Papandreou cabinet, and the Caserta agreement which made the British General Scobie commander-in-chief of the Resistance forces!

THE BRITISH INTERVENTION IN 1944

The communists knew - or should have known - that on the day of
liberation the English would turn against the Greek people to
enforce on that people an 'order' consistent with their interests.
They would then become the principal enemy of these over-protective
allies. On 22 September 1943, Aris Velouchiotis, a member of the
ruling triumvirate of ELAS, wrote a letter to the Political Bureau
of the Communist Party about the British plans:

> If they win, they will impose a fascist regime under another name
> ... At the moment, after the loss of Italy and the course of
> operations in the Soviet Union, they are sure the Germans will
> leave Greece themselves: therefore, if they land here it will be
> against us.

Aris, who had seen the agents from London at work, had correctly
appraised their aims. He was unaware, however, of Churchill's
telegram to General Ismey in September 1943 in which it was said:
'Should the Germans evacuate Greece we must certainly be able to
send 5,000 British troops with armoured cars into Athens', because,
we read in the British leader's 'History', 'the chances of a German
evacuation of the Balkans increased, and with them the possibilities
of a return of the Royal Government, with British support'. (1) On
6 August 1944, Churchill wrote to Eden: 'Either we support
Papandreou, if necessary with force, as we have agreed, or we
disinterest ourselves utterly in Greece'. (2) In his 'History', he
notes, also in August: (3)

> I had asked the Chief of the Imperial General Staff to work out
> the details of a British expedition to Greece in case the Germans
> there collapsed ... It is most desirable to strike out of the
> blue ... to forestall the EAM ... The tardy German withdrawal
> from Athens enabled us however to consolidate the direction of
> Greek affairs on the eve of the decision stroke. I was glad that
> the Greek Government was now at hand in Italy.

Now communists participated in what Churchill himself presented as a
puppet government! They were not unaware, however, of the secret
negotiations between the New Zealand lieutenant, Don Stott, and the
German occupation authorities. They knew that, in fact, many
collaborators were agents of the Intelligence Service and were
slaughtering members of the Resistance with its blessing. After an
operation one of them wrote in his report: 'Our losses - one
German!' As a reward he was appointed deputy commander of the
Athens Cadet School by General Scobie.

A superabundance of documentation makes it possible to accuse the
British Middle East Headquarters of complicity with the enemy in the
interests of preparations to crush the Greek Resistance.

In order to intervene in Greece, Churchill got the go-ahead from
the USA. Roosevelt wrote to him: (4)

> I have no objection to your making preparations to have in
> readiness a sufficient British force to preserve order in Greece
> when the Germans evacuate the country. There is also no
> objection to the use by General Wilson of American transport
> planes that are available to him at that time and that can be
> spared from his other operations.

The British troops landed in Greece only with extreme care as they

did not want to clash with the Germans. There was an interval of
several days between the arrival of the ones and the departure of
the others, in which, despite the proclaimed apprehension of the
Anglo-Saxon leaders, there was no disorder to deplore other than the
fact that, for once, the people were their own masters. If we are
to believe Churchill, there was a 'vacuum' which had to be filled as
fast as possible, since imperialism abhors a vacuum. The first
British troops did not exceed 6,000 men and ELAS, which had 50,000
in its regular army and 100,000 in the people's militia
('politophilaki') could have surrounded these belated 'liberators'
and sent them packing as Tito did. There was nothing in the balance
of forces which compelled EAM-ELAS, which had taken power in
October, to hand it over to the British and the puppet Papandreou.
The latter conceded this himself with astonishment. At the trial of
the Security Batallions (the puppet army raised by the Germans to
fight the Resistance) another enemy of EAM-ELAS, Pyromaglou (second
in command to Zervas, leader of the EDES maquis which was financed
by the British) declared: 'I am certain of this, that EAM could have
seized power three days after the Liberation but, however, failed to
do so'. Let us add that when its 'allies' entered Athens on 14
October, it even encouraged the people to give them an enthusiastic
welcome instead of explaining to them why they had come with tanks
and cannons and what enemy these arms were directed against. (5)

> When we see the other fellow holding something in his hand, we
> should do some investigating. What does he hold in his hand?
> Swords. What are swords made for? For killing. Whom does he
> want to kill with his swords? The people. Having made these
> findings, investigate further - the Chinese people too have hands
> and can take up swords, they can forge a sword if there is none
> handy ... Some of us neglect such investigation and study. Ch'en
> Tu-hsiu, for example, did not understand that with swords one can
> kill people. Some say that this is a plain, everyday truth; how
> can a leader of the Communist Party fail to know it? But you can
> never tell.

The Greek left paid with rivers of blood for its ignorance of this
'plain, everyday truth'.

Under the guise of a sham friendliness the new occupying forces
methodically forged the links which were to bring the Greek people
back under foreign tutelage. The English officers in charge of the
camps in which the men from the Security Batallions were interned
allowed them to keep their arms and instructed them in handling
modern weapons, foreseeing their use against ELAS. The latter, who
had captured them in bitter fighting, handed them over to the
custody of the English military attachés when the latter demanded.
The collaborators were not harrassed. Those who had assumed high
responsibilities were lodged comfortably in the Averoff prison - to
safeguard them from any acts of vengeance by their victims pending
better days. The police and the gendarmerie, guilty of so many
crimes, were left untouched. On the other hand, Papandreou and his
bosses were in haste to disarm ELAS. This was a difficult and risky
enterprise which required considerable reinforcement of the British
expeditionary force and therefore certain delays.

On 7 November Churchill wrote to Eden: (6)

Having paid the price we have to Russia for freedom of action in

Greece, we should not hesitate to use British troops to support
the Royal Hellenic Government under M. Papandreou ... This
implies that British troops should certainly intervene to check
acts of lawlessness. Surely M. Papandreou can close down EAM
newspapers if they call a newspaper strike (?) ... I hope that
the Greek Brigade will arrive soon, and will not hesitate to
shoot when necessary ... we need another eight or ten thousand
foot-soldiers to hold the capital and Salonika ... I fully expect
a clash with EAM and we must not shrink from it, provided the
ground is well-chosen.

The brigade Churchill refers to was composed of the soldiers and
officers with proved Royalist convictions, the remnants left by the
terrible purge carried out by the 'X'ite General Ventiris of the
Greek Army of the Middle East. (7) This brigade was thus a
veritable Praetorian Guard and in the circumstances its despatch to
Greece constituted a definite provocation. The passage from
Churchill we have just quoted leaves no room for doubt about this.

The brigade arrived on 10 November. On 13 November, Papandreou
summoned Othoneos (commander-in-chief of the future Greek Army) to
General Scobie's office. Scobie presumed to dictate to Othoneos his
choice of staff officers. He was particularly opposed to Saraphis
becoming chief and wanted to impose Ventiris. Othoneos denied that
Scobie had any right to involve himself in the organisation and
command of the Greek Army. After a series of more or less acid
exchanges, Papandreou forced him to resign, not bothering to consult
his Ministers.

It was the first clear sign that the British did not want the
peaceful integration of ELAS into the National Army, but its
elimination pure and simple. They were actively preparing for a
trial of strength and now moved the traitors of the Security
Batallions to Italy where they were immediately integrated into
units of the Mountain Brigade and returned to Greece in this
disguise!

After the defeat of Othoneos who had been appointed unanimously
by the Council of Ministers and dismissed under British pressure, on
27 November EAM submitted a plan to Papandreou recommending the
mobilisation of a corp of the National Army comprising the Mountain
Brigade, 'the Holy Column' (a unit composed of Royalist officers),
units of EDES and a Brigade from ELAS equal in strength and arms to
the other forces combined. Papandreou found this 'reasonable' and
gave his consent; but on the following day he published a text which
totally falsified this part of the agreement. EAM then made a last
attempt to find a solution. A proposal was made to the Council of
Ministers that ELAS, EDES and the Mountain Brigade should be
simultaneously dissolved. Papandreou refused and began to make
threats, declaring, 'I hope that the CPG will not push the country
into civil war'. According to his own memoirs the break with EAM
dates from that day. By rejecting out of hand all the plans which
the left put to him he made the confrontation inevitable, in
accordance with the orders which he was receiving from Ambassador
Sir Reginald Leeper and General Scobie. The latter issued a
proclamation notifying ELAS of an order to dissolve itself before 10
December; as a result the EAM Ministers resigned. On 2 December
Papandreou, who was no longer the head of a national unity

government and drew his authority only from the confidence of a
perjured king and the support of foreign troops, repeated Scobie's
proclamation on his own account and ordered the people's militia to
surrender their arms to the police of the fascists and traitors. As
the EAM newspaper pointed out, to have given in to this order would
have meant surrendering the people to their executioners. On 3
November EAM called a successful general strike. An enormous
(authorised) demonstration proceeded through the streets. Just as
the crowd was approaching the Tomb of the Unknown Warrior the police
opened fire, (8) killing twenty-eight people and wounding more than
100. (9)

> According to the declarations made by the journalist Liland Stow
> on New York Radio, the American journalist F. Fontor, a corres-
> pondent of the 'Chicago Sun', had tried twice some weeks earlier
> to alert world public opinion about what was being concocted. He
> asserted that the extreme right would try to provoke a bloody
> clash which would enable Scobie to declare martial law. British
> censorship twice prevented him from sending this warning to his
> newspaper.

On the following day several hundred thousand citizens attended the
funerals of those killed. On the return route members of the 'X'
organisation of sinister memory fired on the demonstrators creating
new victims. The calm displayed by the crowd in the face of such
provocations did not deter Scobie from declaring martial law on the
same day, 4 December, or from calling on ELAS to withdraw from
Athens within forty-eight hours. Then began the trial of strength
which Churchill had long awaited. The people's militia and small
units of ELAS attacked police stations and the den of the 'X'
organisation. The members of the latter were rescued 'in extremis'
thanks to the intervention of British tanks. In the evening
Papandreou resigned. Scobie approached Sophoulis and EAM hastily
declared that it would support a government formed by the liberal
leader. This proves that, until the last minute, the left clung to
the slightest chance of a peaceful settlement. Nevertheless,
Sophoulis declined and Leeper persuaded Papandreou to withdraw his
resignation.

On 5 December at four o'clock in the morning, Churchill
telegraphed to Scobie: (10)

> You may make any regulations you like for the strict control of
> the streets or for the rounding up of any number of truculent
> persons. Naturally ELAS will try to put women and children in
> the van where shooting may occur. You must be clever about this
> and avoid mistakes. But do not hesitate to fire at any armed
> male in Athens who assails the British authority or Greek
> authority with which we are working. It would be well of course
> if your command were reinforced by the authority of some Greek
> Government, and Papandreou is being told by Leeper to stop and
> help. Do not however hesitate to act as if you were in a
> conquered city where a local rebellion is in progress.

The English had 35,000 men at their disposal and faced 8,000 ELAS
men supported by the people's militia armed with old rifles. Most
of the ELAS troops were in the north of Greece and were not to
intervene in the conflict. Its military leaders, Aris Velouchiotis
and Saraphis, received the order to attack the EDES army (at

Epiras), which they destroyed in a few days. However, the decisive
battle took place in the Athens-Piraeus built-up area. In his book
Saraphis says that as the lines of communication were destroyed the
ELAS troops could not get to Athens in time. This explanation is
hardly sufficient. In fact, the EAM leadership, forced to fight,
had by no means decided to carry the struggle through to the end.
On 8, 10, 14 and 18 December it made very conciliatory overtures of
peace to Scobie, which met with demands for surrender pure and
simple. Referring to these peace offers, Churchill telegraphed to
Scobie, 'The clear objective is the defeat of EAM. The ending of
the fighting is subsidiary to this'. At this time, however, ELAS
gained the advantage, driving the British back into a narrow area
comprising the vicinity of Syntagma Square and the 'high-class'
Colonaki district.

On 11 December Field-marshal Alexander landed at Helleniko
Airport, accompanied by Macmillan, Eden's right-hand man. He
telegraphed to Churchill that to him a negotiated settlement
appeared to be indispensable. In reply, he received the order to
summon reinforcements from Italy. At the very moment that the
Ardennes counter-offensive meant that the Anglo-Saxons were losing
thousands of prisoners and considerable equipment; that Brussels and
perhaps Antwerp were threatened, 1,650 transport planes (mostly
American) landed two new British divisions and several colonial
infantry units near Athens.

Churchill wrote: (11)

We were engaged in house-to-house combat with an enemy of whom at
least four-fifths were in plain clothes ... Alexander ... asked
for stern measures against the rebels and permission to bomb
areas inside Athens. On 12 December the War Cabinet gave
Alexander a free hand in all military measures. The fourth
British Division's arrival ... turned the scale.

This optimism was premature and in fact further on we read: (12)

Field-marshal Alexander to Prime Minister 15th December 1944

I fear if rebel resistance continues at the same intensity as
at present I shall have to send further large reinforcements from
the Italian front to make sure of clearing the whole of Piraeus-
Athens.

Prime Minister to Field-marshal Alexander 17th December 1944

The ELAS towards the centre of Athens seems to me a very
serious feature, and I should like your appreciation of whether,
with the reinforcements now arriving, we are likely to hold our
own in the centre of the city and defeat the enemy. Have you any
other reinforcements in view besides the Fourth Division, the
Tank Regiment, and the two remaining brigades of the Forty-Sixth
Division? Is there now any danger of a mass surrender of British
troops cooped up in the city of Athens?

Field-marshal Alexander to Prime Minister 21st December 1944

I estimate that it will be possible to clear the Athens-
Piraeus area and thereafter to hold it securely, but this will
not defeat ELAS and force them to surrender. We are not strong
enough to go beyond this ... During the German occupation they
maintained between six and seven divisions on the mainland, in
addition to the equivalent of four in the Greek islands. Even so
they were unable to keep their communications open all the time,

and I doubt if we will meet less strength and determination than
they encountered.
On 24 December Churchill flew to Athens, making his entry in an
armoured car. He appointed Archbishop Damaskinos Regent and to
ingratiate himself with public opinion he organised a round-table
conference to which representatives of EAM were invited. The latter
agreed to negotiate on an equal footing with politicians among whom
some were old collaborators, while others were totally unaware of
the new Greek realities, e.g. General Plastiras, whom the English
had just brought over from the Côte d'Azur to be Prime Minister.
While not making the withdrawal of the foreign forces a preliminary
demand, EAM's proposals signified in substance a sharing of power
between the left and right. They were rejected without discussion
by the allies of the British and the fighting continued.

Once more, EAM mistakenly believed that it could win a political
victory without throwing all its forces into the military battle.
Its fighters faced the British airforce, armoured cars and artillery
with nothing but light arms. They won some initial successes but
dispersed their efforts and did not exploit their advantage to the
utmost so as to leave the British insufficient time to recover and
bring in reinforcements. Their struggle by no means slackened,
however. They even succeeded in capturing the HQ of the RAF, taking
nearly 600 prisoners. They began to get over their initial lack of
experience in street fighting and devised suitable tactics to
neutralise the enemy's superiority in war material. This was the
moment that EAM-ELAS chose to give the order to evacuate Athens.

ELAS withdrew from Athens on the night of 4/5 January. An
armistice ensued on 15 January. After ten days of negotiations EAM-
ELAS signed the Varkiza agreement on 12 February, under the terms of
which it surrendered its arms. In return it did not get any serious
guarantees safeguarding democratic freedoms. This was an
unprincipled surrender. It handed the Greek patriots over bound and
gagged to the revenge of the fascist trash who, mouthing nothing but
words like 'nation' and 'country' had sold out their country ten
times over. The army which the people built with their blood was
dismantled.

Such an outcome was in no way imposed by the balance of forces,
as can be seen if one considers the following facts:
- With the war continuing in Europe and the Middle East, the
English were only able to divert limited resources to subjugate
Greece.
- The forces which ELAS conserved intact in the provinces were of
such importance that Field-marshal Alexander did not think that it
was possible to guarantee the control of the country.
- The Soviet Union and communists throughout the world were still
the allies of the Western powers. The propaganda campaign to
prepare public opinion for an anti-communist crusade had not yet
been launched. Thus the British intervention was denounced by the
world press. Even in England it was condemned by an enormous
majority at the Trades Union Conference. The MP Strindberg declared
in the House of Commons: 'We are not confronted by a civil war ...
the great majority of the Greek people are on one side and a few
Quislings and Royalists supported by British bayonets are on the
other.'

Roosevelt had to warn Churchill that 'public opinion did not allow him to take (his) side completely in the present conjuncture in Greece'. His Foreign Secretary, Stettinius, went further and made a statement calling for a policy of hands off. In fact, the USA both openly and secretly opposed the re-establishment of the old established powers' colonial or semi-colonial reserves, intending to take their place.

The isolation of the British imperialists who were 'right too soon' did not mean that it was possible to throw them into the sea immediately. One of the weaknesses of the Greek communists was that they never conceived their tasks in the struggle as inscribed in the framework of a protracted war. Another and even more fundamental mistake was their serious underestimation of the power of the people and overestimation of the reactionaries. Lastly, they did not understand that by losing the army the people lost everything.

At its 8th Congress the Communist Party criticised the mistakes made in the Resistance and post-war periods. This critique unilaterally stressed the 'left-wing' mistakes and quickly passed over the right-wing opportunist mistakes. This led Zissis Zographos, a member of the Politbureau, to speak of the December 'defeat' which had 'forced' the EAM and the Communist Party to sign the Varkiza agreement. (13)

THE DAYS AFTER VARKIZA

The British intervention was a warning shot to the Resistance movements in Western Europe. (14) After the Germans' departure they would have to stand aside for new representatives of the powers of money to take over and for order to be re-established. An order which was already being described as pregnant with a Third World War after having given birth to the First and the Second.

The partisans in France and Italy surrendered their arms. In return the PCF was given some posts in the government from which it was ejected by the 'socialist' Ramadier on 4 May 1947, when the reaction no longer needed 'communist' Ministers to keep the social peace, put France back to work and warn of the unleashing of the Indo-China War.

In Greece, Aris Velouchiotis, who had warned his party against the firm intention of the British to eliminate EAM-ELAS, tried to maintain the people's army, for 'without the people's army, the people has nothing' (Mao). Expelled from his party and abandoned by all, he wandered from mountain to mountain for some time and finally fell in an obscure skirmish. According to testimony gathered by Dominique Eudes ('The Kapetanios'), Aris was 'betrayed' by the Communist Party leaders.

Having surrendered their arms, the left forces and in particular the CPG believed - not without some naïvité - that in return they would be granted (as the Varkiza agreement stipulated) the democratic rights for which the British government shows so much respect at home. The communists even went so far as to envisage seriously the possibility of a peaceful transition to a people's democracy and socialism.

An article in 'Revue communiste' by Yanni Zevgou in August 1945

anticipated Khrushchev's argument at the 20th Congress: thus it was
reproduced in the April-May 1966 issue of the EDA paper, 'The Greek
Left'. The author - a member of the CPG leadership - attributed a
prodigious efficacy to the example of the Soviet Union which, he
said, attracted peoples like an 'enormous magnet'. He maintained
that decisive changes had occurred in the balance of forces both
internally and at the international level, without explaining,
however - and for good reason! - how these changes should prevent
the anti-communists from resorting to violence in Greece, as they
were doing at that very moment. He spoke of the 'democratic,
evolutionary road to socialism' and recalled that the Bolshevik
Party took power in Russia 'when it had won a majority in the All-
Russian Congress of Soviets ... that is, a majority of the Russian
people'. Winning the majority was also the objective he set for his
party, whose current slogan he quoted in conclusion: 'Unity -
Order - Calm - Labour - Reconstruction - Culture'.

Zevgou's article ignores both Marxist-Leninist principles and the
Greek realities of that time.

On 5 June the leaders of the Centre Parties, Souphoulis (Prime
Minister), Kaphandaris, Tsuderos (the old Prime Minister in the
Royal Government at Cairo) and Plastiras (the temporary successor
whom the British had provided for Papandreou), signed a note
containing the following statements: (15)

The terror established throughout the country after the December
events by the extreme-right is increasing daily. The way in
which it has developed and spread has made the life of non-
Royalist citizens impossible and excludes even the idea that we
can proceed to a free plebiscite or elections. Right-wing
terrorist organisations the main one of which were partly armed
by the Germans and collaborated with them in every way were not
only neither disarmed nor prosecuted but even rallied openly to
the agents of order with the intention of completely stifling all
democratic thought.

When we recall that the men in the Security Batallions were enrolled
in the 'National Guard' (the future Greek Army) and the officers of
which were chosen by a British military commission, it is not so
surprising that the 'agents of order' should take such an attitude.
As for the police and the gendarmerie, they remained what they had
been under Metaxas and the occupation.

Another demonstration of the CPG's opportunism is the resolution
passed by the 12th Plenum of the Central Committee in June 1945.
The text called for 'the immediate intervention of our three great
friends' to impose the application of the Yalta agreements in
Greece. To be sure, the latter provided for the eradication of
fascism, the punishment of collaborators and guaranteed a democratic
development of the liberated countries; but was it necessary to
raise to the rank of a friend of the Greek people those whose planes
had strafed districts of Athens and whose troops were subjecting
this people to a second occupation in order to guarantee the power
of its exploiters?

At the same meeting of the Central Committee Zachariades declared
that Greece 'had to move between the European-Balkan pole centred on
Russia and the Mediterranean pole centred on England ... by
maintaining a sort of equilibrium between the two'. By proposing

this balancing policy Zachariades sought to be 'realistic', but was premature Nasserism compatible with the perspective of an imminent transition to socialism which was his at this time? This curious mixture of right and left opportunism is a characteristic of a low-level empiricism. We can now understand why the party slogan quoted by Zevgou referred to everything except the departure of the British. On this question and on the elections, the preparations for which took place in a climate of terror, the CPG shed its illusions only gradually. The facts led it more and more to denounce the British occupation and the fascist terror.

This explains the fact that when Partsalidas, one of the principal leaders of the party, insisted on the peaceful transition to socialism at the 7th Congress in October 1945, Zachariades emphasised that it was simply a possibility, and one which was moreover getting less each day. This position was hardly any less opportunist, given the circumstances at this time.

'During the year which followed the signing of the Varkiza agreement there were ... 1,289 dead, 6,671 wounded, 75,000 arrests, 6,567 cases of robbery, 572 attacks on printing houses; also more than 100,000 democrats were subjected to different repressive measures'. (16)

Besides the terror of the fascist gangs encouraged by the 'forces of order', there was also official persecution. The Varkiza agreement stipulated the granting of an amnesty for 'political crimes' committed between 3 December 1944 and 12 February 1945. On the other hand, there was nothing to stop the authorities from prosecuting communists or sympathisers for acts of Resistance, for example, the murder of German soldiers, or else for so-called crimes in common law. (17)

In December 1945, Rentis, the Minister of Justice, declared: 'There are 48,956 individuals being prosecuted as members of EAM-ELAS. We estimate that the total number of persons charged in all, including those already detained, exceeds 80,000.' (18)

These were the conditions in which the campaign for the elections, imposed by the British, opened on 31 March 1946. In his first speech Sophoulis, the Prime Minister and leader of the Liberal Party, declared: 'I have to admit that the conditions necessary for free elections do not exist. The information reaching me from all the regions of Greece proves that only the Monarchist candidates can move about in real safety.' (19)

The Communist Party and a small Centre Party boycotted the elections. Only 49 per cent of those who were eligible participated in the poll and the Royalist Party won it with 611,000 votes in a population of more than 7 million. The winners later claimed that the abstentions had not exceeded 15 per cent of the registered voters!

After their victory the Royalists surmised that they no longer needed to hamper themselves with democratic forms and further increased the persecution of worker militants. Hence they lost no time in hunting down the elected leadership of the Greek trades-union federation (20) and replacing it by 'yellow' unionists led by Makris, who had been appointed to the same post by Metaxas. The fact that he still had it under the Colonels speaks volumes about the confidence he inspires in employers. Paradoxically the communists, who abstained at the elections, did not boycott the plebiscite of 1 September 1946 which restored King George II to the throne. However this vote took place amidst tenfold terror and it was also rigged: '500,000 Democrats were not registered on the electoral lists, while the Royalists were able to vote two or three times.' (21)

However, the picture which we have just painted must be nuanced by insisting on the fact that the military or the right did not impose their dictatorship in this period. A minimum of democracy did allow the classes and fractions of classes in the power bloc to express themselves and to compete freely. While the Royalists had an absolute majority in the House, the King imposed a broad coalition government with the Liberals. The terror only struck the rank-and-file militant, above all in the countryside. In the towns the press was free. This curious situation was made possible by the fact that the communists were to a certain extent cut off from the petty bourgeoisie, which gave a certain assurance to the bourgeois power.

After criticising the CPG call for abstention, Zissis Zographos says in the article which we have already quoted:

The only correct policy in this period would have been to participate in the elections ... in order to realise these principal slogans: 'English instigators of civil war - Out!' 'Normal democratic development!' ... There was then a possibility of this policy winning (as it had the support of the vast majority of the Greek people and the balance of forces on the international level and in the Balkans was favourable).

In reality this 'possibility' did not exist. The repression and terrorism unleashed by the reaction showed that the latter was in no way predisposed to make way for the democratic forces, even in the unlikely event (in view of the absence of freedom) of their victory in the elections. The 'balance of forces in the international level and in the Balkans', favourable or not, did not seem to have any influence whatever on the determination of the government and the fascist gangs to eliminate the left militants.

Nevertheless, the fact remains that the CPG should have participated in the election campaign all the same, at least in the towns, without however fostering illusions about the possibility of liberating the people by the parliamentary and peaceful road but in order to make propaganda, to demonstrate its strength (in the towns), to prove its good intentions, and in this way to attribute responsibility for the civil war to the reaction and to win over waverers. (22)

For a better appraisal of the CPG's policy a comparison with the Chinese Communist Party's line in the same period is instructive, despite the differences in the situations confronting the two parties. The Chinese experience, like that of the Russian revolution, does indeed contain certain lessons of universal validity.

At the beginning of 1946 during discussions with the Chinese Communist Party, the Kuomintang representatives made the following modest proposition: 'Hand over your troops and we will give you freedom'. In contrast to the Greek communists at Varkiza, the Chinese refused, for they had noticed that the bourgeois democratic

parties in the regions controlled by the Kuomintang did not enjoy
any freedom although they had no army, or rather because they did
not have one.

After Japan's surrender on 14 August 1945, the Chinese people
hoped for peace so the CP had put all its efforts into avoiding a
civil war. To this end it signed several agreements in which it
made costly concessions to Chiang Kai-shek. Chiang was seen by
everyone to assume the responsibility for unleashing the civil war
when he violated these agreements and attacked the liberated areas.
While they spoke out against the war, the communists were not under
any illusions about the possibility of averting it indefinitely. In
'The Situation and our Policy', Mao posed only the question: 'Is it
possible ... to localise the civil war or delay the outbreak of a
country-wide civil war?' (23)

He answered in the affirmative and the principal reason he gave
was the presence of 1 million soldiers and more than 2 million men
in the people's militia in the liberated areas.

Nevertheless, he concluded with these words:

Chiang Kai-shek wants to launch a country-wide civil war and his
policy is set; we must be prepared for this. No matter when this
country-wide civil war breaks out, we must be well prepared. If
it comes early, say tomorrow morning, we should also be prepared.

In the same speech, there is a phrase which could be said to be
aimed at the Greek communists in 1944-5: 'We must be clear-headed,
that is, we must not believe in the "nice words" of the imperialists
nor be intimidated by their bluster.' (24)

THE CIVIL WAR

From 1945 self-defence groups were formed to checkmate the
operations of the fascist gangs. On the other hand, hundreds of
militants fleeing political repression hid in the mountains. In the
face of the terrorist frenzy of the right it became a question of
life or death to defend oneself, to give tit for tat.

As Bossuet said: 'What a judicious foresight could not put into
men's minds, a more imperious mistress, I mean experience, has
forced them to believe.' In February 1946, the Central Committee
decided to orient the party towards preparations for armed struggle
to counter 'the unilateral civil war' unleashed by the reaction.
This decision was not followed by any concrete measures and the
'Organisation Conference' held on 16/17 April 1946 'assigned tasks
to party members which had nothing to do with the armed struggle'.
(25) This was a consequence of the communist leaders' wavering
attitude during this period.

They could not participate freely in legal political life; they
did not dare to commit themselves decisively to the armed struggle.
Thus they lost fifteen valuable months without devoting the bulk of
their efforts to preparation for it. Instead, they tried to sit
between two stools, with the inevitable result.

Zographos lists a series of mistakes committed by the leadership
at this time: (26)

- as a consequence of the absence of political, ideological, and
organisational preparation, only a portion - and by no means the

majority - of the party joined the struggle. As secret organisations had not been set up, the party apparatus in the towns was disrupted at the end of 1947 when a wave of arrests followed its outlawing.

- 'The Party leadership did not bother at all to maintain and send in due time the ELAS military cadres into the armed detachments.' From the summer of 1946, hundreds of them - including Saraphis and Bakirdzis - were deported to the islands.

- No political work was undertaken in the army, whereas the situation there was 'very favourable to the popular movement' in 1946.

- The absence for a fairly long time of a military body responsible for leading the armed struggle led to 'the absence of a strategic plan'. 'The detachments which were formed from the spring of 1946 themselves decided what forces they would line up. Thus in 1947 a number among them refused to accept volunteers into their ranks thereby obliging them to return to their villages, where they were unable to avoid arrest'.

Zographos's conclusion is that, strategically speaking, 'The Democratic Army's defeat was ... inevitable'. It is not clear, however, whether he claims that this 'inevitability' was a result of the mistakes which he has identified. Whatever the case, he passed over in silence those which seem to us to be the most serious.

The party never conceived the struggle in which it was involved as a 'protracted war'. Its leaders were impatient and did not have the courage to face up either to the strength of the enemy or to their own weakness. Thus they fell into an opposite but equally serious subjectivist error, the one which led them into the successive surrenders of Lebanon, Caserta and Varkiza. Confronted by an enemy very superior in numbers and military equipment, they should have limited themselves to guerilla war in the first stage, then switched to mobile war when they were in a position to destroy large units, attacking the towns only in the final stage. Generally, they should only have accepted combat provided that they had a crushing local superiority, and they should never have sacrificed forces to preserve one region. By amassing numerous small successes they could have gradually modified the balance of forces and finally achieved a great victory. The transformation of a political superiority (springing from the conformity of the slogans to the needs of the people) into military superiority is only possible in a protracted war, thanks to the mobilisation of the masses to support the army. (27)

The Greek communists did exactly the opposite to all this. Their example is a marvellous lesson in what not to do. We see in it what revolutionaries must do if they want to suffer a short, sharp defeat.

First, on the political level, the Communist Party leadership was unable to define its revolutionary tasks correctly and consequently could not scientifically answer the question: 'Who are our enemies and who are our friends?' so as to bring together in a broad front all those who could be united. Zachariades declared at the 2nd Plenum, 'The approaching revolution will be socialist in nature, and will simultaneously solve the bourgeois-democratic problems which still remain such as foreign domination, land, etc.' (28) In

skipping over the democratic, anti-imperialist stage and claiming to
establish the dictatorship of the proletariat immediately,
Zachariades deepened the split between the working class and the
petty bourgeoisie which had appeared just after 'December'. (29)
This line was concretised in December 1947 in the constitution of a
'Provisional Government of Free Greece' in which only communists
sat.

Let us now look at how the military operations were conducted.
They began with the attack on the gendarmerie post at Litockoron (at
the foot of Mount Olympus) on the night of 30/31 March 1946. The
few hundred maquisards who existed at that time became 2,500 two or
three months later and then 8,000 at the end of the year when the
Democratic Army was created. The latter had 14,250 fighters in
April 1947 and 18,000 in November. Later, and until the summer of
1949, the Democratic Army varied between 20,000 and 25,000 men, to
which must be added some 10,000 recruits in training in the neigh-
bouring peoples' democracies. The strength of the National Army and
the other forces of order rose to 265,000 men.

Until 1948 the Democratic Army carried on guerilla warfare which
enabled it to thwart all the encircling and combing operations
mounted against it, to resolve its supply problems and to disperse
everywhere to win over the population and to reduce the army to
impotence. After the leadership of the CPG moved to the mountains
and with the formation of a 'Provisional Government of Free Greece'
on 23 December 1947, the maquis began to transform themselves into a
regular army fighting a classic war. They regrouped in larger
units: battalions, then brigades and finally divisions. At the end
of 1948 the Democratic Army had eight divisions. On 25 December
1947 it attacked the town of Konitsa at the foot of Mount Grammos
but had to withdraw after six days of fighting. Nevertheless, it
established a permanent base in the Vitsi and Grammos Mountains on
the Albanian/Yugoslav frontier, which it defended by positional
warfare in the summer of 1948 and again in August 1949. This was
its last battle. Faced with the enemy's artillery and air power the
light infantry of the Democratic Army's 'divisions' opposed weakness
to strength by persistently defending its ground. In a war of
attrition it was the Democratic Army which was worn down despite the
excellence of its fortified positions. In December and January 1949
it had successfully attacked the towns of Karthitsa, Naoussa and
Karpenision but had failed and suffered big losses at Edessa and
Florina. Several thousand maquisards took part in each of these
operations. Generally they were forced to withdraw after a few
days, but Karpenision remained in their hands from 21 January 1948
until 9 February 1949. Launching protracted operations with larger
units required considerable supplies. The Democratic Army was quite
simply not in a position to ensure the transport of the necessary
minimum of munitions to central and southern Greece. Even food
supplies became difficult due to the fact that the government had
evacuated the inhabitants of the mountain areas, herding them into
camps near the towns. Such tactics cut both ways, as the experience
of the 'strategic hamlets' in Vietnam demonstrates. But time was
needed to transform the peasants' anger into active revolt. This
brings us back to the problem of protracted war. The 'Provisional
Government' brought the armed struggle to an end in September 1949

after the loss of its base at Grammos-Vitsi. At the beginning of
the year General Markos had been replaced because he advocated a
return to guerilla tactics.

The Resolutions of the 5th Plenum of the Central Committee in
January 1949 implied a final victory in the very same year. It
proclaimed: 'We must learn how to take the enemy's fortified towns.
We must learn not only how to take the towns but also how to defend
them.'

This speaks for itself.

In addition to the mistakes committed by the CPG leadership an
external event – Tito's defection – contributed to the Democratic
Army's rapid defeat. In 1946 Tito had promised considerable
assistance to Zachariades and had encouraged him to embark on an
armed struggle, in contrast to Stalin who proved sceptical about the
Greek communists' chances of success. After his break with the
Comintern Tito stopped his aid and in July 1949 he closed the
frontier completely, which had the immediate effect of removing from
the Democratic Army 4,000 reserves quartered in Yugoslavia, to which
must be added the 2,500 maquisards who were in Bulgaria and the
2,500 who were fighting in eastern Macedonia and Thrace. (30) In
fact, as the Axios Valley between the Yugoslavian frontier and the
Gulf of Salonika was easily guarded, the troops which we have just
mentioned could only have linked up with the main body of the
Democratic Army at the time of the decisive battle by passing
through Yugoslavia. Tito's defection thus deprived the Army of a
third of its forces. (31) However, Tito's 'volte-face' was only
serious because the party leadership did not realise it had to rely
above all on its own forces.

Stricken with famine, lacking ammunition, the combatants of the
Democratic Army, with their poor rifles, took on troops ten times as
strong in number and equipped with ultra-modern American arms.
Under the deluge of fire they fought with an enthusiasm and a
tenacity worthy of a better outcome. The Athens press paid them an
unintended compliment by seriously asking if they were drugged or
suffering from a mental disease which made them fight like
madmen...!

ELAS and the Democratic Army, which pursued one and the same
national liberation struggle, were the inheritors of a tradition
which is several hundred years old. In the entire world hardly any
other people apart from the Vietnamese can pride themselves on such
a tradition of popular armed struggle for independence and freedom.
This gives us hope for the future. As the poet Ritsos says, 'These
trees cannot adapt themselves to a narrower sky.'

STALIN'S RESPONSIBILITIES

Was Stalin responsible for the defeat suffered by the Greek
communists and democrats in the winter of 1944-5? Does the fact
that he 'sold out' the Greek people form part of a policy of
betrayal of the world revolution, based on the theory of socialism
in one country? This is a commonly held thesis which figures as an
established historical truth thanks to its repetition by writers,
some of them Trotskyists, others anti-communists, and lastly others

eager to appear impartial by condemning Churchill and Stalin at the
same time.

We shall show that the mistakes committed by Stalin on this
occasion did not stem from a deliberate wish to impede the spread of
world revolution.

First, let us examine the facts.

As their defeat approached, the Germans manoeuvred to divide the
Allies, indeed to conclude a separate peace with the Western Allies
and conduct a joint war with them against the USSR. Himmler himself
made offers precisely along these lines during 1944 and in April
1945. (32) In the last days of the war, Churchill sent 'Field-
marshal Montgomery ... a telegram asking him not to destroy captured
armaments but to collect it carefully so as to be ready to act
against a new Russian advance conjointly with the defeated German
troops'. (33) Field-marshal Auchinleck and General Ismey received
similar instructions. The Anglo-Saxons manoeuvred to prevent the
Russians from capturing the German armies and went so far as to
co-operate with the 'Dönitz Government'. We have already referred
to British agents' underhand deals with the enemy authorities in
Greece.

In these conditions it was important to avoid all conflict which
involved the risk of unloosing a Third World War before the end of
the Second, which would have been tantamount to a posthumous victory
for Nazism. The danger of such a conflict over the division of the
spoils had appeared very early when in 1943 Churchill advocated a
landing in Greece and later insisted that a Second Front should be
opened not in Normandy but also in the Lower Adriatic with a view to
an offensive towards Vienna which would cut the Russian route.
Therefore there were already signs of difficulties between Great
Britain and the USSR over the Balkans.

Nevertheless, on 31 May 1944, Churchill made it known to
Roosevelt that the Soviets were ready to acknowledge 'predominance'
in Greece for the UK in return for 'predominance' in Rumania for the
USSR, on condition that the USA ratified the agreement. This was
done on 12 June. On 9 October Churchill went to Moscow with Eden.
He said to Stalin: (34)

> Your armies are in Rumania and Bulgaria. We have interests,
> missions, and agents there. Don't let us get at cross purposes
> in small ways ... While this was being translated I wrote out on
> a half-sheet of paper:

Rumania:		
	Russia	90%
	The others	10%
Greece:		
	Great Britain	90%
	(in accord with	
	the USA)	
	Russia	10%
Yugoslavia		50%/50%
Hungary		50%/50%
Bulgaria:		
	Russia	75%
	The others	25%

According to Churchill, Stalin expressed his agreement immediately.

On the following day Eden and Molotov settled the details. It was
evidently a gentleman's agreement which did not figure in the
protocols of the conference.

On 12 October the British Prime Minister gave the following
particulars to his colleagues: (35)

> The system of percentages is ... intended ... to express the
> interest and sentiment with which the British and Soviet
> Governments approach the problems of these countries, and so that
> they might reveal their minds to each other in some way that
> could be comprehended.

Let us note that this agreement did not mean that Stalin undertook
to press the Greek communists not to oppose the British intervention. Even the most extreme advocates of the thesis under
discussion do not go so far as to say this openly. Besides, the
fact that Tito never acknowledged a 50 per cent influence of the
British in Yugoslavia was never invoked by the British as a rupture
of the agreement on Stalin's part.

In order to avoid a dangerous conflict it was necessary and
sufficient that each of the parties should abstain from sending
troops into a country placed in the other's sphere of interest. Can
we blame Stalin for calling a halt at the Greek frontier and not
going to war with the Anglo-Saxons to liberate that country? One
must decide; either one asserts that such a war was desirable in
this historical context in the interests of the revolution or else
one does not condemn Stalin for allowing the British 'carte-blanche'
in Greece.

It is true that he did more, since he refused to criticise them
and appointed an ambassador to the puppet Government in Athens even
before the fighting in the city was over, etc. Stalin's attitude on
this point seems more debatable. Perhaps he thought that it was not
in the interests of the socialist camp beginning to form around the
USSR to initiate a cold war with his allies before the end of the
hot war with his enemies. Be that as it may, his clear neutrality
involved reciprocal obligations on the part of the British, and this
emerges from Churchill's message to Roosevelt on 8 March in which,
after expressing virtuous indignation at the way in which the
Russians had imposed a communist-dominated Government on King
Michael of Rumania, he wrote: (36)

> We were hampered in our protests because Eden and I during our
> October visit to Moscow had recognised that Russia should have a
> largely predominant voice in Rumania and Bulgaria while we took
> the lead in Greece. Stalin kept very strictly to this under-
> standing during the six weeks fighting against the communists and
> ELAS in the city of Athens, in spite of the fact that all this
> was most disagreeable to him and to those around him.

Kedros, who quotes this text, comments (p. 510): 'It is not certain
that Stalin really entertained the feelings Churchill credits him
with.'

Why this venomous scepticism, this guilt by imputation? Because
on 9 February (37)

> when Churchill officially invited Stalin to send a Soviet
> observer to Greece, Stalin answered sarcastically that this
> seemed too dangerous to him seeing that Churchill had allowed
> no one other than the British forces to enter Greece. He

immediately added in a serious tone that he had 'complete
confidence in the British policy in Greece'.

It should not be necessary to emphasise that the 'serious tone' made
the second remark even more sarcastic than the first one.   In
Stalin's mouth 'to have confidence' could only have meant one thing
in this context: not to be under any illusions, to know the truth
about the aims and unscrupulousness of British imperialism.
Stettinius's failure to understand him thus proves only that he
revealed that mixture of cynicism and naïvité which is so frequent
in Americans.

Far from justifying him, this same cold lucidity which Stalin
demonstrated in his reply to Churchill, condemns him.   In fact, he
does not seem to have warned the Greek communists against the foul
blow prepared by the British.   It is even probable that the Soviet
military mission parachuted to the maquis on 26 July 1944 advised
the PESA to participate in the Papandreou Government.   Kedros makes
the following conjectures:

> It is possible that they advised unconditional participation in
> the Papandreou Government in the 'general interest of the allied
> cause' while promising the friendly neutrality of the Soviet
> Government in the event of the EAM leaders 'going it' alone.

This was not good enough.   It was Stalin's duty to urge the
communist leaders to prepare themselves and the masses to resist
ferociously the return of the reaction in the wake of the British,
since those leaders were incapable of understanding this by
themselves.   His silence may be explained by the same error which is
at the root of the mistakes committed by the CPG: he lacked
confidence in the strength of the popular masses and allowed himself
to be intimidated by the apparent power of British imperialism.
Stalin no longer believed that the Greek people could win against
such a formidable enemy.   He did not want to urge on them a hopeless
struggle.

Let us note, however, that the CPG's opportunism had shown itself
before it had the slightest link with the USSR, since as early as
August 1943 Siantos had declared that 'Greece belongs to a region of
Europe in which the British assume all responsibilities'. (38)

We have shown that EAM-ELAS could have defeated an attempt at
foreign intervention, especially if it had not let the enemy wrest
the initiative from it.   In addition we have shown that the reverse
suffered in December was avoidable and very partial.   Even afterwards, victory remained possible and even probable.   The
responsibility for the mistakes rests above all on the CPG's
leadership which Aris Velouchiotis had duly warned.   For his part,
Stalin, who did not usually take the trouble to give advice to
fraternal parties, in this case missed an opportunity to be of real
assistance to his Greek comrades.

At the same time, in those countries which the 'de facto'
division following the war left in the Soviet sphere of influence,
he helped the popular forces to destroy the power of capital and to
take the socialist road. (39)   We do not intend to discuss the
methods (debatable, in fact) which were used from country to
country.   One thing is certain: imperialist interests were radically
eliminated throughout eastern Europe.   To speak, as Kedros does, of
a 'wink from Churchill to his crony (compère) Stalin, is a

formulation more suited to the passion of a pamphleteer than to the calm of a supposedly objective historian.

The Trotskyist theory according to which the Communist leaders were puppets manipulated by Stalin (himself a counter-revolutionary) is invalidated by what happened in China and in Greece immediately after the war.

If we are to believe Djilas, Stalin expressed his point of view on the struggle of the Chinese and the Greek communists at a meeting with the Yugoslav leaders on 10 February 1948.

Stalin did not agree with the launching of armed struggle in Greece, for in his opinion it had no chance of success. He thought that it was necessary to 'cut one's losses' by putting an end to it as quickly as possible.

Someone having mentioned the successes which the Chinese communists had just won, he said: (40)

> Yes, the Chinese comrades have succeeded, but in Greece there is an entirely different situation. The United States is directly engaged there - the strongest state in the world ... true, we, too, can make a mistake. Here, when the war with Japan ended, we invited the Chinese comrades to agree on a means of reaching a modus vivendi with Chiang Kai-shek. They agreed with us in words, but in deeds they did it in their own way when they got home: they mustered their forces and struck. It has been shown that they were right and we were not, but Greece is a different case.

Although Stalin may not have believed that the communists had any chance of winning, the socialist camp did not spare its support for them on the diplomatic and material level, as was duly established in the latter case by a UNO commission of enquiry.

In the same period the USSR supported the armed struggle of the peasants of Telengana in India, the rising of the White Flag communists in Burma, the rising which erupted at Madiun in Indonesia, and national liberation struggles led by the communists of Malaya and Vietnam. As far as China is concerned, despite Stalin's initial doubts, and some blunders (for example, the ambassador of the USSR was the only one to follow Chiang Kai-shek in his retreat to Canton), the USSR gave unconditional political support to the Chinese communists. Thus in an article in 'Bolshevik' on 15 December 1947, the specialist Zhukov exalted 'the admirable Chinese Communist Party forged in struggles'.

The Communist Parties in France and Italy had made the same kind of mistakes as in Greece but more seriously. Despite their preponderant role in the Resistance they tailed behind the bourgeoisie and surrendered their arms at the moment of victory, in return for a few ministerial posts. The first thing Togliatti and Thorez did on their return from Moscow was to enter respectively the Governments of the monarchist Marshall Badoglio and De Gaulle. Thorez imposed the slogan 'One state, one police, one army!' He helped De Gaulle to 'draw the communists' teeth' and to remove from them 'the powers they are usurping and the arms they are exhibiting'. He gave the capitalists assistance by launching a production campaign and opposing strikes, which he blamed on the 'agents of the trusts'. In his interview with 'The Times' he spread illusions about the possibility of a parliamentary road to

socialism. (41) After its eviction from power, the PCF persisted in
calling itself the 'Party of Government'. In its propaganda it put
Moscow, London and Washington on the same level.

Was Stalin responsible for the opportunist line of the Italian
and French communists? Like the right-wing Oppositionists of the
'Unir' group, the Trotskyists argue that he was, but they do not
provide any proof or even any serious evidence in support of their
allegations. This does not prevent the latter from being highly
categorical. They talk about 'total and absolute submission to
Stalinist instructions' (42) and the 'position imposed' on the
French communist leaders, who were only 'executants'. (43) However,
the latter's opportunist line was vigorously criticised at the
founding conference of the Cominform at Szklariska Pareba 22/27
September 1947. Giving in to pressure from Zhdanov and Malenkov,
Duclos had to admit to 'opportunism, legalism, and parliamentary
illusions' on the part of the PCF.

If the PCF and the PCI leadership obeyed only Stalin's
instructions why did they not justify themselves by invoking the
'wise counsels' lavished on them by the 'brilliant' leader of the
world proletariat? This was all the more easy for them as the
meeting was held behind closed doors. At one point, Duclos
apparently stammered that the PCF 'could do nothing before the war
against the Germans had finished in order not to compromise the
relations between the Russians and the Americans', but Djilas
retorted: (44)

> The most effective support for the USSR would have been an action
> to reduce the American influence on the people. The Greeks did
> not hesitate to oppose the English during the war against the
> Germans ... The French communists have become poor representa-
> tives of the policy of the USSR to the French people despite the
> latter's combativity.

As for Kardelj, he recalled that: 'During the war ... we invited the
Italian comrades to study our experience; we liberated half of the
territory and we had an army; but the Italian comrades did not want
to imitate our experience and to take the road of insurrection.'
(45)

In conclusion, it seems clear to us that the development of the
revolutionary struggle in France and Italy would have strengthened
the security of the USSR by preventing the re-establishment and
consolidation of bourgeois state structures in these countries and
by undermining the American rear. This is what enabled Djilas to
ridicule Duclos's claim that the PCF gave up the revolution out of a
concern for the security of the USSR. We know that in this case the
Yugoslav spoke in full agreement with Stalin and that Duclos made no
reply.

In his purely formal self-criticism, Duclos did everything he
could to evade the real problems. This discourse is more damning
than the accusations which he was trying to answer. It provides
proof that, after reaching this stage of ideological degeneration,
the leaders did not need any orders from Stalin to follow an
opportunist line, to capitulate to the pressure of the bourgeoisie.

The Trotskyists and all those who pride themselves on criticising
Stalin from a Marxist point of view push Manicheism to the point of
seeing everywhere the hand of the Evil One enthroned in Moscow. He

was the source of all evil in the workers' movement. According to them, the opportunist leaders made only one mistake: they listened to Stalin. 'The serpent seduced me,' they might say. How does this perspective differ from Carrefour's mythology of the 'secret conductor'?

Chapter 8

CONCLUSION: THE FUNDAMENTAL TRAITS OF TROTSKYISM

We can now isolate the essential aspects of Trotskyism, which might be described as a 'para-Leninism', for although far-reaching in its consequences, the difference which sets it apart from Leninism is sometimes very subtle.

Studying the revolutionary process from the point of view of diachrony, Trotskyism emphasises continuity and the possibility of making non-stop progress: 'The living historical process always makes leaps over isolated "stages" which derive from the theoretical breakdown into its component parts of the process of development in its entirety'; (1) and also the interpenetration, the 'telescoping' of stages, since, according to it, socialist transformations are the order of the day even before the tasks of the bourgeois revolution are completed. Lenin, on the contrary, as a good dialectician, has the correct priorities, putting the emphasis on discontinuity. (2)

Of course, in actual historical circumstances, the elements of the past become interwoven with those of the future; the two paths cross ... But this does not in the least prevent us from logically and historically distinguishing between the major stages of development. We all contrapose bourgeois revolution and socialist revolution; we all insist on the absolute necessity of strictly distinguishing between them.

If this is not done it is no longer possible to distinguish between the principal contradiction and the secondary contradictions, it is impossible to determine the class alliances required by the tasks of the stage, the location of the line of demarcation between friends and enemies; the result is that it is impossible to carry out a correct united front policy which assumes that the contradictions which are secondary objectively are kept so by making concessions to one's allies; thus the proletariat is prevented from taking the leadership of the united front, it is isolated and condemned to impotence.

Considering society in synchrony, in space, so to speak, Trotsky again only saw there the continuity and the unity of the world market. We recall that 'the pressure of cheap commodities' produced by the capitalist countries is one of the factors which makes the construction of socialism impossible in a relatively backward country like Russia. This idea goes back to his first important work: 'Binding all countries together with its mode of production and its commerce, capitalism has converted the whole world into a single economic and political organism.' (3)

By presenting the world (in 1905) as already unified 'into a single economic organism', Trotsky was led to neglect the national peculiarities, the specific concrete conditions (determined by history and the cultural heritage) of the class struggle and the necessity to isolate the peculiar laws of the revolution in each country. In particular, he exaggerated the role of external influences without seeing that these can only act through forces within each of those partial totalities, social formations. This is why he explained all the defeats suffered by different Communist Parties between the two wars through the pernicious influence of Stalin and the Third International.

Mao Tse-tung has shown that: (4)

Contradiction within a thing is the fundamental cause of its development, while its interrelations and interactions with other things are secondary causes ... external causes are the condition of change and internal causes are the basis of change ... In a suitable temperature an egg changes into a chicken, but no temperature can change a stone into a chicken, because each has a different basis ... it is through internal causes that external causes become operative. In China in 1927, the defeat of the proletariat by the big bourgeoisie came about through the opportunism then to be found within the Chinese proletariat itself (inside the Chinese Communist Party).

Trotsky's unilateral emphasis on continuity is the sign of the incomprehension of the Marxist dialectic which led him to ignore the essential implications of the law of uneven development. This law signifies not only that the imperialist powers and monopolies grow at an unequal rate, but also that, in each social formation, the economic base and the political and ideological superstructures evolve at an unequal rate and by leaps, that these instances possess a relative autonomy and a peculiar temporality, and that in each of them the contradictions and their aspects shift (are transformed into their opposite). The revolution explodes when the principal contradiction reaches an explosive phase. The displacement of its aspects then brings about a restructuration of the whole. This contradiction is the nodal point where all the others converge. (5) That such a convergance occurs in the sense of a rupture is rare, as will be clear, and all the more so in several countries at once. This is why, according to Lenin, the victory of the proletariat in one country is the 'typical case', while revolution in several countries can only be a 'rare exception'.

In 'Results and Prospects', Trotsky prophesied the extension of the revolution throughout Europe when the victorious Russian proletariat called on its brothers throughout the world for 'the last fight'. Isaac Deutscher recognised that the tenor of Trotsky's argument suggests that he envisaged the European revolution as a 'unique and continuous' process, basing himself on the general truth that Europe was ripe for socialism, (6) but forgetting the other truth that 'history kept different times in Paris, Rome, London or Moscow'. (7) Why is this? No doubt because humanity does not constitute an integrated whole, because it is divided into distinct social formations, but also because the levels (or instances) of one such formation (economic, political, ideological) always 'keep different times'. For Trotsky, society has a simple structure in which the principal contradiction 'de jure' (proletariat-bourgeoisie) is always and everywhere principal 'de facto' during the whole period of the transition. That is why he saw only the world revolution (and also saw it 'sub specie aeternitatis'). He imagined it as unfolding in a continuous and homogeneous socio-historical time-space. The underground work of the 'old mole', the structure and the articulation of the strata which it has to get through were invisible from the ethereal heights he occupied.

The Trotskyists are ignorant of the dialectic of continuity and discontinuity which is as necessary for an understanding of history as it is for one of microphysics. They roar with laughter when they hear talk of the uninterrupted revolution by stages. For them, it is a contradiction in terms. We know that the concept of the 'break' which Althusser borrowed from Bachelard was inspired in the latter by that of 'discontinuity' in particle physics. If one cannot even grasp the universality of contradiction demonstrated by the unity and opposition of continuity and discontinuity in all the sciences, how could one penetrate its specificity in historical materialism?

It was clear at the time of the campaign which the Trotskyists launched in 1971 against China's international policy that they approached problems in an absolutely unilateral, metaphysical way. They do not understand that a state like Cambodia before Sihanouk's overthrow, or Pakistan, can have a dual nature: progressive, in so far as it defends its autonomy against the superpowers; reactionary, in that it oppresses the people. For them, reactionaries are reactionaries and it is not permissible to apply different policies to them, taking into account their differences so as to isolate the principal enemy of the moment. (8)

The idea Trotsky had of the relation between theory and practice was equally undialectical. For him, theory forecasts practice and practice applies theory. Lenin, on the contrary, constantly listened to the masses. According to him, the party must always be ready to carry out the tasks which the mass movement itself has put on the order of the day. Only the practice of the masses makes it possible to give a concrete content to the general directives which guide the vanguard. Trotsky criticised Lenin's formula of 'the democratic dictatorship of the proletariat and the peasantry' for being algebraic (there was an unknown: what would be the political role of the peasantry?); he, on the contrary, wanted only arithmetic. That is why the term 'prognosis', which we do not find in Lenin's writings, is so frequent in his, where it sometimes occupies the empty place of the 'slogan'. For Trotsky all problems are solved in advance on the basis of 'principles'. The experience of the class struggle invalidates or validates the solution. That is all. Trotsky's dogmatism and its correlate, empiricism, are epitomised in this opposition between arithmetic and algebra.

Lenin's formula that 'theory is a guide to action' was taken literally by Trotsky, who ignored the fundamental mediation which Lenin never forgot, namely, 'the concrete analysis of the concrete situation'. The universal truth of Marxism helps us to carry out this analysis: to think that it could stand in for it is, once more, simply dogmatism.

This dogmatism is cut off from practice and leads practice astray. We have given a typical example of it: the hegemony of the town in the bourgeois revolution, which he made into an axiom: Are 'the belated critics of the permanent revolution ... prepared to extend this elementary proposition to the countries of the East, China, India, etc? Yes or no?'

Obviously not! The fine principle of which Trotsky was so proud proved as useless as an arrow that cannot be unloosed at its target. In a sense it expresses a truth (the domination of the capitalist mode of production) but in its dogmatic interpretation it could only lead the action of Chinese revolutionaries into a dead end. It had to be replaced by another one, that of the encirclement of the towns by the countryside, which has been victoriously applied by the Chinese Communist Party and the Indo-Chinese revolutionaries.

Let no-one object to us that 'the hegemony of the towns' means leadership of the working class. The Chinese Trotskyists drew the conclusion from it that they should put all their efforts into the organisation of the urban proletariat and Trotsky understood it no differently. It was inconceivable to them that the peasantry could be the principal motor-force of the Chinese revolution and that the proletariat could lead the peasantry by organising it in the countryside and re-educating it ideologically.

The same refusal to recognise the revolutionary future of the colonial and semi-colonial peasants led Trotsky to formulate in 'The Class Nature of the Soviet State' the disastrously wrong prognosis that 'the revolutionary centre of gravity has shifted definitely to the West' (p. 31).

Trotsky did not understand the immense importance of Marx's indications on the necessity of combining proletarian revolution with peasant war even in a country as industrialised as Germany. After belatedly rallying to Lenin, he continued to underestimate the peasantry's revolutionary potential, to refuse to define the party's political line in terms of the necessary alliance with it, and to formulate slogans appropriate to its wide mobilisation.

Thus the traits which distinguish Trotskyism from Marxism as well as from Leninism are 'deviations' which separate it not from petrified dogmas, to which it appears to remain scrupulously faithful, but from reality. For if it is true that in political action it is necessary to proceed from reality while holding firmly to principles, it is no less true that one cannot hold firmly to principles unless one proceeds from reality.

We have given a few indications regarding Trotsky's sociologism in which Parvus's persisting influence is apparent. This deviation can at least adopt the guise of Marxism. Trotsky completely threw off this disguise when he explained historical events through individual or collective psychology. His 'History of the Russian Revolution' constantly speaks of the 'leaping movement of ideas and passions' and 'swift changes of mass views and moods'. 'The dynamic of revolutionary events', Trotsky tells us, 'is directly determined by swift, intense and passionate changes in the psychology of classes.' (9) Further on, he explains that Stalin and Kamenev were in agreement in March 1917, 'notwithstanding their opposite characters' because their personalities 'supplemented each other'. (10)

The pseudo-scientific concepts of Trotskyism such as the 'workers' state' (in which the working class is not in power!), 'bureaucratic caste', Bonapartism, 'Thermidor', etc., are deceptive because they are descriptive and cling to appearances. They quip the Trotskyists with convenient little schemas, thanks to which they have an answer for everything without studying anything. The Trotskyists have understood, they therefore have no need to think! This is the secret of their ideologists' sterile fertility.

What, in fact, is there to say about Trotsky's disciples? He himself applied to them a phrase of Marx's (the latter was quoting Heine): 'I have sown dragons and harvested fleas'. Of course, they are more Trotskyist than their master and their present successes are no less brilliant (if one may say so) than those which they achieved under his leadership after 1929. But their impotence, thirty years after his death, and their facile revolutionism, the revolutionism of people who have never made a revolution but have undermined those of others (whom they call Stalinists) would undoubtedly have inspired some bitter and disillusioned reflections in the writer of the following lines from 'In Defence of Marxism', 'The Fourth International did not by accident call itself the world party of the socialist revolution' (p. 15).

Five years after the 9th Congress of the aforesaid International, this definition retains all its humour, or, if one prefers, its unintentional pathos.

The Trotskyists react with fury when one is bold enough to make such reflections. (11) They appeal to the persecutions which they have suffered. Now Communist victims run into millions everywhere in the world. This does not in any way lessen the gravity of their mistakes (Indonesia) and adds nothing to the value of a victorious correct line (China). Given that supporters of the Fourth International can take advantage of favourable objective conditions just as much as those whom they describe as 'Stalinists', victory must be put down to correct leadership. The Trotskyists cannot concede this. They would condemn themselves.

However, their founding-father wrote in 1937: 'The burning historical need for a revolutionary leadership guarantees the Fourth International an exceptionally rapid rhythm of growth.' (12)

Trotsky was not wrong to link the rapid growth of the Fourth International and the need for a revolutionary leadership. His present disciples will allow us to argue as he did, 'mutatis mutandis', and to deduce from the persisting weakness of their movement in the last thirty years its inability to offer the type of leadership required by the revolutionary masses.

The tragedy of Trotskyism was and still is that in a world polarised between the camp of revolution and that of counter-revolution they could not find a recognisable place anywhere. By arguing that they themselves constituted the pole of the revolution by throwing together the 'Stalinists' and world reaction, they achieved the desired repolarisation; but alas, only in the mind's eye. As this solution to their problem was contradicted too much by the facts, they have pushed the art of 'saving the phenomenon' to the point of paranoia. For them, the most frenetic anti-

communists - Churchill, Truman, McCarthy - were 'Stalinists'
precisely because they opposed the USSR, thus giving it 'the
deceptive appearance of a revolutionary regime'. As a leading
Gaullist, Malraux was a 'Stalinist' and a doubly guilty one, since
he expressed a compromising sympathy for Trotsky's unfortunate
cause. (13)

Thus Trotsky's successors have been driven to a choice between an
activity rarely going beyond a futile and anodine revolutionary
masquerade, the desperate search for a third road (Tito, Castro) and
simply crossing to the other side of the barricades under the
pretext of realism and effectivity. As the latter choice has been
made by important organisations (Ceylon) as well as by many small
groups and individuals, it cannot be attributed to chance but rather
to the awareness of the dead-end which Trotskyist orthodoxy
represents.

We can find a new confirmation of this by now studying the
different incarnations or avatars of Trotskyism and their mis-
adventures. Here we are penetrating the domain of infra-Trotskyism
which is no longer amenable to a sustained theoretical critique in
the absence of that minimum of coherence and rigour which the
founding-father had managed to maintain. It is the last circle of
hell in which the confused multitude of sectarians delivered up to
their obsessions talk agitatedly to themselves.

Chapter 9

CRITICAL NOTES ON SOME TROTSKYIST ORGANISATIONS

THE FOURTH INTERNATIONAL

We have said that the Trotskyists are the dogmatists of a dogmatism. It goes without saying that they are not all so to the same degree. Those in the Fourth International are considered by the Lambertists to be revisionists, and not without reason. To say that they practise a 'creative' Trotskyism might seem a contradiction in terms. It is not if we take it in the sense that Khrushchev was a 'creative Marxist'; in other words a pragmatic opportunist using a Marxist phraseology.

A 'third road' which is a dead-end

The Fourth International has always been searching for a ... third road. Between the imperialist camp and the socialist camp it first chose Tito. The illusion could not be maintained for long because after stabbing the Greek maquis in the back, the Yugoslav hero voted for the UNO intervention in Korea, openly considered sending troops there to fight side by side with the Americans, linked himself to NATO via the Balkan Pact and supported the most reactionary regimes, christening them 'non-aligned', etc. As a result, while continuing to congratulate themselves for the 'positive aspects' of the Yugoslav experience, the leaders of the Fourth International transferred to Fidel Castro their need for a reference point in a real revolution. Once again the bashful suitor went unrequited. Speaking to the Tricontinental Conference in January 1966, Castro violently denounced the Trotskyists' undermining activity in Latin America. (1) In reply, the Fourth International published an open letter in a tone of offended dignity from which it appeared that he had not checked his sources and that he had used dishonest and demagogic arguments, which, after all, should come as no surprise. (2) The Trotskyists in the Fourth International were very embarrassed by Castro's silence about the May–June movement in France. While the Chinese press published enthusiastic articles and millions of Chinese workers demonstrated their support, while 'Pravda' denounced the leftists and supported the established order

even less tactfully than 'Humanité', the Cuban press made no comment
at all.   Shortly after, Fidel Castro had to sanction the social-
imperialist aggression against Czechoslovakia, as did Hanoi Radio
(more discreetly, it is true).

In January 1970, if we are to believe 'Le Monde', Douglas Bravo,
the leader of the Venezuelan guerillas, accused Castro of no longer
aiding the Latin American revolutionary movement and of 'taking the
Soviet line'. (3)

Whatever Bravo's disagreements with Castro, the latter reiterated
his support for Soviet positions, attacking the 'leftists' in a
speech delivered on the occasion of the Lenin Centenary.   According
to the 'Le Monde' correspondent, he condemned the attacks launched
on Lenin's native land by the extreme-left.   He took to task the
European intellectuals, particularly the French, and then
'reaffirmed the solidarity of the Cuban people with the Soviet Union
and ... recalled his position at the time of the Czechoslovakian
affair'.

Once again the third road has showed itself to be a dead-end.

The Fourth International and China

Although the Trotskyists in the Fourth International parade
'critical support' for China, they are really much more hostile to
it than some bourgeois writers, occasionally less biased.   Jean
Esmein's book on the cultural revolution or the pamphlet the
distinguished economist Joan Robinson has devoted to the same
subject should be compared with some of their texts. (4)

For example, Ernest Mandel's paper, 'La Gauche', wrote on 3
September 1966 (i.e., after the outbreak of the cultural revolution)
that 'China is led by a bureaucracy the nature of which is no
different from the Soviet bureaucracy'.   The CCP is supposedly
characterised by 'the absence of all freedom of tendencies, a rigid
Puritanism and the most frightful "cultural" and ideological
conformism'.

We do not know what life-style the author of this article offers
in contrast to the 'Puritanism' with which he charges the Chinese
communists, nor why attachment to the thought of Mao Tse-tung should
denote a more 'frightful' conformism than his own obstinacy in
wearing Trotskyist blinkers.

The word blinkers is not too strong when we think that for thirty
years the Trotskyists prayed for the coming of an anti-bureaucratic
political revolution but refused to acknowledge it when it did
finally come and used the arguments of the most conservative
Pekinologists to attack it.

Let us examine Livio Maïtan's 'Report on the "Cultural
Revolution" in China' delivered to the 9th World Congress of the
Fourth International. (5)   Maïtan relied mainly on American
sources, choosing, moreover, those which most denigrated China.   On
the basis of the assessments concocted by these 'leading
specialists', he believed himself to be in a position to state that
in 1965 'the per capita consumption had not yet exceeded the 1933
level' (p. 706, n. 1).   How happy were the Chinese in the period of
Chiang Kai-shek and the Japanese occupation!

Moreover, our author's text is studded with strange assertions
which display a total ignorance of everything which concerns China
and its recent history. Here are a few of them (we leave aside many
of the best ones):
- in China there are peasants not living exclusively from the
income of their labour (p. 707);
- there is 'job insecurity';
- there are delays in the payment of wages (Maïtan has made a
general 'problem' of one incident connected with the struggles and
troubles occasioned by the cultural revolution in Shanghai in
January 1967);
- before January 1967 the leadership of the party and the city
council in Shanghai had been 'a stronghold of the Maoist tendency'
(p. 709, n. 21); it seems here that Maïtan may have been led into
error by the fact that Yao Wen-yuan's article against Wu Han (Deputy
Mayor of Peking) of 10 November 1965 was first published by the
Shanghai daily 'Wenhui Pao' - at a time when Yao and Chang Chouen-
Kiao were working in the Shanghai city council.
- During the cultural revolution (p. 710),
    substantial peasant sectors raised demands similar to those that
    took shape after the halting of the movement of the people's
    communes ... relative freedom for private accumulation, an
    expansion of the private plots, the chance to use the 'free'
    market, a decrease in deliveries to the state, etc. It is
    significant that in certain cases it was the Maoists who sought
    to counter-act excessive state intervention, which was attributed
    to Liu Shao-chi.
In this passage it is clear that Maïtan has inverted the Maoist and
Liu Shao-chiist positions. The innocent reader cannot but conclude
that the Maoist favoured private accumulation and the utilisation of
free markets! In fact, the cultural revolution in the countryside
was above all a movement of criticism by the peasants themselves of
Liu Shao-chi's sinister line known as 'San Zi Yi Bao' ('three
freedoms, one forfeit'): extension of individual plots of land,
development of free markets, multiplication of small enterprises
assuming the entire responsibility for their profits and losses, and
the establishment of production norms on a family basis.
M. Maïtan believed he knew, without quoting sources, that the
revolutionary committees 'were not elected but were the product of
agreements at the top' (p. 710). As if preliminary discussions
between revolutionary organisations, old, experienced, revolutionary
cadres and army representatives were incompatible with election or
broad democratic votes by the masses. In fact, it was the latter
who chose the majority of the members of the revolutionary
committees, without the soldiers unless they were in the militia.
Below the district level, in fact, the people's militia, a part of
which is constituted by all the youth who volunteer, took the place
of the army in the 'Triple Combination'. (6)
In conclusion we can say that Maïtan's report bears the stamp of
ignorance and spite. We only criticised it as a reminder, for it
does not deserve to be taken seriously.
The 9th World Congress 'Resolution on the "Cultural Revolution"
in China' which was based on this report, merely systematises its
most schematic conclusions. We learn in it of the CCP leaders that

'These bureaucrats do not hesitate to subordinate the welfare of the
Chinese masses and the interests of the international revolution and
socialism to the protection and promotion of their own power and
privileges' (p. 705). We also learn that 'the turbulent events of
the cultural revolution have weakened its ("Mao's faction's")
position and power. The regime will not be able to regain the
prestige and stability enjoyed before Mao launched the "Great
Proletarian Cultural Revolution"' (p. 702). Yet another 'prognosis'
which history has quickly contradicted, regardless of the
Trotskyists.

Structural reforms

Ernest Mandel denies being a reformist. The struggle for workers'
control, he says forcefully, is not less but more revolutionary than
wage demands, as it 'cannot be carried out in a normally functioning
capitalist system'. (7) In fact, the programme of structural
reforms is all the more bound up with reformist illusions since it
claims to bring the capitalist system into question by the fact that
at the same time it evades the problem of the ways and means
enabling the working class to take power.

    Mandel writes that this programme 'creates a situation of dual
power', and further on that 'the demand for worker's control ...
tends to give birth, first in the factory, later in the country at
large, to an embryonic worker's power'. It would be nice to know
how a 'programme' or a 'demand' can 'create' a power; the
capitalists have power because they command armed forces. Mandel
does not want to know this. He acknowledges, of course, that 'the
overthrow of capitalism requires a total, extraparliamentary
confrontation between embattled workers and the bourgeois state',
but he takes good care not to specify that this will be an armed
confrontation. His 'strategy' is a variant of the peaceful road to
socialism.

    After May-June 1968, the PCF also gave up trying to instil belief
in the parliamentary road to socialism advocated by Khrushchev.
Today, the French revisionists say only that it is a question of
'winning over the majority of the people, that is, of bringing
together in action a superiority of forces such that the
bourgeoisie, isolated, is no longer in a position to resort to civil
war'. (8) 'It is through multiple actions of the masses ... that
the balance of social and political forces can be modified in favour
of democracy and socialism.' (9)

    The revisionists would like to make us believe in miracles. When
and where has the unarmed majority ever imposed its will on the
armed minority? What 'balance of forces' can be in question when
all the force (to kill) is on one side and all the impotence (to
avoid death) is on the other? If the people are unarmed the
bourgeoisie has no need to 'resort to civil war', to suppress
elections peacefully and to send those who protest peacefully to
concentration camps. The peaceful road is the road to dictatorship,
as experience has shown the Brazilian, Indonesian and Greek
communists, victims of their own opportunism and illusions. With
such examples before them, it is clear that the PCF leaders are not

deceived revolutionaries but deceitful counter-revolutionaries.
Those who claim 'not to confuse the peaceful road to socialism with
the parliamentary road' and to rely above all on the 'multiple
actions of the masses' divided and then stifled the mass movement in
May-June 1968 so that it did not embarrass them in the electoral
campaign intended to represent them above all as a 'Party of
Government', aware of its responsibilities, and the enemy of
violence, disorder and illegality.

Despite a more revolutionary phraseology than the PCF's, Mandel
passes over in complete silence the necessity of civil war to
overthrow the bourgeois order. Not from him will one learn how, on
the basis of the present struggles, the masses can prepare
themselves to take up arms at a later stage.

Here is how, according to him, the workers could have won victory
in May-June 1968: (10)

> Had they been educated during the preceding years and months in
> the spirit of workers' control, they would have known what to do:
> elect a committee in every plant that would begin by opening up
> the company books; calculate for themselves the various
> companies' real manufacturing costs and rates of profit;
> establish a right of veto on hiring and firing and on any changes
> in the organisation of the work; replace the foremen and the
> overseers chosen by the boss with elected fellow workers (or with
> members of the crew taking turns at being in charge). Such a
> committee would naturally come into conflict with the employers'
> authority on every level. The workers would have rapidly had to
> move from workers' control to workers' management. But this
> interval would have been used for denouncing the employer's
> arbitrariness, injustice, trickery and waste to the whole country
> and for organising local, regional and national congresses of the
> strike and workers' control committees. These in turn, would
> have furnished the striking workers with the instruments of
> organisation and self-defence indispensable in tackling the
> bourgeois state and the capitalist class as a whole.

Let us point out, first of all, that Mandel begins by asking the
question of what the workers should have done during the general
strike in May-June, and replies by envisaging a workers' control
carried out in factories producing normally, since he talks about a
veto on hiring and firing, elected overseers, etc. It is not clear
why, stripped of the essence of their powers, the bosses should
accept the running of their plants in these conditions even for a
single day. Experience shows that a lock-out and CRS intervention
would have been immediate. Such is not Mandel's view. According
to him, the bourgeois state will grant the workers an 'interval
which they turn to account to make propaganda and to endow
themselves, at the end of multifarious congresses, with "instruments
of self-defence"'. Mandel is very discreet as to the nature of
these 'instruments' and the ability of a congress to provide them.

The paragraph reveals with stunning clarity the true character of
'revolutionary structural reforms'. How can a 'demand' 'give birth'
to a 'power'? A power implies arms or at any rate the ability to
impose one's will on the enemy by violence. But the question of
proletarian violence is taboo for Mandel.

Henri Weber reads Mao

One of the leaders of the 'Ligue communiste', Henri Weber, who
teaches at Vincennes, devoted his course in the year 1969-70 to a
study of Mao's works. In a book on May 1968 which he wrote with
Bensaid, he had already tried to handle Maoist concepts with all the
naïveté of a neophyte and of course got everything muddled up. Here
is what he teaches us in his academic capacity: 'The front of the
class struggle being deliberately blurred and frozen by the worker's
organisations, its secondary aspects could move to the forefront and
the secondary aspect of the contradiction could become the principal
one.' (p. 31.)

In contrast to what Weber implies, the class struggle unfolds in
the university just as much as it does everywhere in society. It is
correct, however, that students who attack bourgeois academic
authorities are not directly subject to exploitation and that their
struggle is located in the superstructure. In a strategic
perspective, this is a secondary sector. However, as young
intellectuals are generally the first to move, the revolutionary
breakthrough is achieved on this front first of all. If this is
what Weber means, we agree, but in that case the concepts which he
explicitly attributes to Mao have taken on a different meaning at
his hands. In Mao, every contradiction, for example the
contradiction between proletariat and bourgeoisie in Russia, has a
principal and a secondary aspect. Before 1917, these aspects were
respectively the bourgeoisie and the proletariat. After 1917, they
were transformed into their opposite: from then on the principal
aspect was the proletariat, the bourgeoisie having become the
secondary aspect. It is obvious that M. Weber confuses the
principal and secondary aspect, the principal and secondary
contradiction and the principal and secondary front.

'Ligue communiste' and 'Lutte ouvrière'

Between the end of 1968 and the spring of 1969, the 'Ligue
communiste', the French section of the Fourth International, engaged
in discussions with 'Lutte ouvrière' with a view to a unification of
the two organisations. These discussions were renewed in March
1970. However, serious political differences remain between them as
the Political Bureau of the 'Ligue communiste' acknowledged in its
letter of 11 March 1970, particularly 'On the nature of the Chinese
and Cuban states (bourgeois according to 'Lutte ouvrière') and on
the Vietnamese revolution'. Here is what the 'Lutte ouvrière' had
to say on the latter question at the time of Ho Chi-minh's death:
the Vietnamese leader 'has never, so to speak, been a communist
committed to the working class and to international socialism'. He
'was always a stranger to the proletariat and its fight'. He fully
agreed with the Communist International which, under Stalin, gave
'total support to the non-proletarian forces, even in their struggle
against the proletariat'. In 1945, 'Ho Chi-minh distinguished
himself in anti-working class repression'. 'After the defeat of
French imperialism at Dien Bien Phu and the declaration of the
Democratic Republic of Vietnam, Ho remained at the head of this

state the same as ever: a bourgeois nationalist.' (11)   Such views
have very little to do with Marxism, but this did not prevent the
'Ligue communiste' from signing a protocol of agreement with 'Lutte
ouvrière' bearing on organisational questions alone (January 1971).
The problems which these pose are easily solved when there is
political unity. The reverse is not true. Thus the fusion of the
two organisations is not any more advanced today (December 1972)
than it was two years ago.

THE LAMBERTISTS: THE OCI

At the beginning of 1951, the Secretary of the Fourth International,
Michel Pablo, published an article (under his real name, Raptis) in
which he stated that 'the overwhelming majority of the forces
opposed to capitalism are at present led or influenced by the Soviet
bureaucracy'. In another text, he argued that a war was imminent
which 'will push the Communist Parties more and more to the left and
the masses will flock to them, hence the necessity for militant
Trotskyists to enter the Communist Parties'. (12)
   In February 1952, the International Executive Committee adopted
a resolution generalising the tactics of entrism. The majority of
the French section, the 'Parti Communiste Internationaliste',
refused to carry out this instruction and was expelled. In October
the following year, several other sections joined the PCI to form
the 'International Committee of the Fourth International'. Among
them were the 'Socialist Labour League' (SLL) led by Healy in Great
Britain, and the 'Socialist Worker's Party' in the USA gave its
support. In 1963, all these sections were reunited with the Fourth
International, with the exception of the Lambertists and the SLL.
(13)   Considerably weakened, the PCI had ceased to call itself a
party in 1958, reducing its activity to the publication of its
journal, 'La Vérité'. In 1961, the Lambertists founded the 'Comité
de la liaison des étudiants révolutionnaires' (CLER), which,
together with the 'Révoltes' groups ensured them a certain
implantation among young people.
   In January 1967, they took the name of the 'Organisation
communiste internationaliste' (OCI) and the following year CLER
became the 'Fédération des étudiants révolutionnaires'. After the
dissolutions of 11 June 1968, these two organisations were replaced
respectively by the 'Organisation Trotskyste' and the 'Alliance des
jeunes pour le socialisme' whose organ is 'Jeune révolutionnaire'.
The Lambertists are also the animators of the 'Fedération des
comités d'alliance ouvrière' whose organ is 'Informations
ouvrières'. Their influence is especially felt in the student
milieu and they have taken advantage of the disintegration of UNEF
to attempt to take it over. Their tactics consist of following the
mass organisations of the Communist Party (CGT, revived UNEF) while
criticising them in order to change their line.
   In July 1970, the decree dissolving the Lambertist organisations
was annulled by the Conseil d'Etat which thereby acknowledged the
respect for law and order which they had demonstrated.

Differences with the Fourth International

In its Manifesto, the OCI characterised the positions of the
International Secretariat (of the Fourth International) as follows:
(14)
> They see the so-called 'colonial revolution' as the motor-force
> of contemporary history. They stated first of all that the
> imminence of the Third World War forced the Kremlin bureaucracy
> to mobilise the workers 'practically' in the struggle for power;
> then they rallied to petty-bourgeois 'anti-nuclear' pacificism
> while proclaiming yet again that the Stalinist apparatus and even
> the reformist apparatus could only any longer evolve towards the
> left, whereas the Russian bureaucratic regime would gradually
> transform itself under the leadership of the Kremlin into a
> socialist democracy.

The OCI further accused the International Secretariat of Pablo,
Frank and Germain of having propagated revisionism from 1950-1
onwards by wishing to substitute a programme of 'structural reforms'
for the programme of transitional demands preparing the masses for
the struggle for power, of having adopted the entrist tactics
advocated by Pablo and of not recognising the necessity for
independent Marxist parties.

The supporters of the Fourth International are not lacking in
good arguments either.

Bensaid and Weber write:
> The rhythm of the political activity of FER-Révoltes is dictated
> by a biennial succession of central initiatives, for the success
> of which the whole organisation works in the intervening periods.
> Every year, generally at the same time, the leadership presents
> the base with a 'new political gimmick' such as: 'Towards 3,500
> revolutionary youth at the Mutualité 30 June 1968!', 'Towards the
> reconstruction of UNEF!' 'A major demonstration of one million
> workers before the Elysée Palace!' or, later: 'Towards ten
> thousand revolutionary youth of Le Bourget!' These arithmetical
> objectives, fixed well in advance, are pursued without any
> consideration of the political conjuncture.

The two authors give the following example of the Lambertists'
extreme sectarianism: according to the latter, 'the NLF of South
Vietnam is a Stalinist organisation which is betraying the interests
of the "Vietnamese workers and peasants". It is in the process of
"strangling the Vietnamese revolution".' (Charles Berg, 'Révoltes',
nos. 13 and 14.) (15)

To speak of 'sectarianism' in this case is to show great
indulgence. It is a question of an openly counter-revolutionary
attitude. We have another example in the support given by the OCI
to Nessali Hadj, whose organisation collaborated with the French
Army in its repression of the Algerian people's struggle for its
national independence.

As for its analysis of the international situation, for the OCI
'there have been no profound changes in the world since 1938'. (16)

Champions of orthodoxy

In fact, in France, for example, the Lambertists feature as the fundamentalists of Trotskyism. They profess an unshakable faith in Trotsky's Transitional Program (1938) which they insist is unalterable. For them, 'what Trotsky wrote is not simply a Marxist programme, it is THE Marxist programme in its essence.' (17) They are very lucky to have such a text at their disposal: it excuses them from any need to draw lessons from experience. Lenin was obliged to change his programme nearly every year in the light of practice. They are content to demonstrate that the great events of recent history have not contradicted Trotsky. We shall now look into how they fulfil this boast.

According to Trotsky, the foundation of the Fourth International was justified by the fact that 'The Communist International and all its Parties had finally passed over to the side of the bourgeois order'. (18) Pierre Broué declares that thanks to this 'Holy Alliance' constituted by the Western imperialists, Stalin, Mao Tse-tung and Ho Chi-minh, 'the world revolution so much dreaded was averted the day after the Second World War'. (19) Only, capitalism has been swept away in Eastern Europe; and revolutions have conquered in Yugoslavia, Albania, China and Vietnam. The communists in Indonesia and Greece suffered defeats at this time but their fight at least demonstrated that they were not counter-revolutionaries. To get round this, the Lambertists rely on a quotation from Trotsky conceding 'the theoretical possibility that, under the influence of a quite exceptional combination of circumstances ... petty-bourgeois parties, including the Stalinists, might go further than they themselves wish along the road of a break with the bourgeoisie'. They draw from it the conclusion that the Communist Parties struggled, took power at the cost of immense sacrifices, crushed reaction and embarked on the construction of socialism but all against their will, as it were, constrained and forced by a combination of circumstances despite their opposite intention. (20) This speaks for itself.

This being so, should we be surprised if the Lambertists resort to debatable methods to discredit the Chinese communists? On the following page of the 'Manifesto' we read: 'Reviving the thesis of the theoreticians of "proletarian nations", the Chinese CP completely abandons the terrain of the international class struggle and Marxism.'

It is hardly necessary to emphasise that this is a gratuitous accusation which the Trotskyists would be hard pressed to substantiate with any reference whatsoever. (21)

The cessation of the development of the productive forces

The Lambertists define the general crisis of capitalism as an economic stagnation that has lasted since 1913! In doing so, they are reaffirming a thesis from the Transitional Program, according to which the productive forces have stopped growing.

Their argument is strange: they invoke the fact that scientific research 'is almost exclusively oriented towards military ends'.

(22) Now, the discoveries thus achieved find civil application fairly quickly. The time between a scientific discovery and its application in production has decreased considerably since the beginning of the century. They also say that technical advances lead to a 'generalised reduction of skill' for masses of workers and intellectuals and that 'military budgets govern the movement of society'. It follows that such a capitalist economy 'cannot be considered a force of culture and civilisation', nor 'be described as progressive'.

Let us note that the last two 'arguments' are purely demagogic: the fact that capitalist economy is neither 'a force of culture and civilisation' nor 'progressive' in no way proves that it does not permit a certain development of the productive forces, though one far short of what is possible. We could say as much about 'dilution of skill'. Even supposing that it was a global reality it could not serve to prove that the Lambertist thesis is well-founded. In fact, the concept of 'productive forces' in Marx includes the instruments of production plus the capacity to put them to work, to make them function. From the beginning the industrial revolution has involved a dilution of skill for one or other category of workers. The introduction of automation does away with some crafts but sufficient skilled personnel are trained to run the new factories. It is false to say, moreover, that dilution in skill is a global phenomenon hitting all categories of the working population. Of course, it affects some sectors – there is at present a decline in the number of craft workers who are employed more and more as detail labourers – but, at the same time, the demand for highly qualified technical personnel is increasing on the whole and it is established that the average length of training is tending to grow in accordance with the needs of the developing capitalist economy.

The Lambertists' argument is thus based on a mixture of errors and truisms without any relation to their thesis. This emerges even more clearly when the leader himself takes the floor. For example, let us examine a paper read on 24 January 1969 at a session of the 'Cercle d'études marxiste'.

This talk by Lambert unfolds in a conceptual fog propitious to all sorts of conjuring tricks. He begins by arguing that 'the productive forces have stopped growing'; he then interprets this thesis to mean that the production of consumption goods for non-military use has stopped growing, which is not the same thing; he then suggests that the 'productive forces are being transformed into destructive forces', apparently meaning that in the USA 10 per cent of them are used for military purposes (23) which, once again, is not the same thing.

By the productive forces Marx meant the ensemble of material and human factors of production. It is therefore a matter of the factors which make the latter possible independently of their current application (production) and the nature of the objects produced. There is no variation in the level of the productive forces available to a firm when it decides to sell its fabrics (for example) to army workshops rather than to civil fashion houses.

Lambert dupes his listeners by the surreptitious use of a series of semantic slides which amount to a string of illegitimate identifications: productive forces = productive forces actually producing = things produced = things produced for non-military purposes.

Now the portion of military spending in the gross national income in the USA rose from 1 per cent in 1929 to 10 per cent in 1968; the productive forces are therefore being transformed into destructive forces and consequently they have stopped growing.   QED.

Not a single one of these concatenations bears examination.

Even if we charitably leave on one side the thesis of the non-growth of the productive forces and discuss only the apparently more reasonable one of the non-increase in material wealth, it still proves that the figures quoted by Lambert by no means corroborate his conclusions.

Of course, the proportion of military spending in the national income has increased, but the latter has tripled since 1929 in the USA and even more in the other capitalist countries.   This is what Lambert fails to mention. (24)

At this juncture, Lambert resorts to a naïvely demagogic argument: to the extent that the productive forces continue to grow, 'capitalism has a future'.   If this is so, 'the political conditions for the revolution are not there', therefore, those who do not accept my thesis renounce the revolutionary perspective and are counter-revolutionaries.

Strange sophism! According to the leader of the OCI, Trotsky denied in 1938 that capitalism has a future.   However, it has survived more or less for more than thirty years.   Lambert denounces those who oppose his thesis, telling them: 'You are arguing that capitalism has a future'.   Indeed yes, if this means that it will not perish tomorrow.   It is none the less true that its grave-diggers are already preparing for its funeral.   A revolutionary cannot say more.

Let us point out that the Lambertists are only providing one variant of the economism of the Second International, for which revolution was the inevitable outcome of the development of the productive forces (Kautsky and the Mensheviks) or its limits under capitalism (Rosa Luxemburg). (25)

Sometimes Lambert wants to prove too much.   Then the data which he appeals to backfire disastrously.   To illustrate the evils of automation, he quotes the president of an American trust whom he makes say this: (26)

> 36.5 million new jobs must be created in the USA by 1970 (this
> was written in 1966); demographic increases will provide 12.5
> million young people ... while the increase in productivity will
> eliminate 24 million jobs mainly because of automation.

In 1970 the number of unemployed in the USA had increased by 1 million in relation to 1966 as a result of the economic crisis which started in 1969.   According to the figures quoted by Lambert (we shall leave the responsibility for them with him) 35.5 million new jobs have therefore been created since 1966.   Is this not proof of an enormous development of the productive forces? (!!!)

It has been said that facts are stubborn.   They undoubtedly are, but the Lambertists will not let them be as stubborn as they are.

THE USSR, PEACEFUL
CO-EXISTENCE AND VIETNAM

This article appeared at a time when the campaign for the formation
of 'Comités Vietnam de Base' was launched. Their role in the
preparations for May-June in France is well-known. Let us add
simply that they stood out not only by a more consistent support for
the Vietnamese people (it was they who popularised the slogan
'Victory to the NLF!') but also by their ability to carry out
sustained work of daily explanation among ordinary people in the
localities. The Trotskyists, on the other hand, were content to
participate in the episodic initiatives of the 'Comité Vietnam
Nationale' which appealed only to intellectuals. They could not, in
any case, support the Vietnamese on the basis of the latter's
slogans with respect to a 'Just war' ('Just' is a moral notion
without any class content for the Trotskyists!); 'the invincibility
of People's War', which they are against, claiming that the
Vietnamese should launch the slogan of socialist revolution and
abandon the alliance with the national petty and middle bourgeoisie.
   At the time, the theme of the international front against
imperialism was the anti-Chinese war-horse of the revisionists, the
Trotskyists and the 'third roaders' in general. Therefore it was
important to show that the Soviets did not demand this front in
order to prepare a decisive riposte to American aggression, but so
as to get the Chinese to 'suspend the polemics' and to agree to a
policy aiming to conclude a compromise with the USA over the heads
of the South Vietnamese. The Chinese refusal brought unshakable
support to the Vietnamese, determined to carry their fight for the
liberation of their country through to the end. The position which
the Trotskyists adopted on this occasion illustrates their
'centrism' which, despite their verbal extremism, prevents them from
tracing a clearer line of demarcation between themselves and
revisionist betrayal and leads them in fact to practise various
forms of tailism with regard to the so-called 'workers'' parties.

A RESOLUTE UNITED FRONT AGAINST AMERICAN IMPERIALISM (1)

   The Chinese Communist Party and the Chinese government always
   wave the flag highest for the struggle against the imperialists

led by the USA, give total support to the revolutionary struggles
of all oppressed nations and defend world peace. (Speech by
Nguyen Minh Phuong - Acting Head of the permanent mission of the
NLF in Peking - on 19 December 1966, the twenty-second
anniversary of the formation of the PLA and the sixth anniversary
of the founding of the NLF.)

Although material aid to the Vietnamese people is important, it
is the thought of Mao Tse-tung which is the invaluable treasure
for us. (Speech by Tran Tu Binh - the Ambassador of the DRV to
China - on 19 December 1966.) (2)

The Vietnamese comrades are in a good position to know the nature of
American imperialism. The above statements forcefully emphasise the
following two principles:
1 The only way to defend world peace is resolute support for the
  struggle of the oppressed peoples against American imperialism, a
  warmonger by nature.
2 The most important support is consistent political support based
  on Marxism-Leninism.
It follows that united action against the US aggressors is only
possible with those who denounce it as the principal enemy and
resolutely combat it. It is impossible with those who are trying to
come to terms with it at the expense of the revolutionary peoples of
the world and who are plotting a Vietnamese Munich.
   For two years the leaders of the CPSU have called for united
action to help Vietnam. Of course unity is a good thing but before
uniting with someone it is necessary to know whether he is a friend
or an enemy, if his aims are in agreement or contradiction with
those which one wants to achieve. To this end we shall examine in
turn:
   (a) The contradictions of the contemporary world and the correct
        conception of the united front against American imperialism.
   (b) The ideology propagated by the Soviet leaders and their
        policy towards the American aggression in Vietnam.

THE FOUR CONTRADICTIONS

The contradictions oppose:
1 the socialist camp to the imperialist camp;
2 the proletariat to the bourgeoisie;
3 the oppressed nations to imperialism;
4 the imperialist countries and monopoly-capitalist groups to each
   other.
These four contradictions are a 'constant throughout the period of
the general crisis of capitalism, which has begun with the October
Revolution and will go on until the world victory of socialism'.
They constitute a connected system, each of them being present in
all the others. Here are two examples:
   (a) the contradiction between the two camps is revealed through
        the other three contradictions;
   (b) the national liberation struggles are an integral part of
        the world socialist revolution. Their character and their
        development are affected by (i) the support of the socialist

camp and the imperialists' fear of seeing this camp
strengthened; (ii) the support of the proletariats of the
advanced capitalist countries; (iii) the inter-imperialist
contradictions which assist their struggles.

The connected character of this system of four fundamental contradictions explains how they can converge. At present they converge
in Asia, Africa and Latin America, the countries dominated by
imperialism, the 'weakest link' in its chain and the 'storm-centre'
of the world. In other words, the third contradiction is the most
explosive at present.

AN ANTI-AMERICAN UNITED FRONT

The peoples of these regions clash everywhere with American
imperialism, its accomplices and puppets. It intervenes everywhere
to repress the peoples' struggles as the international gendarme of
'Western civilisation'. At the same time it tries to impose its
hegemony on the other imperialist countries, which does not happen
without provoking opposition. Thus American imperialism is at one
of the poles of each of the four fundamental contradictions. It is
possible and necessary to isolate it by forming a broad united
front. The latter implies:

   - the combination of all forces resolutely opposed to American
imperialism;

   - the denunciation of the fraud represented by the 'peace
negotiations' proposed by Johnson or his British or other errand
boys as well as all the attempts to give him a 'way out' in Vietnam
thanks to a compromise over the heads of the Vietnamese people.

THERE IS COMPROMISE AND COMPROMISE

Let there be no mistake, this does not mean that there are no
situations in which a compromise with the enemy might not be
necessary; but these are always tactical compromises; truces which
only serve to prepare one's forces better for the next attack. Such
a compromise is akin to a strategic retreat. The aim of the latter,
says Mao, 'is to preserve the strength of the army and to prepare
for the counter-offensive'. Unprincipled compromises are those
which prepare not for the counter-offensive but for a definitive
settlement with the enemy; that is to say, surrender. Is it not
surrender for revolutionaries to renounce revolution? It is, and
more, for there is no third road. One is revolutionary or counter-
revolutionary. He who wants to make his peace with imperialism is
on the threshold of passing lock, stock and barrel over to its side.

WHAT CO-EXISTENCE PROMISES ...

The degeneration of the leaders of the CPSU illustrates this
process. Since the 20th Congress (February 1956) Khrushchev, his
successors and his supporters throughout the world have explained
that the goal of Soviet policy was to banish from social life now

and for ever all wars and not only atomic war. The establishment of
a perpetual peace is necessary since 'the spark of a local war can
set the world alight' and destroy mankind. It is possible before
the world triumph of socialism and the disappearance of class
antagonism, on the other hand, mainly because of the presence of
'reasonable' statesmen at the head of the principal imperialist
countries (President Eisenhower 'is as anxious as we are to ensure
peace,' said Khrushchev). As civil wars are also wars, this noble
ideal of peace will be realised all the more easily if communists
avoid the resort to violence. The latter is no longer necessary, as
it is now possible for them 'to win a solid parliamentary majority'
and to use it to carry out the transition to socialism peacefully.
'The historical mission of the proletariat is to defend peace' and
'peaceful co-existence is the higher form of the class struggle'.

This idea of peaceful co-existence has supposedly already proved
its effectiveness. For example, the Soviet theoretician,
G. Strarushenko wrote (in 'La Vie internationale', October 1963):

At present the policy of peaceful co-existence ... paralyses the
counter-revolutionary aggression of imperialism on the whole
earth (sic), favouring the rise of the national revolutionary
movement of national liberation.

... WHAT IT ACHIEVES

Today, with the examples of Vietnam, Laos, the Congo, Gabon and San
Domingo, this idyllic image of international relations seems hardly
convincing. Besides, these are not contingent defeats of the policy
of 'peaceful co-existence', but its direct result. The Soviet
leaders could make William the Silent's motto their own: 'It is not
necessary to hope to undertake, nor to succeed to persevere.' The
fact that the 'Camp David spirit' was followed by the U-2 incident,
that the Vienna meeting did not prevent the blockade of Cuba, that
the Treaty of Moscow led to the aggression in North Vietnam - none
of these things has dissipated their illusions about the possibility
of an understanding with the imperialists. Are they, besides,
labouring under illusions? Do they also share those which their
propaganda diffuses every day among the masses? (Particularly the
possibility of imposing a general and complete disarmament on the
imperialists?)

Or rather, is this merely a smokescreen behind which they are
pursuing their grand design, a rapprochement with the USA at the
expense of the peoples of the entire world?

Given the principles according to which socialist countries do
not export revolution, peaceful co-existence as Marxist-Leninists
understand it (the maintenance of the system of the four fundamental
contradictions, non-crossing of frontiers by armies) can be imposed
by the balance of forces. On the other hand, the Khrushchevite
'peaceful co-existence' (end to the Cold War, co-operation and
friendship with the imperialists) implies the adversary's agreement.
Seeing Khrushchev begging for their friendship, the imperialists put
their conditions to him. President Johnson formulated them in his
message on 21 January 1964 at the Geneva Conference: (3)

We will be prepared to discuss means of prohibiting the threat or

> use of force, directly or indirectly - whether by aggression,
> subversion, or the clandestine supply of arms - to change
> boundaries or demarcation lines; to interfere with access to
> territory; or to extend control or administration over territory
> by displacing established authorities.

In this way, Johnson asked the Soviet government to co-operate with
him to proscribe the threat to the established powers. As 'Le
Monde' commented: 'This is really the basic problem.'

THE DIVISION OF THE WORLD

The reactionaries have always feared 'subversion' and 'indirect
aggression' much more than a war of conquest unleashed by the USSR.
If they trumpeted that it was an aggressive power aspiring to
conquer the world, they were translating into their own language the
fact that the USSR supported the peoples' revolutionary struggles.
Today we must believe that they are no longer worried about this.
When, after its return from Moscow in 1964, the SFIO delegation
declared that it recognised the USSR's desire for peace, one could
justifiably wonder who converted who. Reading ex-Chancellor
Adenauer's enthusiastic statements after the Tashkent agreement
acclaiming the USSR as a champion of peace makes one sure about
this. Can the word 'peace' mean the same coming from
revolutionaries and from the most reactionary of German
reactionaries? Can we join in united action with those who have
many times proclaimed their willingness to agree and unite with the
American imperialists to share the world? On 10 September 1961
Khrushchev stated that 'We are the strongest countries in the world
and if we unite for peace there can be no war. Then if any madman
wanted wars, we would but have to shake our fingers to warn him
off.' (4) And here is what Gromyko declared on 13 December 1962
(the day after the crisis in the Caribbean): 'If there is agreement
between the government heads of the Soviet Union and the USA, "there
will be a solution of international problems on which mankind's
destinies depend".' (5)

These were fond illusions, for the peoples of the world have not
accepted and will never accept that two statesmen decide their fate.
The spirited development of the struggle of the Vietnamese people
has somewhat upset Khrushchev's plans.

THE IMPERIALISTS PREPARE FOR ESCALATION

Towards the end of 1963, the Americans began to envisage an
extension of the war to North Vietnam in an attempt, by a sort of
'flight forward', to bring to an end a conflict in which they felt
they were getting inescapably bogged down in. By moving from
special war to classic war, they hoped that their superiority in
weapons would give them victory. Thanks to an inspired leak from
the Pentagon, the 'New York Times' announced on 9 June 1964 that the
American general staff had advised the government to bomb targets in
the North. The aim of this announcement and the whole campaign of
official and unofficial statements in which it took place was to
sound out the intentions of the USSR while blackmailing Hanoi.

In the face of such a definite threat, the Soviet Union had one infallible means to dissuade the Americans from firing their shot: a solemn declaration that it would respond to any aggression against the DRV, a member of the socialist camp, exactly as if it were a question of the USSR itself, a demonstration that this warning was serious by strengthening the Vietnamese anti-aircraft defences with the most modern apparatus and also be sending units of the Soviet fleet armed with missiles to the Gulf of Tonkin. The USSR not only carefully abstained from these measures which alone could have preserved peace, but let it be understood, moreover, that it was unconcerned in what was happening in South-east Asia by making it known that it was considering resigning from its offices as co-President of the Geneva Conference.

Marshall Malinowski had already stated on 24 January 1962 that the military power of the Soviet Union protected 'the socialist countries which are friendly to us'. These and other similar statements (cf. 'Pravda' 7 January 1963) were interpreted by the Pentagon experts in a restrictive sense. To dot the i's Valerian Zorin published an article in 'Izvestia' on 30 January 1964 entitled 'The problems of disarmament and the manoeuvres of Peking' in which he claimed that if China seeks to become a nuclear power it is because it 'has aims and pursues special interests which the socialist camp cannot support by military force'. This veiled warning took certain American plans into account. The journal 'The Minority of One' (the editorial committee of which includes four Nobel Prize Winners) published an enquiry in which we read:

> The partly public debate between the government and the army of the United States as to whether an armed intervention in North Vietnam would weaken enemy pressure on the forces engaged in the South only serves to hide a far more secret discussion on the advisability of plunging into a much more total war against the People's Republic of China.

Thus in the conflict that was approaching the USSR denounced China in advance as responsible and declared that it would stand aside. Replying on 8 July to a note from Hanoi on 25 June, the Soviet government was silent about the aid that it could provide in the event of American aggression against North Vietnam. The leaders in Washington interpreted all these facts to mean that they had a green light for such a project. The pattern of events was to bear them out.

DON'T GO TOO FAR!

After an incident totally fabricated by the Americans, the latter bombed five towns in North Vietnam on 4 August 1964. How did the USSR react? Very simply ... it did not react. 'Izvestia' did publish an article entitled 'Don't go too far!' One way of saying that the Americans had not gone too far. A logical position, moreover, since the journal implicitly admitted that the pretext put forward by the USA was true, objecting only that one cannot talk about legitimate defence 'thousands of kilometres away from American territory'. In contrast, the correspondent of the New China News Agency made a point of showing all the improbabilities,

contradictions and absurdities contained in the American account
which, anyway, the serious organs of the Western press discussed
with as much scepticism. The Tass Agency merely declared 'Official
Soviet circles resolutely condemn the aggressive actions of the USA
in the Gulf of Tonking which are leading to a dangerous worsening of
an already delicate situation.' In short, the USSR only blamed the
USA for 'ill-considered or provocative acts and steps'
('L'Humanité', August 1964) which increased 'tension'. The
reactionary press was not taken in: in an article entitled 'Russians
and Americans, the same aim' on 11 August, for example, 'France-
Soir' declared:

> According to the Americans, China now knows that it cannot rely
> on Soviet nuclear protection if it embarks on a warlike
> adventure. For the moment, the Soviets and the Americans
> therefore seem to have the same aim: the re-establishment of
> peace in South-east Asia. They have reached an understanding at
> the expense of Peking. It even seems that President Johnson may
> have been in contact with Khrushchev on this question during the
> crisis.

THE MOSCOW TREATY

In fact, did Khrushchev use the hot-line when he still had the time
(Johnson made a speech announcing the attacks several hours before
the bombers took off), or did he think that the bombing of a
socialist country was not an act liable to endanger world peace ...?
If the two associates did talk it is above all probable, furthermore, that they congratulated each other on the occasion of the
first anniversary of the Moscow Treaty, 'a great step forward
towards détente and complete general disarmament', which was at that
moment being celebrated with great pomp in the USSR.

THE IMPERIALISTS GROW BOLD

Seeing that, in accordance with their expectations and contrary to
its assurances, the USSR was not reacting, the American imperialists
grew bold. The only assurance given by the Soviet leaders, anyway,
was that they 'would not remain indifferent'. President Johnson
reckoned that the indifference or non-indifference of Moscow would
make no difference to him. As early as September, he had taken the
decision to bomb North Vietnam systematically. Perhaps because they
were not conversant with this decision, the Soviet and French
revisionists greeted his success in the Presidential elections as a
victory for peace.

When the bombings in the North became daily in March 1965, 'all
the Soviet soldiers and politicians joined in unison to raise the
spectre of a world war rather than emphasizing the Soviet ability to
exert military pressure locally', it was pointed out ironically by a
Pentagon expert, T. W. Wolfe, in a statement before a sub-committee
of the House of Representatives (11 March 1965).

THE SOVIET DOCTRINE: TOTAL SURRENDER OR TOTAL DESTRUCTION

According to the doctrine taught in manuals of military strategy in the USSR, a local conflict in which the two greatest world powers got involved 'would inevitably degenerate into a thermo-nuclear war' (cf. 'Voiennaia Stratgia', ed. Marshall Sokolovski, p. 299 of the American translation). One can now understand why the USSR did not reply to the bombing of North Vietnamese towns. One might simply ask if a line does exist which would call forth a Soviet reaction if crossed by the American imperialist aggressors. Until 1964, it was thought that this line surrounded the entire socialist camp. Since then, one can reasonably surmise that it only includes the USSR. A question then arises: if the Americans bombed Odessa tomorrow, why should the whole of humanity perish to avenge the inhabitants of Odessa? Would their lives be worth more than those of the inhabitants of Dong Hoi?

There are two answers to this question:

1 The lives of the inhabitants of Odessa are in actual fact more valuable because they are Russian and not Vietnamese. As a Soviet journalist said, 'the man in the street has no need of subtle doctrines; he thinks, as long as the bombs are not falling on my head - that's OK!' ('France nouvelle', 25 September 1963). The Soviet leaders have long since rid themselves of 'the subtle doctrine' of proletarian internationalism and will never take the slightest risk to defend even a socialist country against imperialism.

2 It is not true that a local conflict between the USSR and the USA would necessarily degenerate into a thermo-nuclear war. This thesis is only put forward to justify the USSR's passivity, the real motive of which is its desire to come to terms and to co-operate with the USA.

BETRAYAL BEHIND A FAÇADE OF SUPPORT

Resistance to imperialism is the way to the defence of peace. The real problem is to know if one wants to resist it and if one stands ready to resist it.

The Soviet leaders have been caught off their guard by every aggression of the USA and each ascent on the ladder of escalation. They were not prepared to face up to it either on the material or on the ideological level. How could they be, considering that for more than ten years the facts have constantly contradicted their analyses? Besides, the latter only have an apologetic function for them. Their problem is: how to co-operate with the imperialists while retaining their influence over at least a part of the international communist movement? This influence increases their 'bargaining power' with their American 'partners'. It is necessary to them, moreover, in order to help the Americans. They have thought up two enormous deceptions to fool the peoples:

  - the so-called obstacles which China put in the way of Soviet aid to Vietnam crossing its territory;
  - the unity of action to help Vietnam.

'ANY LIE WILL BE BELIEVED IF IT IS BIG ENOUGH' (GOEBBELS)

Let us look into the first claim. Since March 1965, senior Soviet officials have leaked to Western correspondents in Moscow the news that China was opposing the transit of arms hurried through by the USSR while, in fact, China transmits all the equipment she receives with urgency and absolute priority, and for nothing. The revisionist press reproduced the despatches of the Western agencies, date-line Moscow, which, however, were contradicted by joint Soviet-Vietnamese statements according to which the aid programme to Vietnam was going ahead as planned. In January 1966 the Chinese government sent the Soviet government a note asking it to deny 'the false rumours of the so-called sabotage by China of the aid to North Vietnam'. Moscow refused to accept this note in order not to have to reply one way or the other. In March 1966, the leaders of the CPSU sent a letter to the Communist Parties of Eastern Europe which took up the same accusations. This letter was reprinted in 'Die Welt' and 'Le Monde' and has never been denied. Finally, in a speech given on 20 April 1966, in Budapest, Marshal Malinowski finally had the courage (or the cynicism) to take responsibility for these slanders. He got the reply he deserved. On 4 May, a Chinese spokesman described him as a 'liar', backing this up with the facts. Without using such virulent expressions, Pham Van Dong, the Prime Minister of Vietnam, thanked the Chinese on 25 April for its 'effective assistance as well as its devoted help in delivering aid sent by the Soviet Union and other fraternal European countries'. Later, the Vietnamese comrades repeatedly rejected the slanderous allegations put into circulation by the Soviet renegades. Thus, on 19 June 1966, the Vietnamese Information Agency communicated that:
> A certain number of Western Agencies have recently propagated the rumour according to which the military material provided as aid by the Soviet Union is at present meeting with difficulties hindering its passage across China ... the said information is only a totally fabricated fable contrived with evil provocative intent (see the complete text as well as General Giap's statement in 'Garde Rouge' no. 2).

Nevertheless, the revisionists continue imperturbably to repeat the same lines in accordance with the precept, 'If you throw enough mud some of it will always stick.'

A CONFESSION

What we must remember about this affair is not the disgraceful methods resorted to by the degenerate clique at the head of the CPSU, but the implicit confession which they contain. The revisionists seem to say that it is China's fault if the Vietnamese do not receive sufficient aid. The fact is that Vietnam receives aid well below the possibilities of the USSR both in quantity and quality. While the imperialists do the maximum to win the war, the USSR does the minimum necessary to hide its collusion with them. Washington is even grateful to it for this 'aid' and proclaims continually that the Vietnam war should not prevent closer Soviet-American co-operation.

OUT-DATED ANTI-AIRCRAFT DEFENCE

Let us consider the anti-aircraft defences. Since 1962, the Soviets
have asserted that they possess anti-missile missiles. Now it is a
thousand times more difficult to hit a missile in flight than a
plane. Today the USSR is in the process of installing these
missiles around its big cities. These devices are so costly that
the USA recoiled at the outlay and gave up the idea of installing
them. The Soviet anti-missile missiles are therefore sufficiently
effective to justify such sacrifices. Is it not astonishing to note
that the whole of the Vietnamese anti-aircraft defences have only
rarely inflicted losses exceeding 1·5 per cent on the American
pirates? It is because the missiles provided by the USSR date from
1958 and are totally out of date. According to French military
experts, the ordinary anti-aircraft missiles at France's disposal
are capable of bringing down 80 per cent of the attacker's planes.
We can therefore reasonably suppose that the Soviet missiles are
capable of bringing down at least 60 per cent of them, even if they
are used by inadequately trained Vietnamese personnel. This
percentage would have been even higher if the USSR had trained the
gun crews before the bombing. In this case, it is even quite
certain that the latter would not have begun in the first place.

THE COLD WAR: A MISUNDERSTANDING

Not to prepare to resist aggression is to encourage it. But how
could the Soviet leaders have prevented the imperialists from
wresting the initiative from them when they have always considered
the cold war as a misunderstanding which a tête-à-tête between
statesmen would be enough to clear up. (Look at the spirit of Camp
David which has long haunted revisionist propaganda.) When Mao
says, 'At whatever moment the civil war breaks out we must be ready.
Even if it should arrive very soon, say tomorrow morning, we must
also be ready', he seems to be stating a commonplace like
Demosthenes's statement that 'those who know how to make war
forestall events instead of following them'. Of course this idea is
not difficult to understand; the enemy must still be considered an
enemy. Secure from any attack on their own territory thanks to
their modern arms, the Soviet leaders do not think that their
national interests in other respects are always opposed to those of
the USA. They avoid giving Vietnam means capable of doing too much
damage to the Americans. This would compromise their good relations
with them. Even quantitative level Soviet aid is ridiculously
insufficient. 'During the year 1965 China transported to Vietnam
some 43,000 tons of Soviet equipment', a spokesman of the Chinese
Ministry for Foreign Affairs declared on 4 May 1966. Jean Baby, who
quotes this statement, points out: 'By way of comparison, the
Americans have sent 800,000 tons of military equipment every month,
not including the bombs carried by the planes of the Seventh Fleet.'
The Chinese spokesman added the following specification: 'In the
first quarter of 1966 the USSR asked China for 1,730 trucks to
transport military equipment. China gave its agreement and got the
trucks ready; yet the deliveries carried out represented only 536
trucks' (quoted by Jean Baby, ibid.).

The Soviet leaders help the USA to transfer their forces from Europe to Asia by making concession after concession to them on the questions of Germany and West Berlin. Did they not forego signing a separate peace treaty with the GDR? They themselves have trans- ferred troops from Central Europe to the Far East. Together with the imperialists they help to encircle China, the red base of the revolutionary peoples.

CO-ORDINATION OR SUSPENSION OF THE POLEMICS

The revisionists now criticise China for not co-operating with the other socialist countries to co-ordinate aid to Vietnam. What does this accusation mean? According to the 'People's Daily' on 14 June 1965, 'China provided as much aid to the Vietnamese people as she could.' The Soviet leaders have not dared to make such a statement. According to the estimates of American experts, China provides aid at least equal in value to that of the USSR (some 500 million dollars) although her industrial production is four times lower. We have seen that China does not prevent the aid from other socialist countries reaching its destination. What then, would be the use of the 'co-ordination' which the Soviet Union makes such a fuss about since it would not increase the Chinese aid or theirs? Its only function would be to secure an implicit certificate of good conduct from China for the Soviet policy in Vietnam. This would be no more or less than the suspension of the polemics which the renegades in the Kremlin have been desperately calling for since 1963; that is, since they themselves initiated the public polemic against the Marxist-Leninists. Now the consistent struggle against imperialism is inseparable from the struggle against revisionism and opportunism. This is a position of principle already stated by Lenin.

A NEW TASHKENT

The revisionists do not support the struggle of the Vietnamese people politically. They proclaim their 'right to peace'. But they do not proclaim their right to a just peace based on the four points of the DRNV and the five points of the NLF. They unilaterally emphasise the sufferings of the Vietnamese people and the dangers of world war, but ignore the invincible character of the just war which it is conducting against the aggressor. They describe the NLF as 'representative' not as the sole, authentic representative of the Vietnamese people. The only condition which they have laid down for opening negotiations is a halt to the bombing and a pledge from the Americans to withdraw their troops, not the previous withdrawal of the latter demanded by the Vietnamese. They verbally denounce the fraud of the Americans' peace proposals (while practising secret diplomacy with them on a wide scale) but keep quiet about the acts of their faithful agents, the Tito-Ghandi clique. In this way they are preparing public opinion for a new 'Tashkent'; that is, an agreement based on the maintenance of the territorial 'status quo' and lines of demarcation (the 17th parallel!) which would hand South

Vietnam over to imperialist domination as the Tashkent agreement
handed the people of Kashmir over to the oppression of Indian
chauvinism. They do not even hide their intentions. Did they not
publish in March 1966 in 'Temps nouveaux', no. 6, an article
declaring that 'two roads present themselves to the world, that of
Tashkent or that of Vietnam'?

STRUGGLE AGAINST THE AGENTS OF IMPERIALISM

If the USSR provides a very inadequate and very limited aid to
Vietnam (old stocks of out-dated arms), they do so in order to make
sufficient political capital to be able when the moment arrives to
swing the balance in favour of a solution which would offer 'a way
out for the USA', according to Kosygin's expression. But the
imperialists are not seeking a way out, they want victory. The way
out which the revisionists would like to offer them corresponds to
their fundamental objective: the maintenance of their domination
over South Vietnam. How could there be a united front on this
basis? In addition, to consent to a suspension of the polemic would
be to disarm the peoples ideologically and hand them over to the
penetration of bourgeois ideology and its accomplice, revisionism.
    As the Vietnamese journal, 'Tam Viet Hoa', said on 13 July 1966:
    The only true revolutionaries are those who resolutely combat
    American imperialism, while the modern revisionists have
    successfully arrived at a compromise with American imperialism
    and are renegades who put spokes in the wheels of the revolution.
In conclusion, there is no place for the revisionists in a united
front against American imperialism for the excellent reason that
they are its agents within the workers' movement!
    As Lenin said: (6) 'The fight against imperialism is a sham and
humbug unless it is inseparably bound up with the fight against
opportunism.'

THE JCR IN MAY-JUNE 1968 (1)

What are the reasons for the deep affinities which linked a faction of the Trotskyists and the PSU for quite a time? These affinities led to Charléty. (2) As it does not seem that there has been the least self-criticism on this point, as on many others, we are entitled to ponder and ask some questions.

Let us recall the essential facts: in the first week of May the ex-JCR constituted the secular arm of the UNEF: in the following weeks it concentrated in the Facultés and the new-born co-ordinations; in the decisive week of 24/31 May, it turned up with the PSU at the demonstrations on the 24th and then at Charléty Stadium. Finally, from then on, given 'the Gaullist counter-offensive', it decided that the tide was turning and that its task was to organise the vanguard, and especially as the agitation among the masses was persistent, that it was necessary to guard this newly-born vanguard from the temptations of adventurism and diehard attitudes. The supporters of the 'proletarian resistance' thus found they were labelled 'diehards'.

It was the time when the great ghosts from the past were raised: it was recalled that it had taken years for the workers' movement to recover from its weakness after 'the Commune massacre'. Where did these ideas come from? Less from books or memories than from the revisionist CP. Subsequent events were to demonstrate it fully: the theme of the Commune as the funeral march of the working class is Waldeck Rochet's favourite theme.

As is clear from these facts, one question is unavoidable: what was the reason for this political proximity of the ex-JCR and the PSU?

VANGUARDIST THOUGHT

Its most illuminating expression was that of 'rehearsal' (répétition). 1968 was the dress-rehearsal for the French socialist revolution. Well and good, but when we analyse the contents of this rehearsal the effect becomes frankly burlesque.

Roughly speaking, if things did not work in 1968 it was because there was no vanguard; if there was no vanguard it was because at the decisive moment, the militants of the vanguard did not have the means to instil into the masses the vanguard line, which is that of 'workers' control', the line of 'the revolutionary transition'. This 'repeats' (répète) Trotsky's Transitional Program of 1938. This is not all; this programme is a repetition of Lenin's programme in 1917. And as everyone knows, 1917 was preceded by the rehearsal of 1905. The class struggle is a theatre where the same play is always performed.

Such a vanguardist thought which would have upheld and repeated the first vanguard play acted on the stage, the Bolshevik revolution – that is what was missing in 1968.

Let us read the ex-JCR's action during the revolutionary storm in the light of this theory. The ex-JCR is the vanguard since this thought belongs to it, but in 1968 this vanguard was not in a position to function as a vanguard.

Two consequences: it reacted to the changes in the balance of forces as if it dominated it politically: it put itself in the place of a vanguard which it was not in fact but which it could have been. The week of 24/31 May was decisive: there was a vacuum of power, why? Quite simply because if there had been a vanguard instead of the PCF-CGT, events would have gone quite differently: the power would have been there for the taking (and it would have been taken) ...

Likewise, since the PCF did not react to the counter-offensive of power on 31 May, since from this moment on the power was no longer there to take, the objective could only be to guard the vanguard (the one which ... in the place of the PCF might have changed the face of history).

We can see the practical result: this imaginary identification amounted to following the balance of forces decided by the PCF.

One becomes the revolutionary shadow of the PCF, the projected shadow.

Proletarian resistance is inadmissible in this category of ideas. In fact, its objective is precisely to upset the PCF-Gaullist game. Its objective is that the workers' strength which is repressed ideologically by revisionism should express itself with the help of the revolutionary students.

This expression is the dawn of a proletarian party. A party which is born from the revolutionary struggle of the masses (revolutionary workers and students) against the enemies, the counter-revolution: the establishment and its revisionist accomplices.

Two roads: either one calls oneself (in thought or in words) a vanguard and this leads to a 'paradoxical' political practice.

Or one builds a vanguard, the leading core of the people's cause. And then one proceeds from reality. Which means, among other things that one proceeds from the fact that the masses still do not acknowledge us as the vanguard.

To transform this reality is to show in deeds how one has made history advance.

PETTY-BOURGEOIS REVOLUTIONISM

We have just seen how a vanguardist thought acquires in thought what must be created in matter. We have seen how such a thought implies tailism. In fact, this imaginary vanguard is forced to proceed from the reality produced by those who occupy the place which it wants (the leadership of the working class). In other words it (critically) tails along behind it.

It remains to analyse the following fact: in this specific case, what is the real position adopted by this vanguard in words? If it is not in the van, where is it?

The facts show that the ex-JCR was on the 'left' of the PSU. Why that position?

In answer to this question it is not enough to say that it is no accident if they found each other good comrades since they were both 'leading' the same movement (the student movement); other political groups which had a mass influence in the revolutionary student movement (ex-22 March, ex-UJCML) did not have this putschist orientation.

This coincidence must therefore have been facilitated not only by a common social reference group (the student movement) but by a convergent policy. This is what must be determined.

Ideological convergence was perceptible well before May: the theses of Mandel, the thinker of the ex-JCR and the adaptor of Trotsky's Transitional Program to the conditions of our era, met and partially fused with the theses of petty-bourgeois socialism: the theses of 'revolutionary reformism'. The line of 'worker's control' became the line of 'anti-capitalist structural reforms'.

The line of 'counter-power' has been amalgamated with that of 'dual power'. For the revolutionary reformists, counter-power is the line which consists of opposing one policy by another policy, and one power of decision-making by a counter-power; for example, opposing the power of the bosses by the power of the unions, a plan by a counter-plan, a model of civilisation by another model of civilisation.

We can clearly see that this line proceeds from the forms of imperialist despotism (extension of despotism; new phenomena of distribution of power) and opposes to it a 'reformist' line of action: in fact, instead of determining a policy radically opposed to the present structure of despotism, a policy is proposed which, espousing the forms of despotism as they appear, is nothing but the renewal of the classical tactics of reformism: the imaginary 'nibbling' at power, the real refusal to destroy it because of the refusal to pose concretely the question of the gun which is the pillar of imperialist despotism.

Apparently the Trotskyist case is very different, since here appeal is made to the theme of armed insurrection. But this is only an appearance.

Let us consider Trotsky's Transitional Program, the fundamental reference. It seems to repeat in every aspect the Bolshevik Programme in 1917. But there is a snag: in 1917 the theme of workers' control was dependent on a concrete context from which it derived all its meaning. Divorced from this context it loses all its meaning. What was the context? The existence of Soviets, of a

Red power devised by the masses. What was the essence of this
power? It was a revolutionary power because, thanks to leading
activity of the Bolsheviks, it combined two essential conditions:
the support of the masses and the gun.

It was a power because its base was a mass base and its pillar,
the embryo of the army, had already formed. In other words, in
order to find ourselves in a 1917 type of situation once again, it
would be necessary not only to have its line of 'workers' control'
(for Lenin this was at most a secondary element of the line), but
above all it would be necessary to have settled the question of the
unified arming of the revolutionary classes (and not only of the
proletariat): of the revolutionary classes, of the real majority of
the people. (3)

A flaw, as we see! In 1917, the Soviet was an unprecedented form
of unified armament of the revolutionary classes. We know the
secret of the matter: the inter-imperialist war had abolished the
distance between town and country (fundamental problem of the
Russian revolution), and the same war had given the gun to the
peasant: he was the soldier.

The principal question of the revolution is that of power; that
is, before the dictatorship of the proletariat, that of
revolutionary war: for good reason, it is not the question of
workers' control (or co-management).

When one claims to have rehearsed the big night by emerging from
May 1968 with the line of workers' control, what else is one doing
but to forget the gun even if elsewhere one chatters on about armed
insurrection and the strike pickets who are its first detachments.
Is the solution to the problem supposed to be invented in a month?
Might one not just as well say that one does not regard it as a
problem?

In the context of May 1968 in which the violence was never
politico-military but always politico-ideological (aiming less, in
fact, at destroying the enemy than at arousing friendly forces), it
is clear how this omission of the gun again became current.

Trotsky's continuators and the supporters of the peaceful, extra-
Parliamentary road (PSU) turned up on the same ground. The touching
harmony at Charléty is understandable.

One can see how social base (anti-authoritarian ideological
revolt of a petty-bourgeois character) and ideological base (amalgam
of the Trotskyist line of transition and the revolutionary reformist
line of transition) coincided to produce Charléty.

All this was cemented together by the position vis-à-vis
revisionism entitled 'Stalinist bureaucracy'. Just as the PSU line
implies left unity and the tactics of the PSU are to put pressure on
the left to 'renew' socialism; the tactics of the Trotskyists are to
put pressure on the Stalinist bureaucracy, a workers' party but a
blemished one (it has rejected the line of workers' control).

That is how, at Charléty, the pressure of revolutionary reformism
coincided with the pressure of the line of workers' control; a
double pressure which had to crush revisionism. The facts: far from
being crushed, revisionism emerged strengthened from Charléty.

These are thus strange vanguards.

CH'EN TU-HSIU'S IDEOLOGICAL ITINERARY

As the Trotskyists have presented Ch'en Tu-hsiu as a much more profound and clever theoretician than Mao Tse-tung, we have deemed it useful to bring together here a few passages outlining his ideological itinerary drawn from Y. C. Wang's book, 'Chinese Intellectuals and the West 1872 - 1949'. (1) It emerges fairly clearly from these that the opportunism of his policy had other causes than Stalin's instructions.

The son of a mandarin, Ch'en became Dean of Peking University. He played a big role in the May 4 Movement as editor of the journal 'New Youth'. In 1919, John Dewey, the American philosopher and pedagogue, made a lecture tour in China. It was under the inspiration of his teachings that Ch'en Tu-hsiu wrote an article entitled 'The basis for the realisation of democracy in China' for the December issue of 'New Youth', in which he suggested two programmes: local self-government and a new guild system. The two were possible, he believed, because (pp. 311-12):

> under the traditional laisser-faire policy there had been many self-governing bodies in the Chinese body-politic ... The guilds should be both the employers and the employees because, 'except in a few big factories, railroads and mines ... the status of employers and employees differs little in China'. One of the general principles for the organisation of these self-governing bodies was that 'stress should be given to the practical needs of the group concerned rather than to the broad problems facing the nation!

In another article Ch'en urged the Chinese to study Christianity and to incorporate 'the loftiness and greatness of Jesus Christ into their blood' (p. 312).

In May 1919, 'New Youth' published a special issue devoted to Marxism. 'The spirit that pervaded the issue was one of disapprobation' (p. 316). 'But by May 1920, his stand had completely changed ... (he) switched his belief from (bourgeois) democracy to Marxism-Leninism' (pp. 313-16).

When it was founded in 1921, Ch'en Tu-hsiu was elected General Secretary of the Chinese Communist Party. He remained in this post until the extraordinary meeting of the Central Committee on 7 August 1927, at which his opportunist line was criticised. In 1928-9, he

publicly attacked the party, which led to his expulsion in August
1929. (2) Then he joined the Trotskyists and in December published
his 'Letter to all members of the Chinese Communist Party'.

Arrested in 1932 by the Kuomintang authorities, he was condemned
to thirteen years' imprisonment but was freed by 1937. He died in
1942. (3)

In an article in 1940, Ch'en wrote: 'If Germany and Russia are to
emerge victorious (from the war) humanity will face a dark age for
at least half a century. Only if the capitalistic democracy can be
preserved through a victory by England, France and America can there
be a path to proletarian democracy.'

To those who were shocked by his new views, Ch'en replied (pp.
318-19):

> The difference between the so-called proletarian democracy and
> the capitalistic democracy is only one of scope. There does not
> exist a proletarian democracy with a different content. After
> the October Revolution efforts were made to destroy the substance
> of capitalistic democracy. It was replaced by a mere abstract
> term: proletarian democracy. The result is the Stalinist regime
> in Russia today, which is in turn imitated by Italy and Germany.

Y. C. Wang concludes his intellectual portrait of Ch'en Tu-hsiu in
these terms (pp. 319-20):

> Viewing Ch'en's life as a whole, it is difficult to detect any
> profound conviction on his part. He embraced Democracy and
> Science in 1919, when he was already forty years old. A bare few
> months later he forsook them for Communism. As leader of the
> party, he could not agree with the Comintern line, but yet lived
> by it for 'disciplinary reasons'. These, however, disappeared as
> soon as he lost the secretary-generalship, for contrary to the
> communist practice of democratic centralism ... he started to
> criticise the policy of the Politburo. For this he was expelled,
> and the setback immediately turned his thought to the formation
> of a Trotskyist faction. After his release from prison in 1937,
> his attitude once again changed. Trotsky and Lenin now in turn
> yielded the place of honour to Western Democracy ... What were
> the factors that underlay his volatility? One reason clearly was
> his intellectual shallowness. At no time did Ch'en really
> understand the causes that he either supported or opposed ... A
> year was to elapse between his declaration for democracy and his
> attempt to elaborate on it. When it did appear, the elaboration
> was no more than an adaptation of Dewey's lectures with some
> shallow observations on China's guild system and village
> democracy. As a recent writer has shown, (4) even when Ch'en had
> become totally committed to Marxism-Leninism, he was blissfully
> unaware of the myriad theoretical difficulties confronting Lenin
> and other Marxists.

NOTES

(The following abbreviations occur in the notes that follow: CW = 'Collected Works'; SW = 'Selected Works'.)

INTRODUCTION

1 La Révolution défigurée, 'De la Révolution', p. 111.
2 Cf., for example, the way they are used by Pierre Broué in 'Le Parti bolchevique', and by Livio Maïtan in his report on the cultural revolution in China to the 9th Congress of the Fourth International (Documents of the World Congress of the Fourth International, 'Intercontinental Press', vol. 7, no. 26, 14 July 1969).
3 Cf. 'Le Discours de la guerre'.
4 'Origins of the Chinese Revolution', pp. 78-9.
5 Even before the publication of 'Lessons of October' in October 1924, the journal 'Bolshevik', criticising Trotsky's articles, correctly pointed out that 'Comrade Trotsky evokes Lenin's lifelong comrades, those who constituted the basic cadre of Bolshevism, only in so far as it is essential to recall their mistakes'. (Quoted by P. and I. Sorlin, 'Lénine, Trotsky, Staline, 1921-1927'.)
6 Pierre Naville, 'Le Monde', 5 April 1969.
7 Figuères draws uncritically on the anti-Trotskyist literature of the Stalin era. In this case his source is the collection 'Trotsky et le trotskysme', published in 1937 by the PCF.

CHAPTER 2 AN ATEMPORAL DOGMATISM

1 For a party to 'lead' a revolutionary movement its authority does not have to be acknowledged by its allies. It is necessary and sufficient that its line be consistent and its slogans correct, in accordance with the interests and wishes of the masses, and apt to unite all those who can be united against the principal enemy. Its partners are then compelled to follow it to a certain extent. When they do not, they become isolated and their influence declines owing to the fact that the party

practises a policy of unity and struggle towards them,
supporting them to the extent that they oppose the common enemy,
criticising them in so far as they incline towards a compromise.
For example, the policy of the anti-Japanese united front in
China aimed less at unity with Chiang Kai-shek than at
mobilising the broad masses around communist slogans. Cf. Han
Suyin, 'The Morning Deluge', p. 391.

2 Marx and Engels, SW, vol. 1, p. 282; Die Klassenkämpfe in
Frankreich, Marx and Engels, 'Werke', Bd 7, pp. 89-90.
3 '1905', p. 55.
4 Cf. Trotsky, The permanent revolution, in 'The Permanent
Revolution', p. 60.
5 Ibid., p. 60.
6 Ibid., p. 77.
7 Lenin, CW, vol. 9, p. 56.
8 'Results and Prospects', p. 212.
9 Ibid., p. 201.
10 According to Trotsky this is the title of a pamphlet whose
author was Parvus, ibid., p. 42.
11 CW, vol. 9, p. 25.
12 Ibid., p. 24.
13 'The Permanent Revolution', p. 4.
14 According to Lenin, this formula makes provision only for a
rapport between the classes, not for a political institution
that brings about that rapport, that collaboration. Cf. CW,
vol. 9.
15 CW, vol. 9, p. 46. By petty bourgeois Lenin meant small
independent producers; particularly, therefore, peasant small-
holders.
16 Ibid., vol. 15, p. 60.
17 Ibid., p. 373.
18 Ibid., vol. 24, p. 47.
19 Ibid., p. 49.
20 27 April 1917; ibid., p. 142.
21 Isaac Deutscher, 'Stalin', p. 284; Pierre Broué, 'Le Parti
bolchevique', p. 83.
22 CW, vol. 24, p. 150.
23 Lenin, The proletarian revolution and the renegade Kautsky, SW,
vol. 3, p. 138.
24 'Stalin', pp. 283-4.
25 'Two Tactics of Social Democracy', CW, vol. 9, pp. 84-5.
26 'Stalin', pp. 283-4.
27 E. Mandel, 'The Leninist Theory of Organisation', p. 22.
28 March 1909; CW, vol. 15, p. 371.
29 Bourgeois transformations can be carried out by a feudal power
(as was the case at the time of so-called primitive accumulation
in England, and in Germany under Bismarck) or by a proletarian
power (as was the case from October 1917 to July 1918 in Russia,
and in China from 1947 to 1952).
30 In numerous passages of the book he describes it as 'backwards',
'primitive', etc. Now the Chinese peasants were no less so, and
yet Mao talks of them with the greatest admiration on account of
their revolutionary spirit. 'The eye of the peasant is clear,'
he has said. Judging by the number of peasant insurrections in

the second half of the nineteenth century (roughly 500 per
decade) one can conclude that the Russian peasants were just as
revolutionary.

31   Our differences, article in '1905', p. 316.

32   'Two Tactics of Social Democracy', CW, vol. 9, p. 60.

33   Ibid., vol. 15, p. 374.

34   Trotsky distinguished these two stages, 'in principle', 'in
theory', just as he distinguished the minimum programme from the
maximum programme. But apart from the fact that for him this
distinction disappears at the moment of the seizure of power, it
was not reflected in his propaganda and his choice of slogans:
and with good reason. In his book '1905' he cited Lassalle, who
had drawn from the events of 1848-9 'the unshakable conviction
that no struggle in Europe can be successful unless, from the
very start, it declares itself to be purely socialist' ('1905',
p. 55). The experience of revolutionary struggles since the
beginning of the century would rather warrant the opposite
axiom.

35   Quoted by Stalin in The October Revolution and the tactics of
the Russian communists, in 'Problems of Leninism', vol. 1, p.
185. See also Lenin's 'Testament', in which it is said: 'Our
party relies on two classes and therefore its instability would
be possible and its downfall inevitable if there were no
agreement between these two classes' (CW, vol. 36, p. 594).

36   'The Permanent Revolution' and 'Results and Prospects', pp. 241,
247.

37   Ibid., p. 247.

38   Ibid., p. 237.

39   Ibid., p. 247.

40   Quoted by Stalin in The October Revolution and the tactics of
the Russian communists, in 'Problems of Leninism', vol. 1, p.
193.

41   Speech at the 14th Conference of the Communist Party of the USSR
in a special number of 'Cahiers du bolchevisme', December 1926,
p. 207, quoted by Léo Figuères, 'Le Trotskysme cet antiléninisme', p. 160.

42   At the same time he was relying on the victory of the
proletarian revolution in one or several European countries.
The defeat of the Red Army before Warsaw made him understand
that henceforth the Soviet Union would have to rely above all on
its own forces.

43   Preface to '1905', 1st ed., 12 January 1922, pp. vi-vii.

44   'Speech to the Plenary Assembly of the Moscow Soviet', 20
November 1922, CW, vol. 33, p. 443.

45   Lenin, SW, vol. 3, p. 814. It concerned the article 'On
co-operation' dictated on 4 January 1923; the latter was the
most important of those in which Lenin touched on the problem of
the construction of socialism in the USSR.

46   'The Third International after Lenin', pp. 31-5.

47   Lenin, SW, vol. 3, p. 816.

48   'Problems of Leninism', pp. 158-162.

49   'New Left Review', no. 47, January-February 1968, p. 42.

50   Stalin was also wrong to argue that the possibility of
constructing socialism in one country had always been
acknowledged by the party.

51   'The Permanent Revolution', p. 22.
52   Ibid., pp. 156-7.
53   Ibid., pp. 26-27.
54   Cf., below, 'The fundamental traits of Trotskyism'.
55   'The Permanent Revolution', p. 28. In 'The Third International
     after Lenin', Trotsky spoke of 'the indissolubility of the
     economic and political ties between capitalist countries', which
     is supposed to be the basis of his thesis that 'the way out of
     these contradictions which will befall the proletarian dictator-
     ship in a backward country, surrounded by a world of capitalist
     enemies, will be found in the arena of world revolution' (op.
     cit., p. 40). According to him, the victorious proletariat
     cannot break these links and the danger to its power comes less
     from the threat of military intervention than from the 'pressure
     of cheap commodities'; 'a Ford tractor is just as dangerous as a
     Creusot gun' (ibid., p. 48).
56   Nicolas Krassó, Reply to Ernest Mandel, 'New Left Review', no.
     48, 1968.
57   'Problems of Leninism', p. 122. Nicolas Krassó's critique of
     Trotsky contains some interesting ideas but - it seems to one -
     the author remains in the grip of certain Trotskyist prejudices.
     Thus he writes: 'Stalin effectively wrote off the possibility of
     international revolutions, and made the construction of
     socialism in one country the exclusive task' ('New Left Review',
     no. 44, July-August 1967, p. 79). Krassó admires, moreover, the
     'magnitude' of Trotsky's 'achievement in correctly forecasting
     the basic nature of the October Revolution'. We have seen what
     must be thought of this.
58   Giuliano Procacci (ed.), 'Staline contre Trotsky', p. 155.
59   K. Marx, 'Critique of the Gotha Programme' (Marx and Engels, SW,
     vol. 3). In current usage, 'communism' designates the higher
     stage and 'socialism' the lower stage.
60   Interview in 'The Times', 25 September 1946, quoted by Fernando
     Claudin in 'La Crise du mouvement communiste', vol. 2, p. 684.
     Claudin is mistaken in arguing that Stalin had not formulated
     this thesis before 1946.
61   'Economic problems of socialism in the USSR', in SW, pp. 357,
     358.
62   Ibid., p. 330. Let us notice that Stalin identified the
     difference between town and country with the difference between
     agriculture and industry! (Ibid., p. 332.)
63   Moscow 1969, p. 352.
64   Napoleon, quoted by Lenin, SW, vol. 3, p. 823. The principle of
     'independence, autonomy and self-reliance' is abominated by the
     Trotskyists. By holding firmly to it the Chinese have been able
     to lay the bases of a modern industrial system and powerfully to
     develop their economy without falling into the power of
     imperialism or social imperialism. This is the only country in
     the world with an internal and external debt equal to zero.
65   Quoted in Lin Piao's Report to the 9th Congress of the CCP.
66   Ibid.
67   French leaders of the Fourth International.
68   This debate took place on 19 February 1964. The interventions
     have been published in the 'Cahiers du centre d'études
     socialistes', nos. 52, 53, January 1965.

69   Stuart Schram, 'Documents sur la théorie de la "révolution
     permanent" en Chine', Introduction. In contrast, Enrica
     Collotti-Pischel was correct to conform to the usage of the
     Peking translators, who distinguish in words what is
     distinguishable in meaning and entitled her book, 'La Révolution
     ininterrompue' (Paris, 1964) thus giving primacy to politics
     over philology.
70   'The Permanent Revolution', p. 116.
71   The facts have contradicted this prognosis of Trotsky.
72   'The Chinese revolution and the Chinese Communist Party', SW,
     vol. 2, pp. 330-1.
73   For Mao Tse-tung this term includes agricultural labourers,
     semi-proletarian poor peasants and middle peasants.
74   Revolutionary classes as a whole at a given stage.
75   Mao Tse-tung, 'On the correct handling of contradictions among
     the people', 'Selected Readings from the Works of Mao Tse-tung'.
76   See Chapter 6, below.
77   'The Permanent Revolution', pp. 155-6.
78   Ibid., p. 156.
79   'The Polemic of the General Line of the International Communist
     Movement', p. 203.
80   Ibid., p. 202.
81   If we add his underestimation of the peasantry, the accusation
     of Menshevism which Stalin made against him may be deemed less
     unfair.
82   L. Althusser, 'For Marx', p. 98.
83   'The Permanent Revolution', p. 9.
84   Marx's letter to Engels, 10 December 1869, quoted by Hélène
     Carrère d'Encausse and Stuart R. Schram in 'Marxism and Asia',
     p. 121.
85   Mao Tse-tung, On the correct handling of contradictions among
     the people, in 'Selected Readings from the Works of Mao
     Tse-tung', p. 358.

CHAPTER 3   TROTSKY'S INCAPACITY FOR CONCRETE ANALYSIS

1   'In Defence of Marxism', p. 49.
2   Quoted by Karl Korsch in Die alte Hegelsche Dialektik und die
     neue materialistische Wissenschaft, 'Der Gegner', 1932.
3   Considerations of these displacements makes it possible to pose
     the problem of periodisation in history correctly.
4   'The trade unions, the present situation and Trotsky's mistakes'
     (Lenin, CW, vol. 32).
5   Cf. Isaac Deutscher, 'The Prophet Armed', p. 375.
6   Cf. ibid., pp. 378-9.
7   Lenin, CW, vol. 36, p. 595.
8   Ibid., p. 595.
9   Isaac Deutscher, 'The Prophet Armed', p. 497.
10   Ibid., p. 499.
11   Ibid., p. 501.
12   SW, vol. 3, pp. 573-5. Elsewhere, Lenin declared that 'Trotsky
     made a number of mistakes bearing on the very essence of the
     dictatorship of the proletariat' ('The trade unions, the present
     situation and Trotsky's mistakes', Lenin, CW, vol. 32, p. 22).

13   Lenin, CW, vol. 35, p. 475.
14   The paragraph which follows is a summary of the second part of
     'Considérations quasiment épistémologiques', R. Linhart's
     Introduction to 'Documents des cahiers marxistes-leninistes',
     1965.
15   Among the first measures taken by the popular power in China
     were those which aimed at creating a healthy currency and the
     stabilisation of prices. These results were achieved by March
     1950.
16   'The Prophet Outcast', p. 126.
17   Ibid., p. 110. According to E. Mandel ('New Left Review', no.
     47) the Opposition proposed as an alternative to collectivi-
     sation: a special tax on the rich peasants and the reduction of
     administrative expenses (!).
18   'Problems of Leninism', vol. 2, pp. 423-4. Despite what
     Poulantzas asserts in 'Fascisme et dictature' (246), this
     argument does not imply any thesis of 'the impossibility of the
     revolution in Europe for a long time', but only that it was
     essential not to act as if its victory was certain. According
     to Stalin it was essential not to rely on it but to act in such
     a way as to face up to the least favourable eventuality: that of
     an impending war.
19   'La Proclamation programme des communistes bolcheviqes
     révolutionnaires soviétiques', Lyon, 1969, considers that all
     Stalin's mistakes belong to this latter category.
20   Speech delivered at the First All-Union Congress of Collective-
     Farm Shock Brigaders, 11 February 1933, 'Works', vol. 13, p.
     259.
21   Mosche Lewin, 'La Paysannerie et le pouvoir sovietique, 1928-
     30', as well as Merle Fainsod, 'Smolensk à l'heure de Staline',
     a work which uses the Smolensk archives covering the period
     1917-38. See particularly pp. 205-12, Stalin and Molotov's
     letter of 8 May 1933 (pp. 212-14) which condemned 'the ill-
     considered and widespread arrests in the countryside' and
     'Histoire de la collectivisation', Chapter 12.
22   Lenin to the 11th Congress, CW, vol. 33, p. 283, quoted by
     R. Linhart, La NEP: analyse de quelques caracteristiques de la
     phase de transition sovietique, 'Etudes de planification
     socialiste', no. 3, March 1966.
23   This is also Deutscher's view: 'The Prophet Outcast', p. 108.
24   'The Prophet Armed', p. 515.
25   'The Prophet Unarmed', p. 101.
26   'The New Economics', pp. 81-2.
27   'The Prophet Unarmed', p. 43.
28   Quoted by Deutscher, ibid., p. 44.
29   'Capital', vol. 1, p. 714.
30   Ibid., p. 714.
31   Ibid., p. 766.
32   Op. cit. As Australia at that time was a virgin continent, the
     workers preferred to establish themselves as independent farmers
     on lands that did not belong to anybody instead of submitting to
     wage slavery in the service of Mr Peel.
33   Cf. Charles Bettelheim, Due tipi di accumulazione, 'Il
     Manifesto', no. 5, May 1970. Published in French in 'Les Temps
     modernes', August-September 1970.

CHAPTER 4   A BUREAUCRATIC ANTI-BUREAUCRATISM

1 Quoted by L. Trotsky in Rapport de la délégation sibérienne, 'Spartacus', January-February 1970, p. 88. (See also 'The Prophet Armed', p. 45.)
2 I. Deutscher, 'The Prophet Armed', p. 76.
3 Ibid., p. 90.
4 Ibid., p. 92.
5 In 1906, 'Rosa practically identified party and masses' (Irène Petit in 'Politique aujourd'hui', September 1972). Cf. also Nicolas Krassó, Trotsky's Marxism, 'New Left Review', no. 44, July-August 1967. The passage quoted above concerning substitutionism is from 'Nos tâches politiques', p. 128. On Trotsky's spontaneism cf. ibid., pp. 125, 188.
6 Deutscher, op. cit., p. 92.
7 'Once Again on the Trade Unions', SW, vol. 3, p. 579.
8 'The trade unions, the present situation and Trotsky's mistakes', Lenin, CW, vol. 32.
9 'Once Again on the Trade Unions', loc cit., pp. 566, 588.
10 Central Commissariat of Transport.
11 In 1922 and 1923 he had rejected Lenin's insistent and repeated proposals that he should be appointed Vice-President of the Council of Peoples' Commissars, and that because there had to be two others: Rykov and Kamenev.
12 From the moment when Trotsky entered into opposition to the Central Committee with 'The New Course' (end of 1923) until his exile (end of 1927), he and his supporters were able to publish articles and speeches in the press. Despite or perhaps because of this, he was totally discredited in the eyes of communist militants and of public opinion at the end of this period. The masses have more judgment than is often thought and a polemicist's talent is not enough to make a weak argument strong.
13 'The Prophet Unarmed', p. 91
14 Cf. above 'Planning and NEP'.
15 Lenin himself was not mistaken. In numerous texts he expressed himself in extremely eulogistic terms about Stalin, 'the marvellous Georgian', and in his Testament he said of him that together with Trotsky he was the most prominent member of the Central Committee. In contrast, Trotsky held his rival in contempt and right until the end treated him as a 'dull mediocrity'.
16 At the 13th Congress (May 1924), Trotsky had acknowledged this, declaring: 'The allegation that I am in favour of permitting groupings is incorrect ... It is impossible to make any distinctions between a faction and a grouping' ('The Prophet Unarmed', p. 139).
17 In Mao's texts there is no question of democratic centralism except 'among the people'. A corollary of this is the supervision exercised over the Communist Party 'by the working people and the party membership', as well as other 'democratic parties' (On the correct handling of contradictions among the people, 'Selected Readings from the Works of Mao Tse-tung', p. 380).

18 'In Defence of Marxism', p. 101.
19 'Cahiers Rouges', no. 3, Paris, 1969, p. 35. The same
    E. Mandel repeats in 'Actualité de la théorie léniniste de
    l'organisation...' (1971) that the prohibition of factions
    announced by the 10th Congress at Lenin's instigation 'was a
    mistake'. The fact that from about 1929 the prohibition of
    factions served as a pretext for prohibiting the expression of
    differences on opinion proves Stalin wrong, perhaps, but not
    Lenin.
20 'In Defence of Marxism', p. 97.
21 Ibid., pp. 207, 211.
22 'Some questions concerning methods of leadership', SW, vol. 3,
    p. 119.
23 'On the correct handling of contradictions among the people',
    loc. cit., p. 355.
24 Mao Tse-tung, SW, vol. 4, p. 232.
25 Cf. Chapters 11, 12, 16 of 'Quotations from Chairman Mao
    Tse-tung', the Decision in Sixteen Points of 1966 (in
    J. Robinson, 'The Cultural Revolution in China', p. 84), as
    well as the rules of the Chinese Communist Party adopted by the
    9th Congress.
26 'Talks and writings of Chairman Mao', Translations on Communist
    China, no. 128, Joint Publications Research Service, 21
    December 1970.
27 Mao Tse-tung, 'On the correct handling of contradictions among
    the people', loc. cit., p. 354.
28 Ibid., p. 374.
29 SW, vol. 3, p. 580.
30 Lenin, SW, vol. 3, p. 571.
31 'Nos tâches politiques', p. 128. However, Rosa Luxemburg did
    not always deny the necessity of an organised vanguard and a
    leadership. In 1906, she partially went back on the criticisms
    which she had directed at Lenin in 1904. Neither must it be
    forgotten that in 1919 she founded the German Communist Party
    and called for an International to function as a centralised
    party of the world revolution.
32 'Nos tâches politiques', p. 125.
33 The 'Communist Manifesto' evoked 'a portion of the bourgeois
    ideologists who have raised themselves to the level of
    comprehending theoretically the historical movement as a whole'
    (Marx and Engels, SW, vol. 1, p. 117).
34 CW, vol. 6, pp. 490-1. Let us note, moreover, that the
    precepts concerning the necessity of a party of professional
    revolutionaries and the restriction of internal democracy were
    linked to the conditions of clandestine work. Lenin abandoned
    them as soon as the 1905 revolution made legal activity
    possible.
35 'Works', vol. 1, p. 99.
36 All on his own Ernest Mandel has discovered this idea of the
    brilliant Stalin, whom he has not read, since he does not give
    him his due. Cf. 'The Leninist Theory of Organisation'.
37 Stalin, 'Works', vol. 1, pp. 162-74; CW, vol. 9, p. 388.
38 CW, vol. 8, pp. 92-3.
39 Ibid., vol. 11, pp. 172-3.

40 Ibid., vol. 10, p. 32.
41 Op. cit., supplement to 'Rouge', no. 167, p. 11.
42 Quoted by Yvan Craipeau, in 'Le Mouvement trotskyste en France', p. 196.
43 Ibid., p. 14. Mandel confuses agitation, which is carried out around a few slogans for action aimed at a large number of people, and propaganda, whose purpose is to inculcate many ideas to fewer people; that is, to educate politically the most advanced elements of the masses. Propaganda is concerned with popularising the programme (and the general principles of Marxism–Leninism).
44 This is what the programme is. To draw up a mixture of more or less vague and abstract generalities is within the reach of every organisation that wants to suggest that it has solved all the problems. The political line is the ensemble of tasks, particular measures and methods of work aimed at achieving objectives in the immediate and middle term. An organisation always explicitly or implicitly has such a line orienting its practice. A programme, on the other hand, presupposes, if it is to be seriously established, that the organisation has reached a certain level in its development. Let us remember that Lenin was opposed to the programme which was drawn up by Plekhanov and adopted by the 2nd Congress because it was too general.
45 Speech at the 8th Congress, CW, vol. 29, p. 155.
46 An allusion to the materialist definition of freedom as knowledge of necessity.
47 'Talks and writings of Chairman Mao', Joint Publications Research Service, 21 December 1970.
48 It is on this point that Marx corrected the 'Communist Manifesto' after drawing lessons from the Commune.
49 CW, vol. 27, pp. 89–90.
50 Quoted by Michael Lowy, 'La Théorie de la révolution chez le jeune Marx', p. 180. Although Trotskyist, Lowy has a weakness for Luxemburgist spontaneism.
51 CW, vol. 38, p. 205.
52 'On practice', SW, vol. 1, p. 300.
53 SW, vol. 3, pp. 11–16.
54 Ibid., vol. 3, p. 12. However, a unilateral interpretation of this thought of Mao's should be avoided. He does not think that direct contact with the masses and immediate experience are the only sources of knowledge of social reality. Indeed, a few lines later he says, 'Speaking generally, the infant bourgeoisie of China has not been able, and never will be able, to provide relatively comprehensive or even rudimentary material on social conditions, as the bourgeoisie in Europe, America and Japan has done; we have therefore no alternative but to collect it ourselves' (p. 13).
55 Ibid., p. 11.
56 SW, vol. 4, p. 232.
57 Ibid., vol. 1, p. 33.
58 Cf. Remarques théoriques, 'Problèmes de planification', no. 14.
59 Reprinted in 'Peking Review', 20 September 1968.
60 'Talks and Writings of Chairman Mao', loc. cit.

61 After the seizure of power in October 1917, Lenin applied the agrarian programme of the Socialist Revolutionaries instead of his own, when he had spent his life studying the problems of the peasantry. This shows well enough the wholly relative value of a programme.

62 'Nos tâches politiques', p. 128.

63 Isaac Deutscher, 'The Prophet Armed', pp. 93, 190, 470.

64 H. Weber, 'Mouvement ouvrier, stalinisme et bureaucratie', p. 15.

65 SW, vol. 1, p. 478.

66 Ibid., vol. 2, p. 348.

67 'The civil war in France', ibid., vol. 2, p. 219. (Translator's note: Marx is using 'imperialism' here to mean the Bonapartist state.)

68 'The Eighteenth Brumaire', ibid., vol. 1, p. 395.

69 'The Prophet Unarmed', pp. 460, 462.

70 'The Prophet Outcast', pp. 54-5.

71 'La Défence de l'USSR et l'opposition'.

72 In his Introduction to the French edition of his 'Stalin', Isaac Deutscher states: 'In my opinion, the Russian equivalents of the Jacobin, Thermidorian and Bonapartist phases of the Revolution were mixed in a strange way in Stalinism.' 'Curiouser and curiouser,' said Alice!

73 'In Defence of Marxism', p. 6.

74 Mao says that it is necessary to draw a line of distinction 'between revolution and counter-revolution, between Yenan and Sian. Some do not understand that they must draw this line of distinction. For example, when they combat bureaucracy, they speak of Yenan as though "nothing is right" there and fail to make a comparison and distinguish between the bureaucracy in Yenan and the bureaucracy in Sian.' (Mao Tse-tung, 'Methods of work of party committees', SW, vol. 4, p. 381.) (Translator's note: The English edition, 1969, p. 381, includes the following note: 'Yenan was the headquarters of the Central Committee of the Communist Party of China from January 1937 to March 1947; Sian was the centre of the reactionary rule of the Kuomintang in Northwestern China. Comrade Mao Tse-tung cited the two cities as symbols of revolution and counter-revolution.')

75 Lenin, 'The immediate tasks of the Soviet government', SW, vol. 2, p. 728.

76 Lenin, 'The tax in kind', ibid., vol. 3, p. 658.

77 Lenin, 'The immediate tasks...', ibid., vol. 2, p. 730.

78 Lenin to the 7th Congress of the RCP(B), ibid., vol. 2, p. 661.

79 In our view this is one factor but not the most important one, for this danger of restoration was real in China before the cultural revolution although the range of incomes was relatively very narrow. It still persists despite considerable progress in the sense of a radical equality carried into effect after this revolution.

80 'The Revolution Betrayed', p. 240.

81 Ibid., p. 238.

82 Trotsky drew on a text of Rakovsky for the latter idea - 'Les Dangers professionnels du pouvoir', the French title of the 'Letter to Valentinov', published in 'De la bureaucratie', 1971.

83 'The Revolution Betrayed', p. 55.
84 Ibid., p. 55.
85 'The Soviet Union and the Fourth International', p. 14.
86 Op. cit., p. 61. The USSR and the GDR have therefore reached
    this stage.
87 Cf. Bettelheim, 'La Transition vers l'économie socialiste'.
88 'The Class Nature of the Soviet State' and 'The Workers' State
    and the Question of Thermidor and Bonapartism', p. 48.
89 La Révolution défigurée, in 'De la Révolution', p. 104.
90 Lettre à Boris Souvarine, 25 April 1929, 'Politique de
    Trotsky', p. 316.
91 'In Defence of Marxism', p. 45.
92 'The Class Nature of the Soviet State', p. 58; Bonapartisme
    bourgeois ou bonapartisme sovietique, in 'Politique de
    Trotsky', pp. 25-6.
93 'The Soviet Union and the Fourth International', p. 14.
94 Op. cit., p. 240.
95 Ibid., p. 236.
96 'In Defence of Marxism', p. 55.
97 'Stalin'.
98 'In Defence of Marxism', p. 28.
99 'Stalin'.
100 On the nature of the relations of production and of State power
    in Egypt, see the masterly analysis by Mahmoud Hussein, 'La
    Lutte de classes en Egypte de 1945 à 1968', pp. 108-17 and
    pp. 163-86.
101 To clarify how the dictatorship of the proletariat can exist
    when the working class has lost power, Trotsky compared such a
    state to a wrecked car which remains a car. This image only
    plagiarises Kautsky's argument that democracy remains democracy
    despite the deformation it suffers from bourgeois domination
    and Hegel's explanation that imperfect empirical states
    nevertheless incarnate the idea of the state just as 'the
    ugliest man, the criminal, the sick man, the cripple, remain
    men nevertheless'. This example illustrates yet again the
    metaphysical (non-dialectical) character of Trotsky's thought.
    On Kautsky's Hegelian inspiration, see Karl Korsch, 'Die
    materialistische Geschichtsauffassung', Europäische
    Verlagsanstalt, 1971, p. 76.
102 Lenin, '"Left-wing" childishness', CW, vol. 27, p. 338; and
    also 'The tax in kind', CW, vol. 32, p. 324. Our attention was
    drawn to the implications of these texts as well as to other
    points discussed here by Jacques Rancière.
103 'The Age of Permanent Revolution: A Trotsky Anthology', p. 228.
104 'The Revolution Betrayed', p. 263. Trotsky did not talk about
    Hitlero-Stalinism in this text but it comes to the same thing.
105 Herbert J. Spiro, 'World Politics. The Global System', p. 104.
    This author is probably alluding to Hannah Arendt's 'The
    Origins of Totalitarianism'.
106 'The Revolution Betrayed', pp. 272-3. He did so at the
    suggestion of Victor Serge, a writer who before his death
    became openly anti-communist and surreptitiously pro-American.
107 April 1962, London, HMSO, Cmnd 1681, p. 3.
108 'The USSR in war', republished in 'In Defence of Marxism'.

109 'The Prophet Outcast', pp. 467-8.
110 'Fourth International', vol. 1, no. 4, p. 140.
111 Le Trotskysme vu par un maoiste ... ou la queue de Staline, 'La Vérité', April 1972.
112 'Writings of Leon Trotsky (1939-40)', p. 81.
113 Ibid., p. 17.
114 M. Merleau-Ponty, 'Humanisme ou terreur', p. 165.
115 The references are to be found in On the question of Stalin, in 'Polemic on the General Line of the International Communist Movement', p. 123. (On the question of Stalin is also to be found in 'Peking Review', no. 38, 24 September 1963.)
116 The Chinese have quoted speeches of Khrushchev dating from the great purge of 1935-8, in which he declared: 'We shall totally annihilate the enemies – to the last man – and scatter their ashes to the winds ... We have annihilated a considerable number of enemies, but still not all. Therefore, it is necessary to keep our eyes open. We should bear firmly in mind the words of Comrade Stalin, that as long as capitalist encirclement exists, spies and saboteurs will be smuggled into our country.'
117 'Polemic on the General Line ...', pp. 119-20.
118 Ibid., p. 121.
119 Ibid., p. 123.
120 Here we have a Marxist-Leninist position of principle diametrically opposed to the constant procedure of the Trotskyists. Even a theoretician like Lucien Goldmann is clearly aware of this methodological principle, because he approaches the problems of Marxism with a minimum of seriousness: 'Hence it is in the economic, social and psychological structure of the group which undergoes the influence that the influence's principal causes must be sought' ('The Human Sciences and Philosophy', p. 93).
121 'Polemic on the General Line ...', p. 123.
122 In fact, on the one hand, theory is linked to (indeed governed by) practice (so that a correct theoretical position with regard to Stalin presupposes a revolutionary practice); on the other hand, Marxist investigation illuminates the past in the light of the present, illuminating its hidden tendencies, their meaning and their truth. As Marx said, 'The anatomy of man is a key to the anatomy of the ape.' The investigations carried out in the framework of the cultural revolution by the Chinese masses with a view to judging correctly the historical role of Liu Shao-chi provides an example of the application of this principle.
123 'Polemic on the General Line ...', p. 117.
124 Cf. Henri Pierre, 'L'Express', 17 May 1965. This fact has been confirmed to us by some friends who recently visited the USSR. They themselves had witnessed these reactions of the Russian public. If 'Pravda' censored Stalin's name in publishing the Chinese message of congratulations on the occasion of the 53rd Anniversary of the October Revolution, it was obviously to prevent the attachment displayed by the Chinese to Stalin's memory from enhancing their credit in the eyes of the Soviet people. (Cf. 'Le Monde', 11 November 1970.)

125   Cf. 'Le Monde', 25 November 1969. Also, Eldridge Cleaver's statement in 'The Black Panther', 8 November 1969.

126   'Polemic on the General Line ...', p. 121. Stalin's works are not always rigorous on the scientific level. We find serious mistakes side by side with profound developments of Marxism-Leninism. However, one of his works may be considered a classic: 'The Foundations of Leninism'. It is the only one studied in China. Let us recall that as editor-in-chief of 'Pravda', Stalin prevented the publication of Lenin's 'Letters from Afar', apart from the first one. This was because after the February Revolution in 1917 he had taken up a 'defensist' position. Moreover, Stalin himself admitted in the 'History of the Russian Revolution', of which he was the co-author, that he was opposed to Lenin's 'April Theses' for some ten days.

127   Cf. Roy Medvedev, 'Faut-il réhabiliter Staline?'

128   'Our study and the current situation', SW, vol. 1, p. 164.

129   Cf. the disposition of Léon Blum in vol. 1, p. 1929, of the official French report of the Commission of Enquiry into the events which occurred in France between 1933 and 1945, cited by R. Garaudy, 'Mésaventures de l'antimarxisme', p. 83.

130   On this last point, cf. Major-General Pjotr Grigorenko, 'Der sowjetische Zusammenbruch 1941', Frankfurt-am-Main, 1969.

131   Quoted by Isaac Deutscher, 'Stalin', p. 465.

132   Quoted in 'Polemic on the General Line ...', p. 122.

133   'The Anti-Stalin Campaign and International Communism', p. 120. There are two types of revisionism: one social-fascist and the other social-liberal. Togliatti and the PCI in general belong to the latter type.

134   Marx conceded that the political or ideological superstructure may be dominant despite determination in the last instance by the base. Cf. 'Capital', p. 81n. Cf. also Mao Tse-tung, 'On contradiction', SW, vol. 1, p. 336. 'True, the productive forces, practice and the economic base generally play the principal and decisive role ... but ... in certain conditions, such aspects as the relations of production, theory and the superstructure in turn manifest themselves in the principal and decisive role'. Lastly, cf. Louis Althusser, On the materialist dialectic, 'For Marx', p. 213.

135   'Polemic on the General Line ...', p. 121.

136   Why I came to China at the age of 72, 'Peking Review', no. 38, 24 September 1963, p. 20.

137   'A Great Historic Document', p. 18. The same criticism is directed at Stalin in 'On Khrushchev's Phoney Communism and its Historical Lessons for the World', p. 15. Cf. 'Polemic on the General Line ...'.

138   'The Draft New Constitution', pp. 5, 8.

139   Ibid., p. 12.

140   'Reports and Speeches at the 18th Congress of the CPSU', p. 33.

141   'Economic problems of socialism in the USSR', SW, p. 357.

142   Marx, quoted by Stalin, ibid., p. 354.

143   'The Moscow Trial and Two Speeches by J. Stalin', p. 253. Stalin's 'supposition' seems less obvious if we consider that 'spies, saboteurs and murderers' and other agents of diversion manoeuvre less easily in a socialist society (the milieu hardly

being favourable to them) and penetrate it with more
difficulty.

144 Ibid., p. 250.
145 Ibid., p. 255.
146 Ibid., p. 260.
147 Ibid., pp. 264-5.
148 Ibid., p. 249.
149 When Mao argues that some counter-revolutionaries still exist,
he is careful to add 'of course ... not ... everywhere and in
every organisation', for he knows that this specification is
not superfluous (On the correct handling of contradictions
among the people, 'Selected Readings from the Works of Mao
Tse-tung', p. 364).
150 'The Moscow Trial and Two Speeches by J. Stalin', p. 262.
151 Ibid., p. 263.
152 M. Merleau-Ponty, The USSR and the camps, 'Signs', p. 264.
153 Cf. 'Recueil chronologique des lois et décrets du Présidium du
Soviet suprême et ordonnances du gouvernement de la RFSSR au
1er mars 1940', vol. 9, OGIZ, 1941, quoted by Merleau-Ponty,
op. cit. p. 263.
154 'Reports and Speeches at the 18th Congress of the CPSU', p. 38.
155 In 'On Khrushchev's Phoney Communism...', the Chinese have
written that Stalin 'failed to rely upon the working class and
the masses in the struggle against the forces of capitalism'
(p. 15).
156 Published by 'Scanteia', 13 February 1946 and quoted by
Merleau-Ponty, 'Humanisme ou terreur', p. 75.
157 'Reports and Speeches at the 18th Congress of the CPSU', p. 19.
158 Ibid., pp. 44-5.
159 'The Anti-Stalin Campaign and International Communism', pp.
27-8.
160 'Le Problème chinois', p. 185. The so-called 'Stalin Law' as
formulated by Garaudy seems to be lifted from a passage in the
Introduction to 'The Permanent Revolution' in which Trotsky
declared that 'In an isolated proletarian dictatorship, the
internal and external contradictions grow inevitably along with
the final successes achieved' ('The Permanent Revolution',
p. 9).
161 'The Moscow Trial ...', p. 262.
162 There is a group of Marxist-Leninist-Stalinists who firmly
maintain that Stalin did not refuse to recognise the
continuation of the class struggle after the expropriation of
the owning classes. This is a mark of attachment to the memory
of the Soviet leader which does them honour. But to carry
conviction, arguments are necessary. Theirs are somewhat
confused. They appeal to the Albanians' silence about this
mistake of Stalin's; but not content for their spokesmen to
be ... silent, they claim the Chinese are silent too, although
they do speak. According to them, the editorials of the
central organs of the CCP emanate from people who are not in
any way qualified to express the point of view of their party.
Even if we grant this, we cannot follow these militants in
their conclusions for, besides, we would have to forget how to
read, since Stalin's texts are sufficiently eloquent in
themselves.

163   'Red Flag', no. 8, 1966, in 'The Great Proletarian Cultural
      Revolution in China', p. 4. On 6 March 1970 'Peking Review'
      published an article entitled Who transforms whom? criticising
      N. A. Kairov's 'Pedagogy'. The article in 'Peking Review'
      indifferently quotes the old (1948) or the new (1965) edition
      of it to show that its contents are revisionist and aim to
      transform society in the image of the new type of bourgeoisie
      which was already gaining in strength in the USSR before
      Stalin's death. The latter was the last bulwark against the
      usurpation of central power by the bureaucratic state
      bourgeoisie. The period from the 20th to the 22nd Congress
      must be considered as the phase in which their class
      consolidated its power. Bettelheim traces this usurpation of
      power by the new bourgeoisie back to 1929. It will be possible
      to assess the strength of his arguments when the major study on
      which he is working at present appears.
164   'Concerning Marxism and Linguistics', pp. 3, 6.
165   'The Draft New Constitution', p. 10.
166   'The Prophet Outcast', p. 322.
167   Victor Serge, for example, wrote: 'Defence of man. Respect for
      man ... be he the meanest of men – "class enemy", son or
      grandson of a bourgeois, I do not care' ('Memoirs of a
      Revolutionary', p. 282).
168   'Signs', p. 260.
169   To characterise Stalin as a 'great Marxist-Leninist' after all
      that we have said about his mistakes may seem contradictory,
      but no more so than Lenin's appraisal of Bukharin – 'a most
      valuable and major theorist' who 'has never made a study of
      dialectics and, I think, never fully understood it' (Lenin, CW,
      vol. 36, p. 595).
170   Maurice Thorez and Roger Garaudy, Les Tâches des philosophes
      communistes et la critique des érreurs philosophiques,
      supplement to 'Cahiers du Communisme', nos. 7-8, 1962, p. 14.
171   'On the correct handling of contradictions...', p. 370.
172   'Concerning Marxism and Linguistics', p. 9.
173   Ibid., p. 22.
174   Open Letter to the Central Committee of the Communist Party of
      the Soviet Union, to all Party Organisations and to all
      Communists in the Soviet Union (14 July 1963), 'Polemic on the
      General Line...', p. 526.
175   That these are not empty words is clear from the evidence of
      the Swedish sociologist Jan Myrdal, who writes, 'I found much
      anti-communist literature in the Chinese bookshops' (Jan
      Myrdal, 'Chinese Journey', p. 134).
176   SW, vol. 3, pp. 49-50.

CHAPTER 5   REVISIONIST DEGENERATION OR CULTURAL REVOLUTION

1   'The Soviet Union and the Fourth International', p. 13.
2   The world situation and perspectives, in 'Writings of Leon
    Trotsky (1939-40)', p. 24.
3   Ibid., p. 26.
4   See her statements in the appendix to Jacques Roussel's book,
    'Les Enfants du prophète'.

5 'Intercontinental Press', vol. 7, no. 26, 14 July 1969, p. 678.
6 La Défense de l'USSR et l'opposition (1929), quoted in
   'Politique de Trotsky', pp. 314-15.
7 Paul Yankovitch, 'Le Monde', 11 August 1970, p. 11.
8 'Intercontinental Press', 14 July 1969, p. 678. The flood of
   Trotskyist print swells but the ambiguity and confusion of their
   positions remain. Some Bolivian Trotskyists declare, for
   example, that the 'socialist system' is 'formed from states in
   which the workers have been transformed into the dominant
   force'. If they are 'oppressed and robbed' how can they be the
   'dominant force'? 'Tesis politica de la COB y otros
   documentos', p. 23.
9 Charles Bettelheim, Remarques théoriques, 'Problèmes de
   planification', no. 14, p. 178.
10 P. P. Rey, Sur l'articulation des modes de production, ibid.,
   no. 13, p. 96.
11 'Cahiers de la Gauche prolétarienne', no. 2, 1970, p. 65.
12 La Base sociale du révisionnisme, 'Cahiers marxistes-
   léninistes', no. 14.
13 This is all the more true in that prices are stable, in the
   USSR, for example, in contrast to the galloping inflation that
   characterises the Western economies.
14 Calcul économique, catégories marchandes et formes de propriété,
   'Problèmes de planification', no. 12, p. 8. Also appeared in
   Maspero.
15 Ibid., p. 13.
16 Ibid., p. 31.
17 Ibid., p. 73.
18 Ibid., p. 84.
19 Letter to Paul Sweezy, 18 February 1970, in 'The Transition to
   Socialism', by P. M. Sweezy and C. Bettelheim, p. 43.
20 Cf. G. Kim, A. Kaufman, Le développement non-capitaliste, 'La
   Vie internationale', December 1967, Moscow.
21 According to Henri Weber, the bureaucracy's privileges 'derive
   from state exploitation, not from given relations of production'
   (op. cit., p. 15). In other words, the bureaucracy exploits the
   state and not the labourers. We must admit to an inability to
   understand what this means from a Marxist point of view. Pierre
   Naville defends a thesis no less paradoxical. In the USSR there
   is supposedly a 'mutual exploitation'. Cf. 'Le Salaire
   socialiste', Paris, 1970.
22 Jacques Rancière, Sobre la téoriã de la ideologia (la politica
   de Althusser), pp. 325-6, 354-5: Here Rancière refutes the
   distinction made by Poulantzas between 'relations of production'
   and 'social relations'.
23 Sweezy and Bettelheim, 'On the Transition to Socialism', pp.
   41-4.
24 K. S. Karol, 'Le Monde', 23 July 1970.
25 A term which we borrow from Mahmoud Hussein in La Restauration
   du capitalisme en USSR et la révolution culturelle chinoise,
   Appendix to 'La Lutte des classes en Egypte', p. 365.
26 Terms used by Charles Bettelheim.
27 Quoted in the pamphlet, 'How the Soviet Revisionists Carry Out
   All-Round Restoration of Capitalism in the USSR', pp. 18-19.

28   Ibid., p. 19.
29   J. Pavleski, Projet, May 1969, reproduced in 'Problèmes économiques', 3 July 1969.
30   Theses of the CPSU Central Committee, 'Soviet News', no. 5394, 11 July 1967, p. 21.
31   J. Pavleski, op. cit.
32   France's commercial adviser in Moscow. 'Notes et études économiques', 28 March 1969; reproduced in 'Problèmes économiques', 3 July 1969.
33   Article from 'Est-Ouest', reproduced in 'Problèmes économiques', 6 March 1969.
34   'Cahiers de la gauche prolétarienne', no. 2, 1970, p. 66.
35   'How the Soviet Revisionists Carry Out All-Round Restoration of Capitalism in the USSR', p. 57.
36   Political Testament, 'New Left Review', no. 62, July-August 1970, pp. 40-2.
37   'Le Monde', 23 July 1970.
38   Lenin, CW, vol. 31, p. 229; cf. Une révélation d'une sincérité exceptionnelle, 'Littérature chinoise', April 1970 and 'Le Monde'.
39   On the international policy of the USSR see Appendix I.
40   The best book on this subject is that of Jean Baby, 'La Grande Controverse sino-soviétique'. It preserves all its topical interest.
41   'The Great Proletarian Cultural Revolution in China', p. 25.
42   Ibid., p. 3.
43   Joan Robinson, 'The Cultural Revolution in China', pp. 85-6.
44   'Decision in Sixteen Points' of the Central Committee of the CCP.
45   On Ideological state apparatuses, see Louis Althusser, 'Lenin and Philosophy and Other Essays'; also Idéologie et forces productives, 'Cahiers marxistes-léninistes', no. 15, January-February 1967. The concept of Ideological State Apparatus was produced by Jacques Rancière.
46   Ibid., p. 90.
47   Ibid., p. 87.
48   'Peking Review', no. 14, 3 April 1970.
49   See an article in the Shanghai 'Wenhui Bao' which is translated into French in 'Cahiers de la Chine nouvelle', 22 July 1968, no. 520 (special number); this same article is also published in summary form in 'Mao Tse-tung's 700 millions', 'Idiot International', no. 1. Cf. 'Take the road of the Shanghai Machine Tools Plant in training technicians from among the workers', pp. 6-20.
50   'The Great Proletarian Cultural Revolution in China', pp. 54, 57.
51   'Intercontinental Press', 14 July 1969, p. 702.
52   Ibid., p. 703.
53   'Histoire de la révolution culturelle prolétarienne en Chine', pp. 253-5.
54   'Intercontinental Press', 14 July 1969, p. 713.
55   Mao Tse-tung, SW, vol. 4, p. 191.
56   Resolution on the 'Cultural Revolution' in China, 'Intercontinental Press', 14 July 1969, p. 702. The Trotskyists

are fond of franglais. It is a way of being internationalist.
Meanwhile, we should really like to know how 'positions'
(theses, analysis, appraisals) can be the replica of a ...
dictatorship? (!)

57 Everyone knows that Newton's equations can be regarded as a
special case of those of Einstein if one takes as given speeds
which are much slower than that of light and the absence of
large masses in the vicinity.

58 See the discussion with Victor in 'Les Maos en France' by
Michèle Manceaux. Another terminological difference that will
have been noticed in this book should be explained here. We
write 'the thought of Mao Tse-tung' (pensée de Mao Tse-tung) and
not 'Mao Tse-tung thought' (pensée Mao Tsetung). The second
expression which is used in Peking publications is very old. In
good French 'pensée Mao Tsetung' would mean that Mao was a
thought! When we asked the Chinese comrades the reason for this
innovation, they answered, somewhat embarrassed, that someone in
the translation department must have thought that 'pensée Mao
Tsetung' rendered the Chinese turn of phrase more literally.
Now, in Chinese there is no declension or genitive. It will be
agreed that altering French syntax to render it closer to
Chinese stems from a strange idea of faithfulness in
translation.

59 Cf. the title of Paloczi-Horvath's book, 'Mao Tse-tung, Emperor
of the Blue Ants.

60 Mao Tse-tung, SW, vol. 3, p. 49.

61 'Marxismes imaginaires', p. 42.

CHAPTER 6 STALIN AND TROTSKY ON THE CHINESE REVOLUTION

1 Poulantzas's idea that three aspects define the International's
policy was probably inspired by Merleau-Ponty, who talks of
'the three Marxist themes of the initiative of the masses,
proletarian internationalism and the construction of economic
bases' ('Humanisme ou terreur', pp. 140, 145).

2 Paris, 1970, pp. 242, 253.

3 Agnes Smedley, 'The Great Road, The Life and Time of Chu Teh',
p. 353.

4 Here we have an example of Trotsky's polemical excesses: 'The
Northern Expedition ... incidentally proved to be an expedition
against the proletariat' ('Problems of the Chinese Revolution',
p. 279).

5 Israel Epstein, 'From Opium War to Liberation', pp. 135-6;
Jacques Guillermaz, 'A History of the Chinese Communist Party,
1941-49', pp. 127-8, 135-6; 'Les Sociétés secrètes en Chine', a
collection of texts introduced by Jean Chesneaux, pp. 237-40.

6 A part of the left Kuomintang remained faithful to the end to
the alliance with the communists, particularly Mme Sung
Ch'ing-ling, Sun Yat Sen's widow and now Vice-President of the
People's Republic of China. In 1965 the 'new Kuomintang' still
had seventy-five Deputies in the National Assembly and three
Ministers.

7 The Anniversary of the People's Liberation Army is on 1 August.

Trotsky denounced 'the opportunist policy' of Ho Lung and Yeh
T'ing and described their rising as an isolated adventure and
'a pseudo-communist action à la Makhno' (the Ukrainian
anarchist leader).

8 J. Guillermaz, op. cit., pp. 163-5, and R. C. North, 'Chinese
Communism', pp. 99-104.

9 SW, vol. 3, p. 261.

10 It is therefore impossible that he could have appealed to the
authority of the International (which he denies having done).
Cf. Harold Isaacs, 'The Tragedy of the Chinese Revolution',
p. 59. The document recording Sneevliet's statements to Harold
Isaacs was published by the latter in the 'China Quarterly',
January-March 1971.

11 P. Mif, 'Heroic China', pp. 21-2. He points out, moreover,
that in this period, the communists had started to enter the
Kuomintang individually. According to Conrad Brandt,
E. H. Carr and Stuart Schram, Maring probably acted on his own
initiative and only obtained the approval of the Comintern
after the event. (Cf. S. Schram, 'Mao Tse-tung', p. 70).

12 'La Question chinoise dans l'internationale communiste', texts
introduced by P. Broué, pp. 295-6.

13 'The Prophet Unarmed', p. 317. On this question see Appendix
III.

14 Fernando Claudin, 'La Crise du mouvement communiste...', vol.
1, p. 325.

15 'La Question chinoise dans l'internationale communiste', p. 76;
cf. also T. Mandalian, ibid., p. 288.

16 Ibid., p. 78.

17 Stuart Schram, 'Mao Tse-tung', p. 78.

18 Ibid., p. 79.

19 There is complete agreement on this point between the 'Shanghai
Letter', which the Trotskyists appeal to without having read,
and Mandalian's article already cited.

20 Given the summary manner in which he himself liquidates certain
historical problems, this 'vulgar Trotskyism' is imaginable!

21 Considering the great number of eminent communist military
leaders who came from Whampoa, J. Guillermaz describes it as
the 'first military school of the future Chinese Red Army' (op.
cit., p. 81).

22 Hélène Carrère d'Encausse and Stuart Schram, 'Marxism and
Asia', p. 154.

23 Conrad Brandt, 'Stalin's Failure in China 1924-25', p. 104.

24 'Problems of the Chinese Revolution', p. 100.

25 'The Prophet Unarmed', p. 322.

26 'The Permanent Revolution', p. 122. In his second letter to
Preobrazhensky he said: 'China has no landed nobility; no
peasant class fused by a community of interests against the
landlords. The agrarian revolution in China is directed
against the urban and rural bourgeoisie.' Cf. 'La Question
chinoise dans l'internationale communiste', p. 328. (The
translation has been corrected.)

27 'The Permanent Revolution', p. 92.

28 Trotsky, 'Problems of the Chinese Revolution', p. 145. We
shall not dwell on the fact that Trotsky had argued that the

Chinese Revolution was a revolution for customs autonomy, an absurd definition which he later had to abandon. In fact, Chiang Kai-shek achieved this autonomy as early as 1930 by means which were hardly revolutionary.

29 In his 'Analysis of the classes in Chinese society' (March 1926), Mao Tse-tung had forecast this shift. He wrote: 'The intermediate classes are bound to disintegrate quickly, some sections turning left to join the revolution, others turning right to join the counter-revolution' (SW, vol. 1, p. 14).

30 In the elections for the 2nd Central Executive Committee of the Kuomintang, the right had suffered a defeat in January 1926, and in March of the following year the Kuomintang government was reconstituted in favour of Wang Ching-wei (Chiang Kai-shek's rival), who became its President, and the communists, who were given the Ministries of Agriculture and Labour.

31 Mao Tse-tung, SW, vol. 1, p. 26.

32 M. N. Roy, 'Revolution and Counter-Revolution in China', p. 551.

33 Agnes Smedley, op. cit., p. 242.

34 The Trotskyists often quote the 'Shanghai Letter', but as always they reveal a total blindness to everything in this letter that does not fit in with their petty schemas.

35 'The Prophet Unarmed', p. 326.

36 Quoted by Stalin, 'Marxism and the National and Colonial Question', p. 238.

37 Roy, in an interview with R. C. North cited by the latter in 'Moscow and the Chinese Communists', pp. 90-1.

38 Quoted by Stalin, 'Marxism and the National and Colonial Question', p. 239.

39 'International Press Correspondence' (23 December 1926), quoted in Shanti Swarup, 'A Study of the Chinese Communist Movement', p. 37.

40 'International Press Correspondence' (30 December 1926), quoted in ibid., p. 38.

41 'Communist International', vol. 2, nos. 18-19, 1925, in ibid., p. 38.

42 'Marxism and the National and Colonial Question', p. 240.

43 In contrast, Trotsky unceasingly repeated that the Chinese revolution had been crushed 'by the opportunist leadership. Not the one that had its seat in Canton, Shanghai and Wuhan but the one that was commanding from Moscow'. Cf. 'Problems of the Chinese Revolution', p. 291.

44 It was published in 'Revolyutsionnyi Vostok', no. 2, 1927, and other Comintern publications.

45 Op. cit., p. 220.

46 See below.

47 Pierre Naville also claims that when Mao's report appeared in Moscow, it 'only found an echo in the left Opposition'. Cf. his collection of articles 'La Classe ouvrière et le régime gaulliste', p. 460.

48 Cf. 'Die chinesische Frage auf dem 8 Plenum der Exekutive der Kommunistischen Internationale', p. 146, and in general The May Plenum of the ECCI, 'Communist International', no. 10, vol. 4, 30 June 1927.

49   'Die chinesische Frage', p. 147.
50   Ibid., p. 148.
51   M. N. Roy, 'Revolution and Counter-Revolution in China', pp. 548-9.
52   This was also the view of Borodin, who consistently supported the right-wing of the CCP.
53   Conrad Brandt, 'Stalin's Failure in China 1924-27', pp. 119-20.
54   'Marxism and the National and Colonial Question', p. 249.
55   Tang Leang-li, 'The Inner History of Chinese Revolution', London, 1930, p. 282, cited by R. C. North, 'Moscow and Chinese Communists', p. 107.
56   We describe him in this way ironically for he himself considered Mao to be extremely rightist (cf. 'Revolution and Counter-Revolution in China', p. 615).
57   Quoted by Shanti Swarup, op. cit., p. 207.
58   'Hong-chi', 19 July 1930; quoted in ibid.
59   Ibid., p. 137.
60   This is also the thesis defended by Professors Benjamin Schwartz and Robert C. North in their work. The Indian Sinologist Shanti Swarup has refuted it, drawing on rich unpublished documentation. In these pages we are using the results of his researches.
61   'Origins of the Chinese Revolution', p. 189.
62   'Hong-chi', 19 July 1930; cf. Shanti Swarup, op. cit., p. 207.
63   Letter of the Executive Committee of the International, 23 July 1930; cf. ibid., p. 215.
64   Cf. ibid., p. 254.
65   Ibid., p. 224.
66   Ibid., p. 225.
67   Cf. John Gittings, 'The Sino-Soviet Dispute 1956-63'. Let us note, however, vis-à-vis the second of these decisions, the preponderant influence of the International's military adviser Otto Braun, whose reminiscences have been published in 'Horizont', Berlin-Est, 1969, nos. 23-38.
68   'Jiefang Ribao', 28 May 1943; long extracts translated in 'The Political Thought of Mao Tse-tung', with an introduction by Stuart Schram, p. 423.
69   Talks and writings of Chairman Mao, Translations on Communist China, no. 128, Joint Publications Research Service, 21 December 1970.
70   Ibid. Han Suyin heard echoes of the speeches we quote, which confirm their authenticity. Cf. 'The Morning Deluge', p. 567.
71   'Works', vol. 8, p. 384.
72   The Chinese question after the Sixth Congress (4 October 1928), in 'Problems of the Chinese Revolution', p. 219.
73   Ibid., pp. 216-17. It is as if one said John O'Groats and Land's End were in Cornwall.
74   The Canton insurrection, ibid., p. 135.
75   Ibid., p. 133.
76   What is happening in China?, ibid., p. 233.
77   Ibid., pp. 233-4.
78   Ibid., p. 235.
79   Resolution on some questions in the history of our party, Appendix to 'Our study and the current situation', SW, vol. 3, p. 181.

80 Stalin and the Chinese revolution, in 'Problems of the Chinese Revolution', p. 304.
81 Ibid., pp. 304-5.
82 Cf. Guillermaz, op. cit., pp. 181, 183.
83 Cf. Aux communistes chinois et du monde entier, in 'La Question chinoise dans l'internationale communiste', pp. 344-5. In Trotsky's view, adopted by his Chinese supporters, the principal political slogan had to be the demand for a Constituent Assembly! He accepted indeed that it was 'very likely that China has to go through a relatively prolonged phase of parliamentarism, starting with a Constituent Assembly' (Cf. ibid., p. 144).
84 Ibid., pp. 346-7.
85 SW, Peking, 1965, vol. 4, p. 235.
86 Hsueh Mu-chiao and others, 'The Socialist transformation of the national economy in China'.
87 Op. cit., p. 235.
88 William Hinton, 'China's Continuing Revolution'.
89 Stalin repeatedly emphasised that the national question is basically a peasant question. Cf. particularly The national question in Yugoslavia (1925), in 'Marxism and the National and Colonial Question', p. 200.
90 Mao Tse-tung, SW, vol. 2, pp. 316-17.
91 Lettre aux bolcheviks-léninistes chinois, 'La Lutte des classes'. In this text, Trotsky expresses his conviction that the peasants of the Red Army will clash with the workers of the towns when they penetrate them.
92 Cf. Kang Hsing, Die Entwickung der revolutionären Bewegung in Nicht-Rätechina und die Aufgaben der Kommunistischen Partei, in Wang Ming-Kang Hsing, 'Das revolutionäre China von Heute', XIII Plenum of the Executive Committee of the Communist International, December 1933, p. 81.
93 CW, vol. 22.
94 Ibid., vol. 18, p. 397 and vol. 19, p. 39.
95 On the concept of 'leadership' see above, p. 142.
96 Mao Tse-tung, 'On contradiction', SW, vol. 1, pp. 331-2.
97 'Chinese Literature', no. 1, 1967, pp. 80, 81-2.
98 Deutscher, 'The Prophet Outcast', p. 424.
99 This was recounted by Vergès in the above-mentioned debate and confirmed by Deutscher.
100 Oxford, 1969, pp. 84-5.
101 'The Prophet Outcast', p. 520.
102 Benjamin Schwartz, Introduction to 'Problems of the Chinese Revolution', p. III. In his article Mao Tse-tung et la révolution permanente, published in 1962, Pierre Naville also interprets the victory of the Chinese revolution as the result of the unconscious application of the theory of the permanent revolution (cf. the collection 'La Classe ouvrière et le régime gaulliste'.
103 Op. cit., p. 56. Where Stalin is concerned bourgeois scholars do not feel obliged to respect the appearance of academic seriousness and objectivity. On p. 225, introducing texts by that revolutionary leader, we find this sentence: 'Extracts from Stalin's articles and speeches illustrating his successive

positions on the Chinese question'. The authors ingenuously
alert us to the intention which has governed the selection,
extraction and presentation of these texts.

104 Ibid., pp. 63-4.
105 Ibid., p. 64.
106 Ibid., p. 74.
107 Op. cit., p. 468.
108 The Chinese question after the Sixth Congress, 'Problems of the
Chinese Revolution', p. 221.
109 Cf. Karol, 'The Other Communism', p. 52n.
110 Ibid., p. 54.
111 Ibid., p. 78.
112 Loc. cit.
113 For the benefit of those who are unable to read let me make it
clear that I am criticising Karol for the inaccurate statements
about the way in which the Chinese teach their own history
which appear in Part One of his book under the heading, 'Their
history as they see it today'. J.-J. Marie pretends to
understand that for me 'a version of history is true because it
is so taught in China' (!). Cf. 'La Vérité', April 1972,
p. 205.
114 SW, Peking, 1965, vol. 3, pp. 221-2. This Resolution has not
been reproduced in vol. 3 of the French translation which came
out after the beginning of the Cultural Revolution, probably
because of certain passages concerning Liu Shao-chi and also no
doubt because it was revealed in the course of the Cultural
Revolution that Ch'ü Ch'ui-päi became a traitor before his
death.
115 Op. cit., p. 138.

CHAPTER 7 THE DEFEAT OF THE GREEK COMMUNISTS

1 Winston Churchill, 'History of the Second World War', vol. 5,
pp. 475-6.
2 Ibid., vol. 6, p. 97.
3 Ibid., pp. 247-8.
4 Ibid., p. 100.
5 Mao Tse-tung, SW, Peking, 1965, vol. 4, pp. 14-15.
6 Churchill, op. cit., vol. 6, p. 250.
7 'X' was an organisation financed by the English supposedly to
carry out Resistance work, but which collaborated with the
Germans in their persecution of communism. Its leader was a
failed politician, Colonel (now General) Grivas, later the head
of EOKA in Cyprus under the name of Dighenis.
8 Here is how Churchill related this event: 'Communist supporters,
engaging in a banned demonstration, collided with the police and
civil war began' ('History', vol. 6, p. 251). It would be
impossible to tell more lies in so few words. They were not
supporters. Only a minority were communists. The demonstration
was not banned. The police made a cowardly attack for which no
one would accept responsibility but which was premeditated for
all that. The war which began was not a civil war for it was
essentially between the British soldiery and the people of

9   A. Kedros, 'La Résistance grecque', p. 488.
10 Churchill, 'History', vol. 6, p. 252. Papandreou was there to
    help Scobie massacre his fellow countrymen. If it had not been
    him it would have been someone else, it is not very important.
    'Some Greek government', Churchill said. This 'some' says all
    that can be said about the relation between an imperialist power
    and the puppets it uses. On the same day, the British Prime
    Minister wrote to Ambassador Leeper: 'Henceforth you and
    Papandreou will conform to his (Scobie's) directions' (ibid.,
    p. 253). And Papandreou has the effrontery to boast in his
    memoirs about the part that he played in these sad events!
11 Ibid., pp. 259-60.
12 Ibid., pp. 266-9.
13 Cf. La guerre civile en Grèce et ses leçons, 'La Nouvelle Revue
    internationale', November 1964.
14 Even the Chinese Nationalists had some hopes of an American
    Scobie. Cf. Mao Tse-tung, SW, vol. 3, p. 275.
15 Quoted by N. Svoronos, 'Histoire de la Grèce moderne', p. 118.
16 Z. Zographos, op. cit., p. 100.
17 We shall cite an example of which we have personal knowledge:
    the French widow of a doctor executed by the Germans was accused
    of the murder of two people and owed her safety only to her
    nationality.
18 Quoted by Darivas, De la résistance à la guerre civile en Grèce,
    in 'Recherches internationales à la lumière du marxisme', nos.
    44-5, 1964, p. 275.
19 Ibid., p. 273.
20 The elections had taken place under the supervision of
    representatives of the British trade unions.
21 Darivas, op. cit., p. 273.
22 It seems that Stalin had advised participation in the elections.
    In 1950, Zachariades acknowledged that the decision to abstain
    was a tactical mistake.
23 SW, vol. 4, p. 18.
24 Ibid., p. 18.
25 Z. Zographos, loc. cit.
26 As early as August 1948 the number of prisoners detained and
    deported rose to 70,000.
27 These principles of people's war have been developed by Mao
    Tse-tung and victoriously applied in China.
28 Quoted by G. Kousoulas, 'Revolution and Defeat: The Story of the
    Greek Communist Party', p. 223.
29 EAM-ELAS made the mistake of taking with it in its retreat
    thousands of hostages not all of whom were class enemies - far
    from it! In those days ELAS justice was sometimes hasty. These
    blunders, magnified by hostile propaganda, helped to isolate the
    communists. In particular, their allies among the intermediate
    strata, by nature vacillating, had lost confidence in them after
    their defeat and were too afraid of the monarcho-fascist
    repression to continue to follow them.
30 Colonel J. C. Murray, The anti-bandit war, 'The Guerilla and How
    to Fight Him', p. 74.
31 On the night of 4/5 July 1949, Greek government troops traversed
    Yugoslavia with the agreement of the authorities of that country

to encircle the positions of the Democratic Army at
Caïmactsalan. In a letter to Jean Cassou published in 'France
nouvelle' on 8 October 1949, the Minister of Justice in the
Greek Government of the Mountain quoted precise facts which
proved the hostile activity deployed by the Yugoslav leaders
against the Democratic Army.

32 See De Gaulle, 'Mémoires de guerre', pp. 205-6: 'Right up to the
end the last officers of the Reich tried to negotiate separate
deals with the West'.

33 Gilbert Badia, 'Histoire de l'Allemagne contemporaine', vol. 2,
p. 125.

34 Churchill, 'History', vol. 6, p. 198.

35 Ibid., p. 203.

36 Ibid., p. 369.

37 Kedros, 'La Résistance grecque', p. 511.

38 Quoted by C. Tsoucalas, 'La Grèce de l'indépendence aux
colonels', Maspero, 1970, p. 73.

39 To attribute the British invasion in October 1944 to the Yalta
Conference, as is often done, is proof of ignorance, for this
Conference met in February and its object was to settle the fate
of Germany.

40 Milovan Djilas, 'Conversations with Stalin', pp. 164-5.

41 18 November 1946, quoted in 'Histoire du parti communiste
français', Editions sociales, p. 486.

42 Cf. 'Histoire du parti communiste français', Editions Unir, vol.
2, p. 265.

43 Ibid., vol. 3, p. 35.

44 Quoted from the pamphlet 'Stalin contre le revisionnisme: I', a
'Ligne rouge' publication. This pamphlet reproduces the notes
of Eugenio Reale, who accompanied Longo.

45 Ibid. The Yugoslavs made similar criticisms of the Greek
communists, attacking them for being legalists and for not
preparing for the seizure of power.

CHAPTER 8   CONCLUSION: THE FUNDAMENTAL TRAITS OF TROTSKYISM

1 'The Permanent Revolution' and 'Results and Prospects', p. 116.

2 'Two Tactics', CW, vol. 9, p. 85.

3 Preface to F. Lassalle's 'Address to the jury', June 1905;
quoted in 'Results and Prospects', p. 239.

4 'On contradiction', SW, vol. 1, pp. 313-15; cf. also
L. Althusser: 'The internal unevenness has priority and is the
basis for the role of the external unevenness, up to and
including the effects this second unevenness has within social
formations in confrontation', 'For Marx', p. 212.

5 Cf. Mao Tse-tung, op. cit., and also On the materialist
dialectic in 'For Marx' by L. Althusser, basing himself on Mao.

6 'The Prophet Armed', p. 159.

7 Cf. Nicolas Krassó, Trotsky's Marxism, 'New Left Review', no.
44, July-August 1967, p. 83.

8 On this subject I take the liberty of referring to my article on
La Politique internationale de la Chine, which appeared in 'Tel
Quel', no. 50, Summer 1972.

9   'History of the Russian Revolution', vol. 1, p. 16.
10   Ibid., p. 301.
11   Cf. 'Quatrième internationale', November 1964, pp. 61-3.
12   Cf. Bonapartisme bourgeois ou bonapartisme soviétique, 'Rouge'
     classics, no. 2, p. 16.
13   M. Merleau-Ponty, 'Signs', p. 251. He quotes an American
     Trotskyist.

CHAPTER 9   CRITICAL NOTES ON SOME TROTSKYIST ORGANISATIONS

1   He was referring to the Mexican 'Posadists' (a split from the
     Fourth International) who infiltrated Yon Sosa's MR 13 and in
     the end were expelled from it.
2   Cf. 'Quatrième internationale', no. 27, February 1966.
3   'Le Monde', 17 January 1970 (editorial). A new element to add
     to the Fourth International dossier is the fact that, to all
     appearances, the Bolivian police made use of its local branch to
     infiltrate its agents into the ELN and to dismantle its urban
     network. After this setback, Cavaldo 'Chato' Peredo (who had
     succeeded his brother, 'Inti', killed on 8 September 1969) had
     to purge his organisation of Trotskyists and other groups of
     intellectuals who had joined it. Cf. 'Compagni', no. 1, pp.
     11-12.
4   Jean Esmein, 'La Révolution culturelle'; Joan Robinson, 'The
     Cultural Revolution in China'. For references to the best texts
     on the cultural revolution, see the Bibliography.
5   'Intercontinental Press', vol. 7, no. 26, 14 July 1969.
6   M. A. Machiocci gives the example of the revolutionary committee
     governing the port of Tien Sin. It constituted fourteen
     representatives of revolutionary cadres, sixteen of the
     revolutionary masses and three from the people's army:
     'Distribution is made on the following principle: the majority
     ... must be constituted by the representatives of the
     revolutionary masses.' (Cf. 'De la Chine', p. 179.)
7   The debate on workers' control, 'International Socialist
     Review', May-June 1969.
8   Waldeck Rochet's report to the Central Committee of the PCF at
     Champigny (5 and 6 December 1968).
9   Champigny Manifesto, 'Pour une démocratie avancée, pour une
     France socialiste'.
10   The debate on workers' control, p. 3.
11   'Lutte ouvrière', no. 54, 10 September 1969.
12   Quoted by Jean-Jacques Marie, 'Le Trotskysme', pp. 80-1.
13   The SLL and the majority of the 'International Committee' broke
     with the Lambertist OCI in October 1970.
14   Cf. 'Manifeste de l'OCI', December 1967, supplement to 'La
     Vérité', no. 543-4, p. 40.
15   'Mai 1968: une répétition générale', pp. 59-62.
16   Cf. 'La Quatrième internationale', p. 87.
17   Lambert in 'Etudes marxistes', no. 2, February 1969, p. 5.
18   Ibid., p. 6.
19   Pierre Broué, 'Le Parti bolchevique', p. 438.
20   Cf. 'Manifeste le l'OCI', pp. 33-4.

21 The thesis according to which the Eastern nations are all
    proletarian was developed after 1923 by the Tartar Sultan
    Galiev, who had been criticised by Stalin and then expelled from
    the CPSU for nationalism.
22 Op. cit., p. 29.
23 In the other capitalist countries, military spending does not
    usually exceed 4 per cent GNP. The OCI Manifesto of December
    1967 falsely asserts (p. 15) that today the USA gives over 15 to
    20 per cent of its national income to arms production and that
    'this figure ... continues to grow'!
24 According to the Institut National des Statistiques et des
    Etudes Economiques, French industrial production increased four
    times from 1947 to 1969. Whereas the Lambertists proclaimed in
    1960 that the Gaullist power proposed to destroy national
    education, the number of students rose from 195,000 in 1960 to
    700,000 in 1971. In 'Qu'est-ce que l'AJS', H. Weber has
    gathered statistical data which show how far the Lambertist
    theses are from reality.
25 Against Rosa, Lenin argued that 'there is no such thing as an
    impasse in capitalism'.
26 Cf. 'Etudes marxistes', no. 2, p. 15.

APPENDIX I   THE USSR, PEACEFUL CO-EXISTENCE AND VIETNAM

1   Extract from 'Garde Rouge' (monthly of the Union des jeunesses
    communistes - marxiste-léniniste), no. 3, January 1967.
2   Abridged summaries of these speeches in 'Peking Review', no. 52,
    23 December 1966.
3   'Public Papers on the Presidents of the United States: Lyndon B.
    Johnson, Book One, 1963-64', p. 171.
4   Cf. 'A Struggle between Two Lines over the Question of How to
    Deal with US Imperialism', by Fan Hsiu-chu, p. 31.
5   Cf. ibid., p. 31.
6   Lenin, CW, vol. 22, p. 302.

APPENDIX II   THE JCR IN MAY-JUNE 1968

1   Extract from 'Cahiers de la gauche prolétarienne', no. 1, April
    1969.
2   Meeting on 27 May called by the PSU, the union confederation
    CFDT, various university organisations (UNEF, SNES sup) and the
    JCR (Jeunesse communiste révolutionnaire), the ancestor of the
    'Ligue communiste', the French section of the Fourth
    International. Mendès-Frances was present on the platform at
    this meeting.
3   The real majority, which, of course, has nothing to do with any
    electoral majority, is the majority of the politically active
    popular masses, the conscious mobilisation of whom is the task
    of Bolshevik revolutionaries.

APPENDIX III CH'EN TU-HSIU'S IDEOLOGICAL ITINERARY

1 Y. C. Wang, 'Chinese Intellectuals and the West, 1872-1949'.
2 For a summary of his criticisms, see Shanti Swarup, 'A Study of the Chinese Communist Movement', pp. 234-6.
3 Pierre Broué falsely implies that he died in prison. Cf. 'Le Parti bolchevique', p. 438.
4 Cf. Benjamin Schwartz, 'Chinese Communism and the Rise of Mao'.

BIBLIOGRAPHY

TROTSKY'S WRITINGS

'The Age of Permanent Revolution: A Trotsky Anthology', Isaac
Deutscher (ed.), Dell, New York, 1964.
'The Class Nature of the Soviet State' and 'The Workers' State and
the Question of Thermidor and Bonapartism', New Park Publications,
London, August 1968.
'De la Révolution', Editions de Minuit, Paris, 1963. (Includes
'Cours Nouveau' (1923), 'La Révolution défigurée' (1927-9), 'La
Révolution permanente' (1928-31), 'La Révolution trahie' (1936).)
'The Death Agony of Capitalism and the Tasks of the Fourth
International (The Transitional Program)', Merit Pamphlet, 4th ed.,
New York, 1970.
'History of the Russian Revolution', 2 vols, Gollancz, London, 1932.
'In Defence of Marxism', Merit Publishers, New York, 1965.
'The New Course', Cresset Press, London, 1965.
'1905', Allen Lane The Penguin Press, London, 1972.
'Nos tâches politiques', Editions Pierre Belfond, Paris, 1970.
'Our Political Tasks', Connolly Books, Belfast, 1969.
'The Permanent Revolution' and 'Results and Prospects', Pioneer
Publishers, New York, 1965.
'Politique de Trotsky', texts selected and introduced by Jean
Baechler, Armand Colin, Paris, 1968.
'Problems of the Chinese Revolution', Pioneer Publishers, New York,
1932.
Rapport de la délegation siberienne, 'Spartacus', 1970.
'The Revolution Betrayed', Faber & Faber, London, 1937.
'The Soviet Union and the Fourth International', G. A. Aldred, 145
Queen St., Glasgow, 1934.
'Stalin', MacGibbon & Kee, London, 1968.
'The Third International After Lenin', Pioneer Publishers, New York,
1936.
'Writings of Leon Trotsky (1939-40)', Merit Publishers, New York,
1964.

ANTHOLOGIES

'De la Bureaucratie', Maspero, Paris, 1971.
'La Question chinoise dans l'internationale communiste (1926-27)',
texts introduced by P. Broué, EDI, Paris, 1965.
'Staline contre le révisionnisme', Sections I, II, III, 'Ligne
rouge' publication.
'Staline contre Trotsky', texts collected and introduced by Giuliano
Procacci, Maspero, Paris, 1965.
'Trotsky et le trotskysme', Editions Norman Bethune, Paris, 1937.

OTHER TROTSKYIST WRITINGS

AVENAS, D. and BROSSAT, A. (1971), 'De l'Antitrotskysme, éléments
d'histoire et de théorie', Maspero, Paris.
BENSAID, D. and WEBER, H. (1968), 'Mai 1968, une répétition
générale', Maspero, Paris.
BROUE, PIERRE (1963), 'Le Parti bolchevique', Editions de Minuit,
Paris.
DEUTSCHER, ISAAC (1949), 'Stalin', Oxford University Press.
DEUTSCHER, ISAAC (1967), 'The Unfinished Revolution 1917-67', Oxford
University Press.
'Etudes marxistes', no. 2, February 1969.
GERMAIN, E., De la bureaucratie (1965-7), 'Cahiers Rouges', no. 3,
Maspero, Paris.
Ho Chi Minh, un combattant du nationalisme, pas du socialisme,
'Lutte ouvrière', no. 54, 10 September 1969.
'Intercontinental Press', vol. 7, no. 26, 14 July 1969.
LOWY, MICHAEL (1970), 'La Théorie de la révolution chez le jeune
Marx', Maspero, Paris.
MANDEL, E. (May-June 1969), The debate on workers' control,
'International Socialist Review'.
MANDEL, E. (1971), 'The Leninist Theory of Organisation', Prinkipo
Press, London.
Manifeste de l'OCI, December 1967, supplement to 'La Vérité', no.
543.
MARIE, J.-J., Des mains très sales, and Toute honte bue ..., 'La
Vérité', no. 556.
NAVILLE, PIERRE (1964), 'La Classe ouvrière et le régime gaulliste',
EDI, Paris.
NAVILLE, PIERRE (1970), 'Le Salaire socialiste', Paris.
PREOBRAZHENSKY, E. (1965), 'The New Economics', Clarendon Press,
Oxford.
'Quatrième internationale', nos 23 (November 1964), 27 (February
1966), 37 (May 1969), 45 (September 1970).
Quelques enseignements de notre histoire, supplement to 'La Vérité',
no. 548.
'Tesis politica de la COB y otros documentos', UMSA, La Paz, 1970.
WEBER, H. (1966), 'Mouvement ouvrier, stalinisme et bureaucratie',
3rd ed., Paris.
WEBER, H. (1971), Qu'est-ce que l'AJS?, 'Cahiers Rouges', Maspero,
Paris.

ON TROTSKY AND TROTSKYISM

'Cahiers de la gauche prolétarienne', no. 1, April 1969.
CRAIPEAU, YVAN (1971), 'Le Mouvement trotskyste en France', Editions Syros, Paris.
DEUTSCHER, ISAAC (1970a), 'The Prophet Armed', Oxford University Press.
DEUTSCHER, ISAAC (1970b), 'The Prophet Outcast', Oxford University Press.
DEUTSCHER, ISAAC (1970c), 'The Prophet Unarmed', Oxford University Press.
FRANK, PIERRE (1970), 'La IVme Internationale', Maspero, Paris.
FIGUERES, LEO (1969), 'Le Trotskysme, cet antiléninisme', Editions Sociales, Paris.
KRASSÓ, NICOLAS (July-August 1967), Trotsky's Marxism, 'New Left Review', no. 44.
KRASSÓ, NICOLAS (1968), Reply to Ernest Mandel, 'New Left Review', no. 48.
MANDEL, ERNEST (January-February 1968), Trotsky's Marxism: an anti-critique, 'New Left Review', no. 47. (N.B. the Krassó-Mandel debate was published in a pamphlet, 'Trotsky's Marxism', an Australian Left Review Discussion Pamphlet, 1968.)
MARIE, J.-J. (1970), 'Le Trotskysme', Flammarion, Paris.
PROCACCI, G. (1965), (ed.), 'Staline contre Trotsky', Maspero, Paris.
'Que Faire?', pamphlet no. 3, UJC(M.-L.) Publications, Paris, 1967.
ROUSSEL, JACQUES (1972), Les enfants du prophète, 'Spartacus'.

CLASSICS

Engels, Friedrich

'Anti-Dühring', Progress Publishers, Moscow, 1969.

Engels, Friedrich, and Karl Marx

'Ausgewahlte Schriften', 2 vols, Dietz Verlag, Berlin, 1960.
'Selected Works', 3 vols, Progress Publishers, Moscow, 1972.

Lenin

'Collected Works', Foreign Languages Publishing House, Moscow, 1961.
'Selected Works', Foreign Languages Publishing House, Moscow, 1961.

Karl Marx

'Capital', Lawrence & Wishart, London, 1970.
'Die Klassenkampfe in Frankreich', Dietz Verlag, Berlin, 1964.

Stalin

'Concerning Marxism in Linguistics', published by Soviet News,
London, 1950.
'The Draft New Constitution', issued by the Anglo-Russian
Parliamentary Committee, London, 1936.
'L'Homme, le capital le plus précieux', following 'Pour une
formation bolchevik', Editions Sociales, Paris, 1948.
'Marxism and the National and Colonial Question', Martin Lawrence,
London, 1973.
'The Moscow Trial (January 1937) and Two Speeches', compiled by
W. P. and Z. K. Coates, issued by the Anglo-Russian Parliamentary
Committee, London, 1937.
'Problems of Leninism', 11th ed., Foreign Languages Publishing
House, Moscow, 1947.
'Reports and Speeches at the 18th Congress of the CPSU(B)', Foreign
Languages Publishing House, Moscow, 1939.
'Selected Works', Stanford University Press, California, 1971.
'Works', 13 vols, Lawrence & Wishart, London, 1955.

Mao Tse-tung

'On the Problem of Agricultural Co-operation', Foreign Language
Publishers, Peking, 1967.
'Selected Readings from the Works of Mao Tse-tung, Foreign Language
Publishers, Peking, 1967.
'Selected Works of Mao Tse-tung', Foreign Language Publishers,
Peking, 1960 edition.
Talks and writings of Chairman Mao, Translations on Communist China,
no. 128, Joint Publications Research Service, China and Asia, vol.
9, no. 6, July 1970-June 1971, reel no. 136.

MARXIST THEORY

ALTHUSSER, LOUIS (1969), 'For Marx', Allen Lane The Penguin Press,
London.
ALTHUSSER, LOUIS (1972), 'Lenin and Philosophy and Other Essays',
New Left Books, London.
BETTELHEIM, CHARLES, Calcul économique, catégories marchandes et
formes de propriété, 'Problèmes de planification', nos 11, 12.
BETTELHEIM, CHARLES, 'Calcul économique et formes de propriété',
Maspero, Paris, 1969. 'Economic Calculation and Forms of Property',
Routledge & Kegan Paul, London, 1975.
BETTELHEIM, CHARLES, Remarques théoriques, 'Problèmes de
planification', no. 14.
BETTELHEIM, CHARLES (1969), 'La Transition vers l'économie
socialiste', Maspero, Paris.
BETTELHEIM, CHARLES (May 1970), Due tipi di accumulazione, interview
in 'Il Manifesto', no. 5.
BETTELHEIM, CHARLES and SWEEZY, PAUL (1971), 'On the Transition to
Socialism', Monthly Review Press, New York and London.
'Cahiers de la gauche prolétarienne', no. 2, 1970.

GARAUDY, R. et al. (1956), 'Mésaventures de l'antimarxisme',
Editions Sociales, Paris.
GLUCKSMANN, ANDRE (1967), 'Le Discours de la guerre', L'Herne,
Paris.
GOLDMANN, LUCIEN (1969), 'The Human Sciences and Philosophy', Cape,
London.
HUSSEIN, MAHMOUD (1969), 'La Lutte des classes en Egypt de 1945 à
1968', Maspero, Paris.
KORSCH, KARL (1932), Die alte Hegelsche Dialektik und die neue
materialistische Wissenschaft in 'Der Gegner', no. 11/12.
KORSCH, KARL (1971), 'Die materialistische Geschichtsauffassung und
andere Schriften', Europäische Verlagsanstalt, Frankfurt-am-Main.
MANCEAUX, MICHELE (1972), 'Les Maos en France', Gallimard, Paris.
MERLEAU-PONTY, MAURICE (1964), 'Signs', Northwestern University
Press, Evanston, Illinois.
'Octobre', Revue du cercle de sociologie de l'UJC(M.-L.) no. 2.
RANCIERE, JACQUES (1970), Sobre la teoria de la ideologia (la
politica de Althusser), in 'Lectura de Althusser', Galerna, Buenos
Aires.
REY, PIERRE-PHILIPPE (1973), Sur l'articulation des modes de
production, in 'Problèmes de planification', nos 13, 14. Also in
'Les Alliances de classes', Maspero, Paris.
Rosa Luxemburg et nous, debate in 'Politique aujourd'hui', September
1972.

HISTORICAL STUDIES AND DOCUMENTS

USSR and the Comintern

CLAUDIN, FERNANDO (1972), 'La Crise du mouvement communiste, du
Komintern au Kominform', Maspero, Paris.
DESANTI, DOMINIQUE (1970), 'L'Internationale communiste', Payot,
Paris.
DJILAS, MILOVAN (1962), 'Conversations with Stalin', Rupert Hart-
Davis, London.
FAINSOD, MERLE (1967), 'Smolensk à l'heure de Staline', Fayard,
Paris.
GITTINGS, JOHN (1964), 'The Sino-Soviet Dispute 1956-63', Oxford
University Press.
GRIGORENKO, PJOTR (1969), 'Der sowjetische Zusammenbruch 1941',
Possev-Verlag, Frankfurt-am-Main.
'How the Soviet Revisionists Carry Out the All-Round Restoration of
Capitalism in the USSR', Peking, 1968.
KIM, G. and KAUFMANN (1966), 'La Paysännerie et le pouvoir
soviétique, 1928-30', Mouton, Paris and the Hague.
LINHART, ROBERT (March 1966), La NEP: analyse de quelques
caracteristiques de la phase de transition sovietique, 'Etudes de
planification socialiste', no. 3.
MEDVEDEV, ROY (1969), 'Faut-il réhabiliter Staline?', Editions du
Seuil, Paris.
POULANTZAS, NICOS (1970), 'Fascisme et dictature', Maspero, Paris.
'Proclamation programme des communistes bolcheviques
révolutionnaires soviétiques', Editions de l'Avenir, Lyon, 1969.

'La Russie soviétique de 1917 à 1932', Documents des cahiers
marxistes-léninistes, preceded by Robert Linhart's Considerations
quasi épistémologiques pour aider a la lecture des textes présentés.
SORLIN, R. and I. (1961), 'Lenine, Trotsky, Staline, 1921-1927',
Armand Colin, Paris.
VARGA, EUGENE (July-August 1970), Political testament, 'New Left
Review', no. 62.
WEISSBERG, ALEXANDER, 'Conspiracy of Silence'.

PCF

'Histoire du parti communiste français', 3 vols, Editions Unir.
'Histoire du parti communiste français', Editions sociales, Paris,
1964.
'Manifeste de Champigny: Pour une démocratie avancée, pour une
France socialiste'.
ROCHET, WALDECK (5 and 6 December 1968), Rapport devant le CC de PCF
à Champigny.
THOREZ, M. and GARAUDY, R. (1962), Les Tâches philosophes
communistes et la critique des erreurs philosophiques de Stalin,
Supplement to 'Cahiers du Communisme', nos 7-8.

China

BABY, JEAN (November, 1967), 'Défense et illustration de la
révolution culturelle', Centre culturel France-Chine, 136, Quai du
Port, Marseille.
BABY, JEAN (1966), 'La Grande Controverse sino-sovietique', Grasset,
Paris.
BIANCO, LUCIEN (1971), 'Origins of the Chinese Revolution', Oxford
University Press.
BING, DOV (October/December 1971), Sneevlit and the early years of
the CCP, 'China Quarterly'.
BLUMER, GIOVANNI (1968), 'Die chinesische Kulturrevolution 1965-
1967', Europäische Verlagsanstalt, Frankfurt-am-Main.
BRANDT, CONRAD (1967), 'Stalin's Failure in China 1924-27', Harvard
University Press, Cambridge, Mass.
'Cahiers marxistes-leninistes', Theoretical and Political Organ of
the Union des Jeunesses Communistes (marxiste-leniniste), nos 14,
15, 17 (1967-8).
CHESNEAUX, JEAN (1965), 'Les Sociétés secrètes en Chine' (Collection
of documents introduced by Jean Chesneaux), Julliard, Paris.
'Chinese Literature', no. 1 of 1967 and 1970.
COLOTTI-PISCHEL, ENRICA (1964), 'La Revolution ininterrompue',
Julliard, Paris.
DAUBIER, JEAN (1970), 'Histoire de la révolution culturelle en
Chine', Maspero, Paris.
'Die chinesische Frage auf den 8 Plenum der Exekutive der
Kommunistischen Internationale Mai 1927', Verlag Carl Hoym Nachf,
Hamburg-Berlin.
EPSTEIN, ISRAEL (1964), 'From Opium War to Liberation', New World
Press, Peking.

ESMEIN, JEAN (1970), 'La Révolution culturelle', Editions du Seuil, Paris.

FOA, L. NATOLI A. (July–August 1970), Dalle Guardie Rosse al IX Congresso, 'Il Manifesto'.

GARAUDY, R. (1967), 'Le Problème chinois', Seghers, Paris.

'A Great Historic Document', Foreign Language Publishers, Peking, 1967.

'The Great Proletarian Cultural Revolution' (ten pamphlets), Foreign Language Publishers, Peking, 1966.

GUILLERMAZ, JACQUES (1972), 'A History of the Chinese Communist Party 1921-49', Methuen, London.

HINTON, WILLIAM (March 1969), 'China's Continuing Revolution', China Policy Study Group, London.

HSÜEN MU-CHIA, HEÜEH MU-CHIAO and others (1960), 'The Socialist Transformation of the National Economy in China', China Knowledge Series, Foreign Language Publishers, Peking.

ISAACS, H. (1951), 'The Tragedy of the Chinese Revolution' (revised edition), Stanford University Press, California.

ISAACS, H. (January–March 1971), Documents on the Comintern and the Chinese Revolution, 'China Quarterly'.

KAROL, K. S. (1967), 'China. The Other Communism', Heinemann, London.

LIN PIAO (1965), 'Long Live the Victory of People's War', Foreign Language Publishers, Peking.

LIN PIAO (1970), Report to the 9th National Congress of the Communist Party of China, 'Important Documents on the Great Proletarian Cultural Revolution in China', Foreign Language Publishers, Peking.

MACCIOCCHI, MARIA-ANTONIETTA (1972), 'Daily life in revolutionary China', Monthly Review Press, New York.

MYRDAL, JAN (1965), 'Chinese Journey', Chatto & Windus, London.

NORTH, R. C. (1966), 'Chinese Communism', Weidenfeld & Nicolson, London.

NORTH, R. C. (1963), 'Moscow and the Chinese Communists', 2nd ed., Stanford University Press, California, 1963.

'Polemic on the General Line of the International Communist Movement', Foreign Language Publishers, Peking, 1965.

Que se passe-t-il dans le mouvement communiste international?, 'Cahiers du Centre d'Etudes socialistes', nos 52-3, January 1965.

ROBINSON, JOAN (1969), 'The Cultural Revolution in China', Penguin Books, Harmondsworth.

ROY, M. N. (June 1946), 'Revolution and Counter-Revolution in China', Renaissance Publishers, Calcutta.

SCHRAM, STUART (1963), 'Documents sur la théorie de la "révolution permanente" en Chine', Mouton, The Hague and Paris.

SCHRAM, STUART (1969), 'The Political Thought of Mao Tse-tung', Penguin Books, Harmondsworth.

SCHRAM, STUART, and CARRERE d'ENCAUSSE, HELENE (1969), 'Marxism and Asia', Allen Lane The Penguin Press, London.

SMEDLEY, AGNES (1956), 'The Great Road: The Life and Time of Chu Teh', Monthly Review Press, New York.

SUYIN, HAN (1972), 'The Morning Deluge', Cape, London.

SWARUP, SHANTI (1966), 'A Study of the Chinese Communist Movement (1924-34)', Clarendon Press, Oxford.

'Take the road of the Shanghai Machine Tools Plant in training
technicians from among the workers', Foreign Language Publishers,
Peking, 1968.
WANG MING-KANG HSING (1934), 'Das revolutionäre China von Heute',
XIII Plenum des EKKI, December 1933, Verlagsgenossenschaft
Ausländischer Arbeiter in der UdSSR, Moskow-Leningrad.
WANG, Y. C. (1966), 'Chinese Intellectuals and the West, 1872-1949',
University of North Carolina Press.

Greece

CHURCHILL, W. S. (1950), 'History of the Second World War', 6 vols,
Cassell, London.
DARIVAS, B. (1964), De la résistance à la guerre civile en Grèce,
'Recherches Internationales à la lumière du marxisme', nos 44-5.
EUDES, D. (1972), 'The Kapetanios, Partisans and Civil War in Greece
1943-49', New Left Books, London.
'Forty Years of the CPG 1918-58' (a collection of documents),
Editions Politiques et Littéraires (in Greek).
KEDROS, ANDRE (1966), 'La Résistance grecque', Robert Laffont,
Paris.
KOUSOULAS, GEORGE (1965), 'Revolution and Defeat: The Story of the
Greek Communist Party', Oxford University Press.
'Laïkos Dromos', no. 13.
MURRAY, COLONEL J. C. (1962), The anti-bandit war, in 'The Guerilla
and How to Fight Him', Praeger, New York.
O'BALLENCE, EDGAR (1966), 'The Greek Civil War', Faber & Faber,
London.
SVORONOS, N. G. (1964), 'Histoire de la Grèce moderne', PUF, Paris.
TSOUCALAS, CONSTANTINE (1969), 'The Greek Tragedy', Penguin Books,
Harmondsworth.
VOUKMANOVIC-TEMPO, S. (1950), 'Über die Volksrevolution in
Griechenland', Belgrade.
ZEVGOU, YANNI (April/May 1966), Evolution démocratique (1945),
published in 'La Gauche héllenique', nos 33-34 (in Greek).
ZOGRAPHOS, Z. (November 1964), La guerre civile en Grèce et ses
leçons, 'La Nouvelle Revue internationale'.